AnnualRecipes
2009

Pillsbury Annual Recipes 2009

Our recipes have been tested in the Pillsbury Kitchens and meet our standards of easy preparation, reliability and great taste.

For more great recipes, visit pillsbury.com

PUBLISHED BY

Taste of Home Books
Reiman Media Group, Inc.
5400 S. 60th St., Greendale, WI 53129
www.tasteofhome.com

This edition published by arrangement with Wiley Publishing, Inc.

Printed in U.S.A.

Taste of Home® is a registered trademark of Reiman Media Group, Inc.

Bake-Off® is a registered trademark of General Mills.

The trademarks referred to herein are trademarks of General Mills, Inc., or its affiliates, except as noted.

Yoplait® is a registered trademark of YOPLAIT Marques Internationales SAS (France) used under license.

All recipes were originally published in different form by Pillsbury Easy Meals™ Magazine and Pillsbury® Magazines, both trademarks of General Mills, Inc.

International Standard Book Number (10):
0-89821-713-X
International Standard Book Number (13):
978-0-89821-713-1
International Standard Serial Number:
1930-7349

CREDITS
General Mills, Inc.
EDITORIAL DIRECTOR: JEFF NOWAK
MANAGER, COOKBOOKS: LOIS TLUSTY
RECIPE DEVELOPMENT AND TESTING: PILLSBURY TEST KITCHENS
PHOTOGRAPHY: GENERAL MILLS PHOTO STUDIOS

Reiman Media Group, Inc.
VICE PRESIDENT, EXECUTIVE EDITOR/BOOKS: HEIDI REUTER LLOYD
SENIOR EDITOR/BOOKS: MARK HAGEN
EDITOR: MICHELLE BRETL
ART DIRECTOR: GRETCHEN TRAUTMAN
CONTENT PRODUCTION SUPERVISOR: JULIE WAGNER
LAYOUT DESIGNERS: KATHY CRAWFORD, NANCY NOVAK
PROOFREADERS: AMY GLANDER, LINNE BRUSKEWITZ
INDEXER: JEAN DUERST
GRAPHIC DESIGN INTERN: HEATHER MILLER

CREATIVE DIRECTOR: ARDYTH COPE
CREATIVE DIRECTOR/CREATIVE MARKETING: JAMES PALMEN
VICE PRESIDENT/BOOK MARKETING: DAN FINK
CHIEF MARKETING OFFICER: LISA KARPINSKI
EDITOR IN CHIEF: CATHERINE CASSIDY
PRESIDENT, FOOD & ENTERTAINING: SUZANNE M. GRIMES
PRESIDENT AND CHIEF EXECUTIVE OFFICER: MARY G. BERNER

FRONT COVER PHOTOGRAPHS:
Mini Chicken Pot Pies, Pg. 266; Peanut Butter Mole Enchiladas, Pg. 166; Thai Peanut Chicken and Noodles, Pg. 145; Black-Bottom Banana Cream Pie, Pg. 314; and Grilled Flank Steaks with Rosemary-Balsamic Glaze, Pg. 218.

PAGE 5 PHOTOGRAPHS:
Ground Beef and Twice-Baked Potato Pie, Pg. 123; Toffee-Banana Brownies, Pg. 308; Spicy Chicken and Orzo Skillet, Pg. 120; and Chicken Crescent Pot Stickers, Pg. 83.

BACK COVER PHOTOGRAPHS:
Chipotle Rice Casserole, Pg. 161; Chocolate Surprise Pecan Pie, Pg. 327; Easy Barbecue Pork Sandwiches, Pg. 183; and Meaty Mostaccioli, Pg. 136.

contents

Pillsbury

"Wow Them With The Very Best Recipes From Pillsbury In This Annual Cookbook!"

introduction

It's so easy to impress your family members, friends… everyone you cook for when you rely on the timeless, trusted recipes from Pillsbury. And you'll find the best of the best from the past year right at your fingertips inside the all-new *Pillsbury Annual Recipes 2009*.

From cover to cover, this fourth edition of our popular cookbook series is packed with scrumptious recipes and expert kitchen hints—more than 400 in all! Every dish was featured in a 2008 Pillsbury Classic® Cookbook…so you can rest assured that each one is a proven winner with families just like yours.

Whether you want a quick weekday dinner, elegant appetizer platter, eye-catching holiday dessert or popular potluck salad, you can choose from standout specialties throughout 12 big chapters. Just turn the page to start off with Breakfast & Brunch, featuring rich Banana-Filled Caramel-Chocolate Crepes (p. 20), Ham 'n Eggs Crescent Brunch Pizza (p. 15) and many more sunrise sensations.

For delicious hors d'oeuvres, munchies and beverages, the Snacks & Sippers and Entertaining Appetizers chapters will have you covered. Enjoy everything from Buffalo Chicken Dip (p. 35) to Spicy Spanish Sausages (p. 65).

If a family-pleasing main dish is on your list, turn to entrees such as Italian Pot Roast (p. 121), Shrimp Tetrazzini (p. 170)

and Biscuit Chicken Pot Pie (p. 180) in the Main Dishes, Comforting Casseroles and Slow Cooker Specialties chapters. Then complete your menu with Home-Style Roasted Vegetables (p. 96) or another favorite from Sides, Soups & Salads.

Looking for dishes that appeal to children? The Cooking for Kids chapter gives you playful Taco Monster Mouths (p. 267) and other fun-filled foods. Or delight people of all ages with Chocolate Truffle Meringues (p. 294), Easy Apple Pie Foldover (p. 324) and more temptations in Cookies, Brownies & Bars and All-American Pies & Treats.

New in this 2009 edition, two seasonal chapters offer festive recipes for every occasion. For example, you can jump-start your Easter holiday celebration with Bunny Puffs (p. 197) from the Spring & Summer Sensations chapter…or get everyone in the Christmas spirit with Marshmallow Santas (p. 262) from Fall & Winter Favorites.

Because every recipe in this beautiful cookbook includes a color photo and step-by-step directions, even novice cooks can whip up success. In fact, many dishes rely on brand-name convenience products you've trusted for years, and each dish has been prepared and approved by the experts in the Pillsbury Test Kitchen.

It's all here for you in *Pillsbury Annual Recipes 2009*. And there's more! Read on…

AT-A-GLANCE ICONS

With today's busy lifestyles, family cooks have less time than ever to spend in the kitchen. To help make the most of it, we've highlighted the easy recipes in this book with an icon that looks like the one at left...so you can quickly find them for yourself. These dishes call for 6 ingredients or less OR are ready to cook in 20 minutes or less OR are ready to eat in 30 minutes or less.

At the top of each recipe, we've also included "Prep" and "Ready in..." times. That way, you'll know exactly how long it takes to prepare each dish from start to finish.

Are you watching your diet...or cooking for someone else who is? Then you'll appreciate the low-fat icon, located next to recipes that contain 10 grams of fat or less (main dishes) or 3 grams of fat or less (all other recipes). And to provide even more information, we've included Nutrition Facts with the majority of this book's recipes.

Plus, you'll spot a number of Pillsbury Bake-Off® Contest Winners—the recipes judged to be the very best in our popular contests over the years. These exceptional dishes shared by home

cooks from across the country are sure to be winners in your own home. As you page through this book, simply look for the Bake-Off® icon next to desserts, main dishes, appetizers and more.

HOW TO FIND A RECIPE

This cookbook is indexed in two helpful ways. Look up any major ingredient, and you'll find a list of the recipes in which it is included.

For instance, if you'd like to make a main dish with chicken, turn to "chicken" in the general index to find dozens of delicious options.

The alphabetical index starts on page 344. Once you have found a few favorite recipes for your family, you can easily locate them by title the next time you want to make them.

Or perhaps you just want to page through this book and look at all the mouth-watering photos until you find one that's perfect for dinnertime tonight, breakfast tomorrow or your get-together on the weekend.

One thing's certain...whichever Pillsbury favorites you serve, they're sure to become some of your most-requested, best-loved recipes ever!

Breakfast & Brunch

Rise and shine! These bright morning delights will get sleepyheads to the table in a hurry.

BANANA-FILLED CARAMEL-
CHOCOLATE CREPES
PG. 20

TROPICAL SUNSHINE FLATCAKES
WITH ORANGE CREAM
PG. 11

TASTE-OF-THE-ISLANDS
BREAKFAST ROLLS
PG. 26

QUICK AND FRUITY
CRESCENT WAFFLES
PG. 22

Upside-Down Caramel-Apple Biscuits

LAUREEN PITTMAN | RIVERSIDE, CALIFORNIA

BAKE-OFF® CONTEST 43, 2008

PREP TIME: 35 MINUTES (READY IN 1 HOUR 5 MINUTES)
SERVINGS: 8

e EASY

- ¼ cup Land O Lakes® butter
- ½ cup Smucker's® caramel ice cream topping
- ¼ cup packed Domino® or C&H® dark brown sugar
- 6 cups sliced peeled Granny Smith apples (about 4 medium)
- ½ cup Fisher® Chef's Naturals® chopped pecans
- 1 can (16.3 oz) Pillsbury® Grands!® Flaky Layers Butter Tastin'® refrigerated biscuits (8 biscuits)

1) Heat oven to 350°F. In 12-inch nonstick skillet, cook butter and caramel topping over medium-high heat, stirring occasionally, until melted and bubbly. Stir in brown sugar and apples. Cook over medium-high heat 12 to 15 minutes, stirring occasionally, until the apples are tender.

2) Meanwhile, spray 8 (10-ounce) custard cups or 8 (12-ounce) ramekins with Crisco® Original No-Stick cooking spray. Sprinkle 1 tablespoon pecans in each cup. Spoon about ⅓ cup caramel-apple mixture evenly over pecans in each cup.

3) Separate biscuits; gently stretch each biscuit until large enough to cover caramel-apple mixture. Place biscuits on top of caramel-apple mixture in each cup. Place cups on large cookie sheet with sides.

4) Bake 18 to 23 minutes or until golden brown. Place cups on cooling rack; cool 5 minutes. Place heatproof serving plate upside down on each cup; carefully turn plate and cup over to remove cakes. Serve warm.

HIGH ALTITUDE (3500-6500 FT.): When cooking apples, stir frequently to avoid scorching.

Nutrition Information Per Serving:		
Calories: 420	From Fat:	180
Total Fat		20g
Saturated Fat		6g
Trans Fat		3g
Cholesterol		15mg
Sodium		670mg
Total Carbohydrate		56g
Dietary Fiber		2g
Sugars		30g
Protein		5g

Sweet Onion Pinwheels

PREP TIME:	15 MINUTES (READY IN 35 MINUTES)
SERVINGS:	16 PINWHEELS

 EASY

- ½ cup chopped sweet onions
- ¼ cup shredded Italian cheese blend (1 oz)
- 2 tablespoons cream cheese, softened
- 1 tablespoon mayonnaise or salad dressing
- 1 can (8 oz) Pillsbury® Place 'n Bake™ refrigerated crescent rounds
- 2 teaspoons chopped fresh chives

1) Heat oven to 375°F. Lightly spray cookie sheet with cooking spray. Mix onions, cheeses and mayonnaise until well blended and soft.

2) Unroll dough on work surface, but do not separate. Firmly press perforations to seal. Spread cheese mixture evenly over dough. Starting with 1 short side, roll up rectangle; pinch edges to seal. Cut roll into 16 slices (about ¾ inch wide). Place cut side down on cookie sheet. Sprinkle with chives.

3) Bake 12 to 15 minutes or until golden brown. Immediately remove from cookie sheet; cool 3 minutes. Serve warm.

HIGH ALTITUDE (3500-6500 FT.): No change.

Nutrition Information Per Serving:

Calories:	70	From Fat:	45
Total Fat		5g	
Saturated Fat		2g	
Trans Fat		1g	
Cholesterol		0mg	
Sodium		135mg	
Total Carbohydrate		6g	
Dietary Fiber		0g	
Sugars		1g	
Protein		2g	

 tip

Store fresh chives in a glass of water in the refrigerator for up to one week. To easily chop fresh chives, simply use a kitchen scissors to snip them into the desired length.

Caramel Chai Crescent Ring

PREP TIME: 35 MINUTES (READY IN 1 HOUR 5 MINUTES)
SERVINGS: 12

¹/₄ cup butter (do not use margarine)

¹/₂ cup packed brown sugar

2 tablespoons maple syrup or corn syrup

2 tablespoons whipping cream

2 tablespoons granulated sugar

1 tablespoon ground cinnamon

¹/₂ teaspoon ground ginger

¹/₂ teaspoon ground nutmeg

¹/₄ teaspoon ground cloves

2 cans (8 oz each) Pillsbury® refrigerated reduced-fat crescent dinner rolls

2 tablespoons butter, melted

16 large marshmallows

¹/₄ cup chopped nuts

1) Heat oven to 350°F. In 1-quart saucepan, melt ¹/₄ cup butter. With 1 to 2 tablespoons of the melted butter, grease bottom and side of 12-cup fluted tube cake pan. To remaining melted butter, stir in brown sugar and syrup. Heat just to boiling, stirring occasionally. Remove from heat; stir in cream.

2) In small bowl, mix granulated sugar, cinnamon, ginger, nutmeg and cloves. Unroll dough from both cans and separate into 16 triangles. Brush each triangle with melted butter. Sprinkle about ¹/₂ teaspoon granulated sugar mixture onto each triangle to within ¹/₄ inch of edges. Top each with marshmallow. Roll up, starting at shortest side of triangle and rolling to opposite point. Completely cover marshmallow with dough; firmly pinch edges to seal. Arrange 8 balls in buttered pan. Sprinkle with nuts; spoon half of brown sugar mixture over dough. Place remaining 8 balls alternately over bottom layer. Spoon remaining brown sugar mixture over balls.

3) Bake 25 to 28 minutes or until golden brown. Cool 3 minutes. Place heatproof serving platter upside down over pan; turn pan and platter over. Remove pan. Serve warm.

HIGH ALTITUDE (3500-6500 FT.): Bake 27 to 30 minutes.

Nutrition Information Per Serving:	
Calories: 290	From Fat: 130
Total Fat	14g
Saturated Fat	7g
Trans Fat	0g
Cholesterol	20mg
Sodium	350mg
Total Carbohydrate	38g
Dietary Fiber	0g
Sugars	21g
Protein	3g

Tropical Sunshine Flatcakes with Orange Cream

AUDREY MADYUN | TOLEDO, OHIO

BAKE-OFF® CONTEST 43, 2008

PREP TIME: 30 MINUTES (READY IN 40 MINUTES)
SERVINGS: 8

FLATCAKES

- 1 tablespoon Crisco® pure vegetable oil
- 1/2 cup Fisher® Chef's Naturals® pecan chips
- 1 can (13.9 oz) Pillsbury® refrigerated orange flavor sweet rolls with icing (8 rolls)

TOPPING

- 2 tablespoons Land O Lakes® butter
- 2 firm ripe medium bananas, sliced (2 cups)
- 2 tablespoons lime juice
- 1 cup fresh or canned, drained, pineapple tidbits
- 1 jar (12 oz) Smucker's® pineapple ice cream topping
- 1 can (15 oz) mandarin orange segments in light syrup, drained

ORANGE CREAM

- 1 1/4 cups whipping cream
- Icing from can of sweet rolls

1) Heat oven to 400°F. Generously brush 1 tablespoon oil on 1 large cookie sheet or 2 small cookie sheets.

2) Cut waxed paper or cooking parchment paper into 16 (6-inch square) sheets. Sprinkle about 1 1/2 teaspoons pecans on 1 sheet. Place 1 orange roll on pecans; sprinkle 1 1/2 teaspoons pecans on top of roll. Top with another waxed paper square. Using rolling pin, roll evenly until orange roll is 4 1/2 inches in diameter; remove waxed paper. Place roll on cookie sheet. Repeat with remaining rolls, placing 1 inch apart on cookie sheet. Set icing aside. Bake 8 to 10 minutes or until golden brown.

3) Meanwhile, in 10-inch skillet, melt butter over medium-high heat. Add bananas, lime juice and pineapple; cook 1 minute, stirring frequently. Reduce heat to medium-low. Gently stir in the pineapple topping; cook 3 to 4 minutes, stirring occasionally, until warmed. Gently stir in mandarin orange segments.

4) In medium bowl, beat whipping cream and icing with electric mixer on High speed until soft peaks form. To serve, top flatcakes with warm pineapple topping and orange cream.

HIGH ALTITUDE (3500-6500 FT.): No change.

Nutrition Information Per Serving:	
Calories: 560	From Fat: 250
Total Fat	28g
Saturated Fat	11g
Trans Fat	2.5g
Cholesterol	50mg
Sodium	380mg
Total Carbohydrate	72g
Dietary Fiber	2g
Sugars	46g
Protein	4g

Breakfast Baklava

WENDY CONNICK | CULVER CITY, CALIFORNIA

Pillsbury Bake-Off®

BAKE-OFF® CONTEST 43, 2008

PREP TIME: 35 MINUTES (READY IN 1 HOUR)
SERVINGS: 8

SYRUP

- 1/4 cup Domino® or C&H® granulated sugar
- 1/2 cup honey
- 1/3 cup water
- 2 teaspoons lemon juice
- 1/8 teaspoon ground cinnamon
  Dash salt
- 3 whole cloves or dash ground cloves

NUT FILLING

- 1/2 cup Fisher® Chef's Naturals® sliced blanched almonds
- 1/4 cup Fisher® Chef's Naturals® walnut halves and pieces
- 1 tablespoon Domino® or C&H® granulated sugar
- 1/2 teaspoon ground cinnamon
  Dash salt, if desired

BISCUITS

- 1 can (16.3 oz) Pillsbury® Grands!® Flaky Layers Butter Tastin'® refrigerated biscuits (8 biscuits)

1) Heat oven to 350°F. Generously spray 8 (2-3/4x1-1/4-inch) nonstick muffin cups with Crisco® Original No-Stick cooking spray.

2) In 1-quart saucepan, mix syrup ingredients; heat to boiling. Remove from heat; cool 10 minutes. Discard whole cloves.

3) Meanwhile, in food processor bowl with metal blade, place filling ingredients. Cover; process with on-and-off pulses until finely chopped. Set aside.

4) Separate dough into 8 biscuits. Separate each biscuit into 3 layers. Place 1 biscuit layer in bottom of 1 muffin cup. Brush dough with syrup; top with 1-1/2 teaspoons nut filling and drizzle with 1-1/2 teaspoons syrup. Place second biscuit layer on top; press edge of second biscuit into side of bottom biscuit. Brush with syrup; top with 1-1/2 teaspoons nut filling and drizzle with 1-1/2 teaspoons syrup. Top with third biscuit layer. Brush with syrup; sprinkle with 1 teaspoon nut filling. Repeat with remaining biscuits. Reserve remaining syrup (about 1/2 cup).

5) Bake 18 to 22 minutes or until deep golden brown. Cool 1 minute. Remove from pan. Serve warm with remaining syrup.

HIGH ALTITUDE (3500-6500 FT.): No change.

Nutrition Information Per Serving:	
Calories: 370	From Fat: 140
Total Fat	16g
Saturated Fat	2.5g
Trans Fat	3g
Cholesterol	0mg
Sodium	570mg
Total Carbohydrate	52g
Dietary Fiber	1g
Sugars	31g
Protein	6g

"Tealightful" Fruit Bowl

| PREP TIME: | 20 MINUTES (READY IN 20 MINUTES) | EASY | LOW FAT |
| SERVINGS: | 14 (1/2 CUP EACH) | | |

SALAD

- 1 container (16 oz) fresh strawberries, halved (about 3 cups)
- 2 cups whole dark sweet cherries or 2 fresh mangoes, peeled, pitted, chopped
- 1 cup seedless green grapes
- 1 cup fresh blueberries

DRESSING

- ¼ cup pomegranate juice or grape juice
- 1 tablespoon balsamic vinegar
- 1 tablespoon honey
- 1 teaspoon instant tea mix

1) In large bowl, mix salad ingredients.

2) In jar with tight-fitting lid, shake dressing ingredients until well mixed. Pour dressing over salad; toss gently to coat. Serve immediately.

HIGH ALTITUDE (3500-6500 FT.): No change.

Nutrition Information Per Serving:

Calories:	50	From Fat:	0
Total Fat			0g
Saturated Fat			0g
Trans Fat			0g
Cholesterol			0mg
Sodium			0mg
Total Carbohydrate			11g
Dietary Fiber			1g
Sugars			9g
Protein			0g

tip

To fix this salad up to 2 hours in advance, leave the strawberries whole or hold off on adding the dressing until serving time.

Peach-Berry Smoothie

| PREP TIME: | 5 MINUTES (READY IN 5 MINUTES) | EASY | LOW FAT |
| SERVINGS: | 4 (1 CUP EACH) | | |

- 2 containers (6 oz each) Yoplait® Original 99% Fat-Free strawberry yogurt
- 1 cup sliced fresh or frozen peaches or nectarines
- 1 cup sliced fresh strawberries
- 1 cup crushed ice

1) In blender, place all ingredients. Cover; blend on high speed 30 to 60 seconds or until smooth.

2) Pour into 4 glasses. Serve immediately.

HIGH ALTITUDE (3500-6500 FT.): No change.

Nutrition Information Per Serving:

Calories:	120	From Fat:	10
Total Fat			1g
Saturated Fat			0.5g
Trans Fat			0g
Cholesterol			5mg
Sodium			40mg
Total Carbohydrate			24g
Dietary Fiber			1g
Sugars			19g
Protein			3g

Biscuits with Sausage–Apple Gravy

PREP TIME: 30 MINUTES (READY IN 30 MINUTES)
SERVINGS: 4

 EASY

4 Pillsbury® Grands!® frozen buttermilk biscuits (from 25-oz bag)

2 teaspoons butter or margarine

1 medium apple, cored, coarsely chopped (about 1¼ cups)

1 lb bulk pork sausage

3 tablespoons all-purpose flour

2¼ cups fat-free (skim) milk

½ teaspoon onion salt

⅛ teaspoon coarse ground black pepper

Dash ground red pepper (cayenne)

1) Heat oven to 375°F. Bake biscuits as directed on bag.

2) Meanwhile, in 10-inch nonstick skillet, melt butter over medium heat. Add apple pieces; cook 4 to 7 minutes, stirring occasionally, until crisp-tender. Remove; cover and keep warm.

3) Increase heat to medium-high. In the same skillet, crumble sausage; cook 4 to 6 minutes, stirring frequently, until no longer pink. Add 1 tablespoon of the flour, stirring constantly, until brown. Stir in remaining flour. Stir in milk with wire whisk. Cook about 3 minutes, stirring constantly, until mixture thickens. Stir in apple pieces, onion salt and peppers.

4) Split the warm biscuits; place biscuits on 4 serving plates. Top with the sausage-apple gravy.

HIGH ALTITUDE (3500-6500 FT.): No change.

Nutrition Information Per Serving:

Calories:	470	From Fat:	240
Total Fat			26g
Saturated Fat			9g
Trans Fat			4g
Cholesterol			55mg
Sodium			1230mg
Total Carbohydrate			38g
Dietary Fiber			1g
Sugars			13g
Protein			20g

tip

If you have fresh sage leaves, try adding 1 teaspoon finely chopped fresh leaves to the gravy. Orange wedges make an attractive garnish.

Ham 'n Eggs Crescent Brunch Pizza

BOBBY BRAUN | MARIETTA, GEORGIA

BAKE-OFF® CONTEST 32, 1986

PREP TIME: 30 MINUTES (READY IN 1 HOUR 10 MINUTES)
SERVINGS: 8

1 can (8 oz) Pillsbury® refrigerated crescent dinner rolls

4 eggs

1/2 teaspoon Italian seasoning

1/2 teaspoon salt, if desired

1 to 1 1/4 cups cubed, cooked ham

1 to 1 1/4 cups shredded mozzarella cheese (4 to 5 oz)

1 box (9 oz) Green Giant® frozen cut broccoli, thawed, drained

1 jar (4.5 oz) Green Giant® sliced mushrooms, drained

2 tablespoons chopped green bell pepper

1 large tomato, peeled, seeded, diced (about 1 cup)

2 tablespoons grated Parmesan cheese

1) Heat oven to 350°F.

2) Separate dough into 8 triangles. Place triangles in ungreased 12-inch pizza pan or 13x9-inch pan; press over bottom and 1/2 inch up sides to form crust. Seal perforations. Beat eggs, Italian seasoning and salt with fork or wire whisk; pour into dough-lined pan. Top with ham, mozzarella cheese, broccoli, mushrooms, bell pepper and tomato; sprinkle with Parmesan cheese.

3) Bake 30 to 40 minutes or until eggs are set and crust is golden brown.

HIGH ALTITUDE (3500-6500 FT.): No change.

Nutrition Information Per Serving:

Calories:	240	From Fat:	120
Total Fat			14g
Saturated Fat			5g
Trans Fat			1.5g
Cholesterol			125mg
Sodium			670mg
Total Carbohydrate			15g
Dietary Fiber			2g
Sugars			4g
Protein			15g

Strawberry-Kiwi-Almond Tart

PREP TIME: 25 MINUTES (READY IN 45 MINUTES)
SERVINGS: 12

1 package (7 oz) almond paste

¼ cup butter or margarine, softened

2 tablespoons all-purpose flour

1 egg

1 can (8 oz) Pillsbury® refrigerated crescent dinner rolls

¼ cup apricot preserves

2 cups sliced fresh strawberries (about 1 lb)

2 kiwifruit, peeled, halved lengthwise and sliced

Nutrition Information Per Serving:	
Calories: 230	From Fat: 110
Total Fat	13g
Saturated Fat	4g
Trans Fat	1g
Cholesterol	30mg
Sodium	180mg
Total Carbohydrate	26g
Dietary Fiber	2g
Sugars	15g
Protein	4g

1) Heat oven to 375°F. In food processor bowl with metal blade, place the almond paste. Cover; process with on-and-off pulses until finely ground. Add butter, flour and egg; process until smooth. Set aside.

2) On ungreased cookie sheet, unroll the dough into 1 large rectangle. Press into 12x9-inch rectangle, firmly pressing perforations to seal. Fold ½ inch of the dough edges over, forming crust rim.

3) Spread almond paste mixture over dough to within rim.

4) Bake 15 to 20 minutes or until crust is golden brown. Immediately spread preserves over tart. Arrange fruit over warm tart. Serve warm or cool.

HIGH ALTITUDE (3500-6500 FT.): No change.

Bacon Breadstick Focaccia

PREP TIME: 15 MINUTES (READY IN 40 MINUTES)
SERVINGS: 6

 EASY

1 can (11 oz) Pillsbury® refrigerated breadsticks (12 breadsticks)

10 slices packaged precooked bacon (from 2.1-oz package)

1 egg, beaten

1 slice packaged precooked bacon, finely chopped

½ teaspoon chopped fresh parsley, if desired

Nutrition Information Per Serving:	
Calories: 190	From Fat: 60
Total Fat	6g
Saturated Fat	3g
Trans Fat	0g
Cholesterol	45mg
Sodium	510mg
Total Carbohydrate	25g
Dietary Fiber	0g
Sugars	3g
Protein	8g

1) Heat oven to 375°F. Unroll dough; separate into 12 strips. Starting at center of ungreased cookie sheet, coil bacon with dough strips into a loose spiral, pinching ends together securely as strips are added.

2) Drizzle or brush egg over dough, using all of egg to fill crevices. Sprinkle with chopped bacon and parsley. Bake 20 to 25 minutes or until edges are deep golden brown. Cut into wedges; serve warm.

HIGH ALTITUDE (3500-6500 FT.): No change.

Crescent Lemon Honey Buns

MRS. PAT NEAVES | KANSAS CITY, MISSOURI

 Bake-Off®   BAKE-OFF® CONTEST 25, 1974

PREP TIME:	15 MINUTES (READY IN 35 MINUTES)
SERVINGS:	12 ROLLS

⊖ EASY

1 package (3 oz) cream cheese, softened

¹⁄₄ cup sugar

¹⁄₄ cup coconut, if desired

1 tablespoon honey

1 teaspoon lemon juice

1 can (8 oz) Pillsbury® refrigerated crescent dinner rolls

GLAZE

¹⁄₂ cup powdered sugar

1 teaspoon butter or margarine, softened

1 tablespoon lemon juice

1) Heat oven to 350°F. In small bowl, mix cream cheese, sugar, coconut, honey and lemon juice with wooden spoon until smooth. Grease cookie sheet.

2) Unroll dough onto work surface and separate into 2 large rectangles. Overlap long sides to form 13x7-inch rectangle; firmly press edges and perforations to seal. Spread cream cheese mixture on rectangle. Starting with 1 long side, roll up; press edge to seal. With serrated knife, cut into 12 slices. Place cut side down on cookie sheet.

3) Bake 15 to 20 minutes or until golden brown. In small bowl, mix the glaze ingredients; spread on warm rolls. Cover and refrigerate any remaining rolls.

HIGH ALTITUDE (3500-6500 FT.): No change.

Nutrition Information Per Serving:

Calories:	140	From Fat:	60
Total Fat		7g	
Saturated Fat		3g	
Trans Fat		1g	
Cholesterol		10mg	
Sodium		170mg	
Total Carbohydrate		18g	
Dietary Fiber		0g	
Sugars		12g	
Protein		2g	

Three-Pepper Galette

PREP TIME: 15 MINUTES (READY IN 50 MINUTES)
SERVINGS: 6

 EASY

1   Pillsbury® refrigerated pie crust (from 15-oz box), softened as directed on box

¼   medium green bell pepper, cut into 2x¼-inch strips (about ½ cup)

¼   medium red bell pepper, cut into 2x¼-inch strips (about ½ cup)

¼   medium yellow bell pepper, cut into 2x¼-inch strips (about ½ cup)

⅓   cup milk

2   eggs

1   container (4 oz) garlic-and-herbs spreadable cheese

¼   cup shredded Italian cheese blend

Fresh basil leaves, if desired

1) Heat oven to 400°F. Place pie crust in 9-inch glass pie plate. Arrange half the peppers in pie plate.

2) In small bowl, beat milk, eggs and spreadable cheese with electric mixer at low speed until well blended. Pour egg mixture over peppers in pie plate. Place remaining peppers over top of egg mixture. Fold edge of crust over filling, pleating crust slightly as necessary.

3) Bake 20 to 30 minutes or until crust is golden brown and center is set. Sprinkle with cheese blend. Bake 3 to 5 minutes longer or until cheese is melted. Sprinkle with basil. Serve immediately.

HIGH ALTITUDE (3500-6500 FT.): Increase first bake time to 25 to 30 minutes.

Nutrition Information Per Serving:

Calories:	280	From Fat: 110
Total Fat		12g
Saturated Fat		6g
Trans Fat		0g
Cholesterol		95mg
Sodium		590mg
Total Carbohydrate		33g
Dietary Fiber		0g
Sugars		6g
Protein		10g

Mascarpone-Filled Cranberry-Walnut Rolls

PAMELA SHANK | PARKERSBURG, WEST VIRGINIA

BAKE-OFF® CONTEST 43, 2008

PREP TIME:	25 MINUTES (READY IN 1 HOUR)
SERVINGS:	6

ROLLS

¹/₄ cup sweetened dried cranberries, coarsely chopped

¹/₃ cup Fisher® Chef's Naturals® chopped walnuts

¹/₂ cup Domino® or C&H® granulated sugar

1 teaspoon ground cinnamon

1 can (12 oz) Pillsbury® Golden Layers® refrigerated buttermilk biscuits (10 biscuits)

¹/₂ cup mascarpone cheese or cream cheese, softened

¹/₄ cup Land O Lakes® unsalted or salted butter, melted

GLAZE

1 tablespoon mascarpone cheese or cream cheese, softened

1 cup Domino® or C&H® confectioners' powdered sugar

1 to 2 tablespoons milk

1) Heat oven to 350°F. Lightly spray 8- or 9-inch round cake pan with Crisco® Original No-Stick cooking spray.

2) In small bowl, mix the cranberries and walnuts; set aside. In another small bowl, mix the granulated sugar and cinnamon; set aside.

3) Separate dough into 10 biscuits; press each biscuit into 3-inch round. Place heaping 1 teaspoon of the mascarpone cheese on center of each biscuit. Bring all sides of dough up over filling, stretching gently if necessary, and gather in center above filling to form a ball; firmly pinch edges to seal. Roll each biscuit in melted butter, then roll in sugar-cinnamon mixture. Place 1 biscuit in center of pan. Arrange remaining biscuits, seam sides down and sides touching, in circle around center biscuit. Pour remaining butter over biscuits; sprinkle with remaining sugar-cinnamon mixture.

4) Reserve ¹/₄ cup cranberry-walnut mixture; sprinkle remaining mixture over biscuits.

5) Bake 28 to 33 minutes or until biscuits are golden brown. Place heatproof serving plate upside down on pan; carefully turn plate and pan over. Let stand 1 minute, then carefully remove pan.

6) Sprinkle reserved cranberry-walnut mixture over coffee cake. In medium bowl, stir glaze ingredients until smooth. Drizzle glaze over top of rolls. Serve warm.

HIGH ALTITUDE (3500-6500 FT.): No change.

Nutrition Information Per Serving:		
Calories: 530	From Fat: 240	
Total Fat		26g
Saturated Fat		11g
Trans Fat		3g
Cholesterol		40mg
Sodium		610mg
Total Carbohydrate		68g
Dietary Fiber		0g
Sugars		43g
Protein		5g

Banana-Filled Caramel-Chocolate Crepes

SHERRY SMITH | BUNKER HILL, WEST VIRGINIA

BAKE-OFF® CONTEST 43, 2008

PREP TIME: 1 HOUR 25 MINUTES (READY IN 1 HOUR 25 MINUTES)
SERVINGS: 12 (2 CREPES EACH)

CREPES

- 1 box (19.5 oz) Pillsbury® traditional fudge brownie mix
- 1 cup Pillsbury BEST® all-purpose flour
- 3 Eggland's Best eggs, beaten
- 1¹/₂ cups milk
- ¹/₂ cup Crisco® pure vegetable oil

FILLING

- 1 cup Land O Lakes® unsalted or salted butter
- ¹/₂ cup Domino® or C&H® granulated sugar
- 2 teaspoons vanilla
- 1 tablespoon finely grated lemon peel
- 6 large firm ripe bananas, cut into ¹/₄-inch slices

TOPPINGS

- ¹/₂ cup Smucker's® caramel ice cream topping
- ³/₄ cup frozen (thawed) whipped topping
- 2 tablespoons Domino® or C&H® confectioners' powdered sugar
- ¹/₄ cup Fisher® Chef's Naturals® chopped walnuts

1) In large bowl, stir together brownie mix, flour, eggs, milk and oil until smooth.

2) Spray 10-inch skillet with Crisco® Original No-Stick cooking spray; heat over medium heat. Pour about ¹/₄ cup batter onto center of skillet. Immediately rotate skillet until thin layer of batter covers bottom. Cook over medium heat about 1 minute, turning once, until top appears slightly dry.

3) Remove crepe to cutting board, flipping crepe over so first cooked side is facing up. Immediately roll up crepe; place on plate to cool. Cover with kitchen towel. Repeat with remaining batter.

4) In large saucepan, cook butter and granulated sugar over medium heat, stirring frequently, until sugar is dissolved. Stir in vanilla and lemon peel until well mixed. Add banana slices; gently toss until coated and slightly softened.

5) Fill 1 crepe at a time, keeping remaining crepes covered. Gently unroll crepe; fill with slightly less than ¹/₄ cup banana filling. Reroll crepe; place seam side down on platter. Repeat with remaining crepes. Top crepes with drizzle of caramel topping and dollop of whipped topping. Sprinkle tops lightly with powdered sugar; sprinkle with walnuts. Serve immediately.

HIGH ALTITUDE (3500-6500 FT.): Increase flour to 1-1/2 cups. When cooking crepes, heat skillet over medium-low heat.

Nutrition Information Per Serving:	
Calories: 610	From Fat: 280
Total Fat	31g
Saturated Fat	13g
Trans Fat	0.5g
Cholesterol	90mg
Sodium	190mg
Total Carbohydrate	75g
Dietary Fiber	2g
Sugars	47g
Protein	7g

Onion and Herb Tart

PREP TIME: 20 MINUTES (READY IN 30 MINUTES)
SERVINGS: 18

 EASY   LOW FAT

- 1 can (8 oz) Pillsbury® refrigerated crescent dinner rolls
- 1 large sweet onion (about 12 oz)
- 2 teaspoons olive oil
- 2 teaspoons chopped fresh rosemary leaves or 1 teaspoon dried rosemary leaves, crushed
- 2 tablespoons packed brown sugar
- 4 oz coarsely chopped Brie cheese

1) Heat oven to 375°F. Grease or spray large cookie sheet. Unroll dough into 1 large rectangle on cookie sheet; press into 13x9-inch rectangle, firmly pressing perforations to seal. Fold edges over $1/2$ inch to form edges on crust. Bake 9 minutes.

2) Meanwhile, cut root end off onion, creating flat surface. Place flat surface on cutting board; cut onion in half vertically and peel off outer layer. Place large flat side down; cut into $1/8$-inch slices. In 10-inch skillet, heat oil over medium heat. Add onion and rosemary; cook 8 to 10 minutes, stirring frequently, until onions are caramelized. Stir in brown sugar.

3) Arrange cheese evenly over partially baked crust; top with onions.

4) Bake 4 to 6 minutes longer or until the crust is golden brown. Cut into 6 rows by 3 rows. Serve warm.

HIGH ALTITUDE (3500-6500 FT.): No change.

Nutrition Information Per Serving:

Calories:	90	From Fat:	45
Total Fat			5g
Saturated Fat			2g
Trans Fat			0.5g
Cholesterol			5mg
Sodium			140mg
Total Carbohydrate			8g
Dietary Fiber			0g
Sugars			3g
Protein			2g

Quick and Fruity Crescent Waffles

RENEE HEIMERL | OAKFIELD, WISCONSIN

Pillsbury Bake-Off®   BAKE-OFF® CONTEST 43, 2008

PREP TIME: 25 MINUTES (READY IN 25 MINUTES)
SERVINGS: 4

e EASY

¹/₄ cup Fisher® Chef's Naturals® pecan pieces

1 can (8 oz) Pillsbury® refrigerated crescent dinner rolls (8 rolls)

¹/₂ cup Smucker's® Simply Fruit® blueberry spreadable fruit

1 container (6 oz) Yoplait® Original 99% Fat-Free mountain blueberry yogurt

1 firm ripe banana, cut into ¹/₄-inch slices

¹/₂ cup whipped cream from aerosol can

¹/₄ teaspoon ground cinnamon

Fresh blueberries, if desired

1) Heat oven to 200°F. Heat square or rectangular waffle maker. Spray with Crisco® Original No-Stick cooking spray.

2) Meanwhile, in 8-inch nonstick skillet, toast the pecans over medium heat 5 to 7 minutes, stirring frequently, until lightly browned. Remove from skillet; set aside.

3) Separate crescent dough into 8 triangles. Place 2 or 3 triangles at a time on waffle maker, leaving at least ¹/₂ inch of space around each triangle. Close lid of waffle maker; cook 1 to 2 minutes or until golden brown. Place cooked waffles on cookie sheet in oven to keep warm.

4) In 1-quart saucepan, heat spreadable fruit and yogurt over medium heat 2 to 3 minutes, stirring occasionally, until hot.

5) To serve, stack 2 crescent waffles, slightly overlapping, on each of 4 serving plates. Spoon ¹/₄ of the fruit sauce over each serving; top each serving with ¹/₄ of the banana slices and 1 tablespoon of the pecans. Top with whipped cream; sprinkle lightly with cinnamon. Garnish with blueberries.

HIGH ALTITUDE (3500-6500 FT.): No change.

Nutrition Information Per Serving:		
Calories: 450	From Fat:	170
Total Fat		19g
Saturated Fat		6g
Trans Fat		3g
Cholesterol		10mg
Sodium		470mg
Total Carbohydrate		63g
Dietary Fiber		5g
Sugars		35g
Protein		7g

tip

Don't have the spreadable fruit on hand to use for this yummy breakfast treat? Smucker's® blueberry preserves may be substituted.

Choco-Peanut Butter-Banana Breakfast Strudel

VICKI FELDMAN | MANLIUS, NEW YORK

BAKE-OFF® CONTEST 43, 2008

PREP TIME: 25 MINUTES (READY IN 2 HOURS 20 MINUTES)
SERVINGS: 16 SLICES

Pillsbury BEST® all-purpose flour

1 can (10.1 oz) Pillsbury® Big & Buttery refrigerated crescent dinner rolls (6 rolls)

$1/3$ cup Jif® creamy peanut butter

$1/2$ cup hazelnut spread with cocoa

2 firm ripe small bananas

1 egg white (from 1 Eggland's Best egg), beaten

1 tablespoon cinnamon-sugar (from 3.62-oz jar)

Nutrition Information Per Serving:

Calories:	170	From Fat:	80
Total Fat			9g
Saturated Fat			2g
Trans Fat			1g
Cholesterol			0mg
Sodium			170mg
Total Carbohydrate			18g
Dietary Fiber			1g
Sugars			9g
Protein			3g

1) Heat oven to 350°F. Line cookie sheet with regular foil and lightly spray with Crisco® Original No-Stick cooking spray, or line cookie sheet with nonstick foil.

2) Sprinkle flour lightly on sheet of waxed paper. Unroll dough on floured paper into 1 long rectangle; press perforations to seal. Cover with another sheet of waxed paper; with rolling pin, roll to make 18x9-inch rectangle.

3) Spread peanut butter over rectangle to within 1 inch of edges. Spread hazelnut spread over peanut butter.

4) Cut bananas into about $1/8$-inch slices; arrange slices with sides touching in 2 rows down center of hazelnut spread.

5) Fold in the short ends of rectangle 1 inch. Starting at one long side of rectangle, roll up tightly; pinch edge of dough to seal. Remove from waxed paper; place seam side down on foil-lined cookie sheet. Brush with egg white; sprinkle with cinnamon-sugar.

6) Bake 20 to 25 minutes or until deep golden brown. Immediately transfer strudel on foil to cooling rack. Cool 30 minutes.

7) Loosely wrap foil around strudel; refrigerate 30 minutes to 1 hour or until chilled. To serve, cut into 1-inch slices, using serrated knife. Wrap and refrigerate any remaining strudel.

HIGH ALTITUDE (3500-6500 FT.): No change.

Cherry-Almond Streusel Danish

JEAN GOTTFRIED | UPPER SANDUSKY, OHIO

BAKE-OFF® CONTEST 43, 2008

PREP TIME: 25 MINUTES (READY IN 55 MINUTES)
SERVINGS: 8 DANISH

STREUSEL TOPPING

2 tablespoons Domino® or C&H® granulated sugar

2 tablespoons Pillsbury BEST® all-purpose flour

$1/2$ teaspoon ground cinnamon

1 tablespoon Land O Lakes® unsalted or salted butter

$1/4$ cup Fisher® Chef's Naturals® sliced almonds

DANISH

3 oz cream cheese (from 8-oz package), softened

$1/4$ cup Domino® or C&H® confectioners' powdered sugar

$1/2$ teaspoon vanilla

1 cup cherry pie filling with more fruit (from 21-oz can)

$1/2$ teaspoon almond extract

1 can (16.3 oz) Pillsbury® Grands!® flaky layers refrigerated original biscuits (8 biscuits)

3 tablespoons Land O Lakes® unsalted or salted butter, melted

ICING

1 tablespoon cream cheese, softened

$1/2$ cup Domino® or C&H® confectioners' powdered sugar

$1/4$ teaspoon vanilla

1 to 2 teaspoons water

1) Heat oven to 350°F. In small bowl, mix the granulated sugar, flour and cinnamon. Cut in 1 tablespoon butter, using fork, until mixture is crumbly. Add almonds; toss and set aside.

2) In another small bowl, mix 3 oz cream cheese, $1/2$ cup powdered sugar and $1/2$ teaspoon vanilla with electric mixer on Medium speed until smooth. In third small bowl, mix pie filling and almond extract.

3) Separate the biscuits; press each biscuit into 5-inch round. On the center of each biscuit round, spoon the pie filling with 4 or 5 cherries and heaping 2 teaspoons cream cheese mixture. Bring all sides of dough up over filling, stretching gently if necessary, and gather in the center above filling; firmly pinch edges to seal. Dip tops and sides into melted butter, dip into streusel; lightly press streusel on tops and sides. Place seam sides down, 2 inches apart, on ungreased cookie sheet.

4) Bake 18 to 22 minutes or until golden brown. Remove from cookie sheet to cooling rack. Cool 5 minutes.

5) In small bowl, mix 1 tablespoon cream cheese, $1/2$ cup powdered sugar and $1/4$ teaspoon vanilla. Stir in the water, 1 teaspoon at a time, until the icing is smooth and creamy. Place icing in small resealable food-storage plastic bag; cut small tip off 1 bottom corner of the bag. Squeeze icing in zigzag pattern on tops of cooled Danish.

HIGH ALTITUDE (3500-6500 FT.): No change.

Nutrition Information Per Serving:	
Calories: 410	From Fat: 190
Total Fat	21g
Saturated Fat	9g
Trans Fat	4g
Cholesterol	30mg
Sodium	590mg
Total Carbohydrate	50g
Dietary Fiber	0g
Sugars	27g
Protein	6g

Cranberry-Pecan Crescent Sausage Wraps

LISA KRAMER | MADISON, INDIANA

BAKE-OFF® CONTEST 43, 2008

PREP TIME: 35 MINUTES (READY IN 1 HOUR 20 MINUTES)
SERVINGS: 32

€ EASY

½ cup sweetened dried cranberries, coarsely chopped

1 cup orange juice

1 can (8 oz) Pillsbury® refrigerated crescent dinner rolls (8 rolls)

32 cocktail-size smoked link sausages (from 16-oz package)

½ cup packed Domino® or C&H® light brown sugar

⅔ cup Fisher® Chef's Naturals® chopped pecans

Nutrition Information Per Serving:

Calories:	120	From Fat:	70
Total Fat			8g
Saturated Fat			2.5g
Trans Fat			0.5g
Cholesterol			10mg
Sodium			210mg
Total Carbohydrate			9g
Dietary Fiber			0g
Sugars			7g
Protein			3g

1) Heat oven to 400°F. In small bowl, mix cranberries and orange juice. Let stand 15 minutes.

2) Meanwhile, separate dough into rectangles; press each into 8x4-inch rectangle. Cut each rectangle into 8 (about 2-inch) squares.

3) Place 1 sausage on each square; wrap dough around sausage. Pinch edges to seal. Place the rolls seam side down in 13x9-inch (3-quart) glass baking dish. Bake 10 to 15 minutes or until light golden brown.

4) Meanwhile, drain orange juice from cranberries into 2-quart saucepan; reserve cranberries. Stir brown sugar into orange juice. Cook over medium heat 2 to 3 minutes, stirring occasionally, until sugar is dissolved.

5) Remove sausage rolls from oven. Pour orange juice mixture evenly over sausage rolls. Sprinkle with cranberries and pecans. Bake 10 to 13 minutes longer or until golden brown and bubbly. Serve warm.

HIGH ALTITUDE (3500-6500 FT.): In Step 3, bake 15 to 18 minutes.

Strawberry-Orange Fruit Dip

PREP TIME: 15 MINUTES (READY IN 15 MINUTES)
SERVINGS: 12 (2 TABLESPOONS DIP EACH)

€ EASY

1 package (8 oz) cream cheese, softened

¼ cup powdered sugar

½ teaspoon grated orange peel

½ cup chopped strawberries (about 3 oz)

Assorted fruit for dipping, as desired

Nutrition Information Per Serving:

Calories:	80	From Fat:	60
Total Fat			7g
Saturated Fat			4g
Trans Fat			0g
Cholesterol			20mg
Sodium			55mg
Total Carbohydrate			4g
Dietary Fiber			0g
Sugars			3g
Protein			1g

1) In small bowl, beat cream cheese, powdered sugar and orange peel with electric mixer on Low speed until smooth. Stir in strawberries.

2) Serve with assorted fruit for dipping. Cover and refrigerate any remaining fruit dip.

HIGH ALTITUDE (3500-6500 FT.): No change.

Taste-of-the-Islands Breakfast Rolls

PATTY COLON | EGG HARBOR CITY, NEW JERSEY

Pillsbury Bake-Off®   BAKE-OFF® CONTEST 43, 2008

PREP TIME: 15 MINUTES (READY IN 40 MINUTES)
SERVINGS: 5 ROLLS

e EASY

ROLLS

1 to 3 teaspoons Crisco® all-vegetable shortening

1 can (17.5 oz) Pillsbury® Grands!® flaky supreme refrigerated cinnamon rolls with icing (5 rolls)

1/2 cup Smucker's® pineapple ice cream topping, drained

1/2 cup Fisher® dry-roasted macadamia nuts, chopped

TOPPING

Icing from can of cinnamon rolls

1 tablespoon coconut-flavored rum or 1/2 teaspoon rum extract

1/2 cup toasted flaked coconut, if desired

GARNISHES

Fresh pineapple rings or chunks

Fresh mint leaves

1) Heat oven to 350°F. Grease cookie sheet with shortening.

2) Unroll cinnamon roll dough, cinnamon side up. Set icing aside. Spoon pineapple topping evenly over cinnamon rolls. Sprinkle nuts over pineapple topping.

3) Reroll the dough into pinwheel shape; separate into 5 rolls. Place 2 inches apart on cookie sheet. Bake 20 to 23 minutes or until golden brown.

4) Pour icing into small bowl; stir in rum. Spread icing on rolls; sprinkle with coconut. Place on serving platter; garnish with pineapple rings and mint.

HIGH ALTITUDE (3500-6500 FT.): Heat oven to 325°F. Decrease pineapple topping to 1/4 cup. Bake 22 to 25 minutes.

Nutrition Information Per Serving:	
Calories: 560	From Fat: 250
Total Fat	28g
Saturated Fat	7g
Trans Fat	5g
Cholesterol	0mg
Sodium	640mg
Total Carbohydrate	72g
Dietary Fiber	2g
Sugars	40g
Protein	5g

Tuna Divan Crescent Squares

PREP TIME: 20 MINUTES (READY IN 1 HOUR)
SERVINGS: 8

e EASY

1 can (8 oz) Pillsbury® crescent dinner rolls

1 cup shredded Swiss cheese (4 oz)

1 box (9 oz) Green Giant® frozen cut broccoli, cooked, well drained

4 eggs

1 can (10¾ oz) condensed cream of broccoli soup

2 tablespoons mayonnaise or salad dressing

½ teaspoon onion powder

½ teaspoon dried dill weed

1 can (6 oz) water-packed tuna, drained

1 jar (2 oz) diced pimiento, drained

1) Heat oven to 350°F. Unroll dough and separate into 2 long rectangles; place lengthwise in ungreased 13x9-inch pan. Press in bottom and ½ inch up sides to form crust; press edges and perforations to seal. Sprinkle cheese over the crust; arrange broccoli over cheese.

2) In medium bowl, beat eggs slightly with wire whisk. Beat in soup, mayonnaise, onion powder and dill weed. Stir in tuna and pimiento. Pour evenly over broccoli. Bake 28 to 32 minutes or until filling is set. Cut into squares; serve warm.

HIGH ALTITUDE (3500-6500 FT.): Bake 30 to 34 minutes.

Nutrition Information Per Serving:	
Calories: 280	From Fat: 160
Total Fat	17g
Saturated Fat	6g
Trans Fat	1.5g
Cholesterol	125mg
Sodium	600mg
Total Carbohydrate	17g
Dietary Fiber	1g
Sugars	5g
Protein	15g

tip

If you're out of pimiento and aren't planning a trip to the store, just use ¼ cup chopped red bell pepper instead.

Apricot-Almond Coffee Cake

PREP TIME: 20 MINUTES (READY IN 1 HOUR 20 MINUTES)
SERVINGS: 12

 EASY

Nutrition Information Per Serving:	
Calories: 190	From Fat: 80
Total Fat	9g
Saturated Fat	3g
Trans Fat	1g
Cholesterol	10mg
Sodium	170mg
Total Carbohydrate	24g
Dietary Fiber	1g
Sugars	15g
Protein	3g

1 package (3 oz) cream cheese, softened

1/2 cup almond paste, crumbled

1 can (8 oz) Pillsbury® refrigerated crescent dinner rolls

1/3 cup apricot preserves

1/2 cup powdered sugar

2 teaspoons milk

1 tablespoon sliced almonds

1) Heat oven to 375°F. Grease or spray cookie sheet. In small bowl, beat cream cheese with electric mixer on Low speed until smooth and creamy. Beat in the almond paste until well mixed.

2) Unroll dough onto cookie sheet; press into 13x7-inch rectangle, firmly pressing perforations to seal. Spoon the cream cheese mixture lengthwise down center 1/3 of rectangle; spoon preserves on top of mixture.

3) On each long side of dough rectangle, make cuts 1 inch apart to edge of filling. Fold opposite strips of dough over filling and cross in center to make a braided appearance; seal ends.

4) Bake 18 to 22 minutes or until golden brown. Remove from cookie sheet to cooling rack. Cool completely, about 40 minutes.

5) In small bowl, mix powdered sugar and milk until smooth; drizzle over coffee cake. Garnish with sliced almonds. Serve warm or cool.

HIGH ALTITUDE (3500-6500 FT.): No change.

tip

You may assemble this coffee cake up to 2 hours ahead of time—just cover it with plastic wrap and store it in the fridge. Uncover and bake it as directed in the recipe.

Poblano–Chorizo Egg Bake

PREP TIME: 40 MINUTES (READY IN 1 HOUR 50 MINUTES)
SERVINGS: 12

2 large poblano chiles

1 lb fresh bulk chorizo sausage

2 cans (8 oz each) Pillsbury® Place 'n Bake™ refrigerated crescent rounds

1 can (15 oz) Progresso® black beans, drained, rinsed

1 cup plum (Roma) tomatoes, seeded and coarsely chopped (about 4)

1 cup shredded Cheddar cheese (4 oz)

1 cup shredded Monterey Jack cheese (4 oz)

10 eggs

1½ cups milk

½ teaspoon ground cumin

Salt and pepper, if desired

2 tablespoons milk

⅔ cup nacho-flavored tortilla chips, crushed

Salsa, if desired

Nutrition Information Per Serving:

Calories:	520	From Fat:	300
Total Fat			33g
Saturated Fat			14g
Trans Fat			0g
Cholesterol			230mg
Sodium			960mg
Total Carbohydrate			31g
Dietary Fiber			3g
Sugars			6g
Protein			26g

1) Set oven control to broil. Place chiles on broiler pan. Broil with tops 2 inches from heat, turning frequently, 6 to 8 minutes or until skins are blistered and lightly charred. Transfer chiles to resealable food-storage plastic bag; seal bag and place in bowl of ice water 5 to 10 minutes. Remove skin by running fingers down each chile. Cut stem and top off each chile. Cut slit down the side and remove seeds. Coarsely chop chiles; set aside.

2) Heat oven to 350°F. Spray bottom only of 13x9-inch (3-quart) glass baking dish with cooking spray.

3) In 10-inch skillet, cook sausage over medium-high heat about 7 minutes or until thoroughly browned, breaking into small pieces. Drain well; move to plate lined with paper towel. Pat with towel to remove additional grease.

4) Separate dough into total of 16 rounds. Cut each of 9 rounds into 4 pieces. Arrange pieces evenly in baking dish. Cut remaining 7 rounds in half for topping; set aside.

5) Spread sausage, black beans, tomatoes and both cheeses evenly in pan over crescent pieces.

6) In large bowl, beat eggs, 1½ cups milk, the cumin, chopped chiles, salt and pepper with wire whisk until well blended. Pour over mixture in baking dish. Press down with back of spoon, making sure all ingredients are covered with egg mixture.

7) Dip reserved crescent halves into 2 tablespoons milk and roll in crushed chips. Place around edge of pan.

8) Bake 52 to 57 minutes or until edges are deep golden brown and center is set. Let stand 10 minutes before serving. Cut egg bake into squares. Serve with salsa.

HIGH ALTITUDE (3500-6500 FT.): No change.

CHEESY CHICKEN AND
ARTICHOKE BITES
PG. 43

Snacks & Sippers

Satisfy the munchies and quench your thirst with these irresistible finger foods, beverages and more.

BEST MINTED ICED TEA
PG. 48

MICROWAVE DILL TATER SNACKS
PG. 47

GLAZED PECANS
PG. 40

Wild Mushroom Pizza

PREP TIME:	15 MINUTES (READY IN 35 MINUTES)
SERVINGS:	48

🅗 LOW FAT

1 teaspoon olive oil

1 can (13.8 oz) Pillsbury® refrigerated classic pizza crust

1 tablespoon butter or margarine

1 lb assorted fresh wild mushrooms (shiitake, oyster, crimini), cut into ¹/₄-inch-thick slices

1 teaspoon dried thyme leaves, crushed

Salt and pepper to taste, if desired

1 package (8 oz) ¹/₃-less-fat cream cheese (Neufchâtel), softened

4 oz fontina cheese, shredded

1 cup shredded mozzarella cheese (4 oz)

Fresh thyme leaves, if desired

1) Heat oven to 400°F. Brush large cookie sheet with oil. Unroll dough; place on oiled cookie sheet. Starting at center, press out the dough into 15x10-inch rectangle. Bake 8 to 10 minutes or until crust is very light brown.

2) Meanwhile, in 12-inch skillet, heat butter over medium-high heat until melted. Add the mushrooms; cook about 6 minutes, stirring frequently, until well browned; drain. Stir in thyme, salt and pepper.

3) Spread the cream cheese evenly over crust. Sprinkle fontina cheese over cream cheese. Spread the cooked mushrooms over cheese. Sprinkle mozzarella cheese over mushrooms.

4) Bake 10 to 12 minutes longer or until cheese is melted and crust is golden brown. Cool 5 minutes. Cut into 8 rows by 6 rows. Sprinkle pizza with thyme leaves.

HIGH ALTITUDE (3500-6500 FT.): No change.

Nutrition Information Per Serving:		
Calories: 50	**From Fat:**	25
Total Fat		3g
Saturated Fat		1.5g
Trans Fat		0g
Cholesterol		10mg
Sodium		110mg
Total Carbohydrate		4g
Dietary Fiber		0g
Sugars		0g
Protein		3g

Spicy Chicken Mini Burritos

PREP TIME: 45 MINUTES (READY IN 45 MINUTES)
SERVINGS: 16 MINI BURRITOS

- 1 teaspoon vegetable oil
- 1 tablespoon finely chopped onion
- 1 garlic clove, finely chopped
- 2 cups shredded cooked chicken
- 2 to 3 tablespoons chopped jalapeño chiles
- 1/2 teaspoon ground cumin
- 3/4 cup salsa verde or green salsa
- 16 Old El Paso® flour tortillas (6-inch; from 10.5-oz packages)
- 1 cup shredded Mexican-style Cheddar Jack cheese with jalapeño peppers (4 oz)
- 1 medium plum (Roma) tomato, chopped (about 1/2 cup)
- 1/3 cup chopped fresh cilantro

1) In 10-inch nonstick skillet, heat oil over medium heat. Add the onion and garlic; cook 2 to 3 minutes, stirring occasionally, until crisp-tender. Stir in the chicken, jalapeño chiles, cumin and salsa verde; cook 4 to 6 minutes or until hot. Keep warm.

2) Heat tortillas as directed on package. Spoon 2 level tablespoons chicken mixture and 1 tablespoon shredded cheese in center of each tortilla. Top with tomato and cilantro. Fold 1/3 of tortilla down over filling; fold sides toward center. Fold remaining side up and turn over. Serve immediately.

HIGH ALTITUDE (3500-6500 FT.): No change.

Nutrition Information Per Serving:

Calories:	140	From Fat:	50
Total Fat		6g	
Saturated Fat		2g	
Trans Fat		1g	
Cholesterol		20mg	
Sodium		290mg	
Total Carbohydrate		14g	
Dietary Fiber		0g	
Sugars		1g	
Protein		9g	

Roast Beef 'n Swiss Tortilla Roll-Ups

PREP TIME: 10 MINUTES (READY IN 10 MINUTES)
SERVINGS: 16 APPETIZERS

 EASY

2 tablespoons Caesar ranch dressing

2 flour tortillas (7- to 8-inch)

2 large leaf lettuce leaves, torn to fit tortilla

4 oz thinly sliced deli roast beef

4 slices ($\frac{3}{4}$ oz each) Swiss cheese product

2 teaspoons diced red onion

Pickle wedges, if desired

Nutrition Information Per Serving:		
Calories: 60	From Fat:	35
Total Fat		4g
Saturated Fat		1.5g
Trans Fat		0g
Cholesterol		10mg
Sodium		70mg
Total Carbohydrate		3g
Dietary Fiber		0g
Sugars		0g
Protein		4g

For a change of pace the next time you fix these, use smoked turkey or ham instead of the roast beef and try Cheddar cheese in place of the Swiss.

1) Spread 1 tablespoon dressing on each tortilla, covering entire surface. Top each with lettuce leaf and half of beef, cheese and onion. Roll up each tortilla tightly.

2) To serve, cut roll-ups into 1-inch slices. Insert cocktail toothpick into each to secure. Serve with pickle wedges.

HIGH ALTITUDE (3500-6500 FT.): No change.

Lemon-Ginger Tingler

PREP TIME: 10 MINUTES (READY IN 15 MINUTES)
SERVINGS: 6 (1 CUP EACH)

 EASY   LOW FAT

1¹/₂ cups sugar

1 cup water

1¹/₂ cups fresh lemon juice (about 8 lemons)

3 cups ginger ale, chilled

1) In 1-quart saucepan, cook sugar and water over medium heat, stirring constantly, until sugar is dissolved. Remove from heat; cool to room temperature.

2) Stir in lemon juice. Store mixture in tightly covered nonmetal container or jar in refrigerator.

3) For each serving, in tall glass, mix ¹/₂ cup chilled mixture and ¹/₂ cup ginger ale. If desired, add ice.

HIGH ALTITUDE (3500-6500 FT.): No change.

Nutrition Information Per Serving:		
Calories: 270	From Fat:	0
Total Fat		0g
Saturated Fat		0g
Trans Fat		0g
Cholesterol		0mg
Sodium		25mg
Total Carbohydrate		66g
Dietary Fiber		0g
Sugars		62g
Protein		0g

Buffalo Chicken Dip

PREP TIME: 10 MINUTES (READY IN 15 MINUTES)
SERVINGS: 32 (2 TABLESPOONS DIP EACH)

 EASY

1 cup chunky blue cheese dressing

2 to 3 tablespoons buffalo wing sauce

2 cans (10 oz each) chunk chicken, drained, chopped

2 packages (8 oz each) cream cheese, softened

2 medium stalks celery, finely chopped (1 cup)

1 bag (8 oz) Gardetto's® Special Request roasted garlic rye chips, as desired

Nutrition Information Per Serving:		
Calories: 100	From Fat:	80
Total Fat		9g
Saturated Fat		3.5g
Trans Fat		0g
Cholesterol		25mg
Sodium		200mg
Total Carbohydrate		1g
Dietary Fiber		0g
Sugars		0g
Protein		4g

1) In large microwavable bowl, mix dressing, sauce, chicken and cream cheese. Cover; microwave on High 2 to 3 minutes or until hot. Stir in celery.

2) Spoon chicken dip into serving dish. Serve with roasted garlic rye chips.

HIGH ALTITUDE (3500-6500 FT.): No change.

Peach Chutney Pinwheels

LAURIE BENDA | MADISON, WISCONSIN

BAKE-OFF® CONTEST 43, 2008

PREP TIME: 20 MINUTES (READY IN 55 MINUTES)
SERVINGS: 32 APPETIZERS

ⓔ EASY   ⓕ LOW FAT

1/4 cup Smucker's® peach preserves

2 teaspoons finely chopped red onion

1 teaspoon water

1/8 teaspoon ground cinnamon

1/8 teaspoon ground cloves

1/8 teaspoon ground nutmeg

1/8 teaspoon crushed red pepper flakes

1/8 teaspoon salt

1/8 teaspoon pepper

1 can (8 oz) Pillsbury® refrigerated crescent dinner rolls (8 rolls)

1/4 cup cream cheese spread (from 8-oz container)

1/2 teaspoon balsamic vinegar

1) In 1-quart saucepan, stir together preserves, onion, water, cinnamon, cloves, nutmeg, pepper flakes, salt and pepper. Heat over medium-high heat until mixture begins to simmer. Reduce heat to medium-low; cook 1 minute, stirring frequently. Remove from heat; set aside.

2) Unroll the crescent dough. Divide into 4 rectangles; press perforations to seal. Spread 1 tablespoon cream cheese over each rectangle, to within 1/2 inch of edge of 1 short end of rectangle.

3) Stir vinegar into the cooled peach chutney. Spread 1/4 of chutney (about 1 tablespoon) over cream cheese on each rectangle. Starting at short end covered with cream cheese, gently roll up each rectangle. Pinch seam to seal. Place rolls on cutting board or large plate; cover with plastic wrap and refrigerate 20 minutes for easier slicing.

4) Heat oven to 375°F. Line 2 cookie sheets with foil; spray foil with Crisco® Original No-Stick cooking spray.

5) Cut each roll into 8 slices, using serrated knife. Place on cookie sheets. Bake 12 to 15 minutes or until golden brown. Immediately remove from cookie sheets. Serve warm.

HIGH ALTITUDE (3500-6500 FT.): No change.

Nutrition Information Per Serving:		
Calories: 40	From Fat:	20
Total Fat		2g
Saturated Fat		1g
Trans Fat		0g
Cholesterol		0mg
Sodium		80mg
Total Carbohydrate		5g
Dietary Fiber		0g
Sugars		2g
Protein		0g

Herb Cheese Spread

PREP TIME: 20 MINUTES (READY IN 2 HOURS 20 MINUTES)
SERVINGS: 10 (2 TABLESPOONS DIP AND 2 APPLE SLICES EACH)

 EASY   LOW FAT

1 container (8 oz) fat-free cream cheese spread (1 cup), softened

2 oz feta cheese, crumbled ($^1/_2$ cup)

1 oz blue cheese, crumbled ($^1/_4$ cup)

$^1/_2$ teaspoon dried basil leaves

$^1/_2$ teaspoon dried rosemary leaves, crushed

1 tablespoon finely chopped chives or green onion tops

2 red or green apples or pears, cut into 20 slices each, or assorted crackers

1) In medium bowl, beat cream cheese, feta cheese, blue cheese, basil and rosemary with electric mixer on medium speed, or with spoon until well mixed. Cover; refrigerate about 2 hours or until thoroughly chilled.

2) To serve, place in serving bowl; sprinkle with chives. Serve with fruit or crackers.

HIGH ALTITUDE (3500-6500 FT.): No change.

Nutrition Information Per Serving:

Calories:	60	From Fat:	20
Total Fat		2.5g	
Saturated Fat		1.5g	
Trans Fat		0g	
Cholesterol		10mg	
Sodium		230mg	
Total Carbohydrate		5g	
Dietary Fiber		0g	
Sugars		4g	
Protein		5g	

Like to use fresh herbs instead of dried? Use 1 teaspoon chopped fresh basil leaves and 1 teaspoon finely chopped fresh rosemary.

Mini Fruit Pizzas

PREP TIME: 25 MINUTES (READY IN 40 MINUTES)
SERVINGS: 20 FRUIT PIZZAS

 EASY

1 package (18 oz) Pillsbury® Ready To Bake!™ refrigerated sugar cookies (20 cookies)

1 package (8 oz) cream cheese, softened

2 tablespoons frozen limeade concentrate

1/2 cup powdered sugar

3 cups fresh blueberries, sliced strawberries and kiwifruit

Powdered sugar, if desired

1) Bake cookies as directed on package. Cool completely, about 10 minutes.

2) Meanwhile, in medium bowl, beat the cream cheese, limeade concentrate and powdered sugar with electric mixer on medium speed until smooth.

3) Spread each cookie with 1 tablespoon cream cheese mixture. Arrange fruit on top of each. Serve immediately, or cover and refrigerate up to 2 hours before serving. Sprinkle with powdered sugar just before serving.

HIGH ALTITUDE (3500-6500 FT.): No change.

Nutrition Information Per Serving:		
Calories: 180	From Fat:	90
Total Fat		10g
Saturated Fat		4.5g
Trans Fat		2g
Cholesterol		20mg
Sodium		100mg
Total Carbohydrate		21g
Dietary Fiber		1g
Sugars		13g
Protein		2g

 tip

To add even more flavor and flair to these sweet treats, sprinkle them with some toasted slivered almonds or a bit of shredded lemon peel.

Spanish Salsa with Crispy French Bread

PREP TIME: 20 MINUTES (READY IN 40 MINUTES)
SERVINGS: 32 (1 SLICE BREAD AND 2 TABLESPOONS SALSA EACH)

e EASY   **lf** LOW FAT

BREAD

32 very thin diagonal slices French bread

Cooking spray

SALSA

1 cup finely chopped fresh mushrooms

1 tablespoon chopped fresh parsley

1 tablespoon balsamic or red wine vinegar

2 teaspoons dried basil leaves

1/4 teaspoon salt

6 plum (Roma) tomatoes, finely chopped

2 medium green onions, sliced (2 tablespoons)

1 jar (6 oz) marinated artichoke hearts, drained, finely chopped

1 can (4 1/4 oz) chopped ripe olives, drained

1) Heat oven to 325°F. Line cookie sheet with foil. Place the bread slices on cookie sheet; spray lightly with cooking spray. Bake 7 to 10 minutes or until very crisp. Place bread slices on cooling rack; cool completely.

2) Meanwhile, in decorative bowl, mix salsa ingredients. Let stand at room temperature 20 minutes to blend flavors, or refrigerate until serving time. Serve salsa with crispy bread slices.

HIGH ALTITUDE (3500-6500 FT.): No change.

Nutrition Information Per Serving:

Calories: 30	From Fat: 5
Total Fat	1g
Saturated Fat	0g
Trans Fat	0g
Cholesterol	0mg
Sodium	100mg
Total Carbohydrate	4g
Dietary Fiber	0g
Sugars	0g
Protein	0g

tip

 Love to dip? Instead of using this salsa to top off French bread slices, serve it alongside a bowl of your favorite tortilla chips.

Very Berry Iced Tea

PREP TIME: 10 MINUTES (READY IN 10 MINUTES)
SERVINGS: 8 (1 CUP EACH)

 EASY   LOW FAT

4 cups water

3 tablespoons instant iced tea mix

3 cups raspberry-kiwi fruit juice, chilled

1/2 cup fresh raspberries

1) In 2-quart pitcher, mix all ingredients except raspberries. Stir in raspberries.

2) Serve tea over ice in glasses.

HIGH ALTITUDE (3500-6500 FT.): No change.

Nutrition Information Per Serving:	
Calories: 50	From Fat: 0
Total Fat	0g
Saturated Fat	0g
Trans Fat	0g
Cholesterol	0mg
Sodium	5mg
Total Carbohydrate	12g
Dietary Fiber	0g
Sugars	9g
Protein	0g

Glazed Pecans

PREP TIME: 20 MINUTES (READY IN 50 MINUTES)
SERVINGS: 16 (2 TABLESPOONS EACH)

 EASY

2 tablespoons butter

2 tablespoons packed dark brown sugar

2 tablespoons maple-flavored syrup or real maple syrup

2 cups pecan halves (8 oz)

Nutrition Information Per Serving:	
Calories: 130	From Fat: 100
Total Fat	12g
Saturated Fat	2g
Trans Fat	0g
Cholesterol	0mg
Sodium	10mg
Total Carbohydrate	6g
Dietary Fiber	1g
Sugars	3g
Protein	1g

1) Heat oven to 350°F. Line cookie sheet with cooking parchment paper. In 12-inch skillet, melt butter over medium heat. Add brown sugar and syrup; mix well. Cook until bubbly, stirring constantly.

2) Add pecans; cook 2 to 3 minutes, stirring constantly, until coated. Spread mixture onto parchment-lined cookie sheet.

3) Bake 6 to 8 minutes or until golden brown. Cool completely, about 30 minutes. Store pecans in tightly covered container up to 2 weeks.

HIGH ALTITUDE (3500-6500 FT.): No change.

Garlic Cream Cheese Crostini

| PREP TIME: | 10 MINUTES (READY IN 15 MINUTES) |
| SERVINGS: | 20 CROSTINI |

 EASY   LOW FAT

20 (¹/₂-inch-thick) slices French bread

1 tablespoon olive or vegetable oil

¹/₂ cup garlic-and-herb cream cheese spread (from 8-oz container)

4 medium green onions, chopped (¹/₄ cup)

Chopped fresh thyme leaves, if desired

Chopped fresh plum (Roma) tomatoes, if desired

1) Set oven control to broil. On ungreased cookie sheet, place bread slices. Lightly brush each with oil. Broil 4 to 6 inches from heat about 1 minute or until light golden brown.

2) In small bowl, mix cream cheese and green onions. Spread mixture on toasted bread slices. Broil about 1 minute longer or until cream cheese bubbles. Garnish with thyme leaves and tomatoes.

HIGH ALTITUDE (3500-6500 FT.): No change.

Nutrition Information Per Serving:

Calories:	50	From Fat:	25
Total Fat			3g
Saturated Fat			1.5g
Trans Fat			0g
Cholesterol			5mg
Sodium			70mg
Total Carbohydrate			5g
Dietary Fiber			0g
Sugars			0g
Protein			1g

tip

Garlic-and-herb cream cheese spread is a soft cream cheese. Look for it alongside the regular cream cheese in your local grocery store.

Red Pepper Hummus with Pita Chips

PREP TIME: 10 MINUTES (READY IN 10 MINUTES)
SERVINGS: 12 (2 TABLESPOONS HUMMUS EACH)

 EASY   LOW FAT

1 can (19 oz) Progresso® chick peas, drained, rinsed

1 tablespoon lemon juice

1 tablespoon olive or vegetable oil

2 garlic cloves, chopped

1/3 cup drained roasted red bell peppers (from a jar)

Chopped fresh parsley

Pita chips, as desired

1) In food processor, place chick peas, lemon juice, oil and garlic. Cover; process 1 to 2 minutes or until smooth. Add the roasted red bell peppers; process 30 to 60 seconds or until peppers are finely chopped. Place in serving bowl. Sprinkle with the parsley. Cover and refrigerate until ready to serve.

2) Serve with pita chips.

HIGH ALTITUDE (3500-6500 FT.): No change.

Nutrition Information Per Serving:		
Calories: 70	From Fat:	20
Total Fat		2g
Saturated Fat		0g
Trans Fat		0g
Cholesterol		0mg
Sodium		50mg
Total Carbohydrate		10g
Dietary Fiber		2g
Sugars		0g
Protein		3g

tip If a food processor is not available, mash the chick peas with a fork. The mixture may be slightly lumpy, but the texture won't interfere with the flavor.

Cheesy Chicken and Artichoke Bites

NOELLE KOMPA | FOREST, VIRGINIA

BAKE-OFF® CONTEST 43, 2008

PREP TIME: 30 MINUTES (READY IN 50 MINUTES)
SERVINGS: 48 APPETIZERS

2 cans (8 oz each) Pillsbury®
refrigerated crescent dinner rolls
(8 rolls each)

6 slices fully cooked bacon (from
2.1-oz package)

1 package (6 oz) refrigerated cooked
chicken breast strips, cubed

1 box (9 oz) Green Giant® frozen
spinach, thawed, squeezed to drain
and thoroughly chopped

1 can (13.75 oz) quartered artichoke
hearts, drained, coarsely chopped

2 medium garlic cloves, finely
chopped

1/2 cup mayonnaise or salad dressing

1/4 cup sour cream

1/2 cup shredded Asiago cheese (2 oz)

1/4 cup grated Parmesan cheese

1) Heat oven to 375°F. Separate dough
from both cans into 8 rectangles; press
perforations to seal. Cut each rectangle
into 6 (2-inch) squares. Press 1 square in
the bottom and up the side of each of
48 ungreased mini muffin cups.

2) Heat bacon as directed on package;
crumble. In large bowl, mix the bacon
and remaining ingredients. Place
1 tablespoon chicken filling in each cup.

3) Bake 12 to 20 minutes or until the edges are golden brown. Immediately
remove from pans to serving platter. Serve warm.

HIGH ALTITUDE (3500-6500 FT.): Bake 16 to 24 minutes.

Nutrition Information Per Serving:	
Calories: 80	From Fat: 45
Total Fat	5g
Saturated Fat	1.5g
Trans Fat	0.5g
Cholesterol	10mg
Sodium	160mg
Total Carbohydrate	5g
Dietary Fiber	0g
Sugars	0g
Protein	3g

Chipotle Pico de Gallo

PREP TIME: 20 MINUTES (READY IN 20 MINUTES)
SERVINGS: 12 (MAKES 3 CUPS)

 EASY   LOW FAT

1 cup coarsely chopped unpeeled seedless cucumber

¹/₂ cup chopped peeled jicama

¹/₂ cup chopped red bell pepper

1 tablespoon lime juice

1 tablespoon honey

¹/₄ teaspoon salt

2 seedless oranges, peeled, coarsely chopped

2 chipotle chiles in adobo sauce (from 11-oz can), chopped

Whole grain tortilla chips, if desired

1) In medium bowl, mix all ingredients except chips.

2) Serve pico de gallo immediately with tortilla chips, or cover and refrigerate until serving time.

HIGH ALTITUDE (3500-6500 FT.): No change.

Nutrition Information Per Serving:

Calories:	25	From Fat:	0
Total Fat			0g
Saturated Fat			0g
Trans Fat			0g
Cholesterol			0mg
Sodium			75mg
Total Carbohydrate			6g
Dietary Fiber			1g
Sugars			4g
Protein			0g

tip

Feel like a meal? With its tangy blend of flavors, this smoky pico de gallo is excellent served with a main dish of grilled pork, chicken or fish.

Chile and Cheese Empanaditas

PREP TIME: 25 MINUTES (READY IN 45 MINUTES)
SERVINGS: 16 APPETIZERS

 EASY

1 cup shredded pepper Jack cheese (4 oz)

$1/3$ cup Old El Paso® chopped green chiles (from 4.5-oz can)

1 box (15 oz) Pillsbury® refrigerated pie crusts, softened as directed on box

1 egg, beaten

1 cup Old El Paso® Thick 'n Chunky salsa

1) Heat oven to 400°F. In small bowl, mix cheese and chiles.

2) With $3\frac{1}{4}$-inch round cutter, cut each pie crust into 8 rounds. Spoon cheese mixture evenly onto half of each dough round. Brush edge of crust rounds with beaten egg. Fold crust rounds in half; press edges with fork to seal. Place on ungreased cookie sheet. Brush tops with egg. Cut small slit in top of each.

3) Bake 12 to 16 minutes or until golden brown. Serve the warm empanaditas with salsa.

HIGH ALTITUDE (3500-6500 FT.): No change.

Nutrition Information Per Serving:

Calories:	130	From Fat:	70
Total Fat		8g	
Saturated Fat		3g	
Trans Fat		0g	
Cholesterol		25mg	
Sodium		310mg	
Total Carbohydrate		12g	
Dietary Fiber		0g	
Sugars		0g	
Protein		2g	

tip

No pepper Jack cheese? Shredded cheddar cheese or Mexican cheese blend are perfectly good substitutes in these Southwestern pastry snacks.

Jalapeño Popper Cups

TRACY SCHUHMACHER | PENFIELD, NEW YORK

Pillsbury
Bake-Off®

BAKE-OFF® CONTEST 43, 2008

EASY

PREP TIME: 15 MINUTES (READY IN 40 MINUTES)
SERVINGS: 20 APPETIZERS

1 can (12 oz) Pillsbury® Golden Layers® refrigerated buttermilk biscuits (10 biscuits)

1 can (4.5 oz) Old El Paso® chopped green chiles, drained

1/2 cup shredded Cheddar cheese (2 oz)

1/3 cup mayonnaise or salad dressing

2 tablespoons cooked real bacon pieces (from 3- to 4.3-oz jar or package)

1 teaspoon dried minced onion

20 Old El Paso® pickled jalapeño slices (from 12-oz jar), drained

1) Heat oven to 375°F. Separate each biscuit into 2 rounds. Press 1 round in bottom and up side of each of 20 ungreased mini muffin cups.

2) In small bowl, mix remaining ingredients except jalapeño slices. Spoon heaping 1 teaspoon mixture into each cup; top each with 1 jalapeño slice.

3) Bake 13 to 19 minutes or until the edges are golden brown. Remove from the pan to serving platter; let stand 5 minutes. Serve warm.

HIGH ALTITUDE (3500-6500 FT.): Bake 16 to 22 minutes.

Nutrition Information Per Serving:		
Calories: 100	From Fat: 60	
Total Fat		6g
Saturated Fat		1.5g
Trans Fat		1g
Cholesterol		5mg
Sodium		290mg
Total Carbohydrate		8g
Dietary Fiber		0g
Sugars		1g
Protein		2g

Microwave Dill Tater Snacks

| PREP TIME: | 20 MINUTES (READY IN 20 MINUTES) |
| SERVINGS: | 20 APPETIZERS |

 EASY   LOW FAT

3 slices lean turkey bacon

10 small red potatoes, unpeeled, halved (about 1¹/₂ lb)

¹/₂ cup reduced-fat sour cream

2 tablespoons sliced green onions (2 medium)

1 teaspoon chopped fresh dill weed

Dash pepper

¹/₄ cup grated Parmesan cheese

Fresh dill weed or parsley, if desired

1) Cook the bacon in microwave as directed on the package. Cool slightly. Crumble; set aside.

2) Place the unpeeled potatoes, cut side down, in 12x8-inch (2-quart) ungreased microwavable dish. Add 2 tablespoons water. Cover tightly with microwavable plastic wrap.

3) Microwave on High 9 to 12 minutes or until tender, rotating dish ¹/₄ turn halfway through cooking. Let stand 3 minutes. Drain; cool slightly.

4) In small bowl, mix sour cream, green onions and 1 teaspoon dill weed. Turn potatoes over. If necessary, trim thin slice off rounded bottom of each potato half to make potatoes stand upright. Top each with dollop of sour cream mixture; sprinkle with bacon. Sprinkle each with pepper and Parmesan cheese. Garnish with fresh dill weed or parsley.

HIGH ALTITUDE (3500-6500 FT.): No change.

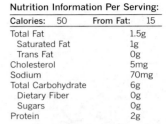

Nutrition Information Per Serving:

Calories:	50	From Fat:	15
Total Fat			1.5g
Saturated Fat			1g
Trans Fat			0g
Cholesterol			5mg
Sodium			70mg
Total Carbohydrate			6g
Dietary Fiber			0g
Sugars			0g
Protein			2g

Bacon–Crab Dip

PREP TIME: 10 MINUTES (READY IN 1 HOUR 10 MINUTES)
SERVINGS: 12 (2 TABLESPOONS EACH)

 EASY

1 package (8 oz) cream cheese, softened

1/2 cup sour cream

2 teaspoons prepared horseradish

1/8 teaspoon pepper

4 imitation crabmeat sticks, chopped (1 cup)

4 slices bacon, crisply cooked, crumbled

2 medium green onions, sliced (2 tablespoons)

Green onion flower, if desired

Toasted bagels, cut into fourths or whole wheat crackers, if desired

Nutrition Information Per Serving:

Calories: 110	From Fat: 90
Total Fat	10g
Saturated Fat	6g
Trans Fat	0g
Cholesterol	35mg
Sodium	220mg
Total Carbohydrate	2g
Dietary Fiber	0g
Sugars	0g
Protein	4g

1) In medium bowl using electric mixer, beat cream cheese and sour cream on medium speed until smooth and fluffy. By hand, stir in remaining ingredients except bagels and onion flower. Cover; refrigerate at least 1 hour to blend flavors.

2) Place dip in serving bowl. Garnish with onion flower. Serve with bagels. Cover and refrigerate any remaining dip.

HIGH ALTITUDE (3500-6500 FT.): No change.

A 6-oz can of crabmeat, drained and cartilage removed, may be substituted for the imitation crabmeat sticks in this dip.

Best Minted Iced Tea

PREP TIME: 10 MINUTES (READY IN 25 MINUTES)
SERVINGS: 12 (1 CUP EACH)

 EASY   LOW FAT

1 quart boiling water (4 cups)

1 cup sugar

1/2 cup instant tea mix

2 to 4 tablespoons slightly crushed fresh mint leaves

2 quarts cold water (8 cups)

1 can (6 oz) frozen lemonade concentrate, thawed

Nutrition Information Per Serving:

Calories: 130	From Fat: 0
Total Fat	0g
Saturated Fat	0g
Trans Fat	0g
Cholesterol	0mg
Sodium	5mg
Total Carbohydrate	33g
Dietary Fiber	0g
Sugars	32g
Protein	0g

1) In 4-quart casserole, mix boiling water, sugar, tea and mint leaves; let stand 15 minutes.

2) Stir in cold water and lemonade. Serve over ice.

HIGH ALTITUDE (3500-6500 FT.): No change.

Ginger Tea Coolers

PREP TIME: 25 MINUTES (READY IN 1 HOUR 15 MINUTES)
SERVINGS: 6 (1 CUP EACH)

 EASY   LOW FAT

3 cups water

1 piece (2 inch) unpeeled gingerroot, finely chopped (2 tablespoons)

1/3 cup sugar

3 tea bags green tea or 3 teaspoons loose green tea

2 cups lime sparkling water

2 cups ice cubes

1 lemon, thinly sliced, if desired

1 lime, thinly sliced, if desired

1 orange, thinly sliced, if desired

1) In 2-quart saucepan, heat the water, gingerroot and sugar to boiling over high heat, stirring to dissolve sugar. Reduce heat. Cover; simmer 5 minutes. Add tea bags; remove from heat. Cover; let steep 15 minutes.

2) Remove tea bags. Cool tea to room temperature, about 10 minutes. Pour through strainer into clean 2-quart pitcher to strain. Refrigerate at least 2 hours until chilled.

3) Just before serving, add sparkling water and ice cubes to pitcher. Garnish with lemon, lime and/or orange slices.

HIGH ALTITUDE (3500-6500 FT.): No change.

Nutrition Information Per Serving:

Calories:	50	From Fat:	0
Total Fat			0g
Saturated Fat			0g
Trans Fat			0g
Cholesterol			0mg
Sodium			5mg
Total Carbohydrate			12g
Dietary Fiber			0g
Sugars			11g
Protein			0g

tip

Green tea is rich in heart-healthy antioxidants. Look for decaffeinated versions of green tea if you'd prefer to skip the caffeine.

Entertaining Appetizers

Invite guests and whip up delicious hors d'oeuvres.
That's all you'll need to get a great party started!

ASPARAGUS STRIPS
PG. 60

BONELESS BUFFALO
CHICKEN APPETIZERS
PG. 84

MUSHROOM-SCALLOP SKEWERS
PG. 78

BLUE CHEESE AND RED ONION JAM
CRESCENT THUMBPRINTS
PG. 61

Chile-Lime Shrimp with Creamy Chipotle Dip

PREP TIME: 15 MINUTES (READY IN 55 MINUTES)
SERVINGS: 12 (2 SHRIMP AND ABOUT 2 TEASPOONS DIP EACH)

 EASY

2 limes

24 uncooked extra-large (16 to 20 per pound) deveined peeled shrimp with tail shells left on (about 1¹/₂ lb)

2 tablespoons olive or vegetable oil

1 garlic clove, finely chopped

¹/₂ teaspoon crushed red pepper flakes

¹/₃ cup mayonnaise or salad dressing

2 tablespoons honey mustard

1 large chipotle chile in adobo sauce (from 7-oz can), finely chopped (1 tablespoon)

1 teaspoon adobo sauce

1 tablespoon chopped fresh cilantro

1) Reserve 1 lime for the garnish. Grate 1 teaspoon peel from other lime. Cut lime in half; squeeze enough juice to measure 2 tablespoons. Set peel and juice aside.

2) Butterfly each shrimp by cutting along the outside curve through the fleshiest part for about 1¹/₂ inches, cutting almost to the inside curve. The shrimp should spread open.

3) In 1-gallon resealable food-storage plastic bag, mix oil, garlic, pepper flakes, lime juice and grated lime peel. Shake lightly to mix. Add the shrimp. Seal the bag; rotate to coat all of shrimp. Refrigerate 30 to 60 minutes to marinate.

4) Meanwhile, in small bowl, mix mayonnaise, honey mustard, chipotle chile and adobo sauce. Cover; refrigerate until serving.

5) Heat oven to 400°F. Remove shrimp from marinade; place in 15x10x1-inch baking pan. Open each shrimp, arranging in pan so that cut portion is on pan with tail tucked in. Discard marinade.

6) Bake 5 to 7 minutes, rearranging shrimp halfway through bake time, until shrimp are pink. Place on serving platter; sprinkle with cilantro. Spoon dip into bowl. Cut reserved lime into wedges. Garnish dip with wedges. Serve shrimp with dip. Store any remaining shrimp and dip in refrigerator.

HIGH ALTITUDE (3500-6500 FT.): No change.

Nutrition Information Per Serving:	
Calories: 110	From Fat: 70
Total Fat	8g
Saturated Fat	4g
Trans Fat	1g
Cholesterol	15mg
Sodium	190mg
Total Carbohydrate	6g
Dietary Fiber	0g
Sugars	1g
Protein	3g

Artichoke Dip with Fresh Herbs

| PREP TIME: | 15 MINUTES (READY IN 40 MINUTES) |
| SERVINGS: | 40 (1 TABLESPOON DIP EACH) |

 EASY LOW FAT

DIP

- 1 cup light sour cream
- 1/2 cup light mayonnaise or salad dressing
- 1/2 cup grated Parmesan cheese
- 1/4 cup chopped fresh parsley
- 2 tablespoons chopped fresh or 1/2 teaspoon dried thyme leaves
- 2 medium green onions, sliced (2 tablespoons)
- 1 can (14 oz) artichoke hearts in water, drained, coarsely chopped
- 1/2 cup diced seeded plum (Roma) tomatoes

DIPPERS

French bread slices or crackers, as desired

1) Heat oven to 350°F. In medium bowl, mix all dip ingredients except tomatoes. Spread in ungreased 9-inch quiche dish, glass pie plate or shallow 1-quart casserole.

2) Bake 18 to 24 minutes or until hot. Top with tomatoes and additional chopped fresh parsley. Serve warm with dippers. Cover and refrigerate any remaining dip.

HIGH ALTITUDE (3500-6500 FT.): No change.

Nutrition Information Per Serving:

Calories: 30	From Fat: 15
Total Fat	2g
Saturated Fat	0.5g
Trans Fat	0g
Cholesterol	0mg
Sodium	65mg
Total Carbohydrate	2g
Dietary Fiber	0g
Sugars	1g
Protein	1g

tip Assemble this dip the night before, then cover it and put it in the fridge. Just before serving, uncover the dip and bake it as directed in the recipe.

Curried Chicken Salad Cups

| PREP TIME: | 20 MINUTES (READY IN 50 MINUTES) |
| SERVINGS: | 15 |

 EASY LOW FAT

- 1/3 cup plain yogurt
- 2 tablespoons purchased mango chutney, large pieces chopped
- 1 teaspoon curry powder
- 1/4 teaspoon salt
- 1 cup finely chopped cooked chicken
- 1/4 cup diced fresh mango
- 2 tablespoons finely chopped red onion
- 2 tablespoons chopped fresh mint leaves
- 1 package (2.1 oz) frozen mini fillo shells (15 shells)

Fresh mint sprigs

Nutrition Information Per Serving:

Calories: 50	From Fat: 15
Total Fat	2g
Saturated Fat	0g
Trans Fat	0g
Cholesterol	10mg
Sodium	65mg
Total Carbohydrate	6g
Dietary Fiber	0g
Sugars	3g
Protein	3g

1) In medium bowl, mix yogurt, chutney, curry powder and salt. Stir in chicken, mango, onion and chopped mint. Cover; refrigerate 30 minutes.

2) Spoon 1 rounded tablespoon chicken mixture into each fillo shell. Top with mint sprig. Serve immediately, or refrigerate until serving.

HIGH ALTITUDE (3500-6500 FT.): No change.

Mini Buffalo Chicken Pastries

PREP TIME: 25 MINUTES (READY IN 40 MINUTES)
SERVINGS: 16 APPETIZERS

1 tablespoon olive oil

1 boneless skinless chicken breast (4 oz), cut in half crosswise

2 tablespoons buffalo wing sauce (from 12-oz jar)

1 tablespoon chopped celery

1 can (8 oz) Pillsbury® refrigerated crescent dinner rolls

1 tablespoon finely chopped fresh parsley

1/2 cup blue cheese dressing

1) Heat oven to 375°F. In 10-inch skillet, heat 2 teaspoons of the oil over medium-high heat until hot. Cook and stir chicken in oil 3 to 5 minutes or until chicken is no longer pink in center. Remove from heat; place chicken on cutting board. Using a fork, pull chicken into shreds; return to skillet. Stir in sauce and celery.

2) Meanwhile, on cutting board, unroll dough and separate into 8 triangles. From the center of 1 longest side to the opposite point, cut each triangle in half, making 16 triangles. Place rounded tablespoonful chicken mixture on center of each triangle. Bring corners to center over filling, overlapping ends; press gently to seal. Place on ungreased cookie sheets. Brush each lightly with remaining 1 teaspoon oil. Sprinkle with chopped parsley.

3) Bake 10 to 13 minutes or until golden brown. Serve warm with blue cheese dressing for dipping.

HIGH ALTITUDE (3500-6500 FT.): No change.

Nutrition Information Per Serving:		
Calories: 100	From Fat:	70
Total Fat		8g
Saturated Fat		1.5g
Trans Fat		1g
Cholesterol		5mg
Sodium		260mg
Total Carbohydrate		6g
Dietary Fiber		0g
Sugars		1g
Protein		3g

Cheese and Crab Cups

PREP TIME: 25 MINUTES (READY IN 50 MINUTES)
SERVINGS: 24 MINIATURE CRAB CUPS

2 tablespoons cornmeal

1 can (13.8 oz) Pillsbury® refrigerated classic pizza crust

1 package (6 oz) chopped pasteurized refrigerated lump crabmeat

1 tablespoon finely chopped red onion

1 tablespoon chopped fresh dill weed or 1 teaspoon dried dill weed

1/2 teaspoon lemon peel

2 teaspoons lemon juice

1/2 cup garlic-and-herbs spreadable cheese (from 4-oz container)

3/4 cup shredded Cheddar cheese (3 oz)

1) Heat oven to 375°F. Spray 24 mini muffin cups with cooking spray. Sprinkle the cornmeal on work surface. Roll or press dough into 18x12-inch rectangle. Cut into 24 (3x3-inch) squares. Place 1 square in each muffin cup.

2) In medium bowl, mix crabmeat, onion, dill, lemon peel, lemon juice, spreadable cheese and 1/2 cup shredded cheese until well mixed. Spoon 1 tablespoon crab mixture into each dough-lined cup.

3) Bake 15 to 18 minutes or until edges just begin to brown. Sprinkle tops with remaining 1/4 cup shredded cheese. Bake about 2 minutes longer or until cheese is just melted. Immediately remove from muffin cups; serve warm or cold.

HIGH ALTITUDE (3500-6500 FT.): No change.

Nutrition Information Per Serving:	
Calories: 80	From Fat: 30
Total Fat	3.5g
Saturated Fat	2g
Trans Fat	0g
Cholesterol	15mg
Sodium	170mg
Total Carbohydrate	9g
Dietary Fiber	0g
Sugars	1g
Protein	4g

Salmon Pastries with Dill Pesto

EDGAR RUDBERG | ST. PAUL, MINNESOTA

BAKE-OFF® CONTEST 43, 2008

PREP TIME: 25 MINUTES (READY IN 50 MINUTES)
SERVINGS: 24 APPETIZERS

$1/2$ cup lightly packed chopped fresh dill weed

$1/3$ cup Crisco® light olive oil

$1/4$ cup Fisher® Chef's Naturals® chopped walnuts

$1/4$ cup fresh lime juice

1 garlic clove

1 tablespoon Dijon mustard

$2/3$ cup shredded Parmesan cheese

Salt and pepper, if desired

$3/4$ lb salmon fillet, thawed if frozen and patted dry

1 box (15 oz) Pillsbury® refrigerated pie crusts, softened as directed on box

Dill weed sprigs

1) Heat oven to 400°F. In food processor bowl with metal blade or in blender, place chopped dill weed, oil, walnuts, lime juice, garlic, mustard, $1/2$ cup of the cheese, the salt and pepper. Cover; process, stopping once to scrape side of bowl, until smooth.

2) If salmon has skin or bones, remove them; rinse fillet and pat dry with paper towel. Cut salmon into 24 (1-inch) cubes.

3) On cutting board, roll 1 pie crust into 12-inch round. Cut into 4 rows by 3 rows to make 12 (4x3-inch) rectangles. Repeat with remaining crust. (Rectangles cut at edge of crust will have rounded side.)

4) Spoon 1 level teaspoon dill pesto onto center of each rectangle; top with 1 salmon cube. Bring 4 corners of each rectangle over filling to center and pinch at top; pinch corners, leaving small openings on sides to vent steam. (For rectangles with rounded side, bring 3 points together at top, pinching to seal.) On ungreased large cookie sheet, place pastries 1 inch apart. Bake 20 to 25 minutes or until golden brown.

5) Place remaining pesto in small resealable food-storage plastic bag. Cut small tip off 1 bottom corner of bag; squeeze bag to drizzle pesto over serving plate. Place pastries on serving plate. Sprinkle pastries with remaining cheese and garnish with dill weed sprigs. Serve warm.

HIGH ALTITUDE (3500-6500 FT.): No change.

Nutrition Information Per Serving:		
Calories: 150	From Fat:	90
Total Fat		10g
Saturated Fat		3g
Trans Fat		0g
Cholesterol		15mg
Sodium		150mg
Total Carbohydrate		9g
Dietary Fiber		0g
Sugars		0g
Protein		4g

Blueberry, Walnut and Brie Tartlets

PREP TIME: 20 MINUTES (READY IN 45 MINUTES)
SERVINGS: 24 APPETIZERS

 EASY

1 can (8 oz) Pillsbury® refrigerated reduced-fat crescent dinner rolls

1/4 cup blueberry or blackberry preserves

1/3 cup coarsely chopped walnuts, toasted

1 round (8 oz) Brie cheese, rind removed, cut into 24 chunks

Fresh blueberries or fresh small sage leaves, if desired

Nutrition Information Per Serving:		
Calories: 80	From Fat:	45
Total Fat		5g
Saturated Fat		2.5g
Trans Fat		0g
Cholesterol		10mg
Sodium		135mg
Total Carbohydrate		7g
Dietary Fiber		0g
Sugars		2g
Protein		3g

1) Heat oven to 350°F. Grease or spray 24 mini muffin cups. Unroll dough and separate into 4 rectangles; firmly press perforations to seal. Cut each into 6 squares. Gently press squares into mini muffin cups (dough will not completely cover inside of cup; do not press too much).

2) Spoon 1/2 teaspoon preserves into each cup. Top with rounded 1/2 teaspoon nuts and cheese chunk.

3) Bake 16 to 19 minutes or until edges are deep golden brown. Cool in pan on cooling rack 5 minutes; remove from muffin cups. Garnish each with fresh blueberries or sage leaves.

HIGH ALTITUDE (3500-6500 FT.): No change.

Roasted Red Pepper Dip

PREP TIME: 10 MINUTES (READY IN 1 HOUR 10 MINUTES)
SERVINGS: 8 (2 TABLESPOONS DIP EACH)

EASY

1 jar (7 or 7.25 oz) roasted red bell peppers, well drained, coarsely chopped

1 tablespoon chopped fresh basil leaves

1 small garlic clove

1/2 cup reduced-fat cream cheese (from 8-oz container)

1 tablespoon sliced almonds, if desired

Asparagus on the Grill, if desired (see recipe on page 195)

Nutrition Information Per Serving:		
Calories: 45	From Fat:	30
Total Fat		3.5g
Saturated Fat		2g
Trans Fat		0g
Cholesterol		10mg
Sodium		60mg
Total Carbohydrate		2g
Dietary Fiber		0g
Sugars		1g
Protein		2g

1) In food processor, place roasted peppers, basil and garlic. Cover; process until finely chopped. Add cream cheese. Cover; process until smooth.

2) Cover dip; refrigerate 1 hour. Just before serving, sprinkle with almonds. Serve with grilled asparagus.

HIGH ALTITUDE (3500-6500 FT.): No change.

Crispy Shrimp Tarts

PREP TIME: 25 MINUTES (READY IN 30 MINUTES)
SERVINGS: 24 APPETIZERS

 EASY   LOW FAT

24 frozen mini phyllo (filo) shells (from two 2.1-oz packages)

$1/2$ cup cream cheese spread (from 8-oz container)

24 frozen cooked deveined peeled medium shrimp

$1/4$ cup Chinese plum sauce

Grated lime peel, if desired

1) Heat oven to 350°F. Place fillo shells on ungreased large cookie sheet.

2) Stir cream cheese to soften. Spoon 1 teaspoon cream cheese into each shell. Top each with 1 shrimp.

3) Bake about 2 minutes or until cream cheese is soft. Remove from cookie sheet; place on serving platter. Top each tart with $1/2$ teaspoon plum sauce and lime peel.

HIGH ALTITUDE (3500-6500 FT.): No change.

Nutrition Information Per Serving:

Calories:	40	From Fat:	15
Total Fat			1.5g
Saturated Fat			1g
Trans Fat			0g
Cholesterol			20mg
Sodium			50mg
Total Carbohydrate			4g
Dietary Fiber			0g
Sugars			0g
Protein			2g

For another seafood version of the tarts, top each one with a piece of cooked crabmeat in place of the shrimp.

Ham Florentine Mini-Cups

PATRICIA INGALLS | WESTERN PATERSON, NEW JERSEY

BAKE-OFF® CONTEST 43, 2008

PREP TIME: 30 MINUTES (READY IN 1 HOUR)
SERVINGS: 24 APPETIZERS

1 box (9 oz) Green Giant® frozen spinach, thawed, squeezed to drain

1/3 cup garlic-and-herbs spreadable cheese

1/4 cup shredded mozzarella cheese (1 oz)

1/4 cup shredded 5-cheese or 6-cheese Italian cheese blend (1 oz)

3 tablespoons freshly grated Pecorino Romano or regular Romano cheese

2 tablespoons finely chopped shallot or onion

1/4 teaspoon garlic powder

1/8 teaspoon salt, if desired

1/8 teaspoon pepper, if desired

1 can (8 oz) Pillsbury® refrigerated crescent dinner rolls (8 rolls)

24 paper-thin slices (about 4-inch diameter) smoked ham (from two 9-oz packages)

Freshly grated Parmesan cheese, if desired

1) Heat oven to 375°F. In medium bowl, mix all ingredients except rolls, ham and Parmesan cheese until well blended. Set mixture aside.

2) Unroll the dough. Separate dough into 4 rectangles; press perforations to seal. Cut each rectangle into 6 (2-inch) squares. Press 1 square in bottom and up side of each of 24 ungreased mini muffin cups.

3) Pat each ham slice dry with paper towel. Place 1 ham slice over dough in each cup (edges of ham will be higher than side of cup). Spoon rounded 1 teaspoon spinach mixture onto ham in center of each cup.

4) Bake 14 to 18 minutes or until crust is golden brown and filling is hot. To prevent excessive browning of ham, cover lightly with foil after the first 5 minutes of baking. Cool in pan 1 minute. Gently remove from pan; let stand 3 minutes. Sprinkle lightly with grated Parmesan cheese before serving. Serve warm.

HIGH ALTITUDE (3500-6500 FT.): No change.

Nutrition Information Per Serving:		
Calories: 80	From Fat:	40
Total Fat		4.5g
Saturated Fat		2g
Trans Fat		0.5g
Cholesterol		10mg
Sodium		260mg
Total Carbohydrate		4g
Dietary Fiber		0g
Sugars		0g
Protein		4g

Creamy Shrimp Dip

PREP TIME: 25 MINUTES (READY IN 25 MINUTES)
SERVINGS: 32 (2 TABLESPOONS DIP AND 1 PIECE RED BELL PEPPER EACH)

 EASY   LOW FAT

1 package (8 oz) $^1/_3$-less-fat cream cheese (Neufchâtel), softened

3 to 4 tablespoons fat-free (skim) milk

1 teaspoon lemon-herb seasoning

1 can (4 oz) tiny shrimp, drained

1 tablespoon sliced green onion (1 medium)

1 tablespoon chopped green bell pepper

2 large red bell peppers, cut into 1$^1/_2$-inch pieces

32 leaves flat leaf parsley

Nutrition Information Per Serving:	
Calories: 25	From Fat: 15
Total Fat	1.5g
Saturated Fat	1g
Trans Fat	0g
Cholesterol	15mg
Sodium	80mg
Total Carbohydrate	0g
Dietary Fiber	0g
Sugars	0g
Protein	2g

1) In small bowl, mix cream cheese, milk and lemon-herb seasoning; beat until smooth. Add shrimp, green onion and green bell pepper; mix well.

2) Scoop into red bell pepper pieces. Cover and refrigerate until serving time. Just before serving, top with parsley leaf.

HIGH ALTITUDE (3500-6500 FT.): No change.

Asparagus Strips

PREP TIME: 15 MINUTES (READY IN 35 MINUTES)
SERVINGS: 28 APPETIZERS

 EASY  LOW FAT

1 can (13.8 oz) Pillsbury® refrigerated classic pizza crust

$^1/_4$ cup basil pesto

14 fresh asparagus spears (about 4 oz), trimmed to about 6 inches

$^1/_4$ cup thinly sliced red onion

$^1/_2$ cup shredded mozzarella cheese (2 oz)

$^1/_2$ cup shredded Asiago cheese (2 oz)

Nutrition Information Per Serving:	
Calories: 60	From Fat: 25
Total Fat	2.5g
Saturated Fat	1g
Trans Fat	0g
Cholesterol	0mg
Sodium	150mg
Total Carbohydrate	7g
Dietary Fiber	0g
Sugars	1g
Protein	2g

1) Heat oven to 400°F. Grease large cookie sheet. Unroll dough on cookie sheet. Press to 14x8-inch rectangle. Fold both long sides over about $^1/_2$ inch to form rim, pressing to seal. Bake 8 minutes.

2) Spread dough with pesto. Arrange asparagus and onion on dough. Sprinkle with cheeses.

3) Bake 8 to 10 minutes or until the edges are golden brown and the cheese is melted. Cut crosswise into 14 (1-inch) strips. Cut in half lengthwise to make 28 pieces. Serve warm or cool.

HIGH ALTITUDE (3500-6500 FT.): No change.

Blue Cheese and Red Onion Jam Crescent Thumbprints

PHYLLIS WEEKS-DANIEL | SAN DIEGO, CALIFORNIA

BAKE-OFF® CONTEST 43, 2008

PREP TIME: 30 MINUTES (READY IN 50 MINUTES)
SERVINGS: 32 APPETIZERS

1 package (3 oz) cream cheese, softened

1/2 cup crumbled Gorgonzola cheese (2 oz)

1 can (8 oz) Pillsbury® refrigerated crescent dinner rolls (8 rolls)

1/3 cup Fisher® Chef's Naturals® chopped pecans

1 teaspoon Crisco® 100% extra virgin or pure olive oil

1/3 cup finely chopped red onion

1 tablespoon balsamic vinegar

1/4 cup Smucker's® apricot preserves

1/8 to 1/4 teaspoon dried thyme leaves

1) Heat oven to 375°F. In small bowl, mix cream cheese and Gorgonzola cheese with fork until blended.

2) Unroll dough; separate into 2 rectangles, each about 11 inches long. Place 1 rectangle on cutting board; press perforations together to seal. Spread half of the cheese mixture over dough to within 1/2 inch of the long sides; sprinkle half of the pecans evenly over cheese. Starting at 1 long side, roll up; press seam to seal. Cut roll into 16 (about 3/4-inch) slices with serrated knife; place cut sides down on ungreased large cookie sheet. Repeat with remaining dough, cheese and pecans.

3) Bake 14 to 17 minutes or until golden brown.

4) Meanwhile, in 8-inch nonstick skillet, heat the oil over medium heat. Add onion; cook 3 to 5 minutes, stirring frequently, until soft and lightly brown. Remove from heat. Stir in vinegar, preserves (breaking up large pieces of fruit if necessary) and thyme; set aside.

5) After removing rolls from oven, immediately press back of a teaspoon into center of each roll to make small indentation. Spoon slightly less than 1/2 teaspoon onion jam into each indentation. Remove from cookie sheet. Serve warm.

HIGH ALTITUDE (3500-6500 FT.): Heat oven to 350°F.

Nutrition Information Per Serving:	
Calories: 60	From Fat: 35
Total Fat	4g
Saturated Fat	1.5g
Trans Fat	0g
Cholesterol	0mg
Sodium	90mg
Total Carbohydrate	5g
Dietary Fiber	0g
Sugars	2g
Protein	1g

Samosa Taquitos with Apricot Chutney Sauce

SCOTT HATFIELD | GROVE CITY, PENNSYLVANIA · · · · · · BAKE-OFF® CONTEST 43, 2008

PREP TIME: 25 MINUTES (READY IN 40 MINUTES)
SERVINGS: 12 (1 TAQUITO AND 2 TABLESPOONS SAUCE EACH)

TAQUITOS

3 tablespoons Crisco® pure canola oil

$1/3$ cup finely chopped onion

$1/2$ bag (30-oz size) frozen country-style shredded hash brown potatoes ($4^1/2$ cups)

1 box (9 oz) Green Giant® frozen spinach

1 can (4.5 oz) Old El Paso® chopped green chiles

1 teaspoon salt

1 teaspoon ground coriander

1 teaspoon garam masala

$1/2$ teaspoon ground ginger

1 tablespoon lemon juice

1 package (10.5 oz) Old El Paso® flour tortillas for soft tacos and fajitas (12 tortillas)

SAUCE

1 jar (12 oz) Smucker's® apricot preserves

Remaining Old El Paso® chopped green chiles

1 tablespoon cider vinegar

$1/4$ to $1/2$ teaspoon ground ginger

$3/4$ teaspoon garam masala

$1/8$ teaspoon ground red pepper (cayenne)

1) Heat oven to 400°F. In 12-inch nonstick skillet, heat 2 tablespoons of the oil over medium-high heat. Add the onion and potatoes; cook about 10 minutes, stirring occasionally, until the potatoes are thoroughly cooked and slightly browned.

2) Meanwhile, cook spinach in microwave as directed on box. Drain spinach; cool 5 minutes. Carefully squeeze with paper towels to drain. Pull spinach apart into smaller pieces. Measure 4 teaspoons of the chiles; reserve the remaining chiles for sauce.

3) Stir spinach, 4 teaspoons chiles, the salt, coriander, 1 teaspoon garam masala and $1/2$ teaspoon ginger into potato mixture. Cook over medium heat 2 to 3 minutes, stirring frequently, until mixed and thoroughly heated. Remove from heat; gently stir in lemon juice.

4) Place about $1/4$ cup potato filling on each tortilla, $1/2$ inch from one side. Starting at side with filling, tightly roll up each tortilla around filling; place seam side down on ungreased cookie sheet. Brush taquitos with remaining 1 tablespoon oil.

5) Bake 8 to 11 minutes or until crispy and golden brown.

6) Meanwhile, in medium bowl, stir sauce ingredients until well mixed. Serve warm taquitos with sauce for dipping.

HIGH ALTITUDE (3500-6500 FT.): No change.

Nutrition Information Per Serving:		
Calories: 270	From Fat: 50	
Total Fat		6g
Saturated Fat		1g
Trans Fat		1g
Cholesterol		0mg
Sodium		580mg
Total Carbohydrate		50g
Dietary Fiber		3g
Sugars		16g
Protein		4g

Chopped Salad Bruschetta

PREP TIME: 20 MINUTES (READY IN 20 MINUTES)
SERVINGS: 12 APPETIZERS

 EASY

12 slices (1/2 inch thick) French bread

2 tablespoons olive oil

1 garlic clove, finely chopped

1 medium tomato, seeded, diced
(3/4 cup)

2 tablespoons sliced pimiento-stuffed
green olives

2 tablespoons sliced ripe olives

2 tablespoons diced bell pepper

2 green onions, sliced (2 tablespoons)

1 tablespoon Italian dressing

4 large fresh basil leaves, thinly sliced

1/4 cup shredded Parmesan cheese

1) Heat oven to 375°F. On ungreased cookie sheet, arrange bread slices. In small bowl, mix oil and garlic; brush on bread. Bake 8 to 10 minutes or until dry and toasted. Set aside to cool.

2) In medium bowl, mix the remaining ingredients except basil and Parmesan cheese. With slotted spoon, spoon tomato mixture evenly on toasts. Top with basil and cheese.

HIGH ALTITUDE (3500-6500 FT.): No change.

Nutrition Information Per Serving:

Calories:	60	From Fat:	35
Total Fat			4g
Saturated Fat			1g
Trans Fat			0g
Cholesterol			0mg
Sodium			135mg
Total Carbohydrate			6g
Dietary Fiber			0g
Sugars			0g
Protein			2g

 Here's an easy way to thinly slice a bunch of basil leaves all at the same time: Stack the leaves and roll them lengthwise into a tight roll, then cut across the roll.

Cucumber-Hummus Stacks

PREP TIME: 20 MINUTES (READY IN 20 MINUTES)
SERVINGS: 26 APPETIZERS

 EASY   LOW FAT

1 large cucumber (about 12 oz), unpeeled

1 container (7 oz) roasted red pepper hummus

2 tablespoons crumbled feta cheese

26 slices kalamata or ripe olives

Nutrition Information Per Serving:

Calories:	20	From Fat:	10
Total Fat			1g
Saturated Fat			0g
Trans Fat			0g
Cholesterol			0mg
Sodium			50mg
Total Carbohydrate			2g
Dietary Fiber			0g
Sugars			0g
Protein			0g

1) Using tines of fork, score cucumber lengthwise on all sides. Cut cucumber into 26 (1/4-inch) slices. Blot dry with paper towel.

2) Spoon heaping teaspoon hummus on each cucumber slice. Sprinkle with feta cheese; top with olive slice.

HIGH ALTITUDE (3500-6500 FT.): No change.

Little Apricot Appetizer Tarts

GAIL SINGER | PALM DESERT, CALIFORNIA

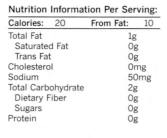 BAKE-OFF® CONTEST 43, 2008

PREP TIME: 35 MINUTES (READY IN 55 MINUTES)
SERVINGS: 24 APPETIZE

 EASY

2 cans (8 oz each) Pillsbury® refrigerated garlic butter crescent dinner rolls (8 rolls each)

1 cup finely shredded pepper Jack cheese (4 oz)

1/4 cup Smucker's® apricot preserves

1/4 cup Fisher® Chef's Naturals® chopped pecans

Nutrition Information Per Serving:

Calories:	90	From Fat:	60
Total Fat			6g
Saturated Fat			2.5g
Trans Fat			0.5g
Cholesterol			10mg
Sodium			220mg
Total Carbohydrate			5g
Dietary Fiber			0g
Sugars			1g
Protein			3g

1) Heat oven to 375°F. Spray 24 mini muffin cups with Crisco® Original No-Stick cooking spray.

2) Unroll each can of dough into a large rectangle; press perforations to seal. Cut each rectangle crosswise into 12 strips, about 1 inch wide. Place each strip in muffin cup, pressing dough to cover bottom and side, making sure all seams are sealed and forming 1/4-inch rim above cup.

3) Spoon 2 teaspoons cheese into each cup. Top each with 1/2 teaspoon preserves and 1/2 teaspoon pecans.

4) Bake 14 to 20 minutes or until crust is deep golden brown. Cool 5 minutes; remove from pan. Serve warm.

HIGH ALTITUDE (3500-6500 FT.): No change.

Spicy Spanish Sausages

PREP TIME: 30 MINUTES (READY IN 30 MINUTES)
SERVINGS: 20

- 1 tablespoon olive oil
- 1/4 cup finely chopped onion
- 3 garlic cloves, finely chopped
- 1 lb cooked chorizo or kielbasa sausage links, cut into 1/2-inch-thick slices
- 1 teaspoon paprika
- 1/2 teaspoon coriander

  Dash ground red pepper (cayenne)
- 1 can (8 oz) tomato sauce
- 1/4 cup dry red wine (such as Rioja, Bordeaux or Merlot) or beef broth

1) In 10-inch skillet, heat oil over medium heat until hot. Add the onion; cook 4 to 5 minutes, stirring occasionally, until softened.

2) Add the garlic; cook and stir 30 to 60 seconds or until fragrant. Add the sausage slices; cook 2 to 4 minutes or until lightly browned, turning once.

3) Stir in paprika, coriander and ground red pepper. Add tomato sauce and wine; cook about 5 minutes to reduce slightly, stirring occasionally. Serve warm with cocktail toothpicks.

HIGH ALTITUDE (3500-6500 FT.): No change.

Nutrition Information Per Serving:

Calories:	120	From Fat:	80
Total Fat		9g	
Saturated Fat		3.5g	
Trans Fat		0g	
Cholesterol		20mg	
Sodium		340mg	
Total Carbohydrate		2g	
Dietary Fiber		0g	
Sugars		0g	
Protein		6g	

tip

Serve these spicy sausages in Asian soup spoons with salted almonds and Spanish olives for a Spanish tapas flair.

Olive Deviled Eggs

PREP TIME: 25 MINUTES (READY IN 50 MINUTES)
SERVINGS: 24 DEVILED EGGS

12 eggs
1/2 cup finely chopped celery
5 tablespoons ranch dressing
1 teaspoon yellow mustard
1/4 teaspoon salt
Sliced ripe olives, if desired

1) In 4-quart saucepan, place eggs in single layer. Add enough water to cover eggs by 1 inch. Heat to boiling. Immediately remove from heat; cover and let stand 15 minutes.

2) Drain water from eggs; rinse eggs with cold water. Place eggs in bowl of ice water; let stand 10 minutes.

3) To remove shell, crack it by tapping gently all over; roll between hands to loosen. Peel, starting at large end.

4) Cut eggs lengthwise in half. Into medium bowl, slip out yolks; mash with fork. Stir in celery, dressing, mustard and salt until well blended.

5) Spoon yolk mixture into egg white halves. Top eggs with ripe olives.

HIGH ALTITUDE (3500-6500 FT.): In Step 1, boil eggs 5 minutes, then remove from heat; cover and let stand 15 minutes.

Shrimp Deviled Eggs

PREP TIME: 25 MINUTES (READY IN 50 MINUTES)
SERVINGS: 24 DEVILED EGGS

12 eggs

1/2 cup finely chopped celery

5 tablespoons ranch dressing

1 teaspoon yellow mustard

1/4 teaspoon salt

Salad shrimp, if desired

Paprika, if desired

1) In 4-quart saucepan, place eggs in single layer. Add enough water to cover eggs by 1 inch. Heat to boiling. Immediately remove from heat; cover and let stand 15 minutes.

2) Drain water from eggs; rinse eggs with cold water. Place eggs in bowl of ice water; let stand 10 minutes.

3) To remove shell, crack it by tapping gently all over; roll between hands to loosen. Peel, starting at large end.

4) Cut eggs lengthwise in half. Into medium bowl, slip out yolks; mash with fork. Stir in celery, dressing, mustard and salt until well blended.

5) Spoon yolk mixture into egg white halves. Top eggs with salad shrimp. Sprinkle with paprika.

HIGH ALTITUDE (3500-6500 FT.): In Step 1, boil eggs 5 minutes, then remove from heat; cover and let stand 15 minutes.

For a different presentation, cut the hard-cooked eggs crosswise instead of lengthwise and stand each deviled egg in an egg cup (as shown in the photo).

Deviled Eggs with a Twist

PREP TIME: 25 MINUTES (READY IN 50 MINUTES)
SERVINGS: 24 DEVILED EGGS

12 eggs

1/2 cup finely chopped celery

5 tablespoons ranch dressing

1 teaspoon yellow mustard

1/4 teaspoon salt

Chopped fresh plum (Roma) tomatoes, if desired

Chopped green onions, if desired

1) In 4-quart saucepan, place eggs in single layer. Add enough water to cover eggs by 1 inch. Heat to boiling. Immediately remove from heat; cover and let stand 15 minutes.

2) Drain water from eggs; rinse eggs with cold water. Place eggs in bowl of ice water; let stand 10 minutes.

3) To remove shell, crack it by tapping gently all over; roll between hands to loosen. Peel, starting at large end.

4) Cut eggs lengthwise in half. Into medium bowl, slip out yolks; mash with fork. Stir in celery, dressing, mustard and salt until well blended.

5) Spoon yolk mixture into egg white halves. Top eggs with tomatoes and green onions.

HIGH ALTITUDE (3500-6500 FT.): In Step 1, boil eggs 5 minutes, then remove from heat; cover and let stand 15 minutes.

Nutrition Information Per Serving:	
Calories: 50	From Fat: 40
Total Fat	4g
Saturated Fat	1g
Trans Fat	0g
Cholesterol	105mg
Sodium	85mg
Total Carbohydrate	0g
Dietary Fiber	0g
Sugars	0g
Protein	3g

Gorgonzola, Fig and Walnut Tartlets

LANA MCDONOGH | SAN MARCOS, CALIFORNIA

BAKE-OFF® CONTEST 43, 2008

PREP TIME: 20 MINUTES (READY IN 35 MINUTES)
SERVINGS: 24 APPETIZERS

 EASY

1 Pillsbury® refrigerated pie crust (from 15-oz box), softened as directed on box

6 dried figs or pitted dates, coarsely chopped ($1/3$ cup)

1 tablespoon packed Domino® or C&H® dark brown sugar

$1/8$ to $1/4$ teaspoon ground cinnamon

$1/4$ cup Fisher® Chef's Naturals® chopped walnuts

$1/2$ cup crumbled Gorgonzola cheese (2 oz)

1 tablespoon honey

1) Heat oven to 425°F. Unroll pie crust on flat surface. Using 2-inch cookie cutter, cut 24 rounds from pie crust, rerolling the crust scraps if necessary. Gently press 1 round in bottom and up side of each of 24 ungreased mini muffin cups.

2) In small bowl, mix figs, brown sugar, cinnamon and walnuts. Spoon slightly less than 1 teaspoon fig mixture into each cup. Break up any larger pieces of cheese. Top each tartlet with slightly less than 1 teaspoon cheese.

3) Bake 7 to 11 minutes or until bubbly and golden brown. Remove tartlets from pan to serving plate. Drizzle tartlets with honey. Serve warm.

HIGH ALTITUDE (3500-6500 FT.): No change.

Nutrition Information Per Serving:

Calories:	60	From Fat:	30
Total Fat			3.5g
Saturated Fat			1g
Trans Fat			0g
Cholesterol			0mg
Sodium			60mg
Total Carbohydrate			6g
Dietary Fiber			0g
Sugars			2g
Protein			0g

Guacamole Appetizer Triangles

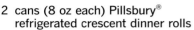

PREP TIME: 20 MINUTES (READY IN 2 HOURS 10 MINUTES)
SERVINGS: 60 APPETIZERS

e EASY   **lf** LOW FAT

2 cans (8 oz each) Pillsbury® refrigerated crescent dinner rolls

1/2 teaspoon ground cumin

1/2 teaspoon chili powder

1 container (8 oz) pineapple cream cheese spread

1 container (8 oz) guacamole

1/2 cup diced seeded plum (Roma) tomatoes

1/4 cup cooked real bacon pieces

1/4 cup sliced ripe olives

1/4 cup chopped fresh cilantro

1) Heat oven to 375°F. Separate dough into 4 long rectangles. Press rectangles to make crust in bottom of ungreased 15x10x1-inch pan, firmly pressing the perforations to seal. Sprinkle with cumin and chili powder.

2) Bake 13 to 17 minutes or until crust is golden brown. Cool completely, about 30 minutes.

3) In medium bowl, mix cream cheese and guacamole. Spread evenly over crust. Cover with plastic wrap; refrigerate 1 to 2 hours.

4) Just before serving, top with tomatoes, bacon, olives and cilantro. Cut into 6 rows by 5 rows. Cut each square diagonally to make 60 small triangles.

HIGH ALTITUDE (3500-6500 FT.): No change.

Nutrition Information Per Serving:

Calories:	45	From Fat:	30
Total Fat			3g
Saturated Fat			1.5g
Trans Fat			0g
Cholesterol			0mg
Sodium			115mg
Total Carbohydrate			4g
Dietary Fiber			0g
Sugars			0g
Protein			1g

Red Pepper and Goat Cheese Bites

ALISON STRUNK | SPRINGFIELD, MISSOURI

Pillsbury Bake-Off®   BAKE-OFF® CONTEST 43, 2008

PREP TIME: 40 MINUTES (READY IN 1 HOUR 5 MINUTES)
SERVINGS: 32 APPETIZERS

8 slices uncooked bacon

1 tablespoon Crisco® 100% extra virgin or pure olive oil

1 cup diced sweet yellow onion (such as Maui or Walla Walla)

1 large red bell pepper, diced (1$\frac{1}{2}$ cups)

$\frac{1}{4}$ teaspoon salt

$\frac{1}{8}$ teaspoon pepper

$\frac{3}{4}$ cup crumbled goat (chèvre) cheese (3 oz)

2 oz cream cheese (from 3-oz package), softened

1 tablespoon chopped fresh parsley

1 can (8 oz) Pillsbury® refrigerated reduced-fat or regular crescent dinner rolls (8 rolls)

1) Heat oven to 350°F. Spray large cookie sheet with Crisco® Original No-Stick cooking spray, or line with cooking parchment paper.

2) In 10-inch skillet, cook bacon over medium heat 10 to 15 minutes, turning occasionally, until crisp. Remove from skillet; drain on paper towels. Crumble bacon; set aside.

3) Discard bacon drippings. Add oil to skillet; heat over medium heat until hot. Add onion and red bell pepper; cook about 15 minutes, stirring occasionally, until soft and tender. Stir in salt and pepper. Place mixture in food processor bowl with metal blade. Cover; process until smooth. Or blend in blender on medium speed about 30 seconds, stopping once to scrape sides, until smooth.

4) In small bowl, mix goat cheese, cream cheese and parsley until smooth.

5) Unroll the dough; separate into 4 rectangles. Press the perforations to seal. Cut each rectangle into 8 (1$\frac{1}{2}$-inch) squares. Place the squares on cookie sheet. Spoon rounded 1 teaspoon red pepper mixture on each square, spreading slightly. Spoon slightly less than 1 teaspoon cheese mixture on the pepper mixture on each square. Top each with about $\frac{1}{4}$ teaspoon crumbled bacon.

6) Bake 15 to 22 minutes or until edges are golden brown. Serve warm, or refrigerate and serve chilled.

HIGH ALTITUDE (3500-6500 FT.): Bake 15 to 18 minutes.

Nutrition Information Per Serving:		
Calories: 60	From Fat:	35
Total Fat		4g
Saturated Fat		2g
Trans Fat		0g
Cholesterol		5mg
Sodium		140mg
Total Carbohydrate		4g
Dietary Fiber		0g
Sugars		1g
Protein		2g

Caramelized Onion Puffs

PREP TIME: 30 MINUTES (READY IN 50 MINUTES)
SERVINGS: 24 APPETIZERS

2 tablespoons butter or margarine

¾ cup coarsely chopped onion

¼ cup finely chopped red bell pepper

2 eggs

½ cup sour cream

¼ teaspoon salt

⅛ teaspoon red pepper sauce

¾ cup finely shredded Cheddar cheese (3 oz)

1 package (8 oz) Pillsbury® refrigerated crescent dinner rolls

1) Heat oven to 400°F. Spray 24 mini muffin cups with cooking spray. In 10-inch skillet, melt butter over medium-high heat. Add ¾ cup onion; cook 5 minutes, stirring occasionally. Reduce heat to medium; add red bell pepper. Cook 5 to 7 minutes longer, stirring occasionally, until onion is softened and golden brown. Remove from heat.

2) In medium bowl, beat eggs. Stir in sour cream, salt and pepper sauce. Stir in cooked onion and ¼ cup of the cheese. Spoon onion mixture evenly into mini muffin cups.

3) Unroll dough into 1 large rectangle; press perforations and edges to seal. Using a 1½-inch biscuit or cookie cutter, cut dough into small rounds. Place dough round on top of onion mixture. Top with remaining cheese.

4) Bake 10 to 15 minutes or until golden brown and set in the center. Cool 5 minutes; run knife around edge of each muffin cup. Serve warm or at room temperature.

HIGH ALTITUDE (3500-6500 FT.): No change.

Nutrition Information Per Serving:		
Calories: 80	From Fat:	50
Total Fat		6g
Saturated Fat		2.5g
Trans Fat		0.5g
Cholesterol		25mg
Sodium		135mg
Total Carbohydrate		4g
Dietary Fiber		0g
Sugars		1g
Protein		2g

tip

Different cheeses may be substituted in these baked puffs. Try replacing the finely shredded Cheddar cheese with Monterey Jack or mozzarella.

Golden Shrimp Shells

| PREP TIME: | 25 MINUTES (READY IN 40 MINUTES) | LOW FAT |
| SERVINGS: | 24 APPETIZERS | |

1 tablespoon olive or vegetable oil

1½ cups frozen cooked salad shrimp, thawed, rinsed and drained (from 7-oz package)

1 tablespoon finely chopped fresh parsley

¼ teaspoon red pepper sauce

1 garlic clove, finely chopped

1 can (8 oz) Pillsbury® refrigerated crescent dinner rolls

1 tablespoon grated Parmesan cheese

Cocktail sauce

1) Heat oven to 375°F. In 10-inch nonstick skillet, heat oil over medium-high heat until hot. Stir-fry shrimp, parsley, pepper sauce and garlic in oil 1 minute. Remove from heat.

2) Remove dough from can in 2 rolled-up sections; do not unroll. Cut each roll into 12 slices; place 1 inch apart, cut side down, on ungreased cookie sheet. Press half of each dough slice to flatten. Place about 1 teaspoon shrimp mixture on flattened half of each slice. Fold the remaining half of dough slice over shrimp; do not seal (openings may occur between dough layers). Sprinkle each with Parmesan cheese.

3) Bake 11 to 13 minutes or until golden brown. Serve warm with cocktail sauce.

HIGH ALTITUDE (3500-6500 FT.): No change.

Nutrition Information Per Serving:

Calories:	50	From Fat:	25
Total Fat		3g	
Saturated Fat		1g	
Trans Fat		0.5g	
Cholesterol		20mg	
Sodium		140mg	
Total Carbohydrate		4g	
Dietary Fiber		0g	
Sugars		0g	
Protein		2g	

Apricot-Gorgonzola Crescent Appetizers

DAVID DAHLMAN | CHATSWORTH, CALIFORNIA   BAKE-OFF® CONTEST 43, 2008

PREP TIME: 10 MINUTES (READY IN 40 MINUTES)
SERVINGS: 12 APPETIZERS

 EASY

1 can (8 oz) Pillsbury® refrigerated crescent dinner rolls (8 rolls)

¼ cup Smucker's® apricot preserves

2 tablespoons Land O Lakes® butter

½ cup crumbled Gorgonzola cheese (2 oz)

½ cup Fisher® Chef's Naturals® chopped pecans

¼ teaspoon freshly ground pepper

Nutrition Information Per Serving:

Calories:	160	From Fat:	90
Total Fat			11g
Saturated Fat			3.5g
Trans Fat			1g
Cholesterol			10mg
Sodium			230mg
Total Carbohydrate			13g
Dietary Fiber			0g
Sugars			5g
Protein			3g

1) Heat oven to 350°F. Spray large cookie sheet with Crisco® Original No-Stick cooking spray. Unroll dough into 1 large rectangle; place on cookie sheet. Press dough into 13x9-inch rectangle; firmly press perforations to seal.

2) In small microwavable bowl, microwave preserves and butter uncovered on High about 30 seconds or until butter is melted; stir until smooth. Spread preserves mixture evenly over dough. Top evenly with cheese and pecans. Sprinkle evenly with pepper.

3) Bake 13 to 19 minutes or until the crust is deep golden brown. Cool 10 minutes. Cut into 12 squares. Serve warm.

HIGH ALTITUDE (3500-6500 FT.): No change.

Endive-Salmon Boats

PREP TIME: 15 MINUTES (READY IN 15 MINUTES)
SERVINGS: 16 APPETIZERS

 EASY   LOW FAT

½ cup whipped cream cheese spread (from 8-oz container)

16 Belgian endive leaves (about 2 heads)

2 oz salmon lox, cut into 2x½-inch strips

4 teaspoons capers, drained

4 teaspoons finely chopped red onion

16 tiny sprigs fresh dill weed

Nutrition Information Per Serving:

Calories:	30	From Fat:	20
Total Fat			2.5g
Saturated Fat			1.5g
Trans Fat			0g
Cholesterol			10mg
Sodium			100mg
Total Carbohydrate			0g
Dietary Fiber			0g
Sugars			0g
Protein			1g

1) Spread about 1 teaspoon whipped cream cheese spread inside each endive leaf.

2) Top each with salmon strip, capers, onion and dill weed.

HIGH ALTITUDE (3500-6500 FT.): No change.

South-of-the-Border Sushi Appetizers

JAN CORBY | MIDDLETOWN, DELAWARE

BAKE-OFF® CONTEST 43, 2008

PREP TIME: 1 HOUR 5 MINUTES (READY IN 2 HOURS 5 MINUTES)
SERVINGS: 32 APPETIZERS

$\frac{1}{2}$ cup uncooked sushi (sticky) or medium-grain rice

$\frac{2}{3}$ cup water

1 tablespoon seasoned rice vinegar

1 box (9 oz) Green Giant® frozen spinach

5 oz imitation crabmeat, shredded (1 cup)

$\frac{1}{2}$ teaspoon ground cumin

$\frac{1}{4}$ teaspoon sea salt or kosher salt

4 Old El Paso® flour tortillas for burritos (from 11.5-oz package)

$\frac{3}{4}$ cup Old El Paso® zesty ranch taco topper

1 medium avocado, pitted, peeled and sliced

1 large or 2 small roasted red bell peppers (from 7-oz jar), cut into $\frac{1}{2}$-inch strips ($\frac{1}{3}$ cup)

1 teaspoon lemon juice

3 tablespoons sesame seed, lightly toasted

Fresh cilantro sprigs

1) Rinse rice in cool water until water runs clear; drain well. Place rice and $\frac{2}{3}$ cup water in 1-quart saucepan. Heat to boiling; reduce heat to low. Cover; simmer 20 minutes (do not uncover). Remove from heat; let stand covered 10 minutes. Place rice in glass or plastic bowl; stir in vinegar. Set aside.

2) Cook spinach in microwave as directed on box. Drain spinach; cool 5 minutes. Carefully squeeze with paper towels to drain; set aside.

3) In small bowl, mix crabmeat, cumin and sea salt; set aside.

4) On each tortilla, spread 1 tablespoon of the taco topper. Spread $\frac{1}{3}$ cup rice mixture over half of each tortilla (if necessary, wet hands with cool water to prevent sticking). Top rice with $\frac{1}{4}$ each of spinach and crabmeat mixture. Place avocado and pepper strips down center of each tortilla; sprinkle with lemon juice. Starting at filled side, carefully and tightly roll up tortillas. Wrap each tortilla roll-up in plastic wrap. Refrigerate at least 1 hour or up to 4 hours before serving.

5) To serve, trim ends from roll-ups; discard. Cut each roll into 8 even slices. If necessary, secure with toothpicks. Sprinkle cut sides with sesame seed. Place roll-ups on serving platter with small dish of remaining $\frac{1}{2}$ cup taco topper; garnish with cilantro sprigs.

HIGH ALTITUDE (3500-6500 FT.): No change.

Nutrition Information Per Serving:

Calories:	80	From Fat:	30
Total Fat			3.5g
Saturated Fat			0.5g
Trans Fat			0g
Cholesterol			0mg
Sodium			200mg
Total Carbohydrate			9g
Dietary Fiber			0g
Sugars			0g
Protein			2g

Meatballs with Fire Roasted Tomato Sauce

| PREP TIME: | 20 MINUTES (READY IN 50 MINUTES) |
| SERVINGS: | 15 (2 MEATBALLS EACH) |

 EASY

MEATBALLS

1 lb lean (at least 80%) ground beef

1/4 cup Progresso® plain bread crumbs

1/2 teaspoon garlic salt

1/4 teaspoon pepper

4 medium green onions, finely chopped (1/4 cup)

1 egg

SAUCE

1 jar (25.5 oz) Muir Glen® fire roasted tomato pasta sauce

3/4 cup dried cherries, chopped

1/2 cup water

2 tablespoons cider vinegar or wine vinegar

Chopped fresh chives, if desired

1) Heat oven to 400°F. In large bowl, mix meatball ingredients. Shape mixture into 30 (1-inch) meatballs. Place in ungreased 13x9-inch pan.

2) Bake uncovered about 15 minutes or until thoroughly cooked and no longer pink in center.

3) In 3-quart saucepan, heat all sauce ingredients exept chives to boiling, stirring occasionally; reduce heat. Stir in meatballs; cover and simmer about 15 minutes or until sauce is hot. Sprinkle with chives. Serve in chafing dish or slow cooker on low heat setting.

HIGH ALTITUDE (3500-6500 FT.): No change.

Nutrition Information Per Serving:

Calories:	110	From Fat:	40
Total Fat			4.5g
Saturated Fat			1.5g
Trans Fat			0g
Cholesterol			35mg
Sodium			200mg
Total Carbohydrate			11g
Dietary Fiber			1g
Sugars			5g
Protein			7g

Greek Cheese Balls

PREP TIME: 15 MINUTES (READY IN 2 HOURS 20 MINUTES)
SERVINGS: 30 (2 CHEESE BALLS AND 2 PITA CHIPS EACH)

 EASY

$^3/_4$ cup chopped walnuts

3 tablespoons chopped fresh oregano leaves

1 package (8 oz) cream cheese, softened

1 package (4 oz) crumbled tomato-basil feta cheese (1 cup)

2 tablespoons mayonnaise or salad dressing

$^1/_4$ cup pitted kalamata olives

$^1/_4$ cup pimiento-stuffed green olives

1 bag (5 oz) baked no-trans-fat garlic pita chips

1) Heat oven to 350°F. In ungreased shallow pan, place walnuts. Bake 6 to 10 minutes, stirring occasionally, until light brown. Cool 5 minutes.

2) Finely chop $^1/_2$ cup of the walnuts. Spread on sheet of waxed paper; mix with oregano.

3) In food processor, place cream cheese, feta cheese and mayonnaise. Cover; process with on-and-off pulses 20 to 30 seconds or until well mixed. Add the kalamata olives and remaining $^1/_4$ cup walnuts. Process by pulsing 4 or 5 times until chopped and mixed. Cover and refrigerate about 1 hour or until firm enough to shape into balls.

4) Using 1 teaspoon for each, shape the cheese mixture into 60 balls. Roll in the walnut-oregano mixture to cover. Place in tightly covered container. Refrigerate about 1 hour or until firm. Serve with pita chips.

HIGH ALTITUDE (3500-6500 FT.): No change.

Nutrition Information Per Serving:	
Calories: 90	From Fat: 60
Total Fat	7g
Saturated Fat	2.5g
Trans Fat	0g
Cholesterol	10mg
Sodium	120mg
Total Carbohydrate	4g
Dietary Fiber	0g
Sugars	0g
Protein	2g

Asian Pork Dumplings

WENDY KO | WALNUT CREEK, CALIFORNIA

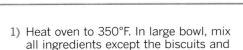

BAKE-OFF® CONTEST 43, 2008

PREP TIME: 50 MINUTES (READY IN 1 HOUR 20 MINUTES)
SERVINGS: 48 APPETIZERS

1¼ lb lean ground pork

1 can (8 oz) sliced or whole water chestnuts, drained, coarsely chopped

1 box (9 oz) Green Giant® frozen spinach, thawed, squeezed to drain

12 medium green onions, thinly sliced (about ¾ cup)

2 tablespoons soy sauce

1 teaspoon granulated garlic or garlic powder

¾ teaspoon ground ginger

¾ teaspoon white pepper or black pepper

2 Eggland's Best eggs

2 cans (16.3 oz each) Pillsbury® Grands!® flaky layers refrigerated original biscuits (8 biscuits each)

1½ cups sweet-and-sour sauce or sweet-spicy chili sauce

1) Heat oven to 350°F. In large bowl, mix all ingredients except the biscuits and sweet-and-sour sauce.

2) Remove 1 can of biscuits from the refrigerator just before filling (keep remaining can of biscuits refrigerated). Separate each biscuit into 3 layers. Press each layer into 3½-inch round, being careful not to tear dough.

3) Spoon 1 rounded tablespoon of pork filling on center of each dough round. Bring all sides of dough up over filling, stretching gently if necessary, and gather in center above filling to form a dumpling; press gathered dough to seal. On ungreased large cookie sheet, place 24 dumplings 2 inches apart.

4) Bake 17 to 27 minutes or until thermometer inserted in the center reads 160°F and sides and tops of dumplings are golden brown. Repeat to make remaining dumplings. Serve warm with sweet-and-sour sauce.

HIGH ALTITUDE (3500-6500 FT.): No change.

Nutrition Information Per Serving:		
Calories: 100	From Fat:	45
Total Fat		5g
Saturated Fat		1.5g
Trans Fat		1g
Cholesterol		15mg
Sodium		260mg
Total Carbohydrate		11g
Dietary Fiber		0g
Sugars		3g
Protein		4g

To make these ahead, cover the unbaked dumplings on a cookie sheet and refrigerate them for up to 2 hours before baking.

Mushroom-Scallop Skewers

PREP TIME: 15 MINUTES (READY IN 25 MINUTES)
SERVINGS: 14 APPETIZERS

 EASY   **f** LOW FAT

¼ cup orange juice

2 tablespoons packed brown sugar

1 teaspoon grated orange peel

½ teaspoon ground ginger

1 garlic clove, finely chopped

14 bay scallops (¼ to ⅓ lb)

14 baby portabello mushrooms (1½ to 2 inches), stems removed

14 slices packaged precooked bacon (from 2.1-oz package)

Fresh orange curls, if desired

1) Heat oven to 425°F. Line 15x10x1-inch pan with cooking parchment paper. In medium bowl, mix orange juice, brown sugar, orange peel, ginger and garlic. Add scallops; toss to coat.

2) Place 1 scallop in each mushroom cap. Wrap each with 1 bacon slice, enclosing scallop. Secure with toothpick. Dip in orange juice mixture; place in pan.

3) Bake 8 to 10 minutes or until the mushrooms are tender and the scallops are opaque. If desired, replace each toothpick with 4-inch wooden skewer.

HIGH ALTITUDE (3500-6500 FT.): No change.

Nutrition Information Per Serving:		
Calories: 40	From Fat:	15
Total Fat		2g
Saturated Fat		0.5g
Trans Fat		0g
Cholesterol		5mg
Sodium		85mg
Total Carbohydrate		3g
Dietary Fiber		0g
Sugars		3g
Protein		3g

Mediterranean Shrimp Antipasto

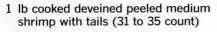

PREP TIME: 35 MINUTES (READY IN 2 HOURS 35 MINUTES)
SERVINGS: 14 (1/2 CUP EACH)

1 lb cooked deveined peeled medium shrimp with tails (31 to 35 count)

1 block (8 oz) feta cheese, cubed

2 cups fresh cauliflower florets

1 medium red bell pepper, cut into 1-inch pieces

16 kalamata or ripe olives

1/2 cup olive oil

1/3 cup red wine vinegar

1/4 cup chopped fresh basil leaves

1/4 cup chopped fresh Italian (flat-leaf) parsley

1 tablespoon fresh grated lemon peel

2 garlic cloves, finely chopped

1) In large resealable food-storage plastic bag or glass baking dish, mix all ingredients. Gently move ingredients around in bag to mix well.

2) Refrigerate at least 2 hours but no longer than 12 hours to blend flavors. Drain before serving. Store in the refrigerator.

HIGH ALTITUDE (3500-6500 FT.): No change.

Nutrition Information Per Serving:

Calories:	160	From Fat:	110
Total Fat		12g	
Saturated Fat		3.5g	
Trans Fat		0g	
Cholesterol		80mg	
Sodium		300mg	
Total Carbohydrate		3g	
Dietary Fiber		0g	
Sugars		2g	
Protein		10g	

Shrimp and Veggie Appetizer Pizza

PREP TIME: 35 MINUTES (READY IN 2 HOURS 50 MINUTES)
SERVINGS: 32 APPETIZERS

2 cans (8 oz each) Pillsbury® refrigerated reduced-fat or regular crescent dinner rolls

8 oz spinach dip (1 cup)

4 oz fresh snow pea pods (1 cup), cut into 1-inch pieces

1 cup cherry tomatoes or grape tomatoes, halved

$1/2$ cup julienne (matchstick-cut) jicama ($1x^1/4x^1/4$ inch)

7 oz cooked deveined peeled salad shrimp, thawed if frozen, tail shells removed

2 tablespoons finely chopped fresh basil leaves

1) Heat oven to 375°F. Grease or spray 15x10x1-inch pan. Unroll both cans of dough; separate into 4 long rectangles. On pan, place 3 rectangles lengthwise, beginning at 1 short end of pan. Place remaining rectangle across other short end of pan, to fill pan with dough. Press dough in bottom and up sides to form crust, firmly pressing perforations to seal.

2) Bake 13 to 17 minutes or until golden brown. Cool completely, about 30 minutes.

3) Spread spinach dip over cooled crust. Arrange peas, tomatoes, jicama and shrimp over dip. Gently press into dip. Sprinkle with basil.

4) Serve immediately, or cover and refrigerate up to 2 hours before serving. To serve, cut into squares, 8 rows by 4 rows.

HIGH ALTITUDE (3500-6500 FT.): No change.

Nutrition Information Per Serving:

Calories: 80	From Fat: 35
Total Fat	4g
Saturated Fat	1.5g
Trans Fat	0g
Cholesterol	15mg
Sodium	170mg
Total Carbohydrate	7g
Dietary Fiber	0g
Sugars	2g
Protein	3g

tip

To easily julienne the jicama, make matchstick-shaped pieces by cutting it into ¼-inch slices, then cutting the ¼-inch strips into 1-inch lengths.

Tuscan Spinach and Tomato "Crustini"

DIANNA WARA | WASHINGTON, ILLINOIS

BAKE-OFF® CONTEST 43, 2008

| PREP TIME: | 20 MINUTES (READY IN 1 HOUR 15 MINUTES) |
| SERVINGS: | 12 APPETIZERS |

EASY

1 Pillsbury® refrigerated pie crust (from 15-oz box), softened as directed on box

2 packages (3 oz each) cream cheese, softened

5 teaspoons basil pesto

1 box (9 oz) Green Giant® frozen spinach, thawed, squeezed to drain

1/3 cup diced red onion

2 small tomatoes, thinly sliced

1 1/2 tablespoons Fisher® dry roasted sunflower kernels

1/3 cup shredded regular or smoked provolone cheese

2 fresh basil leaves, thinly sliced

1) Heat oven to 375°F. Line large cookie sheet with cooking parchment paper, or spray with Crisco® Original No-Stick cooking spray. Unroll the pie crust on cookie sheet.

2) In small bowl, stir together cream cheese and 4 teaspoons of the pesto. Spread cheese mixture over pie crust to within 1 inch of edge. Arrange spinach evenly over cream cheese mixture. Sprinkle onion over spinach. Arrange tomato slices in single layer over onion. Carefully fold 1-inch edge of crust over filling, pleating crust every 2 inches. Brush remaining 1 teaspoon pesto over edge of crust.

3) Bake 20 minutes. Remove from oven; sprinkle the sunflower kernels and provolone cheese evenly over filling. Bake 12 to 14 minutes longer or until cheese is melted and crust is light golden brown.

4) Cool 15 to 20 minutes. Sprinkle with sliced fresh basil leaves. Cut into 12 wedges.

HIGH ALTITUDE (3500-6500 FT.): In Step 3, increase second bake time to 14 to 16 minutes.

Nutrition Information Per Serving:		
Calories: 170		From Fat: 110
Total Fat		12g
Saturated Fat		6g
Trans Fat		0g
Cholesterol		20mg
Sodium		180mg
Total Carbohydrate		11g
Dietary Fiber		0g
Sugars		1g
Protein		3g

Layered Asian Dip

PREP TIME: 35 MINUTES (READY IN 2 HOURS 55 MINUTES)
SERVINGS: 30 (2 TABLESPOONS DIP AND 2 CRACKERS EACH)

TOPPING

- 1 cup cubed cooked chicken
- 2/3 cup shredded carrots
- 1 tablespoon chopped fresh parsley
- 1 garlic clove, finely chopped
- 2 tablespoons soy sauce
- 1/4 teaspoon ground ginger

WONTON DIPPERS

- 30 wonton skins (about 3 1/4-inch square)
- Cooking spray

SAUCE

- 2 tablespoons packed brown sugar
- 2 teaspoons cornstarch
- 1/2 cup water
- 2 tablespoons ketchup
- 1 tablespoon rice wine vinegar
- 2 teaspoons Worcestershire sauce
- 4 drops red pepper sauce

BASE

- 2 packages (8 oz each) 1/3-less-fat cream cheese (Neufchâtel)
- 1 tablespoon milk

GARNISH

- 1/3 cup unsalted cashews, chopped
- 4 medium green onions, sliced (1/4 cup)

Nutrition Information Per Serving:

Calories:	80	From Fat:	35
Total Fat			4g
Saturated Fat			1.5g
Trans Fat			0g
Cholesterol			15mg
Sodium			170mg
Total Carbohydrate			7g
Dietary Fiber			0g
Sugars			2g
Protein			3g

1) In small bowl, mix topping ingredients. Cover and refrigerate 2 to 4 hours.

2) Meanwhile, heat oven to 400°F. Cut each wonton skin in half into two triangles. On 2 large ungreased cookie sheets, arrange wonton skins in single layer. Spray wontons with cooking spray. Bake about 6 minutes or until crisp; cool.

3) In 1-quart saucepan, mix brown sugar and cornstarch. Gradually beat in remaining sauce ingredients with wire whisk. Cook over medium heat about 5 minutes, stirring occasionally with wire whisk, until thick. Cool to room temperature, about 20 minutes.

4) In medium bowl, beat cream cheese and milk with electric mixer on medium speed. Spread on serving platter at least 10 inches in diameter. Just before serving, spoon topping over cheese; drizzle with sauce and sprinkle with cashews and green onions. Serve with crisp wontons.

HIGH ALTITUDE (3500-6500 FT.): No change.

Chicken Crescent Pot Stickers

PREP TIME: 35 MINUTES (READY IN 55 MINUTES)
SERVINGS: 16 POT STICKERS

2 cups shredded cooked chicken

1/4 cup shredded carrots

4 medium green onions, chopped
(1/4 cup chopped)

1/3 cup hoisin sauce

2 tablespoons thick barbecue sauce

1 tablespoon grated fresh gingerroot

2 teaspoons sesame oil

2 teaspoons finely chopped garlic

2 cans (8 oz each) Pillsbury® Place 'n
Bake™ refrigerated crescent rounds

1 egg, beaten

2 tablespoons sesame seed

1) Heat oven to 375°F. Grease or spray large cookie sheet. In medium bowl, mix the chicken, carrots and onions. Stir in the hoisin sauce, barbecue sauce, gingerroot, sesame oil and garlic.

2) Unroll dough from both cans on work surface, but do not separate. Firmly press perforations to seal. Roll or press each into 12x8-inch rectangle. Cut each rectangle into 8 squares. Spoon about 2 tablespoons chicken mixture in center of each square. Bring edges up, pinching together and twisting to form bundle.

3) Place on ungreased cookie sheet. Brush with beaten egg. Sprinkle with sesame seed. Bake 14 to 18 minutes or until golden brown. Serve warm.

HIGH ALTITUDE (3500-6500 FT.): No change.

Nutrition Information Per Serving:	
Calories: 170	From Fat: 80
Total Fat	9g
Saturated Fat	2.5g
Trans Fat	1.5g
Cholesterol	30mg
Sodium	350mg
Total Carbohydrate	15g
Dietary Fiber	0g
Sugars	3g
Protein	8g

Boneless Buffalo Chicken Appetizers

PREP TIME: 20 MINUTES (READY IN 50 MINUTES)
SERVINGS: 12

 EASY

CHICKEN
- $^1/_3$ cup honey
- $^1/_3$ cup chili sauce
- 4 teaspoons soy sauce
- 2 teaspoons red pepper sauce
- 1 teaspoon cider vinegar
- $^1/_8$ teaspoon ground ginger
- $^1/_8$ teaspoon ground cumin
- 4 boneless skinless chicken breasts (1 lb), each cut crosswise into $^1/_2$-inch-wide strips

DIPPING SAUCE
- $^1/_2$ cup blue cheese dressing
- $^1/_4$ cup sour cream
- 2 tablespoons chopped fresh parsley
- 2 tablespoons crumbled blue cheese, if desired

1) In medium bowl, mix all chicken ingredients except chicken. Add chicken; toss to coat well. Cover; refrigerate at least 30 minutes to marinate.

2) Meanwhile, in small bowl, mix dressing and sour cream until well blended. Refrigerate until serving time.

3) Heat 12-inch nonstick skillet over medium-high heat. With slotted spoon, remove chicken from marinade; reserve marinade. Add chicken to skillet; cook and stir 4 minutes. Add reserved marinade; cook over medium-high heat 6 to 7 minutes, stirring occasionally, until sauce thickens and chicken is no longer pink in center.

4) Spoon dipping sauce into small serving bowl; sprinkle with parsley and blue cheese. Place bowl on serving platter; arrange warm chicken around bowl. Serve with cocktail toothpicks.

HIGH ALTITUDE (3500-6500 FT.): No change.

Nutrition Information Per Serving:		
Calories: 140	From Fat:	60
Total Fat		7g
Saturated Fat		1.5g
Trans Fat		0g
Cholesterol		30mg
Sodium		330mg
Total Carbohydrate		10g
Dietary Fiber		0g
Sugars		9g
Protein		9g

tip

Blue cheese gets its distinctive flavor and color from the bacteria used to develop the cheese. The assertive flavor of blue cheese complements the hot spiciness of buffalo chicken recipes.

Spicy Orange-Chicken Charmers

PAULA NAUMANN | SLEEPY EYE, MINNESOTA

 Bake-Off

BAKE-OFF® CONTEST 43, 2008

PREP TIME: 20 MINUTES (READY IN 45 MINUTES)
SERVINGS: 16 APPETIZERS

🄴 EASY

1 teaspoon sesame oil

1/2 lb boneless skinless chicken breast, cut into 1/4-inch pieces

4 medium green onions, sliced (1/4 cup)

1/3 cup Smucker's® sweet orange marmalade

1 teaspoon soy sauce

1 teaspoon cooking sherry, if desired

1/2 teaspoon garlic powder

1/2 teaspoon crushed red pepper flakes

1 can (8 oz) Pillsbury® refrigerated crescent dinner rolls (8 rolls)

1 teaspoon sesame seed

1) Heat oven to 375°F. Lightly spray 16 mini muffin cups with Crisco® Original No-Stick cooking spray. In 12-inch nonstick skillet, heat oil over medium heat. Add chicken and onions; cook 3 minutes, stirring frequently. Reduce heat to medium-low; stir in marmalade, soy sauce, sherry, garlic powder and red pepper flakes. Simmer uncovered about 5 minutes, stirring occasionally, until sauce is thickened and chicken is no longer pink in center. Remove from heat.

2) Meanwhile, unroll dough into 4 rectangles. Cut each rectangle into quarters by making another diagonal cut in addition to the perforation to make a total of 16 triangles.

3) Press largest part of each dough triangle in bottom and up side of muffin cup, leaving triangle points extending over cup. Fill each cup with about 1 tablespoon chicken mixture. For each cup, slightly stretch points of triangles to make longer; twist points together and place on top of filling. Spray shaped rolls lightly with cooking spray; sprinkle with sesame seed.

4) Bake 11 to 19 minutes or until golden brown. Carefully remove from pan to serving plate. Cool 5 minutes before serving. Serve warm.

HIGH ALTITUDE (3500-6500 FT.): Bake 11 to 17 minutes.

Nutrition Information Per Serving:

Calories:	100	From Fat:	35
Total Fat			4g
Saturated Fat			1g
Trans Fat			1g
Cholesterol			10mg
Sodium			140mg
Total Carbohydrate			11g
Dietary Fiber			0g
Sugars			5g
Protein			4g

MANGO-JALAPEÑO-CHICKEN SALAD
IN TORTILLA BOWLS
PG. 91

Sides, Soups & Salads

These standout specialties will complete your menu...or even make a meal by themselves!

CHEESY-TOPPED MASHED POTATO
CASSEROLE
PG. 101

BLT PASTA SALAD
PG. 89

FENNEL POTATO SALAD
PG. 99

Swiss Vegetable Casserole

PREP TIME: 20 MINUTES (READY IN 50 MINUTES)
SERVINGS: 8 (1/2 CUP EACH)

 EASY

2 tablespoons butter or margarine

6 green onions, cut into $1/2$-inch pieces ($1/2$ cup)

2 tablespoons all-purpose flour

$1/4$ teaspoon salt

$1/8$ teaspoon pepper

$1/2$ cups milk

1 cup shredded Swiss cheese (4 oz)

1 bag (1 lb) frozen broccoli, carrots and cauliflower, cooked, drained

$1/4$ cup crushed round buttery crackers

1) Heat oven to 350°F. Spray 1- to $1/2$-quart casserole with cooking spray. In 2-quart saucepan, melt the butter over medium heat. Add the onions; cook and stir 2 to 3 minutes or until tender.

2) Stir in flour, salt and pepper. Gradually add milk, stirring constantly. Cook and stir until the mixture is bubbly and thickened. Remove from heat.

3) Add $3/4$ cup of the cheese; stir until melted. Stir in cooked vegetables. Spoon mixture into casserole. Sprinkle with crushed crackers and remaining $1/4$ cup cheese.

4) Bake 25 to 30 minutes or until topping is golden brown and casserole is bubbly.

HIGH ALTITUDE (3500-6500 FT.): No change.

Nutrition Information Per Serving:		
Calories: 140	From Fat:	80
Total Fat		9g
Saturated Fat		5g
Trans Fat		0g
Cholesterol		25mg
Sodium		170mg
Total Carbohydrate		9g
Dietary Fiber		2g
Sugars		4g
Protein		7g

tip

Want to make this creamy casserole a little lighter? To lower the fat by about 2 grams per serving, use skim milk and reduced-fat Swiss cheese.

No-Fuss Beef Stew

PREP TIME: 20 MINUTES (READY IN 35 MINUTES)
SERVINGS: 4 (1-1/3 CUPS EACH)

 EASY   LOW FAT

2 teaspoons olive oil

1¼ lb boneless beef top sirloin, trimmed of fat, cut into cubes

2 to 3 garlic cloves, finely chopped

1 cup water

⅓ cup all-purpose flour

1 can (10½ oz) condensed beef consommé

1 cup Green Giant® Niblets® frozen whole kernel corn (from 1-lb bag)

3 cups Green Giant® frozen broccoli cuts (from 1-lb bag)

1 cup chopped red bell pepper

Nutrition Information Per Serving:

Calories: 330	From Fat: 70
Total Fat	7g
Saturated Fat	2g
Trans Fat	0g
Cholesterol	80mg
Sodium	440mg
Total Carbohydrate	25g
Dietary Fiber	5g
Sugars	5g
Protein	41g

1) In 4-quart saucepan, heat oil over medium-high heat until hot. Cook beef and garlic in oil; cook, stirring occasionally, until beef is brown.

2) In small bowl, beat water and flour with wire whisk until well blended. Add flour mixture, consommé and corn to meat mixture. Heat to boiling, stirring frequently. Reduce heat to medium-low; cook, stirring occasionally, about 3 minutes. Add the broccoli and bell pepper; cook until thickened and vegetables are tender.

HIGH ALTITUDE (3500-6500 FT.): Thaw frozen vegetables before using.

BLT Pasta Salad

PREP TIME: 25 MINUTES (READY IN 25 MINUTES)
SERVINGS: 6 (1-2/3 CUPS EACH)

 EASY  LOW FAT

1¼ cups uncooked medium pasta shells

4 slices bacon

¼ red onion, thinly sliced (¼ cup)

1 pint (2 cups) cherry tomatoes, cut in half or 3 Roma tomatoes, sliced

½ cup reduced-calorie ranch dressing

6 leaves romaine or iceberg lettuce

Nutrition Information Per Serving:

Calories: 660	From Fat: 370
Total Fat	41g
Saturated Fat	11g
Trans Fat	0g
Cholesterol	90mg
Sodium	960mg
Total Carbohydrate	39g
Dietary Fiber	8g
Sugars	4g
Protein	32g

1) Cook and drain pasta as directed on package, omitting salt. Rinse with cold water; drain well.

2) Meanwhile, in 10-inch nonstick skillet, cook bacon over medium heat about 4 minutes, turning occasionally, until crisp. Drain on paper towels. Crumble into small pieces or cut into thirds.

3) In large bowl, mix pasta, onion and tomatoes; toss gently with dressing to coat. Place lettuce leaf on each of 6 salad plates; divide pasta mixture evenly along plates. Sprinkle each with bacon.

HIGH ALTITUDE (3500-6500 FT.): No change.

Smoky Three-Bean Chili

PREP TIME: 10 MINUTES (READY IN 50 MINUTES)
SERVINGS: 6 (1-1/3 CUPS EACH)

 EASY   LOW FAT

1 tablespoon vegetable oil

1 cup chopped celery

1 medium green bell pepper, chopped (1 cup)

1 medium onion, chopped ($1/2$ cup)

2 cloves garlic, finely chopped

1 can (28 oz) diced tomatoes, undrained

1 can (15 oz) spicy chili beans, undrained

1 can (15 oz) kidney beans, drained, rinsed

1 can (15 oz) black beans, drained, rinsed

1 teaspoon ground cumin

1 teaspoon chili powder

1 teaspoon finely chopped chipotle chile in adobo sauce (from 7- or 11-oz can)

$1/2$ teaspoon adobo sauce (from can of chipotle chiles)

Crushed tortilla chips, if desired

Sliced green onions, if desired

1) In 4-quart saucepan or Dutch oven, heat oil over medium-high heat. Cook celery, bell pepper, onion and garlic in oil 3 minutes.

2) Stir in remaining ingredients except tortilla chips and green onions. Heat to boiling. Reduce heat; cover and simmer 30 to 40 minutes, stirring occasionally, until vegetables are tender and flavors are blended.

3) Top individual servings with tortilla chips and green onions.

HIGH ALTITUDE (3500-6500 FT.): No change.

Nutrition Information Per Serving:

Calories:	310	From Fat:	35
Total Fat		4g	
Saturated Fat		0.5g	
Trans Fat		0g	
Cholesterol		0mg	
Sodium		720mg	
Total Carbohydrate		52g	
Dietary Fiber		16g	
Sugars		8g	
Protein		16g	

Mango-Jalapeño-Chicken Salad in Tortilla Bowls

FRANCES PIETSCH | FLOWER MOUND, TEXAS

PREP TIME: 50 MINUTES (READY IN 50 MINUTES)
SERVINGS: 4

VINAIGRETTE

- 1/2 cup cubed peeled mango
- 2 tablespoons mango nectar (from 12.5-oz can)
- 2 tablespoons white wine vinegar
- 1 tablespoon fresh lime juice
- 1 tablespoon fresh orange juice
- 1 tablespoon honey
- 1/3 cup Crisco® pure canola oil

BOWLS

- 4 Old El Paso® flour tortillas for burritos (from 11.5-oz package)
- 1/2 teaspoon ground cumin
- 1/2 teaspoon salt

SALAD

- 4 cups cubed cooked chicken breast
- 1 1/3 cups cubed peeled mango
- 1 tablespoon fresh lime juice
- 1 1/2 cups cubed peeled avocado (from 2 medium)
- 1/2 cup finely chopped red bell pepper
- 1/2 cup finely chopped red onion
- 1/4 cup finely chopped seeded jalapeño chiles (2 medium)
- 1/4 cup chopped fresh cilantro
- 1 cup shredded iceberg lettuce
- 1/2 teaspoon salt

1) Heat oven to 400°F. Spray insides of 4 ovenproof 2-cup soup bowls with Crisco® Original No-Stick cooking spray. Set aside.

2) In food processor bowl with metal blade or blender, place all vinaigrette ingredients except oil. Cover; process until smooth. With food processor running, slowly pour oil through the feed tube until mixture is thickened. Set aside.

3) Spray 1 side of each tortilla with Crisco® Original No-Stick cooking spray. Sprinkle cumin and 1/2 teaspoon salt evenly over sprayed sides of tortillas. Press tortillas, seasoned sides up, in bowls. Place bowls in 15x10x1-inch pan. Bake 5 to 7 minutes or until edges are golden brown. Remove tortillas from bowls; place upside down on cooling rack. Cool completely.

4) In large bowl, mix the chicken and 1 1/3 cups mango. In small bowl, mix 1 tablespoon lime juice and the avocado. Add avocado and remaining salad ingredients to chicken mixture; mix well. Add vinaigrette; mix well.

5) To serve, spoon chicken salad into tortilla bowls. (Bowls will be full.) Serve immediately.

HIGH ALTITUDE (3500-6500 FT.): No change.

Nutrition Information Per Serving:		
Calories: 740	From Fat:	360
Total Fat		40g
Saturated Fat		5g
Trans Fat		1g
Cholesterol		115mg
Sodium		1000mg
Total Carbohydrate		48g
Dietary Fiber		6g
Sugars		18g
Protein		47g

Tomato, Beef and Barley Soup

PREP TIME: 30 MINUTES (READY IN 45 MINUTES)
SERVINGS: 6 (ABOUT 1-1/3 CUPS EACH)

- 1 lb lean (at least 80%) ground beef
- 2 cans (19 oz each) Progresso® Vegetable Classics hearty tomato soup
- 2 cups water
- 1/2 cup uncooked quick-cooking barley
- 1 cup sliced celery
- 1 cup Green Giant® frozen mixed vegetables (from 1-lb bag)
- 6 tablespoons shredded fresh Parmesan cheese

In place of the hearty tomato soup, try a tomato-basil variety. Serve each bowlful of this soup with a crusty French roll for a satisfying meal.

1) In 4-quart saucepan or Dutch oven, cook beef over medium-high heat 5 to 7 minutes, stirring occasionally, until thoroughly cooked; drain.

2) Stir in soup, water, barley and celery. Heat to boiling, stirring occasionally. Reduce heat to low; simmer uncovered about 15 minutes, stirring occasionally, until barley is tender.

3) Stir in frozen mixed vegetables. Cook 6 to 7 minutes, stirring occasionally, until mixture is hot. Sprinkle each serving with 1 tablespoon cheese.

HIGH ALTITUDE (3500-6500 FT.): Increase water to 2-1/4 cups.

Nutrition Information Per Serving:

Calories:	320	From Fat:	100
Total Fat		11g	
Saturated Fat		4.5g	
Trans Fat		0.5g	
Cholesterol		50mg	
Sodium		890mg	
Total Carbohydrate		35g	
Dietary Fiber		6g	
Sugars		8g	
Protein		20g	

Creamy Bean Soup with Taquito Dippers

SHEILA SUHAN | SCOTTDALE, PENNSYLVANIA

BAKE-OFF® CONTEST 43, 2008

PREP TIME: 30 MINUTES (READY IN 30 MINUTES)
SERVINGS: 4 (1-1/3 CUPS SOUP AND 3 TAQUITOS EACH)

 EASY

1 can (16 oz) Old El Paso® traditional refried beans

1 can (14.5 oz) petite diced tomatoes, undrained

1 cup chicken broth

1/2 cup (from 14-oz can) unsweetened coconut milk (not cream of coconut)

1 can (4.5 oz) Old El Paso® chopped green chiles

1 package (1.25 oz) Old El Paso® taco seasoning mix

6 sticks (0.75 oz each) sharp Cheddar or chipotle Cheddar cheese

1 package (10.5 oz) Old El Paso® flour tortillas for soft tacos and fajitas (12 tortillas)

2 tablespoons Crisco® pure vegetable oil

1/4 cup chopped fresh cilantro, if desired

4 medium green onions, sliced (1/4 cup), if desired

1) Heat oven to 450°F. Line cookie sheet with foil.

2) In 2-quart saucepan, stir refried beans, tomatoes, broth, coconut milk, green chiles and taco seasoning mix; heat to boiling. Reduce heat to low; simmer uncovered about 20 minutes.

3) Meanwhile, cut each cheese stick in half lengthwise to make 2 thin sticks. Place 1 stick on one edge of each tortilla; roll tortilla tightly around cheese. Brush edges of tortillas with water to seal. Place taquitos, seam sides down, on cookie sheet. Brush each lightly with oil. Bake 5 to 7 minutes or until edges of tortillas are golden brown and cheese is melted.

4) Pour soup into serving bowls; garnish with cilantro or onions. Serve with taquitos for dipping.

HIGH ALTITUDE (3500-6500 FT.): No change.

Nutrition Information Per Serving:

Calories:	660	From Fat:	280
Total Fat			31g
Saturated Fat			14g
Trans Fat			2.5g
Cholesterol			45mg
Sodium			2460mg
Total Carbohydrate			71g
Dietary Fiber			9g
Sugars			8g
Protein			23g

White Chicken Chili

PREP TIME: 30 MINUTES (READY IN 30 MINUTES)
SERVINGS: 9 (1 CUP EACH)

 EASY   

LOW FAT

- 1 tablespoon vegetable oil
- 1 large onion, chopped (1 cup)
- 2 garlic cloves, finely chopped
- 1 lb boneless skinless chicken breasts, cut into bite-size pieces
- 3 cans (14 oz each) chicken broth
- 2 cans (15 oz each) cannellini beans, drained
- 2 cans (4.5 oz each) Old El Paso® chopped green chiles, drained
- 1 teaspoon dried oregano leaves
- 1/2 teaspoon ground cumin

  Dash ground red pepper (cayenne), if desired
- 1 1/2 cups shredded Monterey Jack cheese (6 oz)

  Chopped fresh cilantro, if desired

1) In 4-quart saucepan or Dutch oven, heat oil over medium-high heat until hot. Add onion, garlic and chicken; cook and stir until chicken is no longer pink.

2) Stir in remaining ingredients except cheese and cilantro. Heat to boiling. Reduce heat to low; simmer 10 to 15 minutes to blend flavors, stirring occasionally.

3) To serve, spoon chili into soup bowls. Top each serving with cheese and cilantro.

HIGH ALTITUDE (3500-6500 FT.): No change.

Nutrition Information Per Serving:

Calories:	290	From Fat:	90
Total Fat		10g	
Saturated Fat		4.5g	
Trans Fat		0g	
Cholesterol		45mg	
Sodium		1410mg	
Total Carbohydrate		24g	
Dietary Fiber		6g	
Sugars		2g	
Protein		27g	

Spaghetti and Meatball Stew

PREP TIME:	40 MINUTES (READY IN 40 MINUTES)
SERVINGS:	4 (1-1/3 CUPS EACH)

 LOW FAT

2 tablespoons fat-free (skim) milk

1 egg white

1/2 lb lean (at least 90%) ground turkey or extra-lean (at least 90%) ground beef

1/4 cup Progresso® plain bread crumbs

1/4 teaspoon poultry seasoning

1/8 teaspoon pepper

2 cups water

2 cups fat-free tomato pasta sauce

1/2 cup chopped green bell pepper

1 jar (2.5 oz) Green Giant® sliced mushrooms, drained

1 2/3 cups uncooked radiatore (nuggets) pasta (5 oz)

2 tablespoons grated Parmesan cheese

1) Heat oven to 450°F. In medium bowl, mix milk and egg white. Stir in turkey, bread crumbs, poultry seasoning and pepper. Shape into 1-inch balls. Place in ungreased 15x10x1-inch pan. Bake about 10 minutes or until lightly browned and thoroughly cooked.

2) Meanwhile, in 4-quart saucepan, heat water, pasta sauce, bell pepper and mushrooms to boiling. Stir in the pasta. Reduce heat; simmer about 15 minutes or until pasta is of desired doneness, stirring occasionally. Stir in meatballs; heat until hot. Serve sprinkled with Parmesan cheese.

HIGH ALTITUDE (3500-6500 FT.): In Step 2, add an additional 1/4 cup water and simmer 15 to 20 minutes.

Nutrition Information Per Serving:

Calories:	400	From Fat:	90
Total Fat		10g	
Saturated Fat		2.5g	
Trans Fat		0g	
Cholesterol		40mg	
Sodium		850mg	
Total Carbohydrate		55g	
Dietary Fiber		4g	
Sugars		14g	
Protein		23g	

Home-Style Roasted Vegetables

PREP TIME:	15 MINUTES (READY IN 50 MINUTES)	EASY
SERVINGS:	8 (1 CUP EACH)	

2 tablespoons olive or vegetable oil

2 teaspoons dried thyme leaves

1 1/2 teaspoons seasoned salt

1/4 teaspoon pepper

4 medium unpeeled russet potatoes, cut into 1 1/2-inch chunks

1 medium red bell pepper, cut into 1-inch square pieces

2 cups ready-to-eat baby-cut carrots

4 parsnips, peeled, cut into 1/2-inch slices (1 to 1 1/2 cups)

1 onion, cut into 3/4-inch wedges

Nutrition Information Per Serving:		
Calories: 140	From Fat:	35
Total Fat		3.5g
Saturated Fat		0.5g
Trans Fat		0g
Cholesterol		0mg
Sodium		290mg
Total Carbohydrate		25g
Dietary Fiber		4g
Sugars		5g
Protein		3g

1) Heat oven to 450°F. In large bowl, mix oil, thyme, seasoned salt and pepper. Add remaining ingredients; toss to coat. Spread in ungreased 15x10x1-inch pan.

2) Roast 25 minutes; turn and stir vegetables. Roast 25 to 30 minutes longer or until vegetables are tender (carrots will be crisp-tender).

HIGH ALTITUDE (3500-6500 FT.): No change.

Buttercup Squash Casserole

PREP TIME:	10 MINUTES (READY IN 1 HOUR 25 MINUTES)	EASY
SERVINGS:	4 (1/2 CUP EACH)	

1 medium buttercup squash (about 2 1/2 lb)

2 tablespoons packed brown sugar

1/4 teaspoon salt

1/4 teaspoon ground cinnamon

1/4 teaspoon ground nutmeg

2 tablespoons butter or margarine

1 tablespoon chopped fresh chives

1/8 teaspoon ground nutmeg, if desired

1) Heat oven to 350°F. Cut squash into quarters; remove seeds. In ungreased shallow baking pan, place pieces, cut sides down. Bake 45 to 50 minutes or until tender. Cool slightly.

2) Spray 1-quart casserole with cooking spray. Scoop the squash pulp from the skin; place in medium bowl. Discard skin. Add brown sugar, salt, cinnamon, 1/4 teaspoon nutmeg and butter to squash. Mix with potato masher or fork until well blended.

3) Spoon into casserole. Sprinkle with chives and 1/8 teaspoon nutmeg. Bake 20 to 25 minutes or until hot.

HIGH ALTITUDE (3500-6500 FT.): No change.

Nutrition Information Per Serving:		
Calories: 110	From Fat:	5
Total Fat		0.5g
Saturated Fat		0g
Trans Fat		0g
Cholesterol		0mg
Sodium		20mg
Total Carbohydrate		27g
Dietary Fiber		2g
Sugars		20g
Protein		2g

Lemony Leeks and Pasta Salad

PREP TIME: 35 MINUTES (READY IN 1 HOUR 35 MINUTES)
SERVINGS: 8 (1 CUP EACH)

1 large lemon

3 tablespoons olive or vegetable oil

1 cup slivered almonds

3 cups sliced leeks (about 4 leeks)

3 tablespoons capers, drained

$1/2$ teaspoon salt

$1/8$ teaspoon pepper

1 large red bell pepper, roasted, cut into strips

1 large yellow bell pepper, roasted, cut into strips

8 oz ($3^1/2$ cups) uncooked bow-tie (farfalle) pasta

1) Remove peel from lemon, using zester or grater; set aside. Cut white pith from lemon; discard. Cut lemon into $1/4$-inch slices; set aside.

2) In 10-inch skillet, heat the oil over medium-high heat until hot. Cook and stir almonds in oil about 30 seconds or until light brown. With slotted spoon, remove almonds from skillet; set aside.

3) In same skillet, cook and stir lemon slices, lemon peel, leeks, capers, salt and pepper about 1 minute or until vegetables are crisp-tender. Remove from heat. Remove lemon slices; discard. Stir in bell peppers and almonds. Cover; refrigerate at least 2 hours until chilled.

4) Cook pasta to desired doneness as directed on package. Drain; rinse with cold water to cool. In large serving bowl, gently toss pasta, vegetable mixture and almonds.

HIGH ALTITUDE (3500-6500 FT.): No change.

Nutrition Information Per Serving:	
Calories: 290	From Fat: 120
Total Fat	13g
Saturated Fat	1.5g
Trans Fat	0g
Cholesterol	0mg
Sodium	350mg
Total Carbohydrate	35g
Dietary Fiber	4g
Sugars	4g
Protein	8g

Chicken Pasta Soup

PREP TIME: 40 MINUTES (READY IN 40 MINUTES)
SERVINGS: 6 (1-1/3 CUPS EACH)

 LOW FAT

- 2 teaspoons butter or margarine
- 3 boneless skinless chicken breasts, cut into thin strips
- 1 package (8 oz) sliced fresh mushrooms (3 cups)
- 3 cans (14 oz each) fat-free chicken broth with 33% less sodium
- 1½ cups uncooked medium pasta shells (4 oz)
- 1 cup sliced yellow summer squash or zucchini
- ½ cup chopped red bell pepper
- 1 teaspoon Italian seasoning

1) In 4-quart nonstick saucepan or Dutch oven, heat butter over medium heat until hot. Cook chicken and mushrooms in butter, stirring occasionally, until chicken is no longer pink. Stir in remaining ingredients. Heat to boiling.

2) Reduce the heat to low; simmer 10 to 13 minutes or until pasta is tender. Serve immediately.

HIGH ALTITUDE (3500-6500 FT.): In Step 2, simmer 15 to 20 minutes.

Nutrition Information Per Serving:

Calories:	190	From Fat:	35
Total Fat			4g
Saturated Fat			1.5g
Trans Fat			0g
Cholesterol			40mg
Sodium			500mg
Total Carbohydrate			91g
Dietary Fiber			1g
Sugars			1g
Protein			20g

tip

Rotisserie chicken can be used in place of the raw chicken. It's not necessary to cook the chicken with the mushrooms. Instead, simply chop it and add it with the rest of the ingredients.

Fennel Potato Salad

PREP TIME: 45 MINUTES (READY IN 2 HOURS 45 MINUTES)
SERVINGS: 16 (1/2 CUP EACH)

SALAD

8 to 10 new red potatoes (about 1^1/$_2$ lb), sliced

4 hard-cooked eggs

1 medium bulb fennel with stalks and leaves, cored, sliced

^{1}/$_2$ cup sliced celery

^{1}/$_4$ cup chopped onion

DRESSING

1 cup mayonnaise or salad dressing

2 tablespoons Dijon mustard

1 tablespoon chopped fresh chives

1 tablespoon white vinegar

^{1}/$_2$ teaspoon sugar

^{1}/$_4$ teaspoon pepper

1) In 3- to 4-quart saucepan, cook sliced potatoes in small amount of boiling water about 10 minutes or until tender; drain well. Meanwhile, cut eggs into eighths.

2) In large bowl, mix warm potatoes, eggs, fennel, celery and onion. In small bowl, mix dressing ingredients. Spoon dressing over salad; toss gently. Cover; refrigerate 1 to 2 hours or until chilled. Garnish with fennel leaves if desired.

HIGH ALTITUDE (3500-6500 FT.): No change.

Nutrition Information Per Serving:		
Calories: 160	From Fat: 110	
Total Fat		12g
Saturated Fat		2g
Trans Fat		0g
Cholesterol		60mg
Sodium		150mg
Total Carbohydrate		10g
Dietary Fiber		1g
Sugars		2g
Protein		3g

Thai Beef Salad

PREP TIME: 15 MINUTES (READY IN 15 MINUTES)
SERVINGS: 4 (2-1/4 CUPS EACH)

 EASY   LOW FAT

4 teaspoons canola oil

1 tablespoon lime juice

1 tablespoon reduced-sodium soy sauce

1 teaspoon sugar

1/2 teaspoon crushed red pepper flakes

1 bag (10 oz) ready-to-eat romaine lettuce or mixed greens

1/4 cup lightly packed fresh cilantro leaves

1/4 cup lightly packed fresh mint leaves, if desired

6 oz thinly sliced reduced-sodium roast beef (from deli), cut into thin strips (about 1 1/2 cups)

Lime wedges, if desired

1) In small bowl, mix oil, lime juice, soy sauce, sugar and red pepper flakes.

2) In large salad bowl, layer lettuce, cilantro and mint. Arrange beef strips on top; drizzle with dressing. Toss just before serving. Serve with lime wedges.

HIGH ALTITUDE (3500-6500 FT.): No change.

Nutrition Information Per Serving:		
Calories: 190	From Fat: 35	
Total Fat		4g
Saturated Fat		1.5g
Trans Fat		0g
Cholesterol		40mg
Sodium		500mg
Total Carbohydrate		91g
Dietary Fiber		1g
Sugars		1g
Protein		20g

Cheesy-Topped Mashed Potato Casserole

PREP TIME: 15 MINUTES (READY IN 30 MINUTES)
SERVINGS: 4 (1/2 CUP EACH)

 EASY

1 cup hot water

1/4 cup milk

2 tablespoons butter or margarine

1 1/3 cups plain mashed potato mix (dry)

1 tablespoon chopped fresh chives, if desired

1/2 cup bite-size cheese crackers

1/4 cup shredded Cheddar cheese (1 oz)

2 tablespoons butter or margarine, melted

Nutrition Information Per Serving:

Calories: 260	From Fat: 150
Total Fat	16g
Saturated Fat	10g
Trans Fat	1g
Cholesterol	40mg
Sodium	230mg
Total Carbohydrate	23g
Dietary Fiber	1g
Sugars	1g
Protein	5g

1) Heat oven to 375°F. In ungreased 1-quart casserole, mix hot water, milk, 2 tablespoons butter and the mashed potato mix. Cover with plastic wrap, turning back one side to vent steam. Microwave on High 2 to 4 minutes or until moistened.

2) Whip potatoes with fork until fluffy; stir in chives. Smooth top of potato mixture with rubber spatula.

3) Crush crackers. In small bowl, mix crushed crackers, cheese and 2 tablespoons melted butter; sprinkle over top of potatoes.

4) Bake 10 to 15 minutes or until potatoes are hot and topping is crisp.

HIGH ALTITUDE (3500-6500 FT.): No change.

Serve this potato casserole with sliced ham, and add a bowl of greens tossed with mandarin oranges and your favorite vinaigrette dressing.

Mixed Fruit and Cheese Salad

PREP TIME: 15 MINUTES (READY IN 15 MINUTES)
SERVINGS: 6 (1/2 CUP EACH)

 EASY

3/4 cup sliced fresh strawberries

1 tablespoon poppy seed dressing

3/4 teaspoon sugar

1 cup 1-inch pieces cantaloupe

1/2 cup grapes, cut in half

1/2 cup fresh blueberries

2 oz white Cheddar cheese, cut into 1/2-inch cubes

Nutrition Information Per Serving:

Calories: 90	From Fat: 40
Total Fat	4.5g
Saturated Fat	2g
Trans Fat	0g
Cholesterol	10mg
Sodium	80mg
Total Carbohydrate	9g
Dietary Fiber	1g
Sugars	8g
Protein	3g

1) In food processor, place 1/4 cup of the strawberries, the dressing and sugar. Cover; process with quick on-and-off motions until smooth.

2) In medium bowl, mix remaining 1/2 cup strawberries, the cantaloupe, grapes, blueberries and cheese. Pour dressing over fruit mixture; toss.

HIGH ALTITUDE (3500-6500 FT.): No change.

Barley, Corn and Pepper Salad

PREP TIME: 30 MINUTES (READY IN 30 MINUTES)
SERVINGS: 10 (1/2 CUP EACH)

 EASY

SALAD

 1 cup uncooked quick-cooking barley

 1¼ cups Green Giant® Niblets® frozen whole kernel corn

 ½ cup red bell pepper strips

 ½ cup chopped green bell pepper

 ½ cup sliced green onions (8 medium)

DRESSING

 ¼ cup olive oil

 ¼ cup lemon juice

 ¼ cup chopped fresh cilantro

 ½ teaspoon salt

 Coarsely ground black pepper

1) Cook barley to desired doneness as directed on package. Drain; rinse with cold water. Cook corn as directed on bag. Drain; rinse with cold water.

2) In large bowl, mix barley, corn and remaining salad ingredients.

3) In jar with tight-fitting lid, shake dressing ingredients well. Pour salad dressing over salad; toss gently to coat. Serve at room temperature or chilled. Store in the refrigerator.

HIGH ALTITUDE (3500-6500 FT.): No change.

Nutrition Information Per Serving:	
Calories: 150	From Fat: 50
Total Fat	6g
Saturated Fat	1g
Trans Fat	0g
Cholesterol	0mg
Sodium	125mg
Total Carbohydrate	21g
Dietary Fiber	4g
Sugars	2g
Protein	3g

 During summer, take advantage of the availability of fresh corn and use it in place of the frozen corn in this salad.

Mojito Shrimp Salad in Biscuit Bowls

PREP TIME: 15 MINUTES (READY IN 35 MINUTES)
SERVINGS: 5

 EASY

BISCUIT BOWLS

1 can (10.2 oz) Pillsbury® Grands!® flaky layers refrigerated original biscuits

DRESSING

1/4 cup olive or canola oil

2 tablespoons chopped fresh mint leaves

1 tablespoon honey

1 teaspoon grated lime peel

2 tablespoons fresh lime juice

1/4 teaspoon rum extract

1 small garlic clove, finely chopped

SALAD

12 oz cooked deveined peeled medium (32 count) shrimp, tail shells removed

1 can (11 oz) mandarin orange segments, drained

1/2 cup fresh sweet peas (from pods)

5 cups torn leaf lettuce

2 medium green onions, sliced (2 tablespoons)

1) Heat oven to 350°F. On ungreased large cookie sheet, turn 5 (6-oz) custard cups upside down; spray the outsides of cups with cooking spray. Separate dough into 5 biscuits; press each to form 6-inch circle. Press each biscuit over bottom and around side of each cup. Using fingers, press dough around each cup, forming bowl. Bake 15 to 18 minutes or until golden brown. Carefully remove custard cups. Set biscuit bowls aside. Cool completely, about 5 minutes.

2) Meanwhile, in large bowl, mix the dressing ingredients with wire whisk; fold in the shrimp. Set aside. In small microwavable bowl, microwave the peas about 30 seconds or just until heated through. Refrigerate while the biscuit bowls cool.

3) Place biscuit bowls on serving plates. Fold oranges, peas, lettuce and onions into shrimp and dressing. Spoon into biscuit bowls. Serve immediately.

HIGH ALTITUDE (3500-6500 FT.): No change.

Nutrition Information Per Serving:

Calories:	390	From Fat:	190
Total Fat			21g
Saturated Fat			3.5g
Trans Fat			3.5g
Cholesterol			135mg
Sodium			720mg
Total Carbohydrate			31g
Dietary Fiber			1g
Sugars			10g
Protein			20g

Tropical Coleslaw

PREP TIME: 15 MINUTES (READY IN 30 MINUTES)
SERVINGS: 14 (1/2 CUP EACH)

 EASY

1 bag (16 oz) coleslaw mix (shredded cabbage and carrots)

1 can (11 oz) mandarin orange segments, drained

2 medium green onions, chopped (2 tablespoons), if desired

1 container (6 oz) Yoplait Original 99% Fat-Free Key lime pie yogurt

1/4 cup mayonnaise or salad dressing

1 teaspoon grated lime peel

1 tablespoon fresh lime juice

1/4 cup whole cashews

Nutrition Information Per Serving:		
Calories: 70	From Fat:	40
Total Fat		4.5g
Saturated Fat		0.5g
Trans Fat		0g
Cholesterol		0mg
Sodium		40mg
Total Carbohydrate		7g
Dietary Fiber		1g
Sugars		5g
Protein		1g

1) In large bowl, mix coleslaw mix, mandarin oranges and onions.

2) In small bowl, mix yogurt, mayonnaise, lime peel and lime juice; gently fold into coleslaw mixture. Refrigerate at least 15 minutes but no longer than 4 hours to blend flavors.

3) Just before serving, sprinkle with cashews. Cover; refrigerate any remaining coleslaw.

HIGH ALTITUDE (3500-6500 FT.): No change.

Honeydew melon, chopped cauliflower or sticks of jicama could also be tossed into this coleslaw if you like.

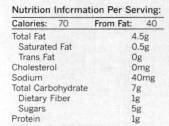

Main-Dish Minestrone

PREP TIME: 50 MINUTES (READY IN 50 MINUTES)
SERVINGS: 6 (1 CUP EACH)

🅕 LOW FAT

³⁄₄ cup water

1 cup chopped onions

2 small unpeeled red potatoes, cubed (1 cup)

¹⁄₂ cup chopped carrot

¹⁄₂ cup chopped celery

¹⁄₃ cup chopped green bell pepper

2 large garlic cloves, finely chopped

1 box (9 oz) Green Giant® frozen spinach

¹⁄₄ cup uncooked rosamarina or orzo pasta (1¹⁄₂ oz) or ¹⁄₄ cup broken spaghetti (1 oz)

2 cans (14 oz each) chicken broth

1 can (15 oz) cannellini beans, drained, rinsed

1 can (8 oz) no-salt-added tomato sauce

¹⁄₄ cup chopped fresh parsley or 1 tablespoon dried parsley flakes

¹⁄₂ teaspoon dried oregano leaves

¹⁄₂ teaspoon dried basil leaves

¹⁄₄ teaspoon salt

¹⁄₄ teaspoon pepper

1) In 4-quart nonstick saucepan or Dutch oven, heat the water to boiling over medium-high heat. Add onions; cook 3 minutes, stirring occasionally. Add potatoes, carrot, celery, bell pepper and garlic; cook 3 minutes, stirring occasionally. Add remaining ingredients. Heat to boiling.

2) Reduce heat; simmer about 20 minutes, stirring occasionally, until potatoes and pasta are tender.

HIGH ALTITUDE (3500-6500 FT.): No change.

Nutrition Information Per Serving:		
Calories: 190	From Fat:	15
Total Fat		1.5g
Saturated Fat		0g
Trans Fat		0g
Cholesterol		0mg
Sodium		720mg
Total Carbohydrate		33g
Dietary Fiber		7g
Sugars		4g
Protein		12g

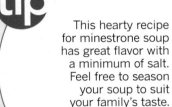

tip

This hearty recipe for minestrone soup has great flavor with a minimum of salt. Feel free to season your soup to suit your family's taste.

Main
Dishes

Families come running for hearty helpings of these
skillet suppers, pasta dishes, meat pies and more.

PATCHWORK POT PIE
PG. 147

CHICKEN PHYLLO BUNDLES
PG. 139

SOUTHWESTERN CHILI SHRIMP
PG. 126

SPICY CHICKEN AND ORZO SKILLET
PG. 120

Loaded Baked Potato Pizza

TRACY MARTINEZ | CHEYENNE, WYOMING

Pillsbury
Bake-Off®   BAKE-OFF® CONTEST 43, 2008

PREP TIME: 35 MINUTES (READY IN 1 HOUR)
SERVINGS: 6

1 can (13.8 oz) Pillsbury® refrigerated classic pizza crust

1 medium white potato

1 tablespoon Crisco® pure olive oil

¼ teaspoon salt

¼ teaspoon pepper

1 box (10 oz) Green Giant® frozen broccoli and cheese sauce

⅔ cup sour cream

1 tablespoon ranch dressing

1 cup shredded Colby-Monterey Jack cheese blend (4 oz)

5 slices cooked bacon, coarsely chopped

1 small tomato, seeded, chopped (½ cup)

2 medium green onions, chopped (2 tablespoons)

1) Heat oven to 375°F. Spray large cookie sheet with Crisco® Original No-Stick cooking spray. Unroll the pizza crust dough on cookie sheet; press dough into 13x9-inch rectangle. Bake 10 to 13 minutes or until crust is light golden brown. Remove from oven; set aside.

2) Meanwhile, pierce the potato with fork; place on microwavable paper towel in microwave oven. Microwave potato 4 to 5 minutes, turning once, until tender. Cover; let stand 5 minutes. When potato is cool enough to handle, peel potato and cut into ¼-inch cubes (1 cup). In small bowl, mix potato, oil, salt and pepper; set aside.

3) Cook broccoli in microwave as directed on box. Empty from pouch into another small bowl to cool slightly; set aside.

4) In another small bowl, mix sour cream and ranch dressing. Spread mixture over pizza crust to within ½ inch of edges of crust. Sprinkle ½ cup of the cheese evenly over sour cream mixture. Sprinkle with bacon.

5) Spread broccoli mixture and potato mixture evenly over bacon. Sprinkle tomato, onions and remaining ½ cup cheese evenly over potato mixture.

6) Bake 15 to 22 minutes longer or until crust is golden brown and cheese is melted. Let stand 5 minutes before cutting.

HIGH ALTITUDE (3500-6500 FT.): No change.

Nutrition Information Per Serving:		
Calories: 410	From Fat: 180	
Total Fat		20g
Saturated Fat		9g
Trans Fat		0g
Cholesterol		45mg
Sodium		1060mg
Total Carbohydrate		42g
Dietary Fiber		2g
Sugars		7g
Protein		14g

Mexican Pesto-Pork Tacos

VANDA POZZANGHERA | PITTSFORD, NEW YORK

BAKE-OFF® CONTEST 43, 2008

PREP TIME: 40 MINUTES (READY IN 40 MINUTES)
SERVINGS: 10 TACOS

FILLING

- 1 package (17 oz) refrigerated fully cooked pork roast au jus
- 2 tablespoons orange juice
- 1/2 teaspoon ground cumin
- 1 medium tomato, chopped (3/4 cup)
- 1 medium avocado, pitted, peeled and chopped (3/4 cup)
- 2 teaspoons lime juice
- 1/2 teaspoon Domino® or C&H® granulated sugar
- 1/4 teaspoon salt

PESTO

- 1 1/2 cups lightly packed fresh cilantro sprigs
- 3/4 cup Fisher® Spanish peanuts
- 2 to 3 garlic cloves
- 1 jalapeño chile, seeded, chopped
- 1/4 cup Crisco® pure olive oil

TACO SHELLS AND CHEESE

- 1 box (4.7 oz) Old El Paso® Stand 'N Stuff® taco shells (10 shells)
- 1 cup shredded Monterey Jack cheese (4 oz)

  Garnishes, if desired

  Lime and orange wedges

  Fresh cilantro sprigs

1) Heat oven to 325°F. In medium microwavable bowl, shred pork; discard juice. Toss pork with orange juice and cumin; set aside. In another medium bowl, mix tomato, avocado, lime juice, sugar and salt.

2) In food processor bowl with metal blade, place 1 1/2 cups cilantro, the peanuts, garlic, chile and oil. Cover; process about 30 seconds or until well blended; set aside.

3) Heat taco shells in oven as directed on box. Meanwhile, cover bowl of pork mixture with microwavable paper towel. Microwave on High 2 to 3 minutes or until warm.

4) To serve, spread about 1 tablespoon pesto over 1 side of each taco shell. Fill each with about 1/4 cup pork mixture, 1 tablespoon tomato-avocado mixture and heaping 1 tablespoon cheese. Serve garnished with lime wedges, orange wedges and cilantro sprigs.

HIGH ALTITUDE (3500-6500 FT.): No change.

Nutrition Information Per Serving:

Calories:	390	From Fat:	250
Total Fat			28g
Saturated Fat			7g
Trans Fat			1.5g
Cholesterol			50mg
Sodium			320mg
Total Carbohydrate			13g
Dietary Fiber			3g
Sugars			2g
Protein			21g

Savory Pork Tenderloins with Herbed Vegetables

PREP TIME: 45 MINUTES (READY IN 45 MINUTES)
SERVINGS: 8

 LOW FAT

2 teaspoons onion powder

2 teaspoons dried thyme leaves

1 teaspoon garlic salt

½ teaspoon pepper

2 to 2¼ lb pork tenderloins

2 tablespoons vegetable oil

2 large red bell peppers, cut into ½-inch pieces

16 medium green onions, diagonally sliced (1 cup)

2 medium bulbs fennel, cored, thinly sliced

¼ teaspoon dried thyme leaves

¼ teaspoon salt

1) Heat gas or charcoal grill. In small bowl, mix onion powder, 2 teaspoons thyme, the garlic salt and pepper. Sprinkle the thyme mixture on all sides of the tenderloins. Immediately place on grill over medium heat. Cover grill; cook 15 to 20 minutes, turning 3 times, until meat thermometer inserted in center reads 160°F.

2) Meanwhile, in 12-inch skillet, heat the oil over medium-high heat until hot. Cook the remaining ingredients in oil 4 to 7 minutes, stirring frequently, until vegetables are tender.

3) To serve, cut tenderloins into slices. Spoon vegetable mixture over slices.

Broiling Directions: Season the tenderloins as directed above. Broil 4 to 6 inches from heat 8 to 13 minutes, turning once, until tender. Make vegetables and serve as directed above.

HIGH ALTITUDE (3500-6500 FT.): Grill pork over medium-low heat.

Nutrition Information Per Serving:		
Calories: 210	From Fat:	70
Total Fat		8g
Saturated Fat		2g
Trans Fat		0g
Cholesterol		70mg
Sodium		280mg
Total Carbohydrate		8g
Dietary Fiber		3g
Sugars		3g
Protein		27g

Turkey, Bacon and Cheese Sandwiches

PREP TIME: 10 MINUTES (READY IN 35 MINUTES)
SERVINGS: 6 SANDWICHES

 EASY

1 can (10.1 oz) Pillsbury® Big & Flaky refrigerated crescent dinner rolls

2 tablespoons Dijon mustard

6 oz thinly sliced cooked turkey (from deli)

3 oz thinly sliced Swiss cheese (from deli)

6 slices precooked bacon

1) Heat oven to 350°F.

2) Unroll dough on work surface; separate into triangles. Spread each triangle with 1 teaspoon mustard. Top each with turkey, cheese and bacon, cutting to fit if necessary. Roll up loosely as directed on can. Place on ungreased cookie sheet; curve into crescent shape.

3) Bake 21 to 23 minutes or until golden brown and cheese is melted.

HIGH ALTITUDE (3500-6500 FT.): No change.

Nutrition Information Per Serving:

Calories: 310	From Fat: 160
Total Fat	18g
Saturated Fat	6g
Trans Fat	2.5g
Cholesterol	45mg
Sodium	620mg
Total Carbohydrate	21g
Dietary Fiber	0g
Sugars	4g
Protein	17g

Italian Sausage-Mashed Potato Pie

PREP TIME: 15 MINUTES (READY IN 1 HOUR 15 MINUTES)
SERVINGS: 6

 EASY

1 pouch (from 7.2-oz box) Betty Crocker® roasted garlic mashed potatoes

¾ cup milk

½ cup water

2 eggs, beaten

1 lb bulk mild Italian pork sausage

1 medium onion, chopped (½ cup)

1 cup tomato pasta sauce

1 teaspoon dried basil leaves

½ cup shredded Parmesan cheese (2 oz)

1) Heat oven to 375°F. Spray 9-inch glass pie plate. Cook 1 pouch potatoes as directed on box—except use ¾ cup milk and ½ cup water; omit margarine. After 5-minute stand time, stir in eggs. Spread cooked potatoes in bottom and up sides of pie plate, forming a crust.

2) Meanwhile, in 12-inch skillet, cook sausage and onion over medium-high heat, stirring frequently, until sausage is no longer pink; drain. Stir in the pasta sauce and basil. Reduce heat to low; cook about 2 minutes, stirring occasionally, until hot. Pour into potato-lined plate.

3) Bake about 25 minutes or until crust edges just begin to turn golden brown. Sprinkle with cheese. Bake about 5 minutes longer or until cheese is melted. Let stand 5 minutes before serving.

HIGH ALTITUDE (3500-6500 FT.): No change.

Nutrition Information Per Serving:

Calories: 530	From Fat: 230
Total Fat	25g
Saturated Fat	13g
Trans Fat	0.5g
Cholesterol	125mg
Sodium	670mg
Total Carbohydrate	41g
Dietary Fiber	4g
Sugars	5g
Protein	34g

Philly-Goes-Mexican Cheese Steak

TENA KERNS | BERKLEY, MASSACHUSETTS

BAKE-OFF® CONTEST 43, 2008

PREP TIME: 40 MINUTES (READY IN 1 HOUR)
SERVINGS: 4 SANDWICHES

1½ lb beef flank steak

1 package (1.25 oz) Old El Paso® taco seasoning mix

6 tablespoons Land O Lakes® unsalted or salted butter, melted

1 garlic clove, finely chopped

1½ teaspoons fresh lime juice

¼ cup water

2 cans (11 oz each) Pillsbury® refrigerated crusty French loaf

½ teaspoon garlic powder

2 tablespoons Crisco® pure canola oil

1 medium onion, thinly sliced

1 medium green bell pepper, thinly sliced

1 medium red bell pepper, thinly sliced

¼ cup finely chopped fresh cilantro, if desired

1 jar (8 oz) cheese dip

1 can (4.5 oz) Old El Paso® chopped green chiles

1) Heat oven to 350°F. Spray large cookie sheet with Crisco® Original No-Stick cooking spray. Cut beef flank steak against the grain into thin strips; set aside. Reserve 2 teaspoons of the taco seasoning mix.

2) In large bowl, mix 3 tablespoons of the butter, remaining taco seasoning mix, garlic, lime juice and water. Add beef; toss to coat. Refrigerate beef mixture while baking bread.

3) Place loaves, at least 2 inches apart, on cookie sheet. With sharp knife, make slits on top of each loaf. In small bowl, stir remaining 3 tablespoons butter, reserved 2 teaspoons taco seasoning mix and the garlic powder until well mixed. Brush seasoning mixture on tops and sides of each loaf. Bake 26 to 30 minutes or until golden brown. Cool 15 minutes.

4) Meanwhile, in 12-inch nonstick skillet, heat 1 tablespoon of the oil over medium-high heat. Add onion and bell peppers; cook 6 to 8 minutes, stirring frequently, until vegetables are tender. Remove vegetables from skillet; set aside.

5) In same skillet, heat remaining 1 tablespoon oil over high heat. Add half of the beef; cook 8 to 10 minutes, stirring frequently, until tender and browned. Transfer cooked beef to a plate; cook the remaining half of beef. Return beef and vegetables to skillet. Stir in cilantro. Keep warm.

6) In small microwavable bowl, stir the cheese dip and green chiles. Cover with microwavable plastic wrap, folding back one edge ¼ inch to vent steam. Microwave on High 3 minutes, stirring after 1 minute 30 seconds, until warm.

7) Cut each bread loaf in half crosswise, then cut each half horizontally ¾ of the way through. To serve, fill each roll with ¼ of the beef mixture; drizzle with cheese sauce. Serve immediately.

HIGH ALTITUDE (3500-6500 FT.): No change.

Nutrition Information Per Serving:		
Calories: 1010	From Fat:	430
Total Fat		48g
Saturated Fat		21g
Trans Fat		1.5g
Cholesterol		140mg
Sodium		2620mg
Total Carbohydrate		88g
Dietary Fiber		3g
Sugars		12g
Protein		57g

Roasted Chicken and Vegetables

PREP TIME: 15 MINUTES (READY IN 1 HOUR 25 MINUTES)   EASY
SERVINGS: 4

¼ cup chicken broth

2 tablespoons olive or vegetable oil

1 teaspoon salt

1 teaspoon dried thyme leaves

1 teaspoon dried tarragon leaves

½ teaspoon pepper

2 medium dark-orange sweet potatoes, peeled, cut into eighths

1½ cups ready-to-eat baby-cut carrots, cut in half lengthwise

1 large onion, cut into 8 wedges

8 garlic cloves, finely chopped

1 cut-up whole chicken (3 to 3½ lb)

1) Heat oven to 425°F. In large bowl, mix broth, oil, salt, thyme, tarragon and pepper. Add vegetables and garlic; toss to coat. Remove vegetables with slotted spoon to ungreased 15x10x1-inch pan, spreading on half of the pan.

2) Add chicken pieces to remaining broth mixture in bowl, turning chicken over to coat all sides. Place the chicken pieces skin-side-down next to vegetables in pan, placing legs and thighs along edge of pan. Drizzle any remaining broth mixture over chicken.

3) Bake 30 minutes. Stir the vegetables and turn the chicken pieces. Bake 30 to 40 minutes longer or until vegetables are tender and juice of chicken is clear when the thickest piece is cut to bone (170°F for breasts; 180°F for thighs and legs).

HIGH ALTITUDE (3500-6500 FT.): No change.

Nutrition Information Per Serving:	
Calories: 410	From Fat: 150
Total Fat	17g
Saturated Fat	3.5g
Trans Fat	0g
Cholesterol	120mg
Sodium	820mg
Total Carbohydrate	22g
Dietary Fiber	4g
Sugars	9g
Protein	41g

Mongolian Steak & String Bean Pot Pies

PREP TIME: 1 HOUR 30 MINUTES (READY IN 2 HOURS 5 MINUTES)
SERVINGS: 4

MARINADE

1/4 cup reduced-sodium soy sauce

3 tablespoons sweet rice wine

1 tablespoon sesame oil

1 teaspoon hoisin sauce

2 tablespoons packed brown sugar

1 tablespoon cornstarch

2 teaspoons grated gingerroot

2 garlic cloves, finely chopped

STEAK AND VEGETABLES

1 lb boneless beef top sirloin steak (3/4 inch thick), trimmed of fat, cut into 2x1/4-inch strips

1 tablespoon butter or margarine

1 garlic clove, finely chopped

4 oz fresh button or beech mushrooms, sliced

2 medium green onions, sliced (2 tablespoons)

1 can (13.8 oz) Pillsbury® refrigerated classic pizza crust

1/2 lb fresh green beans, trimmed, cut into 2-inch pieces

1 tablespoon black or regular sesame seed

1 egg

1 tablespoon water

1) In large bowl, mix marinade ingredients. Add steak strips; stir to coat. Cover and refrigerate 1 hour to marinate.

2) Meanwhile, in 10-inch skillet, melt butter over medium heat. Cook garlic and mushrooms in butter 2 to 3 minutes, stirring occasionally, until the mushrooms are soft. Remove from heat, stir in onions.

3) Unroll pizza dough; cut into 4 rectangles. Spoon 2 tablespoons mushroom mixture onto center of each rectangle. Pull 4 corners of dough to center; twist firmly to seal. Allow side edges to remain open to vent. Place bundles on tray, cover and refrigerate until ready to top meat mixture.

4) Heat oven to 350°F. In 2-quart saucepan, heat 1 cup water to boiling. Add the green beans; cover and cook over medium heat 3 to 4 minutes to blanch. Drain.

5) Drain steak, reserving marinade. In 10-inch skillet, heat reserved marinade to boiling over medium-high heat; cook about 2 minutes or until sauce is thickened. Remove from heat; stir in steak, green beans and sesame seed. Divide mixture evenly among 4 ungreased 10-oz ramekins or custard cups.

6) Place a filled bundle on top of the steak mixture in each ramekin, gently shaping to fit inside. In small bowl, beat egg and water with fork. Brush over tops of bundles.

7) Place ramekins on cookie sheet with sides. Bake 30 to 35 minutes or until dough is golden brown and mixture is bubbly.

HIGH ALTITUDE (3500-6500 FT.): Bake 33 to 38 minutes.

Nutrition Information Per Serving:			
Calories:	560	From Fat:	140
Total Fat			16g
Saturated Fat			5g
Trans Fat			0g
Cholesterol			125mg
Sodium			1330mg
Total Carbohydrate			64g
Dietary Fiber			2g
Sugars			15g
Protein			38g

Thai Chicken Burritos

SHARON KOEBEL | LOVELAND, OHIO

Pillsbury Bake-Off® BAKE-OFF® CONTEST 43, 2008

PREP TIME: 45 MINUTES (READY IN 45 MINUTES)
SERVINGS: 6 BURRITOS

½ cup uncooked basmati rice, rinsed

1 cup water

1 cup Old El Paso® Thick 'n Chunky medium salsa

⅓ cup Jif® Extra Crunchy peanut butter

2 tablespoons teriyaki sauce

2 tablespoons water

¼ cup packed Domino® or C&H® light brown sugar

1 teaspoon chili powder

½ teaspoon ground ginger

1 lb boneless skinless chicken breasts, cut into bite-size pieces

2 teaspoons sesame oil

6 Old El Paso® flour tortillas for burritos (from 11.5-oz package)

6 tablespoons Old El Paso® Thick 'n Chunky medium salsa

6 tablespoons sour cream

1) Cook rice in water as directed on package, omitting butter, if called for.

2) Meanwhile, in small bowl, mix 1 cup salsa, the peanut butter, teriyaki sauce, water and brown sugar; set aside.

3) In large resealable food-storage plastic bag, mix chili powder and ginger. Add the chicken; seal bag and shake until chicken is evenly coated.

4) In 10-inch nonstick skillet, heat the oil over medium-high heat. Add the chicken; cook 3 to 5 minutes, stirring frequently, until chicken is no longer pink in center. Stir in salsa mixture. Reduce heat to low. Cover; simmer 8 to 10 minutes. Stir in cooked rice; cook 2 to 3 minutes longer or until mixture is thoroughly heated.

5) Meanwhile, heat tortillas as directed on package. Spoon ½ cup chicken filling on each warm tortilla to within 1 inch of edge of tortilla. Fold sides of tortilla toward center; fold ends over. Place burritos, folded sides down, on serving plate. Top each burrito with 1 tablespoon salsa and 1 tablespoon sour cream.

HIGH ALTITUDE (3500-6500 FT.): No change.

Nutrition Information Per Serving:		
Calories: 470	From Fat: 160	
Total Fat		18g
Saturated Fat		5g
Trans Fat		1g
Cholesterol		55mg
Sodium		1250mg
Total Carbohydrate		52g
Dietary Fiber		1g
Sugars		13g
Protein		25g

Halibut with Chipotle Butter

PREP TIME: 30 MINUTES (READY IN 30 MINUTES)
SERVINGS: 4

 EASY

1/4 cup butter, softened

1 canned chipotle chile in adobo sauce, chopped

1 teaspoon adobo sauce (from can of chipotle chiles)

1 teaspoon lime juice

2 tablespoons chopped fresh cilantro

1 tablespoon olive oil

1 teaspoon chili powder

1/2 teaspoon garlic salt

1/2 teaspoon ground cumin

4 halibut steaks (6 oz each)

1) Heat gas or charcoal grill. In small bowl, mix butter, chile, adobo sauce, lime juice and cilantro. Refrigerate mixture until serving time.

2) In another small bowl, mix the oil, chili powder, garlic salt and cumin. Brush both sides of each halibut steak with the oil mixture.

3) Place halibut on grill over medium heat. Cover grill; cook 10 to 15 minutes, turning once or twice, until fish flakes easily with fork. Serve halibut topped with butter mixture.

HIGH ALTITUDE (3500-6500 FT.): No change.

Nutrition Information Per Serving:	
Calories: 290	From Fat: 160
Total Fat	17g
Saturated Fat	8g
Trans Fat	0g
Cholesterol	120mg
Sodium	400mg
Total Carbohydrate	1g
Dietary Fiber	0g
Sugars	0g
Protein	32g

Pork Picadillo Pie

PREP TIME: 30 MINUTES (READY IN 1 HOUR 15 MINUTES)
SERVINGS: 6

- 1 box (15 oz) Pillsbury® refrigerated pie crusts, softened as directed on box
- 1 lb boneless pork loin, cut into 1/2-inch cubes
- 1/2 cup chopped onion (1 medium)
- 1 can (14.5 oz) diced tomatoes, undrained
- 1 box (9 oz) Green Giant® Niblets® frozen whole kernel corn
- 1 can (4.5 oz) Old El Paso® chopped green chiles
- 1/2 cup chili sauce
- 1/4 cup sliced pimiento-stuffed green olives
- 1/4 cup raisins
- 1/2 teaspoon ground cumin
- 1/4 teaspoon salt
- 2 teaspoons milk
- 1 tablespoon cornmeal

1) Heat oven to 425°F. Make pie crusts as directed on the box for Two-Crust Pie using 9½- or 10-inch deep-dish glass pie plate.

2) Spray 12-inch skillet with cooking spray; heat over medium-high heat until hot. Add the pork cubes and onion; cook 3 to 5 minutes, stirring occasionally, until pork is no longer pink.

3) Add the tomatoes, corn, green chiles, chili sauce, olives, raisins, cumin and salt. Heat to boiling. Reduce heat to medium; simmer 5 minutes, stirring occasionally, until slightly thickened. Remove from heat; cool 5 minutes.

4) Spoon mixture into crust-lined pie plate. Cut 4 wide slits or small designs in second crust; place crust over pork mixture. Seal edge and flute edge. Brush crust with milk; sprinkle with cornmeal.

5) Bake 25 to 35 minutes or until deep golden brown. Cover crust edge with 2- to 3-inch-wide strips of foil after 10 to 15 minutes of baking to prevent excessive browning. Let pie stand 5 to 10 minutes before serving.

HIGH ALTITUDE (3500-6500 FT.): In Step 3, add 1 tablespoon all-purpose flour with the other ingredients.

Nutrition Information Per Serving:		
Calories: 550	From Fat: 240	
Total Fat		26g
Saturated Fat		9g
Trans Fat		0g
Cholesterol		60mg
Sodium		1240mg
Total Carbohydrate		59g
Dietary Fiber		4g
Sugars		10g
Protein		20g

Crescent Calzones

PREP TIME: 20 MINUTES (READY IN 40 MINUTES)
SERVINGS: 4 CALZONES

 EASY

½ lb bulk Italian pork sausage or ground beef

1 garlic clove, finely chopped

½ cup chopped green bell pepper

1 can (8 oz) Pillsbury® refrigerated crescent dinner rolls

¼ cup pizza sauce

½ cup shredded mozzarella cheese (2 oz)

1 egg, beaten

1) Heat oven to 375°F. Grease or spray cookie sheet. In 10-inch skillet, cook sausage and garlic over medium heat until no longer pink; drain. Stir in bell pepper.

2) On greased cookie sheet, unroll dough and separate into 4 rectangles; press each into 7x4-inch rectangle, firmly pressing the perforations to seal. Spread 1 tablespoon sauce on half of each rectangle to within 1 inch of edge. Sprinkle 2 tablespoons cheese over sauce; top with one-fourth of the sausage mixture. Fold dough over filling; firmly press edges with fork to seal. Brush top of each with egg. With fork, prick top of each to allow steam to escape.

3) Bake 15 to 20 minutes or until deep golden brown. Immediately remove from cookie sheet. Serve warm.

HIGH ALTITUDE (3500-6500 FT.): No change.

Nutrition Information Per Serving:	
Calories: 370	From Fat: 210
Total Fat	24g
Saturated Fat	9g
Trans Fat	3g
Cholesterol	85mg
Sodium	800mg
Total Carbohydrate	25g
Dietary Fiber	1g
Sugars	6g
Protein	15g

Chicken Alfredo Gorgonzola-Walnut Pizza

KATHY SEPICH | GRESHAM, OREGON

BAKE-OFF® CONTEST 43, 2008

PREP TIME: 20 MINUTES (READY IN 40 MINUTES)
SERVINGS: 6

 EASY

2 teaspoons Crisco® light or pure olive oil

1 teaspoon cornmeal

1 can (13.8 oz) Pillsbury® refrigerated classic pizza crust

½ cup refrigerated Alfredo sauce (from 10-oz container)

1 cup shredded Italian cheese blend (4 oz)

¼ cup crumbled Gorgonzola cheese (1 oz)

1 package (6 oz) refrigerated roasted chicken breast strips, chopped

¾ cup sliced fresh mushrooms

½ cup sliced red onion

½ cup Fisher® Chef's Naturals® chopped walnuts

1 garlic clove, finely chopped

¼ cup lightly packed fresh basil leaves, thinly sliced

1) Heat oven to 375°F. Brush large cookie sheet with 1 teaspoon of the oil; sprinkle evenly with cornmeal. Unroll the pizza crust dough on cookie sheet; press the dough into 14x12-inch rectangle. Brush dough with the remaining 1 teaspoon oil. Bake 10 to 14 minutes or until light golden brown.

2) Spread the Alfredo sauce evenly over partially baked crust. Sprinkle with the cheeses, chicken, mushrooms, onion, walnuts and garlic.

3) Bake 10 to 18 minutes longer or until the crust is golden brown. Sprinkle with basil.

HIGH ALTITUDE (3500-6500 FT.): No change.

Nutrition Information Per Serving:		
Calories: 450	From Fat: 210	
Total Fat		24g
Saturated Fat		10g
Trans Fat		0g
Cholesterol		60mg
Sodium		920mg
Total Carbohydrate		36g
Dietary Fiber		1g
Sugars		6g
Protein		23g

Spicy Chicken and Orzo Skillet

PREP TIME: 45 MINUTES (READY IN 45 MINUTES)
SERVINGS: 4 (1-1/2 CUPS EACH)

1 tablespoon olive or vegetable oil

4 boneless skinless chicken breasts, cut into thin bite-size strips

1 garlic clove, finely chopped

1 cup ready-to-eat baby-cut carrots, quartered lengthwise

1 small onion, cut into thin wedges

3/4 cup uncooked rosamarina or orzo pasta (5 1/2 oz)

1 teaspoon ground cumin

1/2 teaspoon Italian seasoning

1/2 teaspoon crushed red pepper flakes

1/2 cup water

1 can (15 oz) chick peas or garbanzo beans, drained, rinsed

1 can (14 oz) chicken broth

2 cups fresh spinach leaves, cut into thin strips

1) In 12-inch skillet, heat the oil over medium-high heat until hot. Add chicken and garlic; cook and stir 3 minutes. Add the carrots and onion; cover and cook 2 to 3 minutes or until vegetables are crisp-tender, stirring once.

2) Stir in all remaining ingredients except spinach. Heat to boiling. Reduce heat; cover and simmer 12 to 15 minutes, stirring occasionally, until most of liquid is absorbed and orzo is tender.

3) Stir in the spinach; cover and cook 2 to 3 minutes longer or until the spinach is wilted.

HIGH ALTITUDE (3500-6500 FT.): No change.

Nutrition Information Per Serving:

Calories:	480	From Fat:	100
Total Fat			11g
Saturated Fat			2g
Trans Fat			0g
Cholesterol			75mg
Sodium			530mg
Total Carbohydrate			52g
Dietary Fiber			8g
Sugars			3g
Protein			42g

Italian Pot Roast

PREP TIME: 20 MINUTES (READY IN 3 HOURS 50 MINUTES)
SERVINGS: 8

 EASY

2 tablespoons olive or vegetable oil

1 bone-in beef chuck roast (3 to 3½ lb)

1 teaspoon salt

1 teaspoon pepper

8 medium potatoes, cut in half (4 cups)

4 carrots, cut into 4 pieces

3 stalks celery, cut into 4 pieces

1 medium onion, quartered

1 tablespoon chopped garlic

1 jar (26 oz) tomato basil pasta sauce

½ cup cold water

¼ cup all-purpose flour

1) Heat oven to 350°F. In 12-inch skillet, heat oil over high heat. Sprinkle beef roast with salt and pepper; place in skillet. Cook about 6 minutes or until beef is browned on both sides.

2) Place beef in large shallow roasting pan. Arrange potatoes, carrots, celery and onion around beef. Sprinkle garlic over beef and vegetables. Pour pasta sauce over top.

3) Cover pan with foil; roast 3 hours to 3 hours 30 minutes or until beef and vegetables are tender.

4) Remove beef from pan; place on serving platter. Cut beef across grain into slices; arrange vegetables over top. Cover with foil to keep warm.

5) Skim excess fat from the drippings in pan. Place 2 cups pan drippings in 1-quart saucepan (if necessary, add water to equal 2 cups). In tightly covered container, shake ½ cup cold water and flour until smooth. With the saucepan over medium-high heat, gradually stir flour mixture into drippings. Heat to boiling, stirring constantly. Boil and stir 1 minute. Serve gravy with beef and vegetables.

HIGH ALTITUDE (3500-6500 FT.): No change.

Nutrition Information Per Serving:	
Calories: 540	From Fat: 240
Total Fat	27g
Saturated Fat	9g
Trans Fat	1g
Cholesterol	100mg
Sodium	870mg
Total Carbohydrate	39g
Dietary Fiber	4g
Sugars	12g
Protein	35g

Hot & Spicy Orange Chicken Pizza

PREP TIME: 30 MINUTES (READY IN 40 MINUTES)
SERVINGS: 4

3 tablespoons garlic and herb marinade

2 tablespoons orange juice

¼ teaspoon ground ginger

¼ teaspoon red pepper sauce

1 boneless skinless chicken breast (6 oz) or 2 boneless skinless chicken breasts (4 oz each)

1 can (13.8 oz) Pillsbury® refrigerated classic pizza crust

1½ cups shredded mozzarella cheese (6 oz)

4 medium sliced green onions (¼ cup)

¼ cup sliced red onion

1 tablespoon chopped fresh cilantro

1) Heat gas or charcoal grill. In small bowl, mix the marinade, orange juice, ginger and pepper sauce. Place 1 tablespoon mixture in shallow bowl; dip chicken in shallow bowl to coat. Place chicken on grill over medium heat. Cover grill; cook 12 to 15 minutes, turning once, until the juice of chicken is clear when center of thickest part is cut (170°F).

2) Meanwhile, heat oven to 425°F. Lightly grease 12- or 14-inch pizza pan. Unroll dough in pan. Starting at center, press out dough with hands. Bake about 8 minutes or until crust begins to brown.

3) Slice chicken breast crosswise into ¼-inch-thick slices; brush marinade mixture onto slices. Spread remaining mixture over partially baked crust. Sprinkle mozzarella cheese over sauce. Sprinkle onions over cheese. Arrange chicken slices on top.

4) Bake 12 to 15 minutes or until cheese is melted. Sprinkle with cilantro. Cut into slices.

HIGH ALTITUDE (3500-6500 FT.): No change.

Nutrition Information Per Serving:

Calories:	440	From Fat:	120
Total Fat			13g
Saturated Fat			7g
Trans Fat			0g
Cholesterol			50mg
Sodium			1260mg
Total Carbohydrate			52g
Dietary Fiber			0g
Sugars			9g
Protein			28g

Ground Beef and Twice-Baked Potato Pie

PREP TIME: 15 MINUTES (READY IN 1 HOUR 5 MINUTES)
SERVINGS: 4

EASY

1 lb lean (at least 80%) ground beef

¼ cup chopped onion

¼ cup Progresso® plain bread crumbs

½ teaspoon dried sage leaves

½ teaspoon salt

1 egg

1 package (1 lb 8 oz) refrigerated garlic mashed potatoes

1 cup shredded Cheddar cheese (4 oz)

¼ cup chopped fresh tomato, if desired

2 slices precooked bacon, chopped, if desired

2 medium green onions, chopped (2 tablespoons), if desired

1) Heat oven to 350°F. In large bowl, mix beef, onion, bread crumbs, sage, salt and egg until well blended. Press in the bottom of ungreased 8-inch square (2-quart) glass baking dish. Spread mashed potatoes evenly over the top. Sprinkle evenly with cheese.

2) Bake uncovered about 50 minutes or until meat thermometer inserted in center of beef mixture reads 160°F. Sprinkle with tomato, bacon and onions.

HIGH ALTITUDE (3500-6500 FT.): No change.

Nutrition Information Per Serving:	
Calories: 570	From Fat: 320
Total Fat	36g
Saturated Fat	17g
Trans Fat	2.5g
Cholesterol	175mg
Sodium	1220mg
Total Carbohydrate	28g
Dietary Fiber	1g
Sugars	2g
Protein	33g

Baja Pie

PREP TIME: 20 MINUTES (READY IN 1 HOUR 5 MINUTES)
SERVINGS: 6

 EASY

5 corn tortillas (6 inch)

1 tablespoon butter or margarine, melted

2 cups shredded deli rotisserie chicken (from 2- to 2½-lb chicken)

1 can (15 oz) Progresso® black beans, drained, rinsed

1 cup Old El Paso® Thick 'n Chunky salsa

2 tablespoons Old El Paso® taco seasoning mix (from 1.25-oz package)

1½ cups shredded Cheddar cheese (6 oz)

1 medium tomato, cut into 6 slices

1 medium avocado, pitted, peeled and chopped

1) Heat oven to 325°F. In 9-inch glass pie plate, arrange tortillas, overlapping and extending to edge or slightly over edge of plate. Brush the edges of tortillas with melted butter.

2) In large bowl, mix chicken, black beans, salsa, taco seasoning mix and ½ cup of the cheese. Spoon chicken mixture onto the tortillas.

3) Bake 25 to 30 minutes or until hot. Sprinkle with remaining 1 cup cheese. Bake 2 to 4 minutes longer or until cheese begins to melt. Top with tomato and avocado.

HIGH ALTITUDE (3500-6500 FT.): Increase first bake time to 28 to 33 minutes.

Nutrition Information Per Serving:	
Calories: 430	From Fat: 180
Total Fat	20g
Saturated Fat	9g
Trans Fat	0g
Cholesterol	75mg
Sodium	1010mg
Total Carbohydrate	35g
Dietary Fiber	10g
Sugars	3g
Protein	27g

tip

When assembling this oven entree, make sure that the corn tortillas you use are fresh. Old tortillas may dry out during baking.

Mediterranean Pizza with Cheese-Stuffed Crust

BARBARA WILLIAMS | LAWRENCEVILLE, GEORGIA

BAKE-OFF® CONTEST 43, 2008

PREP TIME: 25 MINUTES (READY IN 45 MINUTES)
SERVINGS: 8

1½ tablespoons cornmeal

1 can (13.8 oz) Pillsbury® refrigerated classic pizza crust

7 pieces (1 oz each) mozzarella string cheese (from 12-oz package), unwrapped

¼ cup tomato sauce with basil, garlic and oregano or regular tomato sauce (from 8-oz can)

¼ cup chopped fresh basil leaves

½ lb bulk spicy pork sausage

⅓ cup chopped sun-dried tomatoes in oil, drained

1 box (9 oz) Green Giant® frozen spinach, thawed, squeezed to drain

¼ cup sliced ripe olives

¼ cup sliced pimiento-stuffed olives

½ cup crumbled feta cheese (2 oz)

2 cups shredded mozzarella cheese (8 oz)

2 tablespoons Crisco® 100% extra virgin or pure olive oil

½ teaspoon Italian seasoning

½ to 1 teaspoon garlic salt

1) Heat oven to 425°F. Spray 12-inch pizza pan with Crisco® Original No-Stick cooking spray. Sprinkle cornmeal evenly over pan. Unroll pizza crust dough on the pan; press dough to at least 1 inch beyond edge of pan. Place string cheese on dough along inside edge of pizza crust. Fold the edge of dough over the cheese, pressing dough down firmly and covering cheese. Pinch dough to seal.

2) Spread the tomato sauce evenly over the dough. Sprinkle with basil.

3) Heat 10-inch nonstick skillet over medium-high heat. Add sausage; cook 5 to 7 minutes, stirring frequently, until no longer pink; drain. Reduce heat to medium. Stir tomatoes and spinach into sausage until well mixed. Cook 3 to 4 minutes, stirring frequently, until spinach is heated.

4) Spoon the sausage mixture evenly over basil on crust. Top with ripe and pimiento-stuffed olives. Sprinkle with feta and mozzarella cheeses.

5) Brush oil on the edge of crust; sprinkle Italian seasoning and garlic salt on edge of crust.

6) Bake 15 to 18 minutes or until cheese is melted and crust is deep golden brown. Let stand 2 minutes before cutting.

HIGH ALTITUDE (3500-6500 FT.): No change.

Nutrition Information Per Serving:		
Calories: 420	From Fat:	210
Total Fat		23g
Saturated Fat		10g
Trans Fat		0g
Cholesterol		45mg
Sodium		1060mg
Total Carbohydrate		30g
Dietary Fiber		1g
Sugars		5g
Protein		23g

Southwestern Chili Shrimp

PREP TIME:	20 MINUTES (READY IN 20 MINUTES)
SERVINGS:	4

 EASY

SHRIMP

- **2** tablespoons butter or margarine, melted
- **1½** teaspoons chili powder
- **½** teaspoon garlic salt
- **½** teaspoon ground cumin
- **2** teaspoons lime juice
- **1½** lb uncooked deveined peeled large shrimp, tail shells removed if desired

SAUCE

- **¼** cup mayonnaise or salad dressing
- **¼** cup guacamole
- **2** tablespoons chopped fresh cilantro

1) Heat gas or charcoal grill.

2) In large bowl, mix melted butter, chili powder, garlic salt, cumin and lime juice. Add shrimp; toss to coat. Thread shrimp on six 15-inch metal skewers, leaving space between each. Place on grill over medium heat. Cover grill; cook 5 to 10 minutes, turning 2 to 3 times, until shrimp are pink.

3) In small bowl, mix sauce ingredients. Serve sauce with shrimp.

Closed Contact Grill Directions: Heat closed contact grill for 5 minutes. Meanwhile, in large bowl, mix melted butter, chili powder, garlic salt, cumin and lime juice. Add shrimp; toss to coat. With slotted spoon, place shrimp on bottom grill surface. Close grill; cook 4 to 6 minutes or until shrimp are pink. In small bowl, mix sauce ingredients. Serve sauce with shrimp.

HIGH ALTITUDE (3500-6500 FT.): No change.

Nutrition Information Per Serving:			
Calories:	300	From Fat:	180
Total Fat			20g
Saturated Fat			6g
Trans Fat			0g
Cholesterol			265mg
Sodium			600mg
Total Carbohydrate			3g
Dietary Fiber			1g
Sugars			1g
Protein			27g

Chicken-Stuffed Shells with Two Sauces

PREP TIME: 20 MINUTES (READY IN 1 HOUR 5 MINUTES)
SERVINGS: 6

 EASY

18 uncooked jumbo pasta shells

¾ cup lightly packed chopped fresh basil leaves

3 cups diced cooked chicken breast (about 1 lb)

1 cup small-curd cottage cheese

1 egg

2 cups tomato pasta sauce

1 container (10 oz) refrigerated Alfredo sauce

½ cup grated Parmesan cheese

1) Heat oven to 350°F. Spray 13x9-inch (3-quart) glass baking dish with cooking spray. Cook and drain pasta shells as directed on package.

2) In medium bowl, mix ½ cup of the basil leaves, the chicken, cottage cheese and egg. Spoon about 1 heaping tablespoon mixture into each cooked pasta shell.

3) Pour the pasta sauce into baking dish; spread to evenly coat bottom of dish. Place filled shells over sauce, filled sides up. Drizzle Alfredo sauce over shells. Sprinkle with Parmesan cheese. Cover tightly with foil.

4) Bake 35 to 45 minutes or until sauce is bubbly and shells are hot. Sprinkle with remaining basil.

HIGH ALTITUDE (3500-6500 FT.): Heat oven to 375°F. Bake about 40 minutes.

Nutrition Information Per Serving:		
Calories: 560	From Fat:	230
Total Fat		25g
Saturated Fat		13g
Trans Fat		0.5g
Cholesterol		150mg
Sodium		1030mg
Total Carbohydrate		42g
Dietary Fiber		3g
Sugars		10g
Protein		39g

tip

Having a dinner party? Save time by making the filling and sauce the night before. Stuff the cooked shells before your guests arrive, and toss a salad while this dish bakes.

Rotini with Spicy Meat Sauce

PREP TIME: 30 MINUTES (READY IN 30 MINUTES)
SERVINGS: 6 (1-1/2 CUPS EACH)

 EASY

2²/₃ cups uncooked rotini pasta (8 oz)

1 lb lean (at least 80%) ground beef

3 medium stalks celery, chopped (1½ cups)

2 medium onions, chopped (1 cup)

1 small zucchini, sliced, slices quartered (1 cup)

2 cans (14.5 oz each) diced tomatoes with green chiles, undrained

1 can (8 oz) tomato sauce

1 jar (4.5 oz) Green Giant® sliced mushrooms, undrained

1 teaspoon dried basil leaves

½ teaspoon salt

¼ teaspoon pepper

1 cup shredded mozzarella cheese (4 oz)

1) Cook and drain the pasta as directed on the package.

2) Meanwhile, in 12-inch nonstick skillet or 4-quart Dutch oven, cook ground beef, celery and onions over medium-high heat 5 to 7 minutes, stirring occasionally, until beef is thoroughly cooked; drain. Return to skillet.

3) Stir in drained pasta and remaining ingredients except the cheese. Heat to boiling. Reduce the heat to low; simmer uncovered 10 minutes, stirring occasionally. Sprinkle with cheese.

HIGH ALTITUDE (3500-6500 FT.): No change.

Nutrition Information Per Serving:

Calories:	430	From Fat:	120
Total Fat			13g
Saturated Fat			6g
Trans Fat			0.5g
Cholesterol			55mg
Sodium			1190mg
Total Carbohydrate			49g
Dietary Fiber			6g
Sugars			10g
Protein			28g

 tip

Pasta of a similar size and shape may be used in place of the rotini in this recipe. For example, penne pasta would be a nice substitute.

Cilantro-Lime Pork Roll-Ups with Caramelized Onions

KIMBERLY FLUCK | CANON CITY, COLORADO

BAKE-OFF® CONTEST 43, 2008

Bake-Off

PREP TIME: 50 MINUTES (READY IN 1 HOUR 30 MINUTES)
SERVINGS: 8

2 teaspoons grated lime peel

1/4 cup fresh lime juice

2 garlic cloves, finely chopped

1 tablespoon finely chopped fresh cilantro

1/2 teaspoon crushed red pepper flakes

5 tablespoons Crisco® 100% extra virgin or pure olive oil

1 lb boneless pork loin chops (1/2 inch thick) or pork tenderloin, cut into 1/2-inch cubes

2 small onions, thinly sliced

1 can (16 oz) Old El Paso® fat-free refried beans

1 package (11.5 oz) Old El Paso® flour tortillas for burritos (8 tortillas)

2 cups finely shredded pepper Jack or Monterey Jack cheese (8 oz)

1 to 1 1/2 cups Old El Paso® Thick 'n Chunky salsa

1 container (8 oz) sour cream

1) In large resealable food-storage plastic bag, mix lime peel, lime juice, garlic, cilantro, pepper flakes and 1 tablespoon of the oil. Add pork; seal bag and turn to coat with the lime mixture. Refrigerate 30 minutes to 2 hours to marinate.

2) In 12-inch nonstick skillet, heat 1 tablespoon of the oil over medium heat. Add onions; cook 7 to 10 minutes, stirring frequently, until onions turn golden brown. Remove onions from the skillet; keep warm.

3) Heat oven to 375°F. Remove the pork from marinade; drain pork on paper towels to remove excess moisture. Discard marinade.

4) In same skillet, heat 1 tablespoon of the oil over medium-high heat. Add pork; cook 5 to 7 minutes, stirring occasionally, until no longer pink in center. Remove skillet from heat; set aside.

5) Brush 1 tablespoon oil on the bottom and sides of 13x9-inch (3-quart) glass baking dish or 2 (8-inch square) glass baking dishes. In medium microwavable bowl, place refried beans. Cover with microwavable paper towel; microwave on High about 1 minute or until warm.

6) To assemble, spoon 2 tablespoons beans down center of each tortilla. Top with pork, onions and cheese. Roll up tortillas; place seam sides down in baking dish. Lightly brush remaining 1 tablespoon oil over tortillas.

7) Bake uncovered 18 to 24 minutes or until the edges of tortillas are golden brown. Serve with salsa and sour cream.

HIGH ALTITUDE (3500-6500 FT.): No change.

Nutrition Information Per Serving:		
Calories: 510	From Fat:	260
Total Fat		29g
Saturated Fat		12g
Trans Fat		1.5g
Cholesterol		80mg
Sodium		990mg
Total Carbohydrate		37g
Dietary Fiber		3g
Sugars		4g
Protein		25g

Baked Macaroni and Cheese

PREP TIME: 15 MINUTES (READY IN 50 MINUTES)
SERVINGS: 4

 EASY

7 oz uncooked penne pasta (rounded 2 cups)

¼ cup butter or margarine

¼ cup all-purpose flour

½ teaspoon seasoned salt

½ teaspoon ground mustard

¼ teaspoon pepper

¼ teaspoon Worcestershire sauce

2 cups milk

2 cups shredded sharp Cheddar cheese (8 oz)

1) Heat oven to 350°F. Cook and drain the pasta as directed on package.

2) While the pasta is cooking, in 3-quart saucepan, melt butter over low heat. Stir in flour, seasoned salt, mustard, pepper and Worcestershire sauce. Cook over low heat, stirring constantly, until mixture is smooth and bubbly; remove from the heat. Stir in the milk. Heat to boiling, stirring constantly. Boil and stir 1 minute; remove from heat. Using wire whisk, stir in cheese until melted.

3) Gently stir the pasta into the cheese sauce. Spoon into 4 ungreased 8-oz ramekins/gratin dishes or 10-oz custard cups. Place the filled cups in shallow baking pan (or cookie sheet with sides). Bake uncovered 20 to 25 minutes or until bubbly.

HIGH ALTITUDE (3500-6500 FT.): No change.

Nutrition Information Per Serving:

Calories: 630	From Fat: 310
Total Fat	34g
Saturated Fat	21g
Trans Fat	1g
Cholesterol	100mg
Sodium	8500mg
Total Carbohydrate	55g
Dietary Fiber	2g
Sugars	8g
Protein	27g

Three-Cheese Mac

PREP TIME: 15 MINUTES (READY IN 50 MINUTES)
SERVINGS: 4

 EASY

7 oz uncooked penne pasta (rounded 2 cups)

¼ cup butter or margarine

¼ cup all-purpose flour

½ teaspoon seasoned salt

½ teaspoon ground mustard

¼ teaspoon pepper

¼ teaspoon Worcestershire sauce

2 cups milk

1 cup shredded sharp Cheddar cheese (4 oz)

1 package (3 oz) cream cheese, cubed

1 cup shredded Gruyère cheese (4 oz)

1 tablespoon shredded Parmesan cheese

¼ teaspoon Italian parsley, chopped

1) Heat oven to 350°F. Cook and drain pasta as directed on package.

2) While pasta is cooking, in 3-quart saucepan, melt butter over low heat. Stir in flour, seasoned salt, mustard, pepper and Worcestershire sauce. Cook over low heat, stirring constantly, until mixture is smooth and bubbly; remove from heat. Stir in milk. Heat to boiling, stirring constantly. Boil and stir 1 minute; remove from heat. Using wire whisk, stir in Cheddar, cream cheese and Gruyère until melted.

3) Gently stir the pasta into the cheese sauce. Spoon into 4 ungreased 8-oz ramekins/gratin dishes or 10-oz custard cups. Sprinkle with the Parmesan cheese and parsley. Place filled cups in shallow baking pan (or cookie sheet with sides). Bake uncovered 20 to 25 minutes or until bubbly.

HIGH ALTITUDE (3500-6500 FT.): No change.

Mex Mac and Cheese

PREP TIME: 15 MINUTES (READY IN 50 MINUTES)
SERVINGS: 4

EASY

7 oz uncooked penne pasta (rounded 2 cups)

¼ cup butter or margarine

¼ cup all-purpose flour

½ teaspoon seasoned salt

½ teaspoon ground mustard

¼ teaspoon pepper

¼ teaspoon Worcestershire sauce

2 cups milk

8 oz cubed process cheese spread with jalapeño peppers

¼ cup salsa

½ cup corn chips, crushed

1) Heat oven to 350°F. Cook and drain pasta as directed on package.

2) While pasta is cooking, in 3-quart saucepan, melt butter over low heat. Stir in flour, seasoned salt, mustard, pepper and Worcestershire sauce. Cook over low heat, stirring constantly, until mixture is smooth and bubbly; remove from heat. Stir in milk. Heat to boiling, stirring constantly. Boil and stir 1 minute; remove from heat. Using wire whisk, stir in cheese spread until melted. Stir in salsa.

3) Gently stir the pasta into the cheese sauce. Spoon into 4 ungreased 8-oz ramekins/gratin dishes or 10-oz custard cups. Top with crushed corn chips. Place filled cups in shallow baking pan (or cookie sheet with sides). Bake uncovered 20 to 25 minutes or until bubbly.

HIGH ALTITUDE (3500-6500 FT.): No change.

Bacon, Caesar and Mozzarella Panini

CAROLE STRACHAN | HOUSTON, TEXAS

Bake-Off®

BAKE-OFF® CONTEST 43, 2008

PREP TIME: 40 MINUTES (READY IN 50 MINUTES)
SERVINGS: 4 SANDWICHES

1 can (13.8 oz) Pillsbury® refrigerated classic pizza crust

4 teaspoons basil pesto

¼ cup Caesar dressing (creamy or vinaigrette style)

8 oz water-packed fresh mozzarella cheese, drained and cut into 8 slices, or 8 slices (1 oz each) regular mozzarella cheese

¼ teaspoon freshly ground pepper

12 slices cooked bacon

2 plum (Roma) tomatoes, each cut into 4 slices

8 large fresh basil leaves

¼ cup Land O Lakes® butter

1) Heat oven to 375°F. Spray large cookie sheet with Crisco® Original No-Stick cooking spray. Unroll the pizza crust dough on the cookie sheet; press the dough into 16x11-inch rectangle, pulling dough gently if necessary. Bake 9 to 16 minutes or until light brown. Cool about 15 minutes or until cool enough to handle.

2) Cut cooled pizza crust in half lengthwise and crosswise to make 4 rectangles. Remove rectangles from cookie sheet; cut each rectangle in half crosswise for a total of 8 squares.

3) On each of 4 crust slices, spread 1 teaspoon pesto; set aside. On each of remaining 4 slices, spread 1 tablespoon Caesar dressing. Place 2 cheese slices on each crust slice with Caesar dressing. Top cheese with pepper, 3 bacon slices, 2 tomato slices and 2 basil leaves. Top with remaining crust slices, pesto sides down.

4) Heat 12-inch skillet or cast-iron skillet over medium heat until hot. Melt 2 tablespoons of the butter in skillet. Place 2 sandwiches in skillet. Place smaller skillet or saucepan on sandwiches to flatten slightly; keep skillet on sandwiches while cooking. Cook 1 to 2 minutes on each side or until bread is golden brown and crisp and fillings are heated. Remove from skillet; cover with foil to keep warm. Repeat with remaining 2 tablespoons butter and sandwiches.

HIGH ALTITUDE (3500-6500 FT.): No change.

Nutrition Information Per Serving:		
Calories: 760	From Fat: 420	
Total Fat		47g
Saturated Fat		20g
Trans Fat		1g
Cholesterol		90mg
Sodium		1840mg
Total Carbohydrate		51g
Dietary Fiber		0g
Sugars		8g
Protein		32g

Double-Meat Personal Pizzas

PREP TIME: 25 MINUTES (READY IN 25 MINUTES)
SERVINGS: 4 PIZZAS

 EASY

- ½ lb lean (at least 80%) ground beef
- 1 can (13.8 oz) Pillsbury® refrigerated classic pizza crust
- ½ cup pizza sauce
- ¼ teaspoon dried oregano leaves, if desired
- ½ package (3½-oz size) sliced pepperoni
- 2 tablespoons grated Parmesan cheese
- 1½ cups shredded Italian cheese blend or mozzarella cheese (6 oz)

1) Heat oven to 400°F. In 10-inch skillet, cook the beef over medium-high heat 5 to 7 minutes, stirring occasionally, until thoroughly cooked; drain. Lightly spray large cookie sheet with cooking spray. Unroll the dough on work surface. Cut dough into 4 equal pieces; place on cookie sheet. Press out each piece of dough to form 6x5-inch rectangle. With fingers, create slight rim on edge of each dough rectangle. Bake 8 minutes.

2) Spread about 2 tablespoons pizza sauce just to rim of each crust; sprinkle with oregano. Top with pepperoni, beef and cheeses. Bake 8 to 10 minutes until the cheese in center is melted.

HIGH ALTITUDE (3500-6500 FT.): No change.

Nutrition Information Per Serving:

Calories:	570	From Fat:	240
Total Fat			27g
Saturated Fat			13g
Trans Fat			1g
Cholesterol			80mg
Sodium			1510mg
Total Carbohydrate			51g
Dietary Fiber			0g
Sugars			9g
Protein			32g

Quick Fish Tacos

PREP TIME: 30 MINUTES (READY IN 30 MINUTES)
SERVINGS: 5 (2 TACOS EACH)

 EASY   LOW FAT

1 lb white fish fillets, such as tilapia or catfish

2 tablespoons Old El Paso® 40% less-sodium taco seasoning mix (from 1.25-oz package)

3 tablespoons reduced-fat ranch dressing

4 cups coleslaw mix (shredded cabbage and carrots)

1 small jalapeño chile, seeded, finely chopped

10 corn tortillas (6 inch)

1¼ cups sliced radishes (about 10)

Red pepper sauce to taste, if desired

Tomatillo salsa, if desired

1) Heat gas or charcoal grill. Cut 1 (18x12-inch) sheet of heavy-duty foil; spray with cooking spray. Sprinkle both sides of fish fillets with 2 teaspoons of the seasoning mix. Place fish on center of foil sheet. Bring up 2 sides of foil so edges meet. Seal edges, making tight ½-inch fold; fold again, allowing space for heat circulation and expansion. Fold other sides to seal.

2) Place the packet on grill over high heat. Cover grill; cook about 10 minutes, rotating packet ½ turn after 5 minutes, until fish flakes easily with fork. Let cool slightly; cut into bite-size chunks.

3) Meanwhile, in large bowl, mix ranch dressing and remaining 4 teaspoons seasoning mix. Add the coleslaw mix and chile; toss to coat. Let stand 10 minutes. Meanwhile, wrap stack of tortillas in sheet of foil; place on coolest part of grill 5 to 10 minutes, turning occasionally, until steaming.

4) To serve, spoon about ¼ cup fish chunks and ¼ cup coleslaw mixture onto each tortilla; top with 2 tablespoons radishes. Fold tortillas around filling. Serve with pepper sauce and tomatillo salsa.

HIGH ALTITUDE (3500-6500 FT.): Grill fish over medium heat, rotating and flipping packet over after 5 minutes of cooking.

Nutrition Information Per Serving:	
Calories: 240	From Fat: 40
Total Fat	4g
Saturated Fat	0.5g
Trans Fat	0g
Cholesterol	50mg
Sodium	410mg
Total Carbohydrate	30g
Dietary Fiber	4g
Sugars	4g
Protein	21g

Mexican Stuffed-Pepper Biscuit Tostadas

CYNTHIA BOWSER | JONESBOROUGH, TENNESSEE

BAKE-OFF® CONTEST 43, 2008

PREP TIME: 30 MINUTES (READY IN 55 MINUTES)
SERVINGS: 8

2 large bell peppers (any color)

4 cups water

1 lb lean (at least 80%) ground beef

1 package (1.25 oz) Old El Paso® taco seasoning mix

1 cup Old El Paso® Thick 'n Chunky salsa

1 can (16.3 oz) Pillsbury® Grands!® homestyle refrigerated buttermilk biscuits (8 biscuits)

1 Eggland's Best egg, slightly beaten

1 cup shredded Mexican cheese blend or Monterey Jack cheese (4 oz)

½ cup sour cream, if desired

1) Heat oven to 350°F. Lightly spray large cookie sheet with Crisco® Original No-Stick cooking spray.

2) Cut each bell pepper lengthwise into quarters, making 8 pieces; remove the stems, seeds and membranes. In 2-quart saucepan, heat 4 cups water to boiling. Add bell pepper pieces; cook 5 minutes. Drain well on paper towels; set aside.

3) Meanwhile, in 10-inch skillet, cook beef over medium heat 8 to 10 minutes, stirring occasionally, until thoroughly cooked; drain. Stir in taco seasoning mix and salsa until well blended; set aside.

4) Separate dough into 8 biscuits. Place biscuits 2 inches apart on cookie sheet; brush with egg.

5) Press 1 pepper piece, skin side down, on each biscuit. Spoon heaping ¼ cup beef mixture into each pepper, spreading to cover pepper evenly. Sprinkle each with 2 tablespoons cheese.

6) Bake 18 to 22 minutes or until cheese is melted and edges of biscuits are golden brown. Cool 5 minutes. Top each with 1 tablespoon sour cream.

HIGH ALTITUDE (3500-6500 FT.): In Step 5, do not add cheese. In Step 6, bake 20 minutes. Add cheese; bake 3 to 5 minutes longer or until cheese is melted.

Nutrition Information Per Serving:

Calories:	410	From Fat:	180
Total Fat			20g
Saturated Fat			9g
Trans Fat			1.5g
Cholesterol			55mg
Sodium			740mg
Total Carbohydrate			41g
Dietary Fiber			3g
Sugars			5g
Protein			17g

Meaty Mostaccioli

PREP TIME: 20 MINUTES (READY IN 45 MINUTES)
SERVINGS: 4 (1-1/2 CUPS EACH)

 EASY

1 tablespoon olive oil

2 slices uncooked bacon, cut into 1/2-inch pieces

1 medium onion, chopped (1/2 cup)

1/2 lb bulk Italian sausage

1 can (28 oz) whole tomatoes, undrained

1 jar (4.5 oz) Green Giant® sliced mushrooms, undrained

3/4 cup chicken broth

1 teaspoon dried basil leaves

1/4 teaspoon salt

1/4 teaspoon pepper

2 cups uncooked mostaccioli pasta (4 oz)

1) In 12-inch skillet, heat the oil over medium-high heat. Add the bacon, onion and Italian sausage. Cook 4 to 7 minutes, stirring occasionally, until sausage is no longer pink.

2) Stir in tomatoes, mushrooms, broth, basil, salt, pepper and uncooked pasta. Reduce heat to medium-low. Cover; cook 20 to 25 minutes, stirring occasionally, until pasta is tender.

HIGH ALTITUDE (3500-6500 FT.): Increase chicken broth to 1 cup.

Nutrition Information Per Serving:	
Calories: 400	From Fat: 180
Total Fat	20g
Saturated Fat	6g
Trans Fat	0g
Cholesterol	30mg
Sodium	1330mg
Total Carbohydrate	38g
Dietary Fiber	4g
Sugars	8g
Protein	17g

tip

If you don't have a 28-oz can of whole tomatoes, feel free to prepare this dish with 2 cans (14.5 oz each) of diced tomatoes instead.

Spicy Mole Pork Burritos

MIKE BRIGGS | ARLINGTON, VIRGINIA

BAKE-OFF® CONTEST 43, 2008

Pillsbury Bake-Off®

PREP TIME: 35 MINUTES (READY IN 1 HOUR 5 MINUTES)
SERVINGS: 14

BURRITOS

½ cup uncooked regular long-grain white rice

1 cup water

1 small onion, finely chopped (¼ cup)

2 garlic cloves, finely chopped

2 teaspoons chili powder

1 teaspoon ground cumin

¼ teaspoon ground cinnamon

½ teaspoon salt

1 chipotle chile in adobo sauce, finely chopped

2 tablespoons Smucker's® apricot preserves

2 tablespoons Old El Paso® chopped green chiles (from 4.5-oz can)

¼ cup raisins

2 teaspoons unsweetened regular or dark baking cocoa

2 tablespoons Fisher® Chef's Naturals® finely ground almonds

1 lb lean ground pork

½ cup reduced-sodium chicken broth

1 can (10 oz) Old El Paso® mild enchilada sauce

1 can (15 oz) pinto beans, drained, rinsed

14 Old El Paso® flour tortillas for burritos (from two 11.5-oz packages)

2 cups shredded sharp Cheddar cheese (8 oz)

GARNISHES

1½ cups sour cream

Cilantro sprigs

Yellow corn tortilla chips, if desired

1) Cook rice in water as directed on the package. Meanwhile, in small bowl, mix the onion, garlic, chili powder, cumin, cinnamon and salt; set aside. In another small bowl, mix chipotle chile, preserves, green chiles, raisins, cocoa and almonds; set aside.

2) In 12-inch skillet, cook the ground pork over medium-high heat 8 to 10 minutes, stirring occasionally, until no longer pink; drain.

3) Stir onion mixture into pork; cook over medium heat 2 minutes, stirring occasionally. Stir in the preserves mixture, broth and enchilada sauce; heat to boiling. Reduce heat to low. Simmer uncovered 30 minutes, stirring occasionally. Stir in pinto beans and rice; cook 2 to 3 minutes or until hot and bubbly.

4) Meanwhile, heat tortillas as directed on the package. To assemble, spoon slightly less than ½ cup pork filling down center of each tortilla. Sprinkle about 1 tablespoon cheese over filling on each. Fold in ends of each tortilla; fold sides toward center, overlapping edges.

5) To serve, place burritos, folded sides down, on plates. Garnish each serving with about 1 tablespoon sour cream and cilantro sprigs. Serve with chips.

HIGH ALTITUDE (3500-6500 FT.): No change.

Nutrition Information Per Serving:

Calories: 410	From Fat:	180
Total Fat		20g
Saturated Fat		9g
Trans Fat		1.5g
Cholesterol		55mg
Sodium		740mg
Total Carbohydrate		41g
Dietary Fiber		3g
Sugars		5g
Protein		17g

German-Style Sausage Pizza

EVA HUKALO | TOLEDO, OHIO

Bake-Off® BAKE-OFF® CONTEST 43, 2008

PREP TIME: 20 MINUTES (READY IN 45 MINUTES)
SERVINGS: 6

e EASY

---

1 can (13.8 oz) Pillsbury® refrigerated classic pizza crust

1/3 cup Smucker's® apricot preserves

8 oz uncooked bratwurst links (original flavor), casings removed

1 large onion, chopped (1 cup)

1 cup well-drained sauerkraut (from 14-oz can)

1 1/2 cups shredded Monterey Jack cheese (6 oz)

1) Heat oven to 400°F. Spray 12-inch pizza pan with Crisco® Original No-Stick cooking spray. Unroll pizza crust dough on pan; press dough to edge of pan. Bake 8 to 12 minutes or until light golden brown. Brush preserves over dough; set aside.

2) Spray 10-inch skillet with Crisco® Original No-Stick cooking spray. Add sausage, onion and sauerkraut; cook over medium-high heat 5 to 7 minutes, stirring occasionally and breaking up sausage, until sausage is no longer pink. Remove sausage mixture with slotted spoon; spoon evenly over the preserves on crust. Sprinkle cheese over top.

3) Bake 13 to 19 minutes or until cheese is melted and crust is golden brown.

HIGH ALTITUDE (3500-6500 FT.): In Step 3, bake 13 to 17 minutes.

Nutrition Information Per Serving:	
Calories: 420	From Fat: 170
Total Fat	19g
Saturated Fat	9g
Trans Fat	0g
Cholesterol	40mg
Sodium	1150mg
Total Carbohydrate	49g
Dietary Fiber	1g
Sugars	15g
Protein	16g

tip

Kitchen shears or scissors work well for cutting this warm and cheesy pizza into serving portions.

Chicken Phyllo Bundles

PREP TIME: 30 MINUTES (READY IN 55 MINUTES)
SERVINGS: 8

½ cup julienne (matchstick-cut) carrots

2 cups cut-up cooked chicken

½ cup shredded Swiss cheese (2 oz)

4 medium green onions, thinly sliced (¼ cup)

1 box (9 oz) Green Giant® frozen asparagus cuts, thawed, drained

1 package (6.5 oz) garlic-and-herbs spreadable cheese, softened

1 box (16 oz; 40 sheets) frozen phyllo (filo) pastry sheets (14x9 inch), thawed

Butter-flavored cooking spray

Nutrition Information Per Serving:		
Calories: 350	From Fat: 120	
Total Fat		14g
Saturated Fat		7g
Trans Fat		0g
Cholesterol		60mg
Sodium		310mg
Total Carbohydrate		38g
Dietary Fiber		2g
Sugars		2g
Protein		19g

1) Heat oven to 375°F. In small microwavable bowl, place carrots. Cover; microwave on High about 1 minute or until tender. Meanwhile, in medium bowl, gently mix chicken, Swiss cheese, onions, asparagus and spreadable cheese. Stir in carrots.

2) To make 1 bundle, layer 5 phyllo pastry sheets, generously spraying each layer with cooking spray (the sheets can be stacked randomly). Keep the remaining pastry sheets covered with damp cloth until needed to prevent dough from drying out. Place about ½ cup chicken mixture in center of stack of pastry. With both hands, lift pastry stack towards center and twist in center to make bundle (pastry may tear a little). Spray outside of each bundle generously with cooking spray; place on ungreased large cookie sheet. Repeat to make 7 more bundles.

3) Bake 20 to 25 minutes or until pastry is browned and crisp.

HIGH ALTITUDE (3500-6500 FT.): Bake 22 to 27 minutes.

Turkey, Bacon and Brie Panini with Apricot Aioli

KIM FRANTZ | DENVER, COLORADO

BAKE-OFF® CONTEST 43, 2008

PREP TIME: 30 MINUTES (READY IN 30 MINUTES)
SERVINGS: 4 SANDWICHES

 EASY

1 can (13.8 oz) Pillsbury® refrigerated classic pizza crust

8 slices uncooked bacon

¼ cup mayonnaise or salad dressing

¼ cup Smucker's® apricot preserves

6 oz thinly sliced roast turkey breast (from deli)

4 to 5 oz Brie cheese, cut into 4 slices

Parsley sprigs, if desired

1) Heat oven to 375°F. Spray 15x10x1-inch pan with Crisco® Original No-Stick cooking spray. Unroll the pizza crust dough in pan; press dough to edges of pan. Bake 7 to 12 minutes or until light golden brown. Cool 5 minutes.

2) Meanwhile, in 10-inch skillet, cook bacon over medium heat, turning once, until crisp. Remove bacon from skillet; drain on paper towels.

3) In small bowl, make apricot aioli by stirring the mayonnaise and preserves until well mixed. Set aside.

4) Cut pizza crust in half crosswise to make 2 rectangles. Remove rectangles from pan; spread half of the apricot aioli evenly over each rectangle. Top 1 rectangle evenly with turkey, bacon and cheese. Add other rectangle, aioli side down. Cut large sandwich in half crosswise; cut each in half diagonally to make 4 sandwiches.

5) Heat 12-inch skillet over medium heat until hot. Place 2 sandwiches in skillet. Place smaller skillet or saucepan on sandwiches to flatten slightly; keep skillet on sandwiches while cooking. Cook 1 to 4 minutes on each side or until cheese is melted and bread is golden brown. Remove from skillet; cover with foil to keep warm. Repeat with remaining 2 sandwiches. Garnish with parsley sprigs.

HIGH ALTITUDE (3500-6500 FT.): No change.

Nutrition Information Per Serving:	
Calories: 630	From Fat: 260
Total Fat	29g
Saturated Fat	10g
Trans Fat	0g
Cholesterol	90mg
Sodium	1360mg
Total Carbohydrate	61g
Dietary Fiber	0g
Sugars	16g
Protein	32g

Biscuit Tostada Grande

PREP TIME: 30 MINUTES (READY IN 50 MINUTES)
SERVINGS: 6

1 lb lean (at least 80%) ground beef

2 tablespoons Old El Paso® taco or chili seasoning mix (from 1 1/4- to 1 3/8-oz package)

1 can (8 oz) tomato sauce

1 can (4.5 oz) Old El Paso® chopped green chiles, drained

3 to 4 drops red pepper sauce

1 can (12 oz) Pillsbury® Golden Layers® refrigerated buttermilk biscuits

1 cup Old El Paso® refried beans (from 16-oz can)

1 cup shredded mozzarella cheese (4 oz)

1/4 head iceberg lettuce, shredded (about 3 cups)

1 large tomato, chopped (about 1 cup)

1/4 cup sliced or chopped onion

1) In 10-inch skillet, cook the beef over medium-high heat 5 to 7 minutes, stirring frequently, until thoroughly cooked; drain. Add the seasoning mix, tomato sauce, green chiles and red pepper sauce; mix well. Cook until hot and bubbly, stirring occasionally. Reduce the heat; simmer about 5 minutes or until thickened.

2) Heat oven to 400°F. Lightly grease 12-inch pizza pan. Separate dough into 10 biscuits. Place in pan; press over bottom and up side to form the crust. Spread refried beans evenly over dough; top with meat mixture.

3) Bake 16 to 20 minutes or until crust is golden brown. Immediately sprinkle with mozzarella cheese. Garnish with lettuce, tomato and onion.

HIGH ALTITUDE (3500-6500 FT.): No change.

Nutrition Information Per Serving:

Calories:	440	From Fat:	190
Total Fat		21g	
Saturated Fat		8g	
Trans Fat		3g	
Cholesterol		60mg	
Sodium		1660mg	
Total Carbohydrate		39g	
Dietary Fiber		4g	
Sugars		7g	
Protein		25g	

Thai-Style Mexican Chicken Wraps

SARAH LAFON | FRANKLIN, TENNESSEE

BAKE-OFF® CONTEST 43, 2008

PREP TIME: 35 MINUTES (READY IN 35 MINUTES)
SERVINGS: 8

1³⁄₄ lb boneless skinless chicken breasts

1 tablespoon peanut oil

1 package (1.25 oz) Old El Paso® 40% less-sodium taco seasoning mix

¹⁄₂ cup bottled peanut sauce

1 teaspoon red curry paste

2 tablespoons fresh lime juice

2 tablespoons Domino® or C&H® granulated sugar

1 package (11.5 oz) Old El Paso® flour tortillas for burritos (8 tortillas)

¹⁄₂ cup sour cream

2 cups shredded Monterey Jack cheese (8 oz)

2²⁄₃ cups finely shredded lettuce

¹⁄₂ cup very thinly sliced red onion

Decorative toothpicks, if desired

1) Cut chicken into small bite-size pieces. In 12-inch nonstick skillet, heat the oil over medium-high heat until hot. Add chicken; sprinkle with taco seasoning mix. Cook 5 to 7 minutes, stirring frequently, until chicken is no longer pink in center. Remove from heat; cover to keep warm.

2) Meanwhile, in small microwavable bowl, mix peanut sauce, red curry paste, lime juice and sugar. Microwave uncovered on High 30 to 40 seconds or until warm. Stir thoroughly until all of the curry paste is dissolved.

3) Heat tortillas by placing one at a time in 10-inch nonstick skillet or on hot nonstick griddle on medium-high heat 3 to 5 seconds, turning once.

4) To assemble each wrap, spoon about ¹⁄₂ cup chicken mixture down center of 1 tortilla. Top with sour cream, cheese, lettuce and onion. Drizzle with generous 1 tablespoon curry-peanut sauce. Fold 2 sides of tortilla to the middle; secure with toothpick. Serve warm.

HIGH ALTITUDE (3500-6500 FT.): No change.

Nutrition Information Per Serving:		
Calories: 470	From Fat:	220
Total Fat		24g
Saturated Fat		10g
Trans Fat		1.5g
Cholesterol		95mg
Sodium		810mg
Total Carbohydrate		30g
Dietary Fiber		0g
Sugars		5g
Protein		34g

Beef Taco Foldovers

PREP TIME: 20 MINUTES (READY IN 35 MINUTES)
SERVINGS: 5 SANDWICHES

 EASY

½ lb lean (at least 80%) ground beef

¼ cup chopped onion

½ cup black beans, drained (from 15-oz can)

1 can (8 oz) tomato sauce

1 tablespoon Old El Paso® taco seasoning mix (from 1.25-oz package)

1 can (10.2 oz) Pillsbury Grands!® flaky layers refrigerated original biscuits

1 cup shredded Cheddar cheese (4 oz)

5 tablespoons Old El Paso® salsa

5 tablespoons sour cream

Sliced green onions, if desired

Lettuce, if desired

1) Heat oven to 375°F. In 10-inch skillet, cook beef and onion over medium-high heat until beef is brown; drain. Stir in the beans, tomato sauce and seasoning mix. Simmer 3 to 5 minutes, stirring occasionally, until liquid is absorbed.

2) Separate dough into 5 biscuits. Press or roll each to form 5-inch round. Spoon ½ cup meat mixture onto center of each flattened biscuit. Sprinkle cheese evenly onto biscuits. Fold half of biscuit over the filling; press edges with fork to seal. Place on ungreased cookie sheet.

3) Bake 12 to 15 minutes or until golden brown. Top with salsa, sour cream and green onions. Garnish with lettuce.

HIGH ALTITUDE (3500-6500 FT.): Bake 14 to 17 minutes.

Nutrition Information Per Serving:	
Calories: 440	From Fat: 220
Total Fat	25g
Saturated Fat	10g
Trans Fat	4g
Cholesterol	60mg
Sodium	1300mg
Total Carbohydrate	35g
Dietary Fiber	2g
Sugars	9g
Protein	20g

 Mexican chorizo sausage may be used in place of the ground beef in this recipe. If you prefer, omit the Cheddar cheese.

Skillet Chicken Divan

PREP TIME: 35 MINUTES (READY IN 35 MINUTES)
SERVINGS: 4

1 tablespoon butter or margarine

4 boneless skinless chicken breasts (about 1 lb)

Water called for on brown rice package for 1 cup uncooked rice

2 tablespoons Dijon mustard

¹/₄ teaspoon salt

¹/₈ teaspoon pepper

1 cup uncooked quick-cooking brown rice

3 cups Green Giant Select® frozen broccoli florets, thawed (from 14-oz bag)

¹/₂ cup shredded Cheddar or American cheese (2 oz)

1) Melt butter in 10-inch nonstick skillet over medium-high heat. Add chicken; cook 1 to 2 minutes on each side or until browned.

2) Remove chicken from skillet. Add water, mustard, salt and pepper to skillet; stirring with wire whisk until blended. Heat to boiling. Stir in rice; return to boiling. Place chicken pieces and broccoli over rice. Reduce heat to low; cover and simmer about 10 minutes or until most of liquid is absorbed and juice of chicken is clear when center of thickest part is cut (170°F).

3) Sprinkle with cheese; cover and let stand 5 minutes.

HIGH ALTITUDE (3500-6500 FT.): No change.

Nutrition Information Per Serving:		
Calories: 430	From Fat: 120	
Total Fat		13g
Saturated Fat		6g
Trans Fat		0g
Cholesterol		90mg
Sodium		520mg
Total Carbohydrate		42g
Dietary Fiber		8g
Sugars		2g
Protein		36g

Thai Peanut Chicken and Noodles

PREP TIME: 30 MINUTES (READY IN 30 MINUTES)
SERVINGS: 5 (1-1/2 CUPS EACH)

 EASY

2¾ cups uncooked fine egg noodles (6 oz)

¼ cup creamy peanut butter

½ teaspoon finely chopped gingerroot

¼ teaspoon crushed red pepper flakes

¼ cup soy sauce

¼ cup water

1 tablespoon vegetable oil

2 cups small fresh broccoli florets

1½ cups sliced fresh mushrooms (about 4 oz)

1 cup ready-to-eat baby-cut carrots, quartered lengthwise

1 medium red bell pepper, cut into thin bite-size strips

1 package (9 oz) frozen diced cooked chicken, thawed

¼ cup coarsely chopped dry-roasted peanuts

1) Cook and drain noodles as directed on package; cover to keep warm.

2) Meanwhile, in small bowl, beat peanut butter, gingerroot, pepper flakes and 2 tablespoons of the soy sauce with wire whisk until blended. Gradually beat in remaining 2 tablespoons soy sauce and the water until smooth. Set aside.

3) In 12-inch nonstick skillet, heat oil over medium-high heat. Cook the broccoli, mushrooms, carrots and bell pepper in oil 4 to 6 minutes, stirring occasionally, until vegetables are crisp-tender. Add chicken; cook and stir until hot.

4) Reduce heat to medium. Stir peanut butter mixture; stir into the mixture in skillet. Stir in cooked noodles until coated. Cook and stir until hot. Sprinkle with peanuts.

HIGH ALTITUDE (3500-6500 FT.): No change.

Nutrition Information Per Serving:

Calories:	410	From Fat:	170
Total Fat			19g
Saturated Fat			3.5g
Trans Fat			0g
Cholesterol			70mg
Sodium			920mg
Total Carbohydrate			34g
Dietary Fiber			5g
Sugars			5g
Protein			27g

Picadillo Chimichangas

SHERRY ROPER | SAN DIEGO, CALIFORNIA

BAKE-OFF® CONTEST 43, 2008

PREP TIME: 35 MINUTES (READY IN 50 MINUTES)
SERVINGS: 8

¼ cup Crisco® pure canola oil

1 small onion, chopped (¼ cup)

1 garlic clove, finely chopped

1 lb lean (at least 80%) ground beef

1 large tomato, chopped (1 cup)

1 can (4.5 oz) Old El Paso® chopped green chiles

1 package (1.25 oz) Old El Paso® taco seasoning mix

½ cup cinnamon applesauce or plain applesauce

¼ cup raisins

⅓ cup Fisher® Chef's Naturals® sliced almonds

½ cup pimiento-stuffed green olives, coarsely chopped

1 package (11.5 oz) Old El Paso® flour tortillas for burritos (8 tortillas)

1 cup sour cream

4 medium green onions, chopped (¼ cup)

¼ cup chopped fresh cilantro

1) Heat oven to 475°F. Brush large cookie sheet with 1 tablespoon of the oil.

2) In 10-inch skillet, heat 2 tablespoons of the oil over medium heat. Add the onion and garlic; cook 1 to 2 minutes, stirring occasionally, until onion is tender. Stir in beef; cook 8 to 10 minutes, stirring occasionally, until beef is thoroughly cooked; drain.

3) Reduce heat to medium-low. Stir in tomato, chiles, taco seasoning mix, applesauce and raisins; cook 10 minutes, stirring occasionally. Stir in the almonds and olives; cook 1 to 2 minutes or until thoroughly heated.

4) For each chimichanga, spoon ½ cup beef mixture down center of each tortilla. Fold sides of each tortilla toward center; fold ends up. Place seam sides down on cookie sheet. Brush tops and sides of chimichangas with remaining 1 tablespoon oil.

5) Bake 6 to 8 minutes or until chimichangas are golden brown. Cool on cookie sheet 5 minutes. Meanwhile, in small bowl, stir sour cream, green onions and 2 tablespoons of the cilantro.

6) To serve, top each chimichanga with 2 tablespoons sour cream mixture and remaining cilantro.

HIGH ALTITUDE (3500-6500 FT.): Bake 10 to 12 minutes.

Nutrition Information Per Serving:

Calories:	430	From Fat:	240
Total Fat			26g
Saturated Fat			8g
Trans Fat			1.5g
Cholesterol			55mg
Sodium			970mg
Total Carbohydrate			33g
Dietary Fiber			2g
Sugars			7g
Protein			15g

Patchwork Pot Pie

PREP TIME: 15 MINUTES (READY IN 1 HOUR 35 MINUTES)
SERVINGS: 6

 EASY

2 cups diced (¼ to ½ inch) cooked turkey breast

2 cups refrigerated cooked diced potatoes with onions (from 20-oz bag)

2 cups Green Giant® frozen mixed vegetables

1 jar (4.5 oz) Green Giant® sliced mushrooms, drained

½ cup sour cream

1 jar (12 oz) turkey gravy

¼ teaspoon dried sage leaves

1 Pillsbury® refrigerated pie crust (from 15-oz box), softened as directed on box

1) Heat oven to 375°F. Spray 3-quart casserole with cooking spray. In large bowl, mix turkey, potatoes, frozen vegetables, mushrooms, sour cream, turkey gravy and sage; spoon mixture into casserole.

2) Unroll pie crust. Cut into 1½-inch wide strips, then cut in opposite direction, making 1½-inch square pieces (not all will be perfectly square). Starting with rounded-edge pieces around edge of casserole, cover top of mixture with pie crust pieces, overlapping each piece (see photo).

3) Bake 1 hour 15 minutes to 1 hour 20 minutes or until crust is golden brown and edges are bubbly.

HIGH ALTITUDE (3500-6500 FT.): Thaw frozen vegetables before adding to casserole.

Nutrition Information Per Serving:	
Calories: 390 From Fat: 160	
Total Fat	18g
Saturated Fat	7g
Trans Fat	0g
Cholesterol	60mg
Sodium	760mg
Total Carbohydrate	40g
Dietary Fiber	4g
Sugars	4g
Protein	19g

GREEK CHICKEN AND PASTA
PG. 157

Comforting Casseroles

Piping hot from the oven, big spoonfuls of these homey bakes deliver a family dinner-in-one.

ITALIAN PASTA BAKE
PG. 164

CHEESY CHICKEN-TORTILLA LASAGNA
PG. 172

LAYERED BEEF-NOODLE BAKE
PG. 156

Beef Burgundy with Biscuits

PREP TIME: 30 MINUTES (READY IN 1 HOUR 15 MINUTES)
SERVINGS: 5

1 tablespoon vegetable oil

¾ cup thinly sliced onions

1 garlic clove, finely chopped

1 boneless beef round steak (16 oz), cut into 1-inch cubes

1 can (6 oz) tomato paste

1 can (14.5 oz) diced tomatoes, undrained

1 jar (6 oz) Green Giant® whole mushrooms, undrained

⅓ cup red wine or water

¼ teaspoon dried oregano leaves

¼ teaspoon dried basil leaves

1 bay leaf

½ cup green bell pepper strips

1 can (10.2 oz) Pillsbury® Grands!® Flaky Layers refrigerated original or buttermilk biscuits

1) In 10-inch skillet, heat the oil over medium-high heat. Cook onions and garlic in oil; simmer uncovered about 2 minutes, stirring occasionally. Remove with slotted spoon. Add the beef to skillet; cook about 5 minutes or until browned. Stir in onions and garlic, tomato paste, tomatoes, mushrooms, wine, oregano, basil and bay leaf. Cover; simmer about 25 minutes or until meat is tender. Stir in bell pepper; remove bay leaf.

2) Heat oven to 375°F. Separate dough into 5 biscuits; cut each into quarters. Pour hot meat mixture into ungreased 2-quart casserole. Arrange dough wedges, point-side-down, on top of hot meat mixture.

3) Bake 20 to 25 minutes or until biscuits are golden brown.

HIGH ALTITUDE (3500-6500 FT.): Increase red wine or water to ⅔ cup.

Nutrition Information Per Serving:	
Calories: 400	From Fat: 130
Total Fat	15g
Saturated Fat	3.5g
Trans Fat	3.5g
Cholesterol	50mg
Sodium	1100mg
Total Carbohydrate	37g
Dietary Fiber	3g
Sugars	13g
Protein	28g

Green Bean and Chicken Casserole

PREP TIME: 10 MINUTES (READY IN 55 MINUTES)
SERVINGS: 4

 EASY

1 can (10¾ oz) condensed cream of chicken soup

¼ cup milk

1 cup herb-seasoned stuffing crumbs

¼ cup butter or margarine, melted

4 boneless skinless chicken breasts (about 1¼ lb), cut into 1-inch-wide strips

2 cups Green Giant® frozen cut green beans, thawed

Nutrition Information Per Serving:	
Calories: 450	From Fat: 200
Total Fat	23g
Saturated Fat	11g
Trans Fat	1g
Cholesterol	125mg
Sodium	1000mg
Total Carbohydrate	25g
Dietary Fiber	2g
Sugars	4g
Protein	37g

1) Heat oven to 350°F. Lightly spray 11x7-inch glass baking dish with cooking spray. In small bowl, mix cream soup and milk until well blended. In another small bowl, mix stuffing crumbs and melted butter.

2) In baking dish, layer the chicken, green beans, cream soup mixture and stuffing mixture. Bake uncovered about 45 minutes or until the chicken is no longer pink in the center and the mixture is hot and bubbly.

HIGH ALTITUDE (3500-6500 FT.): Heat oven to 375°F. Bake uncovered 40 to 45 minutes.

Give this bake a taste of Thanksgiving dinner by adding a bit of ground sage. Just stir 1/2 teaspoon into the mixture of milk and cream of chicken soup.

Lazy-Day Overnight Lasagna

PREP TIME: 20 MINUTES (READY IN 13 HOURS 35 MINUTES)
SERVINGS: 12

 EASY

- 1 lb mild bulk Italian pork sausage or ground beef
- 1 jar (26 to 28 oz) tomato pasta sauce
- 1 cup water
- 1 container (15 oz) ricotta cheese
- 2 tablespoons chopped fresh chives
- 1/2 teaspoon dried oregano leaves
- 1 egg
- 8 oz uncooked lasagna noodles
- 1 package (16 oz) sliced mozzarella cheese
- 2 tablespoons grated Parmesan cheese

1) In 12-inch skillet, cook sausage over medium-high heat, stirring occasionally, until no longer pink. Drain well. Stir in pasta sauce and water. Heat to boiling. Reduce heat to low; simmer 5 minutes.

2) In medium bowl, mix ricotta cheese, chives, oregano and egg.

3) In ungreased 13x9-inch (3-quart) glass baking dish or lasagna pan, spread 1½ cups of the meat sauce. Top with half each of the uncooked noodles, ricotta cheese mixture and mozzarella cheese. Repeat with 1½ cups meat sauce and remaining noodles, ricotta cheese mixture and mozzarella cheese. Top with remaining meat sauce. Sprinkle with Parmesan cheese. Cover; refrigerate 12 hours or overnight.

4) Heat oven to 350°F. Uncover baking dish; bake 50 to 60 minutes or until noodles are tender and casserole is bubbly. Cover; let stand 15 minutes before serving.

HIGH ALTITUDE (3500-6500 FT.): In Step 4, bake covered 60 minutes. Uncover and bake 10 to 20 minutes longer.

Nutrition Information Per Serving:		
Calories: 380	From Fat: 170	
Total Fat		19g
Saturated Fat		9g
Trans Fat		0g
Cholesterol		65mg
Sodium		700mg
Total Carbohydrate		31g
Dietary Fiber		2g
Sugars		7g
Protein		22g

tip

To give this dish a flavor twist, replace the pork sausage with ground beef or use provolone cheese instead of the mozzarella.

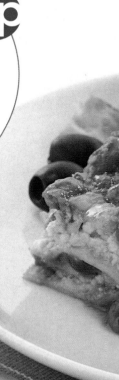

Creamy Ham and Potato Casserole

PREP TIME: 15 MINUTES (READY IN 1 HOUR 20 MINUTES)
SERVINGS: 4 (1-1/4 CUPS EACH)

 EASY

3 cups frozen potatoes O'Brien with onions and peppers (from 28-oz bag)

1½ cups Green Giant® frozen cut green beans

1½ cups finely chopped cooked ham

¾ cup milk

½ cup shredded American cheese (2 oz)

1 can (10¾ oz) condensed 98% fat-free cream of chicken soup with 30% less sodium

Nutrition Information Per Serving:	
Calories: 280	From Fat: 100
Total Fat	11g
Saturated Fat	5g
Trans Fat	0g
Cholesterol	50mg
Sodium	1300mg
Total Carbohydrate	26g
Dietary Fiber	2g
Sugars	5g
Protein	19g

1) Heat oven to 375°F. Spray 8-inch square (2-quart) glass baking dish with cooking spray.

2) In large bowl, mix all ingredients; spoon into baking dish. Bake about 1 hour or until bubbly and hot. Let stand 5 minutes before serving.

HIGH ALTITUDE (3500-6500 FT.): Thaw potatoes and green beans before mixing with other ingredients.

Bow-Ties with Ham

PREP TIME: 30 MINUTES (READY IN 1 HOUR 15 MINUTES)
SERVINGS: 6 (1-1/3 CUPS EACH)

3 cups uncooked bow-tie (farfalle) pasta (6 oz)

1 jar (16 oz) Alfredo pasta sauce

10 medium asparagus spears, cut into 1-inch pieces (about 1 cup)

½ cup sun-dried tomatoes in oil and herbs, drained, chopped

1 cup diced (¼ to ½ inch) cooked ham

1 cup shredded Havarti cheese (4 oz)

Nutrition Information Per Serving:	
Calories: 560	From Fat: 320
Total Fat	35g
Saturated Fat	20g
Trans Fat	1g
Cholesterol	110mg
Sodium	930mg
Total Carbohydrate	41g
Dietary Fiber	3g
Sugars	3g
Protein	22g

1) Heat oven to 350°F. Spray 2-quart casserole with cooking spray. Cook and drain the pasta as directed on package.

2) Meanwhile, in 3-quart saucepan, heat Alfredo sauce over medium heat, stirring frequently, until hot. Gently stir in cooked pasta, asparagus, tomatoes and ham. Stir in ½ cup of the cheese. Pour into casserole.

3) Cover casserole; bake 35 to 45 minutes or until bubbly. Top with remaining cheese.

HIGH ALTITUDE (3500-6500 FT.): No change.

Mediterranean Chicken Bake

PREP TIME: 20 MINUTES (READY IN 55 MINUTES)
SERVINGS: 6 (1-1/4 CUPS EACH)

 EASY

Nutrition Information Per Serving:

Calories:	490	From Fat:	190
Total Fat			21g
Saturated Fat			10g
Trans Fat			0g
Cholesterol			80mg
Sodium			930mg
Total Carbohydrate			45g
Dietary Fiber			4g
Sugars			14g
Protein			32g

- 1 lb boneless skinless chicken breasts, cubed
- 1 medium onion, chopped (1/2 cup)
- 2 medium zucchini, cut into 1/8-inch slices
- 1/2 cup uncooked rosamarina or orzo pasta
- 1/2 cup water
- 2 medium plum (Roma) tomatoes, chopped
- 1 jar (26 oz) roasted tomato and garlic pasta sauce
- 2 cups shredded mozzarella cheese (8 oz)
- 1 teaspoon Italian seasoning
- 6 sheets frozen phyllo (filo) pastry (14x9 inch), thawed (from 1-lb box)
- 3 tablespoons butter or margarine, melted

1) Heat oven to 400°F. Spray 3-quart glass casserole with cooking spray. In 12-inch nonstick skillet, cook the chicken over medium heat 8 to 10 minutes, stirring occasionally, until no longer pink. Stir in onion, zucchini, pasta and water. Cook 5 to 6 minutes, stirring occasionally, until vegetables are crisp-tender.

2) Stir in tomatoes, pasta sauce, cheese and Italian seasoning. Spoon mixture into casserole. Brush top of each of phyllo sheet with melted butter. Crumple each phyllo sheet and place on top of chicken mixture in casserole.

3) Bake uncovered 20 to 30 minutes or until phyllo is golden brown.

HIGH ALTITUDE (3500-6500 FT.): In Step 1, use medium-high heat. Increase water to 3/4 cup. Bake 35 to 45 minutes.

Crescent-Topped Ratatouille Casserole

PREP TIME: 25 MINUTES (READY IN 1 HOUR 10 MINUTES)
SERVINGS: 6

1 tablespoon olive oil or vegetable oil

1 small eggplant (1¼ lb), cut into
¾-inch cubes (4 cups)

1 medium zucchini, sliced

1 medium onion, sliced

1 medium green bell pepper, cut into
1-inch pieces

1 garlic clove, finely chopped

1 can (14.5 oz) diced tomatoes,
undrained

1 can (8 oz) tomato sauce

½ teaspoon dried basil leaves

¼ teaspoon Italian seasoning

⅛ teaspoon coarse ground black
pepper

1 can (15.5 oz) dark red kidney beans,
drained, rinsed

1 can (8 oz) Pillsbury® refrigerated
crescent dinner rolls

2 tablespoons grated Parmesan
cheese

1 tablespoon chopped fresh parsley, if
desired

1) In 10-inch skillet, heat the oil over medium-high heat until hot. Add the eggplant, zucchini, onion, bell pepper and garlic; cook and stir 4 to 6 minutes or until vegetables are lightly browned.

2) Reduce heat to medium-low. Stir in tomatoes, tomato sauce, basil, Italian seasoning and pepper. Cover; simmer about 10 minutes or until vegetables are crisp-tender. Stir in kidney beans; cook 5 minutes longer.

3) Meanwhile, remove dough from can in 2 rolled sections; do not unroll dough. Cut each roll into 4 slices; cut each slice into quarters. Place cheese in 1-quart resealable plastic bag; add crescent pieces, seal and shake to coat.

4) Heat oven to 375°F. Spray 11x8-inch (2-quart) baking dish with cooking spray. Spoon the eggplant mixture into baking dish. Arrange crescent pieces on top.

5) Bake 17 to 20 minutes or until the crescents are golden brown. Sprinkle with parsley.

HIGH ALTITUDE (3500-6500 FT.): No change.

Nutrition Information Per Serving:		
Calories: 320	From Fat:	100
Total Fat		12g
Saturated Fat		3.5g
Trans Fat		2g
Cholesterol		0mg
Sodium		620mg
Total Carbohydrate		43g
Dietary Fiber		8g
Sugars		10g
Protein		11g

tip

The eggplant mixture can be made a day ahead of time, covered and refrigerated. To complete the recipe, heat the ratatouille in the oven or microwave it until bubbly, then add the biscuits and bake as directed.

Layered Beef-Noodle Bake

PREP TIME: 25 MINUTES (READY IN 1 HOUR)
SERVINGS: 6

2½ cups uncooked mini lasagna (mafalda) noodles (4 oz)

1 lb lean (at least 80%) ground beef or lean ground turkey

1 jar (14 or 15 oz) tomato pasta sauce

1 container (8 oz) chives-and-onion cream cheese

½ cup reduced-fat sour cream

3 tablespoons milk

1 box (9 oz) Green Giant® frozen spinach, thawed, squeezed to drain

¼ cup shredded or grated Parmesan cheese

1) Heat oven to 350°F. Spray 12x8- or 11x7-inch (2-quart) glass baking dish with cooking spray. Cook noodles as directed on package. Drain; rinse with hot water.

2) Meanwhile, in 10-inch skillet, cook beef over medium-high heat 5 to 7 minutes, stirring occasionally, until thoroughly cooked; drain. Stir in pasta sauce and cooked noodles.

3) In medium bowl, beat chives-and-onion cream cheese, sour cream and milk with spoon until smooth.

4) Spoon half of the noodle mixture into baking dish. Top evenly with cheese mixture. Spoon spinach evenly over cheese mixture. Top with remaining noodle mixture. Cover with foil.

5) Bake casserole 35 minutes; uncover and sprinkle with Parmesan cheese. Bake about 5 minutes longer or until hot. Cut into squares.

HIGH ALTITUDE (3500-6500 FT.): Heat oven to 375°F.

Nutrition Information Per Serving:

Calories:	460	From Fat:	230
Total Fat			26g
Saturated Fat			13g
Trans Fat			1g
Cholesterol			95mg
Sodium			800mg
Total Carbohydrate			32g
Dietary Fiber			3g
Sugars			9g
Protein			24g

Greek Chicken and Pasta

PREP TIME: 30 MINUTES (READY IN 55 MINUTES)
SERVINGS: 5 (1-1/2 CUPS EACH)

---

2 cups uncooked penne pasta (6 oz)

¼ cup butter or margarine

1 large onion, chopped (1 cup)

¼ cup all-purpose flour

1 can (14 oz) reduced-sodium chicken broth

1 cup crumbled feta cheese or shredded Havarti cheese (4 oz)

3 cups chopped deli rotisserie chicken (from 2- to 2½-lb chicken)

1 jar (6 oz) marinated artichoke hearts, drained, chopped

½ cup sun-dried tomatoes in oil, drained, chopped

½ cup sliced kalamata olives

2 tablespoons chopped fresh parsley

1) Heat oven to 350°F. Spray 11x7-inch (2-quart) glass baking dish with cooking spray. Cook and drain pasta as directed on package.

2) Meanwhile, in 3-quart saucepan, melt butter over medium heat. Add onion; cook 3 minutes, stirring occasionally. Stir in flour; cook and stir 30 seconds. Slowly stir in chicken broth; heat to boiling. Cook 3 to 4 minutes, stirring frequently, until thickened. Remove from heat; stir in cheese. Gently stir in cooked pasta, chicken, artichoke hearts, tomatoes, kalamata olives and parsley. Spoon into baking dish.

3) Bake uncovered 25 to 30 minutes or until hot. Garnish with additional fresh parsley if desired.

HIGH ALTITUDE (3500-6500 FT.): No change.

Nutrition Information Per Serving:		
Calories: 550	From Fat:	230
Total Fat		26g
Saturated Fat		13g
Trans Fat		1g
Cholesterol		125mg
Sodium		1300mg
Total Carbohydrate		44g
Dietary Fiber		4g
Sugars		5g
Protein		37g

Chicken Enchilada Lasagna

PREP TIME: 25 MINUTES (READY IN 1 HOUR 15 MINUTES)
SERVINGS: 6

- 1 can (10 oz) Old El Paso® enchilada sauce
- ½ cup Old El Paso® Thick 'n Chunky salsa
- 1 large deli rotisserie chicken, cubed (4 cups cooked chicken)
- ½ cup sour cream
- ½ cup sliced green onions (8 medium)
- 2 tablespoons Old El Paso® taco seasoning mix (from 1.25-oz package)
- 8 corn tortillas (6 inch), cut in half
- 2 cups shredded Colby-Monterey Jack cheese blend (8 oz)
- 2 cups tortilla chips
- 1 cup chopped tomato (1 large)
- 2 tablespoons sliced ripe olives

  Fresh cilantro, if desired

1) Heat oven to 375°F. Spray 13x9-inch (3-quart) glass baking dish with cooking spray. In small bowl, mix enchilada sauce and salsa; reserve ¼ cup of the mixture. In large bowl, mix remaining enchilada sauce mixture, the chicken, sour cream, ¼ cup of the green onions and the taco seasoning mix.

2) Spoon reserved ¼ cup enchilada sauce mixture in the bottom of baking dish. Arrange 8 tortilla pieces over sauce, overlapping as necessary. Spoon half of the chicken mixture over tortillas; sprinkle with ⅔ cup of the cheese. Repeat layers. Cover with foil.

3) Bake 30 to 35 minutes or until hot. Layer tortilla chips, tomato, olives, remaining ¼ cup green onions and remaining ⅔ cup cheese over top of casserole. Bake uncovered 5 minutes longer. Let stand 10 minutes before serving. Garnish with cilantro leaves.

HIGH ALTITUDE (3500-6500 FT.): No change.

Nutrition Information Per Serving:		
Calories: 520	From Fat: 240	
Total Fat		27g
Saturated Fat		12g
Trans Fat		0.5g
Cholesterol		130mg
Sodium		1430mg
Total Carbohydrate		31g
Dietary Fiber		3g
Sugars		4g
Protein		39g

Sausage and Chicken Cassoulet

PREP TIME: 30 MINUTES (READY IN 1 HOUR 15 MINUTES)
SERVINGS: 6

4 slices bacon, cut into 1-inch pieces

6 bone-in chicken thighs (about 2 lb), skin removed if desired

1 cup ready-to-eat baby-cut carrots

1 medium onion, chopped (1/2 cup)

1 teaspoon dried thyme leaves

1/2 teaspoon salt

1/4 teaspoon pepper

4 oz Polish sausage links, cut into 1/2-inch pieces

2 cans (15 oz each) navy beans, drained, rinsed

1 can (14.5 oz) diced tomatoes with roasted garlic, undrained

1) Heat oven to 350°F. In 12-inch nonstick skillet, cook bacon over medium-high heat until crisp. Remove bacon from skillet; drain on paper towels. Reserve 1 tablespoon drippings in skillet.

2) Add the chicken thighs to skillet; cook over medium-high heat about 4 minutes, turning once, until golden brown. Stir in carrots, onion, thyme, salt and pepper; cook 4 to 5 minutes or until chicken and vegetables are browned. Drain well. Remove chicken from skillet.

3) In ungreased 13x9-inch (3-quart) glass baking dish, mix sausage, beans, tomatoes, bacon, carrots and onion. Top with chicken thighs; cover with foil.

4) Bake about 45 minutes or until juice of chicken is clear when thickest part is cut to bone (180°F) and vegetables are tender.

HIGH ALTITUDE (3500-6500 FT.): No change.

Nutrition Information Per Serving:		
Calories: 440	From Fat:	160
Total Fat		18g
Saturated Fat		6g
Trans Fat		0g
Cholesterol		75mg
Sodium		650mg
Total Carbohydrate		38g
Dietary Fiber		14g
Sugars		4g
Protein		33g

Sausage and Pasta Bake

PREP TIME: 20 MINUTES (READY IN 1 HOUR 20 MINUTES)
SERVINGS: 4 (1-1/2 CUPS EACH)

 EASY   LOW FAT

1½ cups uncooked penne pasta (5 oz)

½ lb bulk Italian pork sausage

1 medium onion, chopped (½ cup)

1 teaspoon dried oregano leaves

½ teaspoon Cajun seasoning

1 cup vegetable juice

1 can (15 to 16 oz) chili beans in sauce, undrained

1 can (14.5 oz) zesty chili-style diced tomatoes, undrained

1) Heat oven to 350°F. Cook and drain pasta as directed on package. Return to pan; set aside.

2) Meanwhile, in 10-inch skillet, cook sausage and onion over medium heat 8 to 10 minutes, stirring occasionally, until sausage is no longer pink; drain. Remove from heat. Stir in oregano and Cajun seasoning.

3) Stir sausage mixture into pasta. Stir in the remaining ingredients. Spoon into ungreased 2-quart casserole. Cover with foil. Bake 50 to 60 minutes or until hot in center.

Nutrition Information Per Serving:

Calories:	390	From Fat:	90
Total Fat			10g
Saturated Fat			3g
Trans Fat			0g
Cholesterol			20mg
Sodium			1470mg
Total Carbohydrate			58g
Dietary Fiber			8g
Sugars			9g
Protein			18g

Don't have Cajun seasoning on hand? Use chili powder instead.

Chipotle Rice Casserole

PREP TIME: 35 MINUTES (READY IN 1 HOUR 10 MINUTES)
SERVINGS: 4 (1-1/2 CUPS EACH)

1/2 cup uncooked regular long-grain white rice

1 cup water

1 jar (7.25 oz) roasted red bell peppers, drained, cut into 1/2-inch pieces

1 can (15 oz) Progresso® black beans, drained, rinsed

1 can (11 oz) Green Giant® Mexicorn® whole kernel corn with red and green peppers, drained

1 can (14.5 oz) diced tomatoes, drained

1 tablespoon chopped fresh cilantro

1 tablespoon canned chipotle chiles in adobo sauce, chopped

1 cup shredded pepper Jack cheese (4 oz)

3 tablespoons vegetable oil

1/4 cup all-purpose flour

1 cup milk

1/2 cup chicken broth

1 teaspoon ground cumin

1 teaspoon garlic salt

2 plum (Roma) tomatoes, sliced

1) Cook rice in water as directed on package. Meanwhile, heat oven to 350°F. Lightly spray 8-inch square (2-quart) glass baking dish with cooking spray. In large bowl, mix roasted peppers, beans, corn, diced tomatoes, cilantro, chipotle chiles, 1/2 cup of the cheese and the cooked rice.

2) In 2-quart saucepan, heat oil over low heat. Stir in flour, using wire whisk. Cook over medium heat, stirring constantly, until mixture is smooth and bubbly. Gradually stir in milk, broth, cumin and garlic salt. Heat to boiling, stirring constantly. Boil and stir about 1 minute or until slightly thickened. Stir into rice mixture in bowl. Spoon mixture into baking dish.

3) Bake 20 to 25 minutes or until bubbly around the edges. Sprinkle with the remaining 1/2 cup cheese. Arrange tomato slices on top. Bake 5 to 8 minutes longer or until cheese is melted.

HIGH ALTITUDE (3500-6500 FT.): Increase first bake time to 25 to 30 minutes.

Nutrition Information Per Serving:

Calories:	580	From Fat:	180
Total Fat		20g	
Saturated Fat		7g	
Trans Fat		0g	
Cholesterol		30mg	
Sodium		1280mg	
Total Carbohydrate		76g	
Dietary Fiber		13g	
Sugars		14g	
Protein		23g	

Seafood and Asparagus Manicotti

PREP TIME: 30 MINUTES (READY IN 1 HOUR 10 MINUTES)
SERVINGS: 6 (2 MANICOTTI EACH)

12 uncooked manicotti pasta shells
(from 8-oz package)

1 jar (26 oz) tomato pasta sauce

1/4 cup dry white wine or nonalcoholic
white wine

3/4 cup half-and-half

1 package (6 oz) frozen cooked salad
shrimp, thawed

6 oz refrigerated imitation crabmeat
sticks (from 12-oz package), cut into
1/4-inch pieces

1 box (9 oz) Green Giant® frozen
asparagus cuts, thawed, coarsely
chopped

1/2 cup chopped sun-dried tomatoes in
oil, drained

1/3 cup cream cheese, softened

2 cups shredded mozzarella cheese
(8 oz)

1/4 cup lightly packed cut-up strips
fresh basil leaves

1) Heat oven to 350°F. Cook and drain the
pasta as directed on package.

2) Meanwhile, in 2-quart saucepan, heat the
tomato pasta sauce and wine to boiling
over medium heat. Reduce heat to low;
simmer 4 minutes. Remove from the
heat; stir in half-and-half. In ungreased
13x9-inch (3-quart) glass baking dish,
spread 1 cup of the tomato pasta sauce.

3) In medium bowl, mix shrimp, imitation
crabmeat, asparagus, tomatoes, cream cheese and 1/2 cup of the
mozzarella cheese. Spoon about 1/4 cup seafood mixture into each pasta
shell. Arrange in baking dish. Pour remaining tomato pasta sauce evenly
over shells.

4) Cover dish with foil. Bake 25 to 30 minutes or until hot. Top with remaining
1 1/2 cups mozzarella cheese. Bake uncovered 5 to 10 minutes longer or
until cheese is melted. Sprinkle with basil before serving.

HIGH ALTITUDE (3500-6500 FT.): Heat oven to 375°F. Bake 10 to 15 minutes after adding cheese.

Nutrition Information Per Serving:		
Calories: 550	From Fat: 200	
Total Fat		23g
Saturated Fat		11g
Trans Fat		0g
Cholesterol		95mg
Sodium		1290mg
Total Carbohydrate		58g
Dietary Fiber		4g
Sugars		16g
Protein		29g

Cravin' Crab Enchiladas

SHARON CHITTOCK | GRASS VALLEY, CALIFORNIA

Pillsbury Bake-Off®

BAKE-OFF® CONTEST 43, 2008

PREP TIME: 40 MINUTES (READY IN 1 HOUR 25 MINUTES)
SERVINGS: 10

ENCHILADAS

- 1 can (19 oz) Old El Paso® mild enchilada sauce
- 1 cup whipping cream
- 2 tablespoons Crisco® pure olive oil
- 1 small onion, coarsely chopped ($1/4$ cup)
- 1 box (10 oz) Green Giant® Niblets® frozen corn and butter sauce, thawed
- 1 can (4.5 oz) Old El Paso® chopped green chiles
- $1/2$ cup lightly packed fresh cilantro, stems removed, coarsely chopped
- $1/4$ cup dry sherry or apple juice
- 1 can (1 lb) pasteurized crabmeat or 3 cans (6 oz each) lump crabmeat, drained
- 10 Old El Paso® flour tortillas for soft tacos and fajitas (from 10.5-oz package)
- 4 cups shredded Cheddar-Monterey Jack or Colby-Monterey Jack cheese blend (1 lb)
- $1/2$ cup chopped green onions (about 8 medium)
- 1 package (2 oz) Fisher® Chef's Naturals® slivered blanched almonds

GARNISHES

- $2/3$ cup sour cream
- Lime wedges

1) Heat oven to 350°F. Spray 13x9-inch (3-quart) glass baking dish with Crisco® Original No-Stick cooking spray.

2) In 2-quart saucepan, heat enchilada sauce and whipping cream to boiling over medium heat, stirring occasionally. Reduce heat to low; simmer uncovered 7 to 10 minutes, stirring occasionally, until sauce mixture is reduced and slightly thickened.

3) Meanwhile, in 12-inch skillet, heat oil over medium-high heat until hot. Add the onion; cook 2 to 3 minutes, stirring occasionally, until softened and translucent (do not brown). Stir in corn, chiles, $1/4$ cup of the cilantro, the sherry and crabmeat until well mixed. Remove from heat.

4) Spoon slightly less than $1/2$ cup crabmeat mixture down center of each tortilla; top each with $1/4$ cup of the cheese. Roll up tortillas; place seam sides down in baking dish. Sprinkle the remaining $1\frac{1}{2}$ cups cheese over enchiladas. Pour sauce mixture over enchiladas.

5) Bake 30 to 35 minutes or until bubbly around the edges. Sprinkle with the remaining $1/4$ cup cilantro, the green onions and almonds. Serve with sour cream and lime wedges.

HIGH ALTITUDE (3500-6500 FT.): No change.

Nutrition Information Per Serving:		
Calories: 530	From Fat:	320
Total Fat		35g
Saturated Fat		17g
Trans Fat		1.5g
Cholesterol		130mg
Sodium		990mg
Total Carbohydrate		26g
Dietary Fiber		2g
Sugars		6g
Protein		26g

Italian Pasta Bake

PREP TIME: 20 MINUTES (READY IN 45 MINUTES)
SERVINGS: 4

 EASY

1½ cups uncooked mostaccioli or penne pasta

½ lb bulk pork Italian sausage

1 medium onion, chopped (½ cup)

1 medium stalk celery, sliced (½ cup)

1 small zucchini, sliced, slices quartered (1 cup)

1 can (15 oz) tomato sauce

1 can (14.5 oz) diced tomatoes with basil, garlic and oregano, undrained

1 jar (4.5 oz) Green Giant® sliced mushrooms, drained

½ cup shredded mozzarella cheese (2 oz)

1) Heat oven to 350°F. Spray 8-inch square (2-quart) glass baking dish with cooking spray. Cook and drain pasta as directed on package.

2) Meanwhile, in 12-inch nonstick skillet, cook the sausage and onion over medium-high heat 5 to 7 minutes, stirring occasionally, until sausage is no longer pink and onion is tender; drain. Stir in the celery, zucchini, tomato sauce, diced tomatoes and mushrooms. Heat to boiling; reduce the heat. Cook 5 to 10 minutes. Remove from heat. Add cooked pasta; stir gently to mix. Pour into baking dish.

3) Spray sheet of foil with cooking spray; place sprayed side down on baking dish and seal tightly. Bake 15 minutes.

4) Uncover; sprinkle with cheese. Bake uncovered 5 to 10 minutes longer or until casserole is bubbly and cheese is melted.

HIGH ALTITUDE (3500-6500 FT.): Heat oven to 375°F.

Nutrition Information Per Serving:		
Calories: 400	From Fat:	110
Total Fat		12g
Saturated Fat		4.5g
Trans Fat		0g
Cholesterol		30mg
Sodium		1280mg
Total Carbohydrate		54g
Dietary Fiber		6g
Sugars		10g
Protein		19g

Pesto-Chicken Manicotti

PREP TIME:	20 MINUTES (READY IN 1 HOUR 15 MINUTES)
SERVINGS:	7 (2 MANICOTTI EACH)

 EASY

1 jar (16 oz) Alfredo pasta sauce

1¹/₂ cups water

1 teaspoon garlic powder

1 package (1¹/₄ lb) uncooked chicken breast tenders (14 tenders; not breaded)

1 teaspoon Italian seasoning

14 uncooked manicotti pasta shells (8 oz)

2 cups shredded mozzarella cheese (8 oz)

1 large tomato, chopped (1 cup)

¹/₃ cup basil pesto

1) Heat oven to 375°F. In medium bowl, mix the pasta sauce, water and garlic powder. In ungreased 13x9-inch (3-quart) glass baking dish, spread about one-third (1 cup) of the pasta sauce mixture.

2) In medium bowl, sprinkle chicken tenders with Italian seasoning. Stuff chicken into uncooked manicotti shells. Place shells on pasta sauce mixture in baking dish. Pour the remaining pasta sauce mixture evenly over shells, covering completely.

3) Cover with foil. Bake 45 to 50 minutes or until shells are tender. Sprinkle with cheese. Bake uncovered 2 to 4 minutes longer or until the cheese is melted. Sprinkle with tomato. Serve with pesto.

HIGH ALTITUDE (3500-6500 FT.): Stir 1/2 cup milk into pasta sauce mixture in Step 1. Increase first bake time to 60 to 65 minutes.

Nutrition Information Per Serving:		
Calories: 600	From Fat: 310	
Total Fat		34g
Saturated Fat		18g
Trans Fat		1g
Cholesterol		120mg
Sodium		610mg
Total Carbohydrate		35g
Dietary Fiber		2g
Sugars		2g
Protein		37g

Peanut Butter Mole Enchiladas

MARGARET MARTINEZ | WESTMINSTER, COLORADO

 BAKE-OFF® CONTEST 43, 2008

PREP TIME:	20 MINUTES (READY IN 50 MINUTES)		EASY
SERVINGS:	8		

SAUCE

2 cans (10 oz each) Old El Paso® mild enchilada sauce

½ cup Jif® creamy peanut butter

½ teaspoon Domino® or C&H® granulated sugar

½ teaspoon ground cinnamon

½ oz bittersweet baking chocolate

ENCHILADAS

1½ cups shredded mild white Cheddar and Monterey Jack cheese blend or Cheddar-Monterey Jack cheese blend

1 package (11.5 oz) Old El Paso® flour tortillas for burritos (8 tortillas)

2 cups cooked chicken breast strips (2¼ x ¼ inch)

¼ cup Fisher® party peanuts, chopped

1 teaspoon lime juice

1 container (8 oz) sour cream

2 tablespoons chopped fresh cilantro

1) Heat oven to 325°F. In 2-quart saucepan, cook enchilada sauce over medium-low heat about 5 minutes, stirring sauce occasionally, until heated. Stir in peanut butter and sugar; cook 1 to 2 minutes or until peanut butter is melted. Remove from heat. Add cinnamon and chocolate; stir until chocolate is melted.

2) Spray 13x9-inch (3-quart) glass baking dish with Crisco® Original No-Stick cooking spray. Spoon about ½ cup sauce over the bottom of the baking dish. Reserve ½ cup cheese. Fill each tortilla with about ¼ cup chicken, 2 tablespoons cheese and heaping 1 tablespoon sauce. Roll up the tortillas; place seam sides down in baking dish. Pour the remaining sauce evenly over the tortillas.

3) Cover loosely with foil; bake 25 to 30 minutes or until thoroughly heated. Sprinkle with the reserved ½ cup cheese. Bake uncovered 2 to 3 minutes longer or until cheese is melted. Sprinkle with peanuts.

4) In small bowl, stir lime juice into sour cream until mixed. Top individual servings with sour cream mixture and cilantro.

HIGH ALTITUDE (3500-6500 FT.): Heat oven to 350°F.

Nutrition Information Per Serving:		
Calories: 500	From Fat:	280
Total Fat		31g
Saturated Fat		12g
Trans Fat		1.5g
Cholesterol		70mg
Sodium		930mg
Total Carbohydrate		31g
Dietary Fiber		1g
Sugars		5g
Protein		25g

Crescent-Topped Turkey Chili Mole

PREP TIME: 35 MINUTES (READY IN 55 MINUTES)
SERVINGS: 6

1 lb ground turkey breast

1 to 2 medium jalapeño chiles, seeded, finely chopped

2 garlic cloves, finely chopped

1 tablespoon chili powder

1/2 teaspoon salt

1/4 teaspoon pepper

2 oz semisweet baking chocolate

1 can (28 oz) or 2 cans (14.5 oz each) Muir Glen® organic fire roasted crushed tomatoes, undrained

1 can (15 to 16 oz) red kidney or pinto beans, drained

1 can (8 oz) Pillsbury® refrigerated crescent dinner rolls

1 tablespoon cornmeal

1 tablespoon chopped cilantro, if desired

1) In 4-quart Dutch oven, cook the turkey, chiles and garlic over medium heat 5 to 8 minutes, stirring occasionally, until the turkey is no longer pink.

2) Stir in the chili powder, salt, pepper, baking chocolate, tomatoes and beans. Heat to boiling, stirring occasionally; reduce the heat. Simmer uncovered 15 minutes, stirring occasionally.

3) Meanwhile, heat oven to 375°F. Lightly spray 12x8-inch (2-quart) glass baking dish with cooking spray. Unroll dough and separate into 2 long rectangles; firmly press perforations to seal. Sprinkle both sides with cornmeal, gently pressing in with palm of hand. Spoon chili mixture into baking dish. Place dough rectangles over chili, leaving center open for steam to escape.

4) Bake 15 to 20 minutes or until the crust is golden brown. Sprinkle with chopped cilantro.

HIGH ALTITUDE (3500-6500 FT.): No change.

Nutrition Information Per Serving:		
Calories: 430	From Fat: 160	
Total Fat		18g
Saturated Fat		7g
Trans Fat		2g
Cholesterol		50mg
Sodium		990mg
Total Carbohydrate		40g
Dietary Fiber		7g
Sugars		8g
Protein		27g

Creamy Tuna and Broccoli Casserole with Bagel Chips

PREP TIME: 10 MINUTES (READY IN 50 MINUTES)
SERVINGS: 6

  EASY LOW FAT

3 cups uncooked rotini pasta

3 cups Green Giant® frozen broccoli cuts

1 can (6 oz) albacore tuna in water, drained

1 can (18 oz) Progresso® Vegetable Classics creamy mushroom soup

¼ cup milk

1½ cups garlic bagel chips (from 6-oz bag), broken into pieces

1) Heat oven to 350°F. Cook and drain pasta as directed on package, adding broccoli 5 minutes before the pasta is done cooking.

2) Return cooked pasta and broccoli to pan; stir in tuna, soup and milk. Spoon into ungreased 8-inch square (2-quart) glass baking dish.

3) Bake 15 minutes. Sprinkle with bagel chips. Bake 10 to 15 minutes longer or until bagel chips are lightly browned and casserole is hot.

HIGH ALTITUDE (3500-6500 FT.): Increase first bake time to 20 minutes.

Nutrition Information Per Serving:			
Calories:	420	From Fat:	70
Total Fat			8g
Saturated Fat			2g
Trans Fat			0g
Cholesterol			10mg
Sodium			700mg
Total Carbohydrate			68g
Dietary Fiber			6g
Sugars			4g
Protein			20g

To make the casserole even creamier, add 1/2 cup sour cream with the milk.

Poblanos Florentine Casserole

GLORIA FELTS | INDIANAPOLIS, INDIANA

BAKE-OFF® CONTEST 43, 2008

PREP TIME: 45 MINUTES (READY IN 2 HOURS 5 MINUTES)
SERVINGS: 9

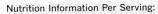

5 fresh poblano chiles (4$\frac{1}{2}$x3 inch)

1$\frac{1}{2}$ cups shredded Chihuahua or Monterey Jack cheese (6 oz)

1 cup shredded Mexican cheese blend (4 oz)

$\frac{1}{3}$ cup ricotta cheese

2 garlic cloves, finely chopped

$\frac{1}{2}$ teaspoon ground cumin

1 box (9 oz) Green Giant® frozen spinach, thawed, squeezed to drain

1 can (12 oz) Pillsbury® Golden Layers® Butter Tastin'® refrigerated biscuits (10 biscuits)

1 can (10 oz) Old El Paso® mild enchilada sauce

2 plum (Roma) tomatoes, chopped, if desired

$\frac{1}{2}$ cup fresh guacamole, if desired

$\frac{1}{2}$ cup sour cream, if desired

1) Set oven control to broil. On cookie sheet, broil chiles with tops 2 inches from heat about 10 minutes, turning frequently with tongs, until all sides are blackened and blistered. Place chiles in paper bag; seal bag. Let chiles steam 15 minutes.

2) Heat oven to 350°F. Lightly spray 8-inch square (2-quart) glass baking dish with Crisco® Original No-Stick cooking spray.

3) In medium bowl, mix the Chihuahua cheese and Mexican cheese blend; reserve $\frac{3}{4}$ cup for topping. In another medium bowl, mix ricotta cheese, garlic, cumin and spinach. Stir in remaining shredded cheeses. Set aside.

4) Wearing food-safe plastic gloves, peel blackened skin from chiles. Cut open chiles; remove the stems, seeds and membranes. Cut each chile in half lengthwise into 2 pieces; pat dry.

5) Separate dough into 10 biscuits. Separate each biscuit into 2 thin layers; flatten slightly.

6) Pour half of the enchilada sauce over the bottom of baking dish. Place 10 biscuit layers on sauce, cutting biscuits if necessary to fit into dish. Top with 5 chile halves; spread spinach mixture over chiles. Top with remaining 5 chiles halves and remaining 10 biscuit layers. Pour remaining enchilada sauce over biscuits.

7) Spray sheet of foil with cooking spray. Cover baking dish with foil, sprayed side down. Bake 55 to 60 minutes or until thoroughly heated and bubbly around edges.

8) Sprinkle with the reserved $\frac{3}{4}$ cup shredded cheeses. Bake uncovered 5 to 8 minutes longer or until cheese is melted. Cool 10 minutes before cutting. Top each serving with tomatoes, guacamole and sour cream.

HIGH ALTITUDE (3500-6500 FT.): No change.

Nutrition Information Per Serving:

Calories:	290	From Fat:	150
Total Fat			16g
Saturated Fat			8g
Trans Fat			2g
Cholesterol			30mg
Sodium			790mg
Total Carbohydrate			23g
Dietary Fiber			1g
Sugars			4g
Protein			12g

Shrimp Tetrazzini

PREP TIME: 20 MINUTES (READY IN 50 MINUTES)
SERVINGS: 4

 EASY

TETRAZZINI

- 8 oz uncooked linguine
- 3 tablespoons butter or margarine
- 3 tablespoons all-purpose flour
- 1/2 teaspoon lemon-pepper seasoning
- 1 can (14 oz) chicken broth
- 1/2 cup half-and-half
- 2 tablespoons dry sherry, if desired
- 1 1/2 cups frozen cooked deveined peeled medium shrimp, thawed, tail shells removed
- 1 cup Green Giant® frozen sweet peas, thawed

TOPPING

- 2 tablespoons butter or margarine, melted
- 1/3 cup Progresso® plain bread crumbs
- 2 tablespoons shredded fresh Parmesan cheese

1) Heat oven to 350°F. Spray 13x9-inch (3-quart) glass baking dish with cooking spray. Cook the linguine as directed on the package.

2) Meanwhile, in 2-quart saucepan, melt 3 tablespoons butter over medium heat. Stir in flour and lemon-pepper seasoning. Stir in broth; heat to boiling, stirring constantly. Stir in half-and-half, sherry, shrimp and peas.

3) Drain linguine; place in 13x9-inch (3-quart) glass baking dish. Pour sauce over linguine; toss to mix.

4) In small bowl, mix 2 tablespoons melted butter and the bread crumbs. Sprinkle over shrimp mixture. Sprinkle with Parmesan cheese. Bake about 30 minutes or until mixture is hot and topping is golden brown.

HIGH ALTITUDE (3500-6500 FT.): Increase half-and-half to 3/4 cup. Sprinkle melted butter and bread crumb mixture over shrimp mixture. Bake 20 minutes; sprinkle with cheese and bake about 10 minutes.

Nutrition Information Per Serving:	
Calories: 580	From Fat: 200
Total Fat	22g
Saturated Fat	13g
Trans Fat	1g
Cholesterol	160mg
Sodium	1080mg
Total Carbohydrate	67g
Dietary Fiber	4g
Sugars	4g
Protein	29g

Spinach and Mushroom Enchiladas with Red Sauce

ROBIN HILL | ARLINGTON, TEXAS

BAKE-OFF® CONTEST 43, 2008

PREP TIME: 45 MINUTES (READY IN 1 HOUR 25 MINUTES)
SERVINGS: 5 (2 ENCHILADAS EACH)

1 can (10 oz) Old El Paso® mild enchilada sauce

1 cup crema Mexicana table cream or sour cream

1 tablespoon Crisco® pure olive oil

1 medium onion, chopped ($\frac{1}{2}$ cup)

3 garlic cloves, finely chopped

1 package (8 oz) sliced fresh baby portabello mushrooms

1 box (9 oz) Green Giant® frozen spinach, thawed, squeezed to drain

$\frac{1}{3}$ cup chopped drained roasted red bell peppers (from 7.25-oz jar)

2 tablespoons Old El Paso® taco seasoning mix (from 1.25-oz package)

$\frac{1}{4}$ cup lightly packed fresh cilantro sprigs

$\frac{1}{2}$ teaspoon ground cumin

$1\frac{1}{4}$ cups shredded pepper Jack or salsa Jack cheese (5 oz)

2 cups shredded quesadilla or mozzarella cheese (8 oz)

10 Old El Paso® flour tortillas for soft tacos and fajitas (from 10.5-oz package)

$\frac{1}{2}$ cup crumbled cotija cheese or fresh mozzarella cheese

1) Heat oven to 350°F. Spray 13x9-inch (3-quart) glass baking dish with Crisco® Original No-Stick cooking spray.

2) In 1-quart saucepan, heat enchilada sauce and $\frac{1}{2}$ cup of the crema Mexicana over medium heat 2 to 3 minutes, stirring occasionally, until warm. Spread $\frac{1}{4}$ cup of the sauce mixture on bottom of baking dish. Set aside remaining sauce.

3) Meanwhile, in 12-inch nonstick skillet, heat oil over medium-high heat. Add onion and garlic; cook 2 to 3 minutes, stirring occasionally, until onion is tender. Stir in mushrooms; cook 7 to 8 minutes, stirring occasionally, until mushrooms are tender.

4) Transfer vegetable mixture to food processor bowl with metal blade. Add the spinach, roasted peppers, taco seasoning mix, 2 tablespoons of the cilantro, the cumin and remaining $\frac{1}{2}$ cup crema Mexicana. Cover; process with on-and-off pulses 6 to 8 times or until the mushrooms are coarsely chopped. Pour the mixture into large bowl; stir in pepper Jack cheese and $1\frac{1}{4}$ cups of the quesadilla cheese.

5) Spoon $\frac{1}{3}$ cup vegetable filling down center of each tortilla. Roll up tortillas; place seam sides down on sauce in baking dish. Pour remaining sauce evenly over tortillas; sprinkle with remaining $\frac{3}{4}$ cup quesadilla cheese and the cotija cheese. Spray sheet of foil with Crisco® Original No-Stick cooking spray; cover baking dish tightly with foil, sprayed side down.

6) Bake 35 to 40 minutes or until thoroughly heated. Chop the remaining 2 tablespoons cilantro; sprinkle over enchiladas before serving.

HIGH ALTITUDE (3500-6500 FT.): Heat oven to 375°F.

Nutrition Information Per Serving:

Calories: 660	From Fat: 390
Total Fat	43g
Saturated Fat	23g
Trans Fat	2g
Cholesterol	110mg
Sodium	1660mg
Total Carbohydrate	41g
Dietary Fiber	3g
Sugars	8g
Protein	29g

Cheesy Chicken-Tortilla Lasagna

PREP TIME: 40 MINUTES (READY IN 1 HOUR 25 MINUTES)
SERVINGS: 8

1 can (10 oz) Old El Paso® enchilada sauce

2 cups chopped plum (Roma) tomatoes (about 4 medium)

2 cups cubed cooked chicken

8 medium green onions, finely chopped (½ cup)

1 can (15 oz) Progresso® black beans, drained, rinsed

1 cup Southwest ranch veggie dip (from 16-oz container)

8 corn tortillas (6 inch), cut in half

1½ cups shredded Mexican cheese blend (6 oz)

¼ cup sliced ripe olives

2 tablespoons chopped fresh cilantro

1) Heat oven to 375°F. Spray 13x9-inch (3-quart) glass baking dish with cooking spray. Spread 2 tablespoons of the enchilada sauce in the bottom of the baking dish.

2) In medium bowl, mix tomatoes, chicken, onions and beans. In another medium bowl, mix remaining enchilada sauce and the veggie dip until well blended.

3) Arrange 8 tortilla pieces over sauce in dish, overlapping as necessary. Spoon half of the chicken mixture over tortillas; sprinkle with ½ cup of the cheese. Spoon half of the sauce mixture over cheese. Repeat layers once, reserving ½ cup cheese.

4) Cover with foil. Bake 40 to 45 minutes or until hot. Sprinkle with reserved ½ cup cheese. Bake uncovered about 5 minutes longer or until cheese is melted. Let stand 5 minutes before serving. Sprinkle with the ripe olives and cilantro.

HIGH ALTITUDE (3500-6500 FT.): No change.

Nutrition Information Per Serving:	
Calories: 420	From Fat: 220
Total Fat	24g
Saturated Fat	5g
Trans Fat	0g
Cholesterol	75mg
Sodium	620mg
Total Carbohydrate	30g
Dietary Fiber	7g
Sugars	3g
Protein	21g

Pork Chop Bake

PREP TIME: 20 MINUTES (READY IN 1 HOUR 15 MINUTES)
SERVINGS: 6 (1 PORK CHOP AND 1 CUP POTATO MIXTURE EACH)

 EASY

- 1 bag (20 oz) refrigerated cooked shredded hash brown potatoes
- 1 can (11 oz) condensed Cheddar cheese soup
- $\frac{1}{2}$ cup sour cream
- $\frac{1}{2}$ cup milk
- 3 cups chopped fresh broccoli florets
- 1 medium onion, chopped ($\frac{1}{2}$ cup)
- 1 tablespoon olive or vegetable oil
- 6 bone-in pork chops ($\frac{1}{2}$ inch thick)
- $\frac{1}{2}$ teaspoon salt
- $\frac{1}{4}$ teaspoon pepper

1) Heat oven to 350°F. In large bowl, mix potatoes, cheese soup, sour cream, milk, broccoli and onion. Spoon mixture into ungreased 13x9-inch (3-quart) glass baking dish. Cover with foil; bake 30 minutes.

2) Meanwhile, in 12-inch skillet, heat oil over medium-high heat. Add 3 of the pork chops; sprinkle with half of the salt and pepper. Cook 3 to 5 minutes on each side or until pork is browned. Repeat with remaining pork chops, salt and pepper.

3) Remove foil from dish. Place chops evenly on top of potatoes, overlapping slightly. Bake 25 to 35 minutes longer or until edges are bubbly and pork is no longer pink in center.

HIGH ALTITUDE (3500-6500 FT.): No change.

Nutrition Information Per Serving:

Calories:	440	From Fat:	170
Total Fat			19g
Saturated Fat			8g
Trans Fat			1g
Cholesterol			90mg
Sodium			770mg
Total Carbohydrate			37g
Dietary Fiber			4g
Sugars			5g
Protein			30g

Slow Cooker Specialties

Uncover a ready-to-eat, home-cooked dinner after a busy day. Just switch on the slow cooker and go!

SLOW COOKER CRANBERRY RIBS
PG. 177

CHIPOTLE PORK ROAST
PG. 176

CHICKEN AND ROASTED
VEGETABLES DINNER
PG. 187

BISCUIT CHICKEN POT PIE
PG. 180

Chipotle Pork Roast

PREP TIME: 25 MINUTES (READY IN 6 HOURS 25 MINUTES)
SERVINGS: 6

2 tablespoons chili powder

1 teaspoon salt

1 teaspoon garlic powder

2 teaspoons ground cumin

9 small unpeeled red potatoes, quartered

3 small sweet potatoes, peeled, quartered

1 medium onion, cut into ¾-inch wedges (about ½ cup)

1 boneless pork shoulder roast (2½ to 3 lb)

2 tablespoons olive or vegetable oil

1 can (8 oz) tomato sauce

1 can (14.5 oz) diced tomatoes, undrained

1 canned chipotle chile in adobo sauce, finely chopped (about ½ tablespoon)

2 tablespoons water

2 tablespoons cornstarch

1) Spray 5- to 6-quart slow cooker with cooking spray. In large bowl, mix chili powder, salt, garlic powder and cumin. Add potatoes, sweet potatoes and onion to bowl; stir to coat. Place vegetables in slow cooker.

2) Remove netting from pork. Rub oil over pork; roll in the spices in bowl to cover. Place pork over vegetables. Pour tomato sauce, tomatoes and chopped chile over pork and vegetables.

3) Cover; cook on Low heat setting 6 to 8 hours.

4) Remove pork and vegetables from slow cooker; cover to keep warm. Pour sauce from cooker into 3-quart saucepan. In small bowl, mix water and cornstarch; stir into sauce. Cook over high heat 5 to 10 minutes, stirring frequently, until thickened. Serve sauce with pork and vegetables.

HIGH ALTITUDE (3500-6500 FT.): No change.

Nutrition Information Per Serving:	
Calories: 580	From Fat: 250
Total Fat	28g
Saturated Fat	9g
Trans Fat	0g
Cholesterol	120mg
Sodium	810mg
Total Carbohydrate	39g
Dietary Fiber	6g
Sugars	8g
Protein	44g

tip

When placing the ingredients in your slow cooker, make sure the potatoes are mostly covered with the liquid to prevent browning.

Slow Cooker Cranberry Ribs

PREP TIME: 50 MINUTES (READY IN 3 HOURS 30 MINUTES)
SERVINGS: 14 (1 RIB EACH)

2 teaspoons ground cumin

2 teaspoons chili powder

2 teaspoons packed brown sugar

3 to 3½ lb pork loin back ribs (about 2 racks)

1 can (16 oz) whole berry cranberry sauce

1 jar (12 oz) beef gravy

2 tablespoons cider vinegar

2 tablespoons packed brown sugar

1 teaspoon salt

½ teaspoon crushed red pepper flakes

2 garlic cloves, finely chopped

1) Set oven control to broil; heat 15 minutes. Line broiler pan with foil.

2) In small bowl, mix cumin, chili powder and 2 teaspoons brown sugar. Rub evenly over racks of ribs. Place ribs on rack in broiler pan. Broil with tops 4 to 6 inches from heat 10 to 15 minutes, turning once, until browned. Cool slightly. Cut into individual ribs.

3) Place ribs in 3½- to 4-quart slow cooker. Reserve half of the cranberry sauce. In medium bowl, mix remaining cranberry sauce and remaining ingredients; pour over ribs.

4) Cover; cook on High heat setting 2 hours 30 minutes to 3 hours or until the ribs are tender.

5) Stir in reserved cranberry sauce; stir from bottom of cooker to coat ribs with sauce. Set cooker to Low heat setting to serve. Ribs will hold on Low heat setting up to 2 hours.

HIGH ALTITUDE (3500-6500 FT.): No change.

Nutrition Information Per Serving:

Calories:	330	From Fat:	90
Total Fat		10g	
Saturated Fat		3.5g	
Trans Fat		0g	
Cholesterol		45mg	
Sodium		950mg	
Total Carbohydrate		35g	
Dietary Fiber		8g	
Sugars		5g	
Protein		25g	

Layered Enchilada Dinner

PREP TIME: 30 MINUTES (READY IN 5 HOURS)
SERVINGS: 6

1 lb lean (at least 80%) ground beef

1 small onion, chopped (about ⅓ cup)

1 garlic clove, finely chopped

1 can (10¾ oz) condensed cream of mushroom soup

1 can (4.5 oz) Old El Paso® chopped green chiles

1 can (10 oz) Old El Paso® enchilada sauce

10 corn tortillas (6 inch)

3 cups shredded Monterey Jack cheese (12 oz)

    Paprika

    Chopped fresh cilantro

1) In 10-inch skillet, cook the ground beef, onion and garlic over medium-high heat, stirring frequently, until the beef is thoroughly cooked; drain. Stir in soup and chiles.

2) Spray 3½- to 4-quart slow cooker with cooking spray. Spread about ¼ cup of the enchilada sauce in the bottom of the slow cooker. Place 4 corn tortillas over the sauce, overlapping and breaking in half as necessary to make an even layer. Top with ⅓ of the beef mixture, spreading evenly. Drizzle with about ¼ cup enchilada sauce. Sprinkle with 1 cup of the cheese.

3) Repeat layering twice, using 3 corn tortillas and half of remaining beef mixture, enchilada sauce and cheese in each layer. Sprinkle paprika over the top.

4) Cover; cock on Low heat setting 4 hours 30 minutes to 5 hours 30 minutes.

5) Let stand about 5 minutes before serving. Sprinkle individual servings with fresh cilantro.

HIGH ALTITUDE (3500-6500 FT.): Use 1 can (19 oz) Old El Paso® enchilada sauce.

Nutrition Information Per Serving:	
Calories: 500	From Fat: 280
Total Fat	31g
Saturated Fat	15g
Trans Fat	1g
Cholesterol	100mg
Sodium	1240mg
Total Carbohydrate	27g
Dietary Fiber	3g
Sugars	3g
Protein	30g

Easy Slow Cooker Stew

PREP TIME: 10 MINUTES (READY IN 6 HOURS 10 MINUTES)
SERVINGS: 8 (1-1/2 CUPS EACH)

 EASY

3 lb beef stew meat

3 large onions, cut into eighths

1 can (14.5 oz) diced tomatoes, undrained

2 cups water

1 tablespoon beef bouillon granules

1 tablespoon packed brown sugar

2 teaspoons salt

1 teaspoon pepper

2 dried bay leaves

1 bag (1 lb) ready-to-eat baby-cut carrots

1 bag (1 lb) Green Giant® frozen cut green beans

1) In 4- to 5-quart slow cooker, mix all ingredients except green beans.

2) Cover; cook on High heat setting 6 to 7 hours, stirring occasionally, adding green beans during last hour of cook time. Before serving, remove and discard the bay leaves.

HIGH ALTITUDE (3500-6500 FT.): Thaw green beans before adding to slow cooker.

Nutrition Information Per Serving:

Calories:	400	From Fat:	190
Total Fat			21g
Saturated Fat			8g
Trans Fat			1g
Cholesterol			100mg
Sodium			1110mg
Total Carbohydrate			19g
Dietary Fiber			4g
Sugars			9g
Protein			34g

Cheesy Ravioli Casserole

PREP TIME: 15 MINUTES (READY IN 6 HOURS 45 MINUTES)
SERVINGS: 10 (1-1/2 CUPS EACH)

 EASY

1 tablespoon olive or vegetable oil

1 medium onion, chopped ($^1/_2$ cup)

1 large garlic clove, finely chopped

2 jars (26 oz each) four cheese-flavored tomato pasta sauce

1 can (15 oz) tomato sauce

1 teaspoon Italian seasoning

2 packages (25 oz each) frozen beef-filled ravioli

2 cups shredded mozzarella cheese (8 oz)

$^1/_4$ cup chopped fresh parsley

Nutrition Information Per Serving:

Calories:	500	From Fat:	150
Total Fat			17g
Saturated Fat			7g
Trans Fat			0g
Cholesterol			40mg
Sodium			1380mg
Total Carbohydrate			65g
Dietary Fiber			4g
Sugars			12g
Protein			23g

1) Spray 5- to 6-quart slow cooker with cooking spray. In Dutch oven or 12-inch skillet, heat oil over medium heat until hot. Cook onion and garlic in oil about 4 minutes, stirring occasionally, until onion is tender. Stir in pasta sauce, tomato sauce and Italian seasoning.

2) Place 1 cup of the sauce mixture in slow cooker. Add 1 package frozen ravioli; top with 1 cup of the cheese. Top with remaining package of ravioli and 1 cup cheese. Pour remaining sauce mixture over top.

3) Cover; cook on Low heat setting 5½ to 6½ hours or until hot. Sprinkle with parsley before serving.

HIGH ALTITUDE (3500-6500 FT.): No change.

Biscuit Chicken Pot Pie

PREP TIME: 10 MINUTES (READY IN 10 HOURS 40 MINUTES)
SERVINGS: 6

 EASY

1¼ lb boneless skinless chicken thighs

1 medium onion, chopped (½ cup)

½ teaspoon poultry seasoning

½ teaspoon dried thyme leaves

¼ teaspoon pepper

1 jar (18 oz) chicken gravy

2 medium stalks celery, cut into ½-inch slices (¾ cup)

1 bag (1 lb) Green Giant® frozen mixed vegetables

6 Pillsbury® Grands!® flaky layers frozen biscuits (from 22.1-oz bag)

1) Spray 3½- to 4-quart slow cooker with cooking spray. Place chicken in cooker. Top with the onion, poultry seasoning, thyme, pepper, gravy and celery.

2) Cover; cook on Low heat setting 8 to 10 hours.

3) Gently stir the frozen vegetables into chicken mixture. Increase heat setting to High. Cover; cook 30 minutes longer.

4) Meanwhile, heat oven to 375°F. Bake biscuits as directed on bag.

5) Spoon about 1 cup chicken mixture onto each of 6 plates. Top with split biscuits.

HIGH ALTITUDE (3500-6500 FT.): Thaw frozen vegetables before using.

Nutrition Information Per Serving:		
Calories: 450	From Fat:	190
Total Fat		22g
Saturated Fat		7g
Trans Fat		2.5g
Cholesterol		60mg
Sodium		1080mg
Total Carbohydrate		37g
Dietary Fiber		4g
Sugars		8g
Protein		28g

Vegetable Beef Soup

PREP TIME: 10 MINUTES (READY IN 7 HOURS 40 MINUTES)
SERVINGS: 6 (1-1/2 CUPS EACH)

 EASY   LOW FAT

1 lb beef stew meat, cut into bite-size pieces if needed

½ lb small red potatoes, each cut into 8 pieces (about 1½ cups)

1 medium onion, chopped (½ cup)

4 garlic cloves, finely chopped

1 teaspoon seasoned salt

½ teaspoon pepper

2 bay leaves

2 cans (14 oz each) beef broth

1 can (14 oz) diced tomatoes, undrained

1 can (15 to 16 oz) great northern beans, drained, rinsed

2 cups Green Giant® frozen mixed vegetables, thawed

1) In 3- to 4-quart slow cooker, mix all ingredients except frozen vegetables.

2) Cover; cook on Low heat setting 7 to 8 hours.

3) Add the mixed vegetables. Increase the heat setting to High. Cover; cook 20 to 30 minutes longer or until vegetables are crisp-tender. Remove bay leaves before serving.

HIGH ALTITUDE (3500-6500 FT.): No change.

Nutrition Information Per Serving:	
Calories: 330	From Fat: 90
Total Fat	10g
Saturated Fat	3.5g
Trans Fat	0g
Cholesterol	45mg
Sodium	950mg
Total Carbohydrate	35g
Dietary Fiber	8g
Sugars	5g
Protein	25g

tip

Because the frozen veggies are added near the end of the cooking time, you can let them thaw in the refrigerator while the soup is cooking in the slow cooker.

Italian Sausage Lasagna

PREP TIME: 25 MINUTES (READY IN 6 HOURS 25 MINUTES)
SERVINGS: 6

¾ lb bulk Italian pork sausage

½ cup chopped onion

2 cans (15 oz each) Italian-style tomato sauce

2 teaspoons dried basil leaves

½ teaspoon salt

1 container (15 oz) part-skim ricotta cheese

1 cup grated Parmesan cheese

3 cups shredded mozzarella cheese (12 oz)

12 uncooked lasagna noodles

1) In 10-inch skillet, cook sausage and onion over medium heat 6 to 8 minutes, stirring occasionally, until sausage is no longer pink; drain. Stir in tomato sauce, basil and salt.

2) In medium bowl, mix ricotta cheese, Parmesan cheese and 2 cups of the mozzarella cheese.

3) Into 3½- to 5-quart slow cooker, spoon ¼ of the sausage mixture. Top with 4 noodles, broken into pieces to fit. Top with half of the cheese mixture and ¼ of the sausage mixture. Top with 4 noodles, remaining cheese mixture and ¼ of the sausage mixture. Top with remaining 4 noodles and remaining sausage mixture.

4) Cover; cook on Low heat setting 6 to 8 hours.

5) About 10 minutes before serving, sprinkle the top of lasagna with the remaining 1 cup mozzarella cheese. Cover; let stand about 10 minutes or until cheese is melted. Cut lasagna into pieces.

HIGH ALTITUDE (3500-6500 FT.): Cook 5 to 7 hours.

Nutrition Information Per Serving:	
Calories: 660	From Fat: 280
Total Fat	31g
Saturated Fat	16g
Trans Fat	0.5g
Cholesterol	90mg
Sodium	1780mg
Total Carbohydrate	52g
Dietary Fiber	4g
Sugars	9g
Protein	43g

tip

Love your lasagna thick and meaty? For thick pieces, use a 3-1/2-quart slow cooker. A larger slow cooker will also work, but your lasagna will be a bit thinner.

Slow Cooker Alfredo Green Bean Casserole

PREP TIME: 10 MINUTES (READY IN 3 HOURS 10 MINUTES)
SERVINGS: 10 (1/2 CUP EACH)

 EASY

2 bags (1 lb each) Green Giant® frozen cut green beans

1 can (8 oz) sliced water chestnuts, drained

1/2 cup roasted red bell peppers (from 7-oz jar), cut into small strips

1/4 teaspoon salt

1 container (10 oz) refrigerated Alfredo pasta sauce

1 can (2.8 oz) French-fried onions

1) Spray inside of 3- to 4-quart slow cooker with cooking spray. In large bowl, mix all ingredients except onions. Stir in half of the onions; spoon the mixture into the slow cooker.

2) Cover; cook on Low heat setting 3 to 4 hours, stirring after 1 to 1½ hours.

3) About 5 minutes before serving, in 6-inch skillet, heat remaining half of onions over medium-high heat 2 to 3 minutes, stirring frequently, until hot. Stir bean mixture; sprinkle with the onions.

HIGH ALTITUDE (3500-6500 FT.): No change.

Nutrition Information Per Serving:

Calories: 190	From Fat: 120
Total Fat	13g
Saturated Fat	7g
Trans Fat	1.5g
Cholesterol	30mg
Sodium	240mg
Total Carbohydrate	13g
Dietary Fiber	3g
Sugars	3g
Protein	4g

Easy Barbecue Pork Sandwiches

PREP TIME: 10 MINUTES (READY IN 10 HOURS 10 MINUTES)
SERVINGS: 6 SANDWICHES

 EASY

1/2 cup barbecue sauce

1/2 cup sweet-and-sour sauce

1 garlic clove, finely chopped

2 lb boneless country-style pork ribs, trimmed of fat, cut into 2-inch pieces

1) In 3½- to 4-quart slow cooker, mix both sauces and the garlic. Stir in pork pieces to coat.

2) Cover; cook on Low heat setting 8 to 10 hours.

3) Remove pork from slow cooker; place on plate. Shred pork by pulling apart with 2 forks. Return pork to sauce in slow cooker; mix well. If desired, to toast rolls, place cut sides up on ungreased cookie sheet; broil 4 to 6 inches from heat 1 to 2 minutes or until toasted. Spoon about ½ cup pork mixture into each roll.

HIGH ALTITUDE (3500-6500 FT.): No change.

Nutrition Information Per Serving:

Calories: 490	From Fat: 180
Total Fat	20g
Saturated Fat	7g
Trans Fat	0.5g
Cholesterol	95mg
Sodium	630mg
Total Carbohydrate	41g
Dietary Fiber	1g
Sugars	11g
Protein	36g

Home-Style Pork Stew

PREP TIME:	15 MINUTES (READY IN 7 HOURS 35 MINUTES)
SERVINGS:	6 (1-1/3 CUPS EACH)

e EASY

1 tablespoon vegetable oil

1½ lb boneless pork shoulder roast, cut into 1½-inch pieces

⅛ teaspoon salt

⅛ teaspoon pepper

8 small unpeeled red potatoes, quartered (4 cups)

2 cups ready-to-eat baby-cut carrots, cut in half lengthwise

1 jar (12 oz) pork gravy

2 tablespoons ketchup

½ teaspoon dried rosemary leaves

¼ teaspoon pepper

⅛ teaspoon ground sage

1½ cups Green Giant® frozen cut green beans, thawed

1) In 10-inch skillet, heat the oil over high heat until hot. Add the pork; sprinkle with salt and ⅛ teaspoon pepper. Cook 3 to 5 minutes, stirring frequently, until pork is browned.

2) In 3½- to 4-quart slow cooker, mix the pork and remaining ingredients except the green beans.

3) Cover; cook on Low heat setting 7 to 8 hours.

4) About 20 minutes before serving, stir the thawed green beans into stew. Increase heat setting to High. Cover; cook 15 to 20 minutes longer or until green beans are tender.

HIGH ALTITUDE (3500-6500 FT.): No change.

Nutrition Information Per Serving:		
Calories: 380	From Fat: 160	
Total Fat		17g
Saturated Fat		6g
Trans Fat		0g
Cholesterol		75mg
Sodium		500mg
Total Carbohydrate		28g
Dietary Fiber		4g
Sugars		5g
Protein		29g

Chicken and Vegetable Tortellini Stew

PREP TIME: 35 MINUTES (READY IN 8 HOURS 35 MINUTES)
SERVINGS: 6 (1-1/2 CUPS EACH)

 LOW FAT

- 2 medium carrots, sliced (about ¾ cup)
- 2 garlic cloves, finely chopped
- 1 lb boneless skinless chicken thighs, cut into ¾-inch pieces
- 1 medium bulb fennel, chopped
- 1 can (19 oz) Progresso® cannellini beans, drained, rinsed
- ½ teaspoon salt
- ¼ teaspoon pepper
- 1 can (14 oz) chicken broth
- 2 cups water
- 1 package (9 oz) refrigerated cheese-filled tortellini
- 1 cup firmly packed fresh baby spinach leaves
- 2 medium green onions, sliced (2 tablespoons)
- 1 teaspoon dried basil leaves
- 2 tablespoons shredded fresh Parmesan cheese

1) In 3½- to 4-quart slow cooker, layer carrots, garlic, chicken, fennel and beans. Sprinkle with salt and pepper. Pour chicken broth and water over top. Stir to combine.

2) Cover; cook on Low heat setting 6 to 8 hours.

3) About 20 minutes before serving, stir the tortellini, spinach, green onions and basil into the chicken mixture. Increase the heat setting to High. Cover; cook 15 to 20 minutes or until the tortellini are tender. Sprinkle individual servings with Parmesan cheese.

HIGH ALTITUDE (3500-6500 FT.): In Step 3, increase cook time on High to 20 to 25 minutes.

Nutrition Information Per Serving:

Calories:	480	From Fat:	160
Total Fat			17g
Saturated Fat			12g
Trans Fat			0.5g
Cholesterol			20mg
Sodium			170mg
Total Carbohydrate			80g
Dietary Fiber			0g
Sugars			69g
Protein			2g

tip

To trim the prep time for this recipe, use washed baby spinach leaves. Select the small quantity needed for the stew from your grocery store's salad bar.

Slow Cooker Bacon Cheeseburger Dip

PREP TIME: 20 MINUTES (READY IN 2 HOURS 20 MINUTES)
SERVINGS: 28 (2 TABLESPOONS DIP, 2 BELL PEPPER STRIPS AND 1 BAGEL CHIP EACH)

 EASY

8 slices bacon

1/2 lb lean (at least 85%) ground beef

1 package (8 oz) cream cheese, cubed

1 package (8 oz) shredded American-Cheddar cheese blend (2 cups)

1 can (10 oz) diced tomatoes with green chiles, undrained

2 tablespoons chopped fresh parsley

2 medium red bell peppers, cut into bite-size strips

1 package (5.25 oz) mini bagel chips

Nutrition Information Per Serving:

Calories:	120	From Fat:	70
Total Fat			8g
Saturated Fat			4g
Trans Fat			0g
Cholesterol			25mg
Sodium			190mg
Total Carbohydrate			5g
Dietary Fiber			0g
Sugars			1g
Protein			6g

1) In 12-inch skillet, cook bacon over medium-high heat, turning occasionally, until bacon is crisp; drain on paper towels. Crumble bacon; reserve 2 tablespoons bacon for the garnish.

2) In same skillet, cook beef over medium-high heat 5 to 7 minutes, stirring occasionally, until thoroughly cooked; drain. Reduce heat to low. Stir in the cream cheese, shredded cheese, tomatoes and crumbled bacon until well mixed and cheese starts to melt.

3) Pour mixture into 1- to 1½-quart slow cooker. Cover; cook on Low heat setting 2 to 3 hours or until hot and bubbly.

4) Stir parsley into dip. Sprinkle with reserved bacon for garnish. Keep on Low heat setting to serve. Serve with bell pepper strips and bagel chips.

HIGH ALTITUDE (3500-6500 FT.): No change.

French Onion Beef

PREP TIME: 30 MINUTES (READY IN 10 HOURS 40 MINUTES)
SERVINGS: 6

1) Cut the beef into 6 serving-sized pieces. Layer half each of beef, mushrooms and onion in 3½- to 4-quart slow cooker; repeat layers. Pour soup over ingredients in slow cooker.

2) Cover; cook on Low heat setting 8 to 10 hours or until beef is tender and no longer pink.

3) Before serving, in medium bowl, mix stuffing mix, melted butter and ½ cup liquid from slow cooker; toss to mix. Place stuffing on top of contents in slow cooker.

4) Increase heat setting to High. Cover; cook 10 minutes longer or until the stuffing is fluffy. Sprinkle with cheese. Cover; cook until cheese is melted before using.

HIGH ALTITUDE (3500-6500 FT.): In Step 4, cook 15 minutes longer or until stuffing is fluffy.

Nutrition Information Per Serving:

Calories:	400	From Fat:	150
Total Fat			17g
Saturated Fat			9g
Trans Fat			0.5g
Cholesterol			85mg
Sodium			970mg
Total Carbohydrate			30g
Dietary Fiber			3g
Sugars			5g
Protein			32g

1¼ lb boneless beef round steak (1/2 to 3/4 inch thick)

1 package (8 oz) sliced fresh mushrooms (3 cups)

1 large onion, sliced, separated into rings

1 can (10¾ oz) condensed French onion soup

1 package (6 oz) 10-minute herb stuffing mix

1/4 cup butter or margarine, melted

1 cup shredded mozzarella cheese (4 oz)

Chicken and Roasted Vegetables Dinner

PREP TIME: 10 MINUTES (READY IN 8 HOURS 25 MINUTES)
SERVINGS: 6 (1-1/2 CUPS EACH)

 EASY

1 lb unpeeled small potatoes (6 to 8), cut into 1-inch pieces (3 cups)

2 cups ready-to-eat baby-cut carrots

1 cup frozen small whole onions (from 1-lb bag), thawed

6 boneless skinless chicken thighs (1¼ lb)

½ teaspoon salt

⅛ teaspoon pepper

1 jar (12 oz) chicken gravy

1½ cups Green Giant® frozen sweet peas, thawed

1) Spray 3- to 4-quart slow cooker with cooking spray. Place vegetables, except peas, in slow cooker. Sprinkle chicken thighs with salt and pepper; place over vegetables in slow cooker. Pour gravy over top.

2) Cover; cook on Low heat setting 8 to 10 hours.

3) Stir in peas. Increase heat setting to High. Cover; cook 15 minutes longer or until peas are tender.

HIGH ALTITUDE (3500-6500 FT.): Cut potatoes into 1/2-inch pieces. Cut carrots in half lengthwise.

Nutrition Information Per Serving:

Calories:	330	From Fat:	90
Total Fat			10g
Saturated Fat			3.5g
Trans Fat			0g
Cholesterol			45mg
Sodium			950mg
Total Carbohydrate			35g
Dietary Fiber			8g
Sugars			5g
Protein			25g

 Chicken thighs make an economical choice for the slow cooker. They also stay moist and tender during the cooking process.

Chicken Tortilla Soup

PREP TIME: 10 MINUTES (READY IN 5 HOURS 10 MINUTES)
SERVINGS: 6 (1-1/2 CUPS EACH)

 EASY LOW FAT

6 boneless skinless chicken thighs (1¼ lb)

1 medium onion, chopped (½ cup)

3 (6-inch) corn tortillas, cut into 1-inch pieces

1½ cups Green Giant® Niblets® frozen whole kernel corn, thawed

1 can (15 oz) chick peas or garbanzo beans, drained, rinsed

1 can (4.5 oz) Old El Paso® chopped green chiles

¾ cup salsa verde

2 cans (14 oz each) chicken broth

1 teaspoon dried oregano leaves

1 teaspoon ground cumin

½ teaspoon ground red pepper (cayenne)

2 tomatoes, seeded, chopped

Chopped fresh cilantro leaves, if desired

1) In 3- to 4-quart slow cooker, mix all ingredients except the tomatoes and cilantro.

2) Cover; cook on Low heat setting 5 to 7 hours or until juice of chicken is clear when center of thickest part is cut (180°F). Stir to break up chicken thighs. Stir in tomatoes before serving. Garnish with cilantro.

HIGH ALTITUDE (3500-6500 FT.): No change.

Nutrition Information Per Serving:

Calories:	330	From Fat:	80
Total Fat			9g
Saturated Fat			2.5g
Trans Fat			0g
Cholesterol			45mg
Sodium			1160mg
Total Carbohydrate			37g
Dietary Fiber			7g
Sugars			5g
Protein			26g

 tip Salsa verde is "green salsa," which is made from tomatillos, green chiles and cilantro. It can be found in the Mexican section of supermarkets.

Au Gratin Potatoes and Ham

PREP TIME: 20 MINUTES (READY IN 9 HOURS 20 MINUTES)
SERVINGS: 7 (1 CUP EACH)

 EASY LOW FAT

6 cups (6 medium) sliced peeled
potatoes

1 medium onion, coarsely chopped
($\frac{1}{2}$ cup)

1$\frac{1}{2}$ cups cubed cooked ham

1 cup shredded American cheese
(4 oz)

1 can (10$\frac{3}{4}$ oz) condensed 98%
fat-free cream of mushroom soup
with 30% less sodium

$\frac{1}{2}$ cup milk

$\frac{1}{4}$ to $\frac{1}{2}$ teaspoon dried thyme leaves

Nutrition Information Per Serving:

Calories: 350	From Fat: 80
Total Fat	9g
Saturated Fat	4.5g
Trans Fat	0g
Cholesterol	35mg
Sodium	860mg
Total Carbohydrate	52g
Dietary Fiber	5g
Sugars	5g
Protein	15g

1) In 3$\frac{1}{2}$- to 4-quart slow cooker, layer half each of the potatoes, onion, ham and cheese; repeat layers. In small bowl, mix soup, milk and thyme; pour over top. Cover; cook on High heat setting 1 hour.

2) Reduce heat setting to Low. Cover; cook 6 to 8 hours longer or until the potatoes are tender.

HIGH ALTITUDE (3500-6500 FT.): No change.

Pulled Pork with Root Beer Sauce

PREP TIME: 35 MINUTES (READY IN 7 HOURS 15 MINUTES)
SERVINGS: 12

1 tablespoon olive or vegetable oil

1 boneless pork loin roast (3 lb)

2 teaspoons salt

$\frac{1}{2}$ teaspoon pepper

1 medium onion, chopped ($\frac{1}{2}$ cup)

2 cans (12 oz each) root beer (3 cups)

1 bottle (12 oz) chili sauce

$\frac{1}{2}$ teaspoon salt

12 sandwich buns

Nutrition Information Per Serving:

Calories: 230	From Fat: 140
Total Fat	16g
Saturated Fat	4g
Trans Fat	0g
Cholesterol	235mg
Sodium	660mg
Total Carbohydrate	7g
Dietary Fiber	2g
Sugars	4g
Protein	14g

1) In 10-inch skillet, heat the oil over high heat. Cook the pork roast in oil 6 to 10 minutes or until brown on all sides.

2) In 3- to 4-quart slow cooker, place pork roast, 2 teaspoon salt, the pepper, onion and 1 cup of root beer. Cover; cook on Low heat setting 7 to 8 hours.

3) About 30 minutes before serving, in 4-quart saucepan or Dutch oven, heat remaining 2 cups root beer, the chili sauce and $\frac{1}{2}$ teaspoon salt to boiling over medium-high heat. Reduce heat to medium. Cook 8 to 10 minutes, stirring occasionally, until mixture is glossy and reduced to 2$\frac{1}{2}$ to 3 cups.

4) Remove pork from slow cooker, discarding the cooking liquid. Shred pork, using 2 forks to pull pork apart. Stir in chili sauce mixture. To serve, spoon about $\frac{1}{2}$ cup pork mixture in each bun.

HIGH ALTITUDE (3500-6500 FT.): In Step 3, reduce heat to medium-low and cook 15 to 20 minutes.

GRILLED FLANK STEAKS WITH
ROSEMARY-BALSAMIC GLAZE
PG. 218

Spring & Summer Sensations

Breeze into seasonal menus with refreshing recipes, from Easter treats to favorites for the Fourth of July.

WATERMELON GRANITA
PG. 210

SHRIMP, MELON AND
PINEAPPLE KABOBS
PG. 196

BERRY-LEMON CHEESECAKE
PG. 215

Brownie Bites with Strawberries and Mango

PREP TIME: 25 MINUTES (READY IN 1 HOUR 30 MINUTES)
SERVINGS: 48

1 box supreme brownie mix with pouch of chocolate flavor syrup

¼ cup water

⅓ cup vegetable oil

2 eggs

⅔ cup whipping cream

1 cup semisweet chocolate chips (6 oz)

Fresh strawberries and mango slices, if desired

1) Heat oven to 350°F. Grease 48 mini muffin cups with shortening, or line with miniature paper baking cups. In medium bowl, stir together brownie mix, water, oil, eggs and chocolate syrup pouch until well blended. Fill muffin cups about ¾ full (about 1 tablespoon batter each).

2) Bake 18 to 20 minutes or until toothpick inserted in edge of brownie bites comes out clean. Cool 10 minutes; turn upside down onto serving plate. Cool completely, about 30 minutes.

3) In 1-quart saucepan, heat whipping cream over low heat just to boiling. Remove from heat; stir in chocolate chips until melted. Let stand about 15 minutes or until mixture coats a spoon.

4) Spoon about 2 teaspoons chocolate mixture onto each brownie. Garnish with fruit.

HIGH ALTITUDE (3500-6500 FT.): Line mini muffin cups with miniature paper baking cups; spray cups with cooking spray. Follow High Altitude directions on brownie mix box for making batter.

Nutrition Information Per Serving:		
Calories: 100	From Fat:	40
Total Fat		4.5g
Saturated Fat		2g
Trans Fat		0g
Cholesterol		15mg
Sodium		50mg
Total Carbohydrate		14g
Dietary Fiber		0g
Sugars		10g
Protein		0g

Rhubarb Upside-Down Desserts

PREP TIME: 15 MINUTES (READY IN 45 MINUTES)
SERVINGS: 4

🅔 EASY

⅓ cup packed brown sugar

2 tablespoons butter or margarine, melted

2 tablespoons dark or light corn syrup

½ teaspoon grated orange peel

1½ cups chopped fresh rhubarb

4 Pillsbury® Grands!® frozen southern-style biscuits (from 25-oz bag)

½ teaspoon granulated sugar

⅛ teaspoon ground cinnamon

1 cup vanilla ice cream

1) Heat oven to 375°F. Spray insides of 4 (6-oz) custard cups with cooking spray. Place custard cups on cookie sheet with sides.

2) In medium bowl, mix brown sugar, butter, corn syrup, peel and rhubarb; divide evenly among custard cups. Top each with 1 biscuit. In small bowl, mix granulated sugar and cinnamon; sprinkle over biscuits.

3) Bake 25 to 28 minutes or until deep golden brown; cool 1 minute. Turn upside down onto 4 plates; remove custard cups. Serve warm with ice cream.

HIGH ALTITUDE (3500-6500 FT.): Bake 30 to 33 minutes.

Nutrition Information Per Serving:		
Calories: 420	From Fat:	170
Total Fat		19g
Saturated Fat		9g
Trans Fat		4.5g
Cholesterol		30mg
Sodium		640mg
Total Carbohydrate		57g
Dietary Fiber		0g
Sugars		31g
Protein		6g

Cheesy Easter Shapes

PREP TIME: 20 MINUTES (READY IN 30 MINUTES)
SERVINGS: ABOUT 23 APPETIZERS (6 BUNNIES, 17 FLOWERS)

 EASY

1 can (13.8 oz) Pillsbury® refrigerated classic pizza crust

3 tablespoons mayonnaise or salad dressing

1 tablespoon ranch dressing and seasoning mix (from 1-oz package)

¼ cup finely shredded Colby-Monterey Jack cheese blend (1 oz)

23 pimiento-stuffed olives, sliced

Sliced carrots, as desired

Fresh chives and finely chopped fresh parsley, if desired

1) Heat oven to 400°F. Unroll dough on work surface; press into 14x10-inch rectangle. Cut 6 dough bunnies with 3½ x 2-inch bunny-shaped cookie cutter and 17 flowers with 2-inch flower-shaped cookie cutter. Place shapes on ungreased cookie sheet. Discard dough scraps.

2) In small bowl, mix the mayonnaise and dressing mix. Add the cheese blend; mix well.

3) Spread each bunny dough shape with about 1 teaspoon mayonnaise mixture and each flower shape with ¼ teaspoon mixture. Decorate with olive slices. Sprinkle with parsley.

4) Bake 6 to 8 minutes or until cheese is melted. Serve hot.

HIGH ALTITUDE (3500-6500 FT.): No change.

Strawberry-Orange Butterfly Biscuits

PREP TIME: 20 MINUTES (READY IN 40 MINUTES)
SERVINGS: 8 BISCUITS

 EASY

1 can (16.3 oz) Pillsbury® Grands!® flaky layers refrigerated original biscuits

3 tablespoons strawberry preserves

Grated peel of 1 medium orange (1 to 2 tablespoons)

1 heaping tablespoon coarse white sparkling sugar

½ cup whipping cream

2 teaspoons sugar

¼ teaspoon vanilla, if desired

1½ pints (3 cups) fresh strawberries, sliced

1) Heat oven to 350°F. Spray large cookie sheet with cooking spray.

2) Separate the dough into 8 biscuits. Separate each biscuit into 2 layers; spread about ½ teaspoon preserves between layers, then put biscuits back together. Pinch edges together to seal. Cut biscuits in half. Place 2 halves on cookie sheet so round edges overlap slightly to look like butterfly; press together where round edges touch. Make 7 more butterfly biscuits.

3) Spread remaining preserves on tops of biscuits; sprinkle each with orange peel and about ½ teaspoon sparkling sugar. Bake 12 to 15 minutes or until golden brown. Cool 5 minutes.

4) Meanwhile, in small bowl, beat whipping cream until soft peaks form. Beat in 2 teaspoons sugar and the vanilla.

5) To serve, arrange strawberry slices on tops of butterfly biscuits for wings; pipe whipped cream to form body and antenna of each butterfly.

HIGH ALTITUDE (3500-6500 FT.): No change.

Nutrition Information Per Serving:

Calories:	290	From Fat:	120
Total Fat			14g
Saturated Fat			5g
Trans Fat			3.5g
Cholesterol			15mg
Sodium			560mg
Total Carbohydrate			38g
Dietary Fiber			1g
Sugars			15g
Protein			5g

Asparagus on the Grill

| PREP TIME: | 25 MINUTES (READY IN 25 MINUTES) |
| SERVINGS: | 6 |

 EASY　　 LOW FAT

1½ lb fresh asparagus spears

1 tablespoon olive or vegetable oil

Salt and pepper to taste

1) Heat gas or charcoal grill.

2) Brush asparagus with oil; sprinkle with salt and pepper. Place on grill or in grill basket (grill "wok") on grill over medium heat. Cover grill; cook 5 minutes. Turn asparagus or shake basket to turn asparagus; cook 3 to 4 minutes longer or until lightly browned and crisp-tender. Place asparagus on serving platter.

HIGH ALTITUDE (3500-6500 FT.): Cook over medium-low heat.

Nutrition Information Per Serving:

Calories:	50	From Fat:	20
Total Fat			2.5g
Saturated Fat			0g
Trans Fat			0g
Cholesterol			0mg
Sodium			15mg
Total Carbohydrate			4g
Dietary Fiber			2g
Sugars			1g
Protein			3g

Margarita Shot-Glass Shrimp

| PREP TIME: | 30 MINUTES (READY IN 30 MINUTES) |
| SERVINGS: | 24 APPETIZERS |

 EASY　　 LOW FAT

Lime wedges, if desired

Coarse salt, if desired

Coarse ground black pepper, if desired

1 cup zesty cocktail sauce

½ cup finely chopped red or yellow bell pepper

1 tablespoon lime juice

2 cans (8 oz each) crushed pineapple in juice, drained

24 cooked deveined peeled large shrimp (about 2 lb)

Cilantro sprigs, if desired

Nutrition Information Per Serving:

Calories:	60	From Fat:	0
Total Fat			0g
Saturated Fat			0g
Trans Fat			0g
Cholesterol			75mg
Sodium			210mg
Total Carbohydrate			6g
Dietary Fiber			0g
Sugars			5g
Protein			8g

1) If desired, rub rims of 24 (2-oz) cordial glasses (shot glasses) with lime wedges; dip rims in coarse salt and pepper.

2) In medium bowl, mix cocktail sauce, bell pepper, lime juice and pineapple. Place about 1 tablespoon sauce mixture in bottom of each glass. Place 1 shrimp in each glass; top each with lime wedge and cilantro sprig. Serve immediately, or cover and refrigerate until serving.

Alternate Method: In medium bowl, mix sauce, bell pepper, lime juice and pineapple. Serve immediately, or cover and refrigerate until serving. To serve, spoon sauce mixture into small bowl; place on serving tray. Arrange shrimp around bowl. Garnish with lime wedges and cilantro.

HIGH ALTITUDE (3500-6500 FT.): No change.

Shrimp, Melon and Pineapple Kabobs

PREP TIME: 20 MINUTES (READY IN 50 MINUTES)
SERVINGS: 16 KABOBS

 EASY   LOW FAT

16 (6-inch) bamboo skewers

SAUCE

3 tablespoons honey

4 teaspoons teriyaki sauce

1 teaspoon lemon juice

KABOBS

1 lb uncooked deveined peeled large shrimp

16 (1-inch) cantaloupe cubes

16 (1-inch) honeydew melon cubes

16 (1-inch) fresh pineapple pieces

Pineapple slices, if desired

Nutrition Information Per Serving:	
Calories: 50	From Fat: 0
Total Fat	0g
Saturated Fat	0g
Trans Fat	0g
Cholesterol	40mg
Sodium	110mg
Total Carbohydrate	7g
Dietary Fiber	0g
Sugars	6g
Protein	5g

1) Soak skewers in water at least 30 minutes before using to prevent burning. Meanwhile in small bowl, mix sauce ingredients; set aside. Alternately thread shrimp, melon and pineapple pieces onto 16 wooden skewers.

2) Set oven control to broil. Place the kabobs on broiler pan with tops 4 to 6 inches from heat. Brush kabobs with sauce; broil 8 to 10 minutes or until shrimp turn pink, turning once and brushing frequently with the sauce. To serve, stick kabobs into fresh pineapple slices, if desired.

HIGH ALTITUDE (3500-6500 FT.): No change.

Spring Spritzer

PREP TIME: 10 MINUTES (READY IN 1 HOUR 10 MINUTES)
SERVINGS: 19 (1/2 CUP EACH)

 EASY LOW FAT

ICE CUBES

Red or green seedless grapes

Water

SPRITZER

1 bottle (24 oz) white grape juice (3 cups), chilled

1 can (12 oz) frozen apple-grape-cherry juice concentrate, thawed

1 cup water

1 bottle (1 liter) club soda (4 cups), chilled

Nutrition Information Per Serving:	
Calories: 80	From Fat: 0
Total Fat	0g
Saturated Fat	0g
Trans Fat	0g
Cholesterol	0mg
Sodium	20mg
Total Carbohydrate	19g
Dietary Fiber	0g
Sugars	17g
Protein	0g

1) Place 2 to 3 grapes in each section of 2 ice cube trays. Fill trays with water; freeze.

2) In 4-quart nonmetal container or punch bowl, mix juice, juice concentrate and 1 cup water. Just before serving, add club soda; stir gently to blend. Add fruit-filled ice cubes.

HIGH ALTITUDE (3500-6500 FT.): No change.

Bunny Puffs

PREP TIME: 20 MINUTES (READY IN 30 MINUTES)
SERVINGS: 8 BUNNY PUFFS

 EASY

- 1 can (8 oz) Pillsbury® refrigerated crescent dinner rolls
- 8 miniature chocolate-covered peanut butter cup candies, unwrapped
- 8 white miniature marshmallows, cut in half
- 4 pink miniature marshmallows, cut in half
- 16 blue miniature candy-coated semi-sweet chocolate baking bits

1) Heat oven to 375°F. Line large cookie sheet with cooking parchment paper; spray paper with cooking spray.

2) Unroll dough and separate into 8 triangles. Place 1 peanut butter cup in center of 1 triangle. Gently stretch corners closest to and farthest from cup together at top of cup, pinching edges together to seal around cup. Pull up third corner; firmly pinch edges to seal. Place on cookie sheet; twist 2 longest tips of dough to make ears. If desired, bend down longer ear. Repeat with remaining dough triangles and peanut butter cups, shaping and trimming dough as needed for desired shape.

3) Bake 8 to 9 minutes or until puffs begin to brown. Place 2 white miniature marshmallow halves and 1 pink marshmallow half on center of each for eyes and nose. Bake 1 to 2 minutes longer or until puffs are golden brown and marshmallows are slightly puffed.

4) For pupils, immediately place 2 blue baking bits on white marshmallows; remove puffs to cooling rack.

HIGH ALTITUDE (3500-6500 FT.): No change.

Nutrition Information Per Serving:

Calories:	140	From Fat:	70
Total Fat			8g
Saturated Fat			3g
Trans Fat			1.5g
Cholesterol			0mg
Sodium			240mg
Total Carbohydrate			15g
Dietary Fiber			0g
Sugars			6g
Protein			3g

Chocolate Mousse Cones

PREP TIME: 2 HOURS (READY IN 3 HOURS)
SERVINGS: 8

1 bag (12 oz) semisweet chocolate chips (2 cups)

1 tablespoon vegetable oil

8 sugar-style ice cream cones with pointed ends

2 eggs

2 tablespoons sugar

2 cups whipping cream

2 cups raspberry sorbet

8 fresh raspberries

Nutrition Information Per Serving:		
Calories: 120	From Fat: 50	
Total Fat		5g
Saturated Fat		2g
Trans Fat		0g
Cholesterol		10mg
Sodium		350mg
Total Carbohydrate		14g
Dietary Fiber		0g
Sugars		2g
Protein		5g

1) To make a holder to hold cones upright, turn an egg carton upside down. Punch holes in 8 of the egg cases to hold the cones. If you don't have an egg carton, use 8 heavy, narrow-rimmed drinking glasses.

2) Place chocolate chips and oil in top of double boiler over simmering water or in medium bowl over saucepan of simmering water. Melt chocolate, stirring as chocolate starts to soften.

3) Dip and twirl top 2 inches of each cone into melted chocolate; quickly remove and place in holder. Refrigerate or freeze until chocolate is hardened, about 1 hour.

4) In small bowl, beat eggs with electric mixer on high speed 3 minutes. Gradually beat in sugar; beat 1 minute longer.

5) In 2-quart saucepan, heat 1 cup of the whipping cream over medium heat just until hot. Gradually stir at least half of the hot cream into eggs, then stir back into hot cream in saucepan. Cook over medium-low heat about 10 minutes, stirring constantly, until mixture thickens (do not boil).

6) Stir in remaining melted chocolate from dipping cones. Cover; refrigerate about 1 hour, stirring occasionally, just until chilled.

7) In chilled medium bowl, beat remaining 1 cup whipping cream on high speed until stiff. Fold chocolate mixture into whipped cream; refrigerate up to 1 hour before serving time.

8) Spoon chocolate mixture into cones, place 1 small scoop sorbet on top of each. Garnish each with fresh raspberry.

HIGH ALTITUDE (3500-6500 FT.): No change.

Hawaiian Appetizer Quesadillas

PREP TIME: 20 MINUTES (READY IN 35 MINUTES)
SERVINGS: 32 APPETIZERS

 EASY   LOW FAT

1 package (11.5 oz) Old El Paso® flour tortillas for burritos (8 tortillas)

Cooking spray

1 cup finely chopped cooked Canadian bacon (about 5 oz)

½ cup crushed pineapple (from 8-oz can), well drained

1 cup finely shredded Mexican cheese blend (4 oz)

½ cup mango or peach salsa, if desired

1) Move oven rack to lowest position; heat oven to 400°F. Spray 1 side of 4 tortillas with cooking spray. On large cookie sheet, place tortillas, sprayed sides down, overlapping in center so tortillas do not hang over edge of sheet. Top evenly with bacon, pineapple, cheese and remaining tortillas. Spray tops of tortillas with cooking spray. Place another cookie sheet on top of tortillas; press down.

2) Bake on the bottom oven rack 8 to 10 minutes or until the bottom tortillas are golden brown. Turn cookie sheets and quesadillas over. Bake about 5 minutes longer or until bottoms are golden brown and cheese is melted. Cut into 8 small wedges; serve warm with salsa.

HIGH ALTITUDE (3500-6500 FT.): No change.

Nutrition Information Per Serving:		
Calories: 60	From Fat:	25
Total Fat		2.5g
Saturated Fat		1g
Trans Fat		0g
Cholesterol		5mg
Sodium		160mg
Total Carbohydrate		6g
Dietary Fiber		0g
Sugars		0g
Protein		3g

tip Feel free to use any kind of shredded cheese you like in these tropical quesadillas. Stir fresh mango or peach pieces into purchased salsa if you can't find mango or peach salsa.

Fiesta Fruit and Shrimp Salad Stacks

ROXANNE CHAN | ALBANY, CALIFORNIA

BAKE-OFF® CONTEST 43, 2008

PREP TIME: 55 MINUTES (READY IN 55 MINUTES)
SERVINGS: 4

1 package (11.5 oz) Old El Paso® flour tortillas for burritos (8 tortillas)

¼ cup Crisco® pure vegetable oil

1 medium avocado, pitted, peeled and diced

½ cup diced peeled jicama

½ cup diced firm ripe banana

1 large orange, peeled, sectioned and chopped

½ cup diced fresh pineapple

2 tablespoons diced red onion

1 cup coarsely chopped cooked deveined peeled shrimp

½ cup diced pepper Jack or Monterey Jack cheese

2 tablespoons chopped fresh mint leaves

3 tablespoons Smucker's® sweet orange marmalade

3 tablespoons sour cream

2 tablespoons lime juice

1 tablespoon chopped chipotle chile in adobo sauce

¼ cup Fisher® honey-roasted peanuts

2 cups shredded lettuce

2 teaspoons grated lime peel

1) Heat oven to 375°F. Generously brush each side of tortillas with oil. Place tortillas on cookie sheets. Bake 8 to 10 minutes, turning after about 4 minutes, until edges are golden brown and crisp. Set aside.

2) Meanwhile, in medium bowl, mix avocado, jicama, banana, orange, pineapple, onion, shrimp, cheese and mint.

3) In small bowl, beat marmalade, sour cream, lime juice and chile with wire whisk until well blended. Reserve 2 tablespoons marmalade dressing. Gently toss remaining dressing with fruit mixture until evenly coated.

4) Place 1 tortilla on each of 4 serving plates. Spoon heaping 1 cup fruit mixture onto each tortilla; top each with another tortilla. Brush reserved dressing over top of each tortilla stack; sprinkle with peanuts. Arrange shredded lettuce around each tortilla stack; garnish with lime peel.

HIGH ALTITUDE (3500-6500 FT.): No change.

Nutrition Information Per Serving:

Calories:	740	From Fat:	360
Total Fat			40g
Saturated Fat			10g
Trans Fat			2g
Cholesterol			95mg
Sodium			880mg
Total Carbohydrate			73g
Dietary Fiber			7g
Sugars			19g
Protein			22g

Peach Crescent Palmiers

PREP TIME: 20 MINUTES (READY IN 35 MINUTES)
SERVINGS: 16

 EASY

3 tablespoons sugar

1 can (8 oz) Pillsbury® refrigerated crescent dinner rolls

2 tablespoons butter or margarine, melted

³/₄ cup pineapple cream cheese spread

1²/₃ cups thinly sliced peaches, halved

Nutrition Information Per Serving:		
Calories: 120	From Fat:	70
Total Fat		8g
Saturated Fat		4g
Trans Fat		1g
Cholesterol		15mg
Sodium		200mg
Total Carbohydrate		10g
Dietary Fiber		0g
Sugars		5g
Protein		2g

1) Heat oven to 375°F. On cutting board sprinkled with 1½ tablespoons of the sugar, separate dough into 4 rectangles; firmly press perforations to seal. Lightly press dough into sugar. Brush rectangles with about 1 tablespoon of the melted butter; sprinkle with remaining sugar. Using 2 rectangles, place one rectangle on top of the other. Starting with the shortest sides, roll up both ends jelly-roll fashion to meet in center. Cut into 8 slices. Repeat with remaining 2 rectangles, forming 16 slices in all. Place the slices, cut side down, 2 inches apart on ungreased cookie sheets. Brush with remaining melted butter.

2) Bake 10 to 13 minutes or until golden brown. Gently recoil cookie if necessary. Immediately remove from cookie sheets. Cool completely.

3) Place cookies on serving plate. Place dollop of cream cheese spread on each cookie. Top each with sliced peaches.

HIGH ALTITUDE (3500-6500 FT.): No change.

 Palmiers, so named because they form a palm leaf shape as the pastry puffs out, can be made the day before, then assembled before serving. Frozen or canned peaches can be substituted; plan on about 11 ounces.

Grilled Greek Chicken Sandwiches

PREP TIME: 30 MINUTES (READY IN 30 MINUTES)
SERVINGS: 2 SANDWICHES

 EASY   LOW FAT

CUCUMBER SAUCE

¼ cup Yoplait® Original Fat-Free plain yogurt

⅓ cup finely chopped seeded cucumber

1 medium green onion, sliced (1 tablespoon)

1 teaspoon grated lemon peel

Dash salt and pepper

SANDWICHES

2 teaspoons lemon juice

1 teaspoon olive or vegetable oil

¼ teaspoon dried oregano leaves

2 boneless skinless chicken breasts

1 pita (pocket) bread (6 inch), cut in half to form pockets

1 small tomato, sliced

2 thin slices red onion

1) Heat gas or charcoal grill. In small bowl, mix sauce ingredients. Set aside. (Sauce may become watery if it stands longer than 30 minutes.)

2) In another small bowl, mix lemon juice, oil and oregano. Brush lemon mixture over the chicken, coating all sides. If desired, sprinkle with salt and pepper.

3) Place chicken on grill over medium heat. Cover grill; cook 15 to 20 minutes, turning once, until juice of chicken is clear when center of thickest part is cut (170°F). Wrap pita bread halves in foil; place on grill 1 to 2 minutes or until warm.

4) Place chicken, tomato and onion inside pita pockets. Top with sauce.

HIGH ALTITUDE (3500-6500 FT.): No change.

Nutrition Information Per Serving:		
Calories: 290	From Fat:	60
Total Fat		7g
Saturated Fat		1.5g
Trans Fat		0g
Cholesterol		75mg
Sodium		340mg
Total Carbohydrate		23g
Dietary Fiber		2g
Sugars		7g
Protein		33g

tip

To broil the chicken, place it on a broiler pan; broil 4 to 6 inches from the heat using the times above as a guide, turning once.

S'more Thumbprint Cookies

PREP TIME: 1 HOUR (READY IN 1 HOUR)
SERVINGS: ABOUT 5 DOZEN COOKIES

1 cup butter, softened

1/2 cup packed brown sugar

1 egg

1 teaspoon vanilla

1 1/3 cups all-purpose flour

1 cup finely ground graham cracker crumbs (16 cracker squares)

1/8 teaspoon salt

120 miniature marshmallows (about 1 1/4 cups)

60 rectangles milk chocolate (from four 1.55-oz bars)

Nutrition Information Per Serving:

Calories: 70	From Fat: 40
Total Fat	4g
Saturated Fat	2.5g
Trans Fat	0g
Cholesterol	10mg
Sodium	40mg
Total Carbohydrate	8g
Dietary Fiber	0g
Sugars	5g
Protein	0g

1) Heat oven to 325°F.

2) In large bowl, beat butter and brown sugar with electric mixer on medium speed until light and fluffy. Add egg and vanilla; beat until blended. Add flour, graham cracker crumbs and salt; on low speed, beat about 1 minute or until stiff dough forms.

3) Shape dough by heaping teaspoonfuls into 60 balls. On ungreased cookie sheets, place balls 2 inches apart. With your thumb, make an indentation in the center of each ball.

4) Bake 10 to 12 minutes or until cookies are firm and edges are just beginning to brown. Lightly press 2 marshmallows in center of each cookie; bake 2 to 3 minutes longer. Top marshmallows on each cookie with 1 rectangle of chocolate; let stand 2 to 3 minutes. With tip of knife, gently spread chocolate over marshmallows. Let stand until chocolate is set.

HIGH ALTITUDE (3500-6500 FT.): Increase flour to 2 cups. Bake 12 to 14 minutes.

Picnic Lemonade

PREP TIME: 10 MINUTES (READY IN 10 MINUTES)
SERVINGS: 22 (1 CUP EACH)

 EASY LOW FAT

2 cans (12 oz each) frozen lemonade concentrate

1 can (12 oz) frozen white grape juice concentrate

17 1/2 cups cold water

1) In large nonmetal container, mix all ingredients. Refrigerate until serving.

2) Serve over ice.

HIGH ALTITUDE (3500-6500 FT.): No change.

Nutrition Information Per Serving:

Calories: 70	From Fat: 40
Total Fat	4g
Saturated Fat	2.5g
Trans Fat	0g
Cholesterol	10mg
Sodium	40mg
Total Carbohydrate	8g
Dietary Fiber	0g
Sugars	5g
Protein	0g

Cheesecake Shot-Glass Desserts

PREP TIME: 30 MINUTES (READY IN 1 HOUR)
SERVINGS: 12 DESSERTS

2 packages (8 oz each) cream cheese, softened

¾ cup sugar

1 tablespoon coffee-flavored liqueur or 1 teaspoon chocolate extract

2 teaspoons grated lemon peel

4 tablespoons chocolate cookie crumbs

Chocolate-covered coffee beans or grated chocolate

4 tablespoons graham cracker crumbs

Blueberries and raspberries

1) In large bowl, beat cream cheese and sugar with electric mixer on medium speed until smooth. Divide mixture in half; place in separate bowls. Stir coffee liqueur into half; stir lemon peel into remaining half of cream cheese mixture.

2) Spoon 2 teaspoons chocolate cookie crumbs into the bottoms of six 2-oz cordial glasses (shot glasses). Top with 2 tablespoons liqueur cream cheese mixture. Sprinkle with 2 teaspoons chocolate cookie crumbs and another 2 tablespoons liqueur cream cheese mixture. Top each with coffee bean.

3) Spoon 2 teaspoons graham cracker crumbs into the bottoms of six 2-oz cordial glasses (shot glasses). Top with 2 tablespoons lemon cream cheese mixture. Sprinkle with 2 teaspoons graham cracker crumbs and another 2 tablespoons lemon cream cheese mixture. Top each with blueberries and raspberries. Refrigerate desserts at least 30 minutes before serving.

HIGH ALTITUDE (3500-6500 FT.): No change.

Nutrition Information Per Serving:		
Calories: 210	From Fat: 130	
Total Fat		14g
Saturated Fat		9g
Trans Fat		0.5g
Cholesterol		40mg
Sodium		135mg
Total Carbohydrate		19g
Dietary Fiber		0g
Sugars		16g
Protein		3g

tip

This is a great opportunity to use any souvenir shot glasses you have on hand. Or, use 2-ounce plastic cups available in party supply stores.

Dipped Cream Cheese Strawberries

PREP TIME: 25 MINUTES (READY IN 1 HOUR 25 MINUTES)
SERVINGS: 12 STRAWBERRIES

1 package (1 lb) fresh strawberries

6 oz cream cheese (from 8-oz package), softened

24 vanilla wafer cookies, finely crushed (3/4 cup)

3 tablespoons powdered sugar

1 teaspoon grated orange peel

1 bag (12 oz) semisweet chocolate chips (2 cups)

2 oz bittersweet baking chocolate, chopped

1/2 cup white vanilla baking chips

1 teaspoon vegetable oil

1) Rinse strawberries; pat dry with paper towels. Line cookie sheet with waxed paper. In medium bowl, beat cream cheese, cookie crumbs, powdered sugar and orange peel with electric mixer on medium speed until mixed. Press about 1 rounded tablespoon cream cheese mixture over the bottom half of each strawberry, molding to fit the strawberry. Place the strawberries on cookie sheet. Refrigerate 30 minutes.

2) In 1-quart saucepan, melt semisweet chocolate chips and bittersweet chocolate over low heat, stirring frequently. Holding strawberry by the leaves, dip each strawberry into chocolate mixture, covering cheese mixture. Place on cookie sheet. Refrigerate about 30 minutes or until chocolate is completely set.

3) In small microwavable bowl, microwave vanilla baking chips and oil uncovered on High 1 minute, stirring every 30 seconds, until melted. Continue to microwave at 15-second intervals if necessary to melt chips. Drizzle melted vanilla chips over dark chocolate on strawberries. Place each in paper baking cup. Store in tightly covered container in refrigerator no longer than 24 hours.

HIGH ALTITUDE (3500-6500 FT.): No change.

Nutrition Information Per Serving:

Calories:	330	From Fat:	180
Total Fat			20g
Saturated Fat			12g
Trans Fat			0g
Cholesterol			15mg
Sodium			90mg
Total Carbohydrate			34g
Dietary Fiber			3g
Sugars			27g
Protein			4g

Grilled Southwestern Corn

PREP TIME: 15 MINUTES (READY IN 15 MINUTES)
SERVINGS: 4 (1 EAR EACH)

 EASY

4 medium ears fresh corn, husks removed

¼ teaspoon salt

2 teaspoons finely chopped fresh cilantro

1 tablespoon canola or olive oil

¼ teaspoon ground cumin

⅛ teaspoon garlic powder

⅛ teaspoon ground red pepper (cayenne)

1) Heat gas or charcoal grill. Carefully brush grill rack with canola oil. Place the corn directly on grill over medium-high heat. Cover grill; cook 8 to 10 minutes, turning occasionally, until lightly browned on all sides.

2) Meanwhile, in small bowl, mix the salt and cilantro; set aside.

3) In 8-inch nonstick skillet, mix 1 tablespoon oil and the cumin. Cook over medium heat about 30 seconds, stirring frequently, until fragrant. Stir in garlic powder and red pepper. Brush cumin mixture over hot corn; sprinkle with cilantro-salt mixture.

HIGH ALTITUDE (3500-6500 FT.): Grill over medium heat 10 to 12 minutes.

Nutrition Information Per Serving:

Calories: 160	From Fat: 40
Total Fat	4.5g
Saturated Fat	0.5g
Trans Fat	0g
Cholesterol	0mg
Sodium	160mg
Total Carbohydrate	25g
Dietary Fiber	4g
Sugars	3g
Protein	

Mascarpone-Filled Fresh Strawberries

PREP TIME: 20 MINUTES (READY IN 20 MINUTES)
SERVINGS: 20

 EASY

1 quart fresh strawberries

1 container (8 oz) mascarpone cheese

3 tablespoons powdered sugar

1 teaspoon milk

½ teaspoon almond extract

Sliced almonds

Nutrition Information Per Serving:

Calories: 60	From Fat: 30
Total Fat	3.5g
Saturated Fat	2.5g
Trans Fat	0g
Cholesterol	10mg
Sodium	0mg
Total Carbohydrate	6g
Dietary Fiber	0g
Sugars	3g
Protein	0g

1) Using larger strawberries, trim tops and bottoms of strawberries to level. Using small melon baller, scoop out center of each strawberry.

2) In medium bowl, mix the cheese, powdered sugar, milk and extract until smooth. Spoon cheese mixture into small resealable food freezer plastic bag or pastry bag fitted with star tip; seal bag. Cut small hole in bottom corner of plastic bag. Squeeze the bag to pipe the cheese mixture into strawberries; top with almonds.

HIGH ALTITUDE (3500-6500 FT.): No change.

Fresh Tomato-Basil Caprese Kabobs

PREP TIME: 30 MINUTES (READY IN 1 HOUR 30 MINUTES)
SERVINGS: 34 KABOBS

¼ cup extra-virgin olive oil

2 tablespoons lemon juice

⅔ cup coarsely chopped fresh basil or lemon basil leaves

¼ teaspoon salt

¼ teaspoon freshly ground black pepper

1 pint red cherry tomatoes

1 pint yellow cherry tomatoes

2 medium zucchini or yellow squash, cubed

1 lb fresh mozzarella cheese, cubed

34 (6-inch) bamboo skewers

Fresh basil leaves, if desired

1) In large bowl, mix oil, lemon juice, basil, salt and pepper, using wire whisk. Add tomatoes, zucchini and cheese. Cover and refrigerate about 30 minutes.

2) Drain vegetables, reserving olive oil mixture. Thread skewers alternately with tomatoes, zucchini and cheese; top with basil leaf. Serve kabobs with reserved olive oil mixture.

HIGH ALTITUDE (3500-6500 FT.): No change.

Nutrition Information Per Serving:

Calories:	60	From Fat:	40
Total Fat			4.5g
Saturated Fat			2g
Trans Fat			0g
Cholesterol			5mg
Sodium			90mg
Total Carbohydrate			2g
Dietary Fiber			0g
Sugars			0g
Protein			4g

Italian Chopped Salad Pizzas

BOB GADSBY | GREAT FALLS, MONTANA

Bake-Off

BAKE-OFF® CONTEST 43, 2008

PREP TIME: 40 MINUTES (READY IN 55 MINUTES)
SERVINGS: 4 INDIVIDUAL PIZZAS

2 tablespoons Crisco® pure olive oil

Cornmeal, if desired

3 oz thickly sliced pancetta, chopped (3⁄4 cup)

5 cups chopped iceberg or romaine lettuce

1 1⁄2 cups (1⁄2-inch cubes) skinned rotisserie chicken breast

3⁄4 cup cubed fresh mozzarella cheese

2 plum (Roma) tomatoes, chopped (3⁄4 cup)

1⁄4 cup sun-dried tomatoes in oil, drained and chopped

3 tablespoons fresh basil leaves, thinly sliced

1 can (13.8 oz) Pillsbury® refrigerated classic pizza crust

2 teaspoons Italian seasoning

1⁄2 cup shredded Asiago cheese (2 oz)

1⁄2 to 3⁄4 cup red wine vinaigrette dressing

1⁄4 cup crumbled sweet or regular Gorgonzola cheese, if desired

Basil sprigs

1) Heat oven to 425°F. Lightly brush large cookie sheet with 1 tablespoon of the oil; sprinkle with cornmeal. In 8-inch skillet, cook pancetta over medium-high heat, stirring occasionally, until crisp; drain.

2) In large bowl, mix lettuce, chicken, mozzarella cheese, plum tomatoes, sun-dried tomatoes, sliced basil and pancetta; set aside.

3) Unroll pizza crust dough; cut into 4 rectangles, using pizza cutter. Place rectangles on cookie sheet. Press each rectangle into 8x6-inch oval, folding over edges of dough to form a rim. Brush remaining 1 tablespoon oil over dough ovals; sprinkle evenly with Italian seasoning and Asiago cheese. Bake 11 to 13 minutes or until crusts are golden brown and cheese is melted.

4) Pour dressing over salad mixture; toss to mix. Mound about 2 cups of the salad mixture onto each pizza crust; sprinkle with Gorgonzola cheese. Garnish with basil sprigs.

HIGH ALTITUDE (3500-6500 FT.): No change.

Nutrition Information Per Serving:

Calories:	690	From Fat:	320
Total Fat			35g
Saturated Fat			11g
Trans Fat			0g
Cholesterol			85mg
Sodium			1810mg
Total Carbohydrate			55g
Dietary Fiber			2g
Sugars			12g
Protein			37g

Chipotle Burgers with Guacamole

PREP TIME: 45 MINUTES (READY IN 45 MINUTES)
SERVINGS: 8

BURGERS

2½ lb lean (at least 80%) ground beef

1 can (4.5 oz) Old El Paso® chopped green chiles (¼ cup)

3 tablespoons chopped canned chipotle chiles in adobo sauce, undrained

8 slices Cheddar or Monterey Jack cheese, if desired

8 burger buns, split

2 medium tomatoes, sliced

GUACAMOLE

2 large avocados (about 1 lb), pitted, peeled and cubed

1 tablespoon lime juice

¼ teaspoon red pepper sauce

¼ teaspoon salt, if desired

1 garlic clove, finely chopped

1) Heat gas or charcoal grill. In large bowl, mix the ground beef, green chiles and chipotle chiles. Shape into 8 patties, about ¾ inch thick.

2) In medium bowl, mash the guacamole ingredients, using pastry blender or fork.

3) Place patties on grill over medium heat. Cover grill; cook 13 to 15 minutes, turning once, until meat thermometer inserted in center of patties reads 160°F. Top each patty with cheese slice; cook just until cheese is melted. To toast buns, place cut sides down on grill during last 1 to 2 minutes of cook time.

4) Layer buns with tomato slices, burgers and guacamole.

HIGH ALTITUDE (3500-6500 FT.):
No change.

Nutrition Information Per Serving:	
Calories: 440	From Fat: 230
Total Fat	25g
Saturated Fat	8g
Trans Fat	1.5g
Cholesterol	90mg
Sodium	520mg
Total Carbohydrate	24g
Dietary Fiber	5g
Sugars	4g
Protein	29g

tip

Make just the guacamole in this recipe when you want an accompaniment for a Mexican dinner or a south-of-the-border snack assortment.

Watermelon Granita

PREP TIME: 25 MINUTES (READY IN 4 HOURS 25 MINUTES)
SERVINGS: 10 (1 CUP EACH)

 EASY   LOW FAT

3 tablespoons lime juice (juice of 2 to 3 limes)

1 cup water

¹/₂ cup sugar

6 cups 1-inch cubes seeded watermelon

Nutrition Information Per Serving:	
Calories: 70	From Fat: 0
Total Fat	0g
Saturated Fat	0g
Trans Fat	0g
Cholesterol	0mg
Sodium	0mg
Total Carbohydrate	17g
Dietary Fiber	0g
Sugars	16g
Protein	0g

1) In 1-quart saucepan, mix lime juice, water and sugar. Cook over low heat about 5 minutes, stirring occasionally, until sugar is dissolved. Cool slightly, about 5 minutes.

2) In blender or food processor, place watermelon. Cover; blend on high speed about 2 minutes or until smooth. Add lime juice mixture; blend until well mixed. Pour into ungreased 13x9-inch glass baking dish. Cover; freeze 1 hour.

3) Scrape with fork to distribute ice crystals evenly. Every 30 minutes, repeat scraping procedure for at least 3 hours until mixture is consistency of fine ice crystals. Scoop into chilled dessert cups to serve.

HIGH ALTITUDE (3500-6500 FT.): No change.

Grilled Sweet Potatoes with Orange-Ginger Butter

PREP TIME: 20 MINUTES (READY IN 20 MINUTES)
SERVINGS: 4

 EASY   LOW FAT

2 medium dark-orange sweet potatoes (8 oz each), peeled, cut in half lengthwise

¹/₄ cup water

1 tablespoon butter or margarine, melted

1 teaspoon grated orange peel

¹/₂ teaspoon grated gingerroot

¹/₄ teaspoon salt

Nutrition Information Per Serving:	
Calories: 100	From Fat: 25
Total Fat	3g
Saturated Fat	2g
Trans Fat	0g
Cholesterol	10mg
Sodium	190mg
Total Carbohydrate	16g
Dietary Fiber	2g
Sugars	5g
Protein	1g

1) Heat gas or charcoal grill. In 8- or 9-inch square glass baking dish, place sweet potatoes and water. Cover with plastic wrap, folding back one edge ¼ inch to vent steam. Microwave on High 4 to 6 minutes or just until tender; drain.

2) Meanwhile, in small bowl, mix remaining ingredients; set aside.

3) Place potatoes on grill. Cook uncovered over medium heat 3 to 5 minutes, turning frequently and brushing with butter mixture, until potatoes are tender and lightly browned.

HIGH ALTITUDE (3500-6500 FT.): No change.

Berry Ice Cream Pie

PREP TIME: 25 MINUTES (READY IN 2 HOURS 55 MINUTES)
SERVINGS: 8

FILLING

3 cups (1½ pints) vanilla ice cream

2 cups (1 pint) raspberry sherbet

1 box (10 oz) frozen raspberries in syrup, thawed

CRUST

1¼ cups vanilla wafer crumbs (41 wafers)

½ cup finely chopped pecans

¼ cup butter or margarine, melted

SAUCE

3 tablespoons sugar

1 tablespoon cornstarch

Reserved raspberry liquid

2 tablespoons orange juice

1 container (6 oz) fresh raspberries, if desired

1) Place ice cream and sherbet in refrigerator to soften. Place thawed raspberries in syrup in strainer over 2-cup glass measuring cup on counter to drain and save liquid for sauce.

2) Heat oven to 375°F. In medium bowl, mix crust ingredients; press in bottom and up side of ungreased 9-inch glass pie plate. Bake 5 to 8 minutes or until the edge just begins to brown. Cool completely, about 15 minutes.

3) Scoop 1½ cups ice cream into crust. In large bowl, fold drained raspberries into sherbet. Spoon over ice cream. Scoop remaining ice cream over top. Freeze at least 2 hours until firm.

4) Meanwhile, in 1-quart saucepan, mix the sugar and cornstarch. Stir in the reserved raspberry liquid. Cook over medium heat, stirring constantly, until mixture becomes clear and thickened. Stir in orange juice; cool at room temperature at least 10 minutes before serving. Serve individual servings of pie with sauce. If desired, garnish with fresh raspberries. Cover and store pie in freezer, sauce in refrigerator.

HIGH ALTITUDE (3500-6500 FT.): Bake 8 to 11 minutes.

Nutrition Information Per Serving:		
Calories: 390	From Fat: 180	
Total Fat		20g
Saturated Fat		9g
Trans Fat		1g
Cholesterol		40mg
Sodium		160mg
Total Carbohydrate		49g
Dietary Fiber		4g
Sugars		36g
Protein		4g

Colorful Marinated Olive Kabobs

PREP TIME:	20 MINUTES (READY IN 2 HOURS 20 MINUTES)	
SERVINGS:	36 KABOBS	e EASY f LOW FAT

MARINADE

- ¼ cup olive oil
- ¼ cup chopped fresh dill weed
- 2 thin slices orange, quartered
- 2 thin slices lemon, quartered
- 2 garlic cloves, quartered

KABOBS

- 1 cup pitted assorted olives (kalamata, niçoise, green)
- 2 yellow or orange bell peppers, cut into 1-inch squares
- 18 cherry tomatoes, halved

Cocktail picks, fresh rosemary twigs or toothpicks

1) In food-storage plastic container or resealable food-storage plastic bag, mix marinade ingredients. Add olives and bell pepper squares; cover container or seal bag. Turn to coat well with marinade. Refrigerate 2 hours or overnight, occasionally turning container or bag to coat with marinade.

2) To serve, remove olives and pepper squares from marinade; discard marinade. Arrange tomatoes, cut side down, on serving plate. Thread 1 olive and 1 pepper square onto each cocktail pick. Insert each into tomato half for base.

HIGH ALTITUDE (3500-6500 FT.): No change.

Nutrition Information Per Serving:		
Calories: 10	From Fat:	5
Total Fat		1g
Saturated Fat		0g
Trans Fat		0g
Cholesterol		0mg
Sodium		35mg
Total Carbohydrate		1g
Dietary Fiber		0g
Sugars		0g
Protein		0g

Grilled Chicken Margherita Pizzas

PREP TIME: 35 MINUTES (READY IN 35 MINUTES)
SERVINGS: 4

- 1 tablespoon olive oil
- 1 garlic clove, finely chopped
- 2 boneless skinless chicken breasts (about 8 oz)
- 1/2 teaspoon seasoned salt
- 4 Old El Paso® flour tortillas (8 inch)
- 1 1/2 cups finely shredded mozzarella cheese (6 oz)
- 2 plum (Roma) tomatoes, thinly sliced (about 10 oz)
- 1/4 cup sliced fresh basil leaves

1) Heat gas or charcoal grill. In small bowl, mix oil and garlic. Brush chicken breasts with 1 teaspoon of the oil mixture; sprinkle with seasoned salt. Place on grill over medium-high heat. Cover grill; cook 12 to 18 minutes, turning once, until juice of chicken is clear when center of thickest part is cut (170°F). Reduce heat to medium-low.

2) On ungreased cookie sheets, place tortillas. Brush with remaining oil mixture. Cut chicken into strips. Arrange chicken strips over tortillas. Sprinkle each with 1/4 cup of the cheese. Top evenly with tomato slices; sprinkle with remaining cheese and basil.

3) With wide spatula, carefully slide the pizzas onto grill over medium-low heat. Cover grill; cook 3 to 5 minutes, rotating pizzas to avoid hot spots, until cheese is melted and crusts are crisp. Slide pizzas back onto cookie sheets.

HIGH ALTITUDE (3500-6500 FT.): In Step 1, grill over medium-low heat. In Step 3, grill over low heat.

Nutrition Information Per Serving:

Calories:	370	From Fat:	160
Total Fat			18g
Saturated Fat			7g
Trans Fat			1g
Cholesterol			55mg
Sodium			730mg
Total Carbohydrate			25g
Dietary Fiber			0g
Sugars			2g
Protein			27g

Grilled Summer Vegetable Pasta

PREP TIME: 35 MINUTES (READY IN 35 MINUTES)
SERVINGS: 6 (1-1/2 CUPS EACH)

8 oz uncooked linguine

4 medium tomatoes, chopped

1/3 cup coarsely chopped fresh basil leaves

6 tablespoons olive or vegetable oil

1/2 teaspoon salt

1/4 teaspoon coarse ground black pepper

2 garlic cloves, finely chopped

1/2 eggplant, cut into 1/2-inch slices

1 medium red bell pepper, quartered

1 medium yellow summer squash, cut in half lengthwise

1 medium onion, cut into 1/2-inch slices

4 oz chèvre (goat) cheese, crumbled

1/3 cup shredded fresh Parmesan cheese

1) Heat gas or charcoal grill. In Dutch oven or 4-quart saucepan, cook the linguine to desired doneness as directed on the package.

2) Meanwhile, in large bowl, mix tomatoes, basil, 4 tablespoons of the oil, the salt and pepper; set aside.

3) In small bowl, mix the remaining 2 tablespoons oil and the garlic. In ungreased 15x10x1-inch pan, place the eggplant, bell pepper, summer squash and onion. Brush with the oil-garlic mixture.

4) Place eggplant, bell pepper, summer squash and onion pieces directly on grill over medium heat. Cover grill; cook 8 to 12 minutes, turning frequently, until vegetables are crisp-tender.

5) Coarsely chop vegetables; add to tomato mixture. Add chèvre; mix gently.

6) Drain linguine; place on serving platter. Top with vegetable mixture and Parmesan cheese.

HIGH ALTITUDE (3500-6500 FT.): No change.

Nutrition Information Per Serving:

Calories: 440	From Fat: 200
Total Fat	22g
Saturated Fat	7g
Trans Fat	0g
Cholesterol	20mg
Sodium	550mg
Total Carbohydrate	45g
Dietary Fiber	5g
Sugars	7g
Protein	14g

tip

To broil, place the vegetables on a broiler pan and broil 4 to 6 inches from heat, using the time provided in the recipe above as a guide.

Berry-Lemon Cheesecake Squares

PREP TIME: 50 MINUTES (READY IN 1 HOUR 20 MINUTES)
SERVINGS: 8

PASTRY SQUARES

- 1 box (15 oz) Pillsbury® refrigerated pie crusts, softened as directed on box
- 1 teaspoon milk
- 2 teaspoons sugar

FILLING

- ½ cup whipping cream
- 1 package (8 oz) cream cheese, softened
- ¼ cup sugar
- 1 to 2 teaspoons grated lemon peel

BERRIES

- 1 cup fresh blackberries
- ½ cup fresh raspberries
- ½ cup fresh blueberries

1) Heat oven to 450°F. Unroll crusts on lightly floured work surface. With rolling pin, roll each crust to 11½ inches in diameter. Cut 1 (8½-inch) square out of center of each round. Cut 4 squares from each large square, making 8 (4¼-inch) squares. Fold up all sides of each square ½ inch and roll inward to form thick crust edge. Brush the edges with milk; sprinkle with 2 teaspoons sugar. Place on ungreased large cookie sheet. Bake 6 to 8 minutes or until light golden brown. Cool completely, about 10 minutes.

2) Using small cookie cutters, cut shapes out of crust scraps. Place on ungreased cookie sheet. Bake 2 to 3 minutes or until lightly browned. Cool completely, about 5 minutes.

3) Meanwhile, in small bowl, beat whipping cream with electric mixer on high speed until stiff peaks form. In another small bowl, beat cream cheese, ¼ cup sugar and the lemon peel on medium speed until fluffy. Fold in whipped cream. Spoon rounded 3 tablespoons mixture into each pastry square. Arrange berries and crust cutouts over filling. Cover and refrigerate any remaining squares.

HIGH ALTITUDE (3500-6500 FT.): No change.

Nutrition Information Per Serving:	
Calories: 420	From Fat: 260
Total Fat	29g
Saturated Fat	14g
Trans Fat	0g
Cholesterol	55mg
Sodium	310mg
Total Carbohydrate	39g
Dietary Fiber	1g
Sugars	10g
Protein	3g

Fresh Berry Dessert Bites

PREP TIME: 45 MINUTES (READY IN 2 HOURS 40 MINUTES)
SERVINGS: 40 BARS

CRUST

2¼ cups all-purpose flour

⅔ cup sugar

½ teaspoon grated lemon peel

¼ teaspoon salt

1 cup butter or margarine, cut into tablespoon-size pieces

TOPPING

1 package (8 oz) cream cheese, softened

2 tablespoons packed brown sugar

1 container (6 oz) Yoplait® Original 99% Fat-Free lemon burst yogurt

1 teaspoon grated lemon peel

40 fresh raspberries (about 6½ oz)

40 fresh blackberries (8 oz)

40 fresh blueberries (about 3 oz)

1) Heat oven to 350°F. Grease or spray 15x10x1-inch pan. In large bowl, mix all crust ingredients except butter. Using pastry blender, cut in butter until the mixture looks like fine crumbs; press evenly in pan.

2) Bake 18 to 20 minutes or until the edges are light golden. Cool completely, about 40 minutes.

3) In large bowl, beat cream cheese and brown sugar with electric mixer on low speed until blended. Add yogurt and 1 teaspoon lemon peel; beat until blended. Spread mixture over crust. Refrigerate at least 1 hour but no longer than 24 hours.

4) Cut into 10 rows by 4 rows. Arrange 1 of each kind of berry on each bar. Store in refrigerator.

HIGH ALTITUDE (3500-6500 FT.): No change.

Nutrition Information Per Serving:		
Calories: 110	From Fat:	60
Total Fat		7g
Saturated Fat		4g
Trans Fat		0g
Cholesterol		20mg
Sodium		65mg
Total Carbohydrate		12g
Dietary Fiber		0g
Sugars		5g
Protein		1g

Flip-Flop Fun Cookies

| PREP TIME: | 35 MINUTES (READY IN 35 MINUTES) |
| SERVINGS: | 12 COOKIES |

 EASY

4 rectangles (1½ x 1 inch each)
   vanilla-flavored candy coating
   (almond bark; from 20-oz package)

1 roll Fruit by the Foot® chewy fruit
   snack (from 6-roll box)

12 peanut butter sandwich cookies
   (from 1-lb package)

12 miniature candy-coated chocolate
   baking bits

   Brown sugar, if desired

1) In 1-quart saucepan, melt candy coating
   over low heat, stirring occasionally.

2) Meanwhile, unroll fruit snack roll. Using
   kitchen scissors, cut 12 (4½ x ¼-inch)
   strips from fruit snack roll. Remove
   paper. Fold each strip in half, forming a
   V shape.

3) Dip tops and sides of cookies into
   melted candy coating; lift out with fork
   or tongs, letting excess drip off. Place
   cookies, coated side up, on cookie
   sheets. Before coating sets, carefully
   attach fruit snack pieces to make tops of
   flip-flop sandals, placing the point of
   V shape near one end of cookie, and
   ends at other end of cookie. Place
   baking bit at tip of V shape. Let stand
   until set, about 10 minutes.

4) Spoon brown sugar onto tray to look like
   sand; arrange cookies on brown sugar.

   HIGH ALTITUDE (3500-6500 FT.): No change.

Nutrition Information Per Serving:

Calories:	130	From Fat:	60
Total Fat			6g
Saturated Fat			3g
Trans Fat			0.5g
Cholesterol			0mg
Sodium			60mg
Total Carbohydrate			16g
Dietary Fiber			0g
Sugars			10g
Protein			1g

Personalize this
playful food for
your guests by
decorating the
flip-flop cookies
with your own
selection of candy.

Grilled Flank Steaks with Rosemary-Balsamic Glaze

PREP TIME: 25 MINUTES (READY IN 4 HOURS 25 MINUTES)
SERVINGS: 8

Ⓕ LOW FAT

2 beef flank steaks (1 lb each)

⅓ cup balsamic vinegar

2 tablespoons packed brown sugar

1 tablespoon chopped fresh or
1 teaspoon dried rosemary leaves

3 garlic cloves, finely chopped

½ teaspoon salt

½ teaspoon pepper

½ cup reduced-sodium beef broth

2 teaspoons cornstarch

1) Trim the fat from the beef flank steaks. Make cuts about ½ inch apart and ⅛ inch deep in diamond pattern on both sides of the beef. Place in shallow glass dish. In small bowl, mix the vinegar, brown sugar, rosemary, garlic, salt and pepper; pour evenly over the beef. Cover; refrigerate at least 4 hours but no longer than 24 hours, turning occasionally.

2) Heat gas or charcoal grill. Carefully brush grill rack with canola oil. Remove beef from marinade; reserve marinade. Place beef on grill over medium heat. Cover grill; cook about 12 minutes for medium doneness, turning after 6 minutes.

3) Meanwhile, in 1-quart saucepan, heat reserved marinade to boiling over medium-high heat. Boil 3 to 4 minutes or until reduced by half. In small bowl, mix broth and cornstarch; stir broth mixture into marinade. Cook about 2 minutes, stirring occasionally, until thickened.

4) Place beef on cutting board; cut diagonally into thin slices. Place slices on serving platter. Spoon sauce over beef.

HIGH ALTITUDE (3500-6500 FT.): Cook about 16 minutes for medium doneness, turning after 8 minutes.

Nutrition Information Per Serving:		
Calories: 190	From Fat:	70
Total Fat		8g
Saturated Fat		3g
Trans Fat		0g
Cholesterol		50mg
Sodium		200mg
Total Carbohydrate		5g
Dietary Fiber		0g
Sugars		4g
Protein		26g

Strawberries and Cream Tart

PREP TIME: 40 MINUTES (READY IN 1 HOUR 10 MINUTES)
SERVINGS: 10

CRUST

1 Pillsbury® refrigerated pie crust (from 15-oz box), softened as directed on box

FILLING

1 package (8 oz) cream cheese, softened

1/3 cup sugar

1/4 to 1/2 teaspoon almond extract

1 cup whipping cream, whipped

TOPPING

4 cups fresh strawberries, washed, hulled, halved

1/2 cup semisweet chocolate chips

1 tablespoon shortening

1) Heat oven to 450°F. Bake pie crust as directed on box for One-Crust Baked Shell, using 10-inch tart pan or 9-inch glass pie plate. Cool on cooling rack 15 minutes.

2) In large bowl, beat cream cheese with electric mixer on medium speed until fluffy. Gradually add sugar and almond extract; beat well. Fold in whipped cream. Spoon into crust.

3) Arrange strawberry halves over filling. Refrigerate while making drizzle. In 1-quart saucepan, melt the chocolate chips and shortening over low heat, stirring constantly, until smooth. Drizzle over the strawberries and filling. Refrigerate until set, about 30 minutes. Cover and refrigerate any remaining tart.

HIGH ALTITUDE (3500-6500 FT.): No change.

Nutrition Information Per Serving:

Calories: 350	From Fat: 220
Total Fat	25g
Saturated Fat	13g
Trans Fat	0.5g
Cholesterol	55mg
Sodium	160mg
Total Carbohydrate	28g
Dietary Fiber	1g
Sugars	15g
Protein	3g

tip For a different look, use whole strawberries and dip the pointed end of each into melted chocolate so it is half covered. Set them stem-end-down on a waxed paper-lined tray. Chill until set; arrange on top of the chilled filling.

Buffalo-Style Grilled Chicken

PREP TIME: 20 MINUTES (READY IN 2 HOURS 20 MINUTES)
SERVINGS: 4 (1 BREAST AND 1/4 CUP DRESSING MIXTURE EACH)

 EASY

1/3 cup red pepper sauce

2 teaspoons canola oil

1/2 teaspoon garlic powder

1/8 teaspoon salt

4 boneless skinless chicken breasts

1/2 cup blue cheese dressing

2 tablespoons crumbled blue cheese, if desired

1 tablespoon reduced-fat sour cream

4 medium stalks celery

1) In heavy-duty resealable food-storage plastic bag, stir pepper sauce, oil, garlic powder and salt. Add chicken, turning to coat with marinade; seal bag. Refrigerate at least 2 hours but no longer than 24 hours.

2) Heat gas or charcoal grill. Carefully brush grill rack with canola oil.

3) Remove chicken from bag. Place chicken on grill over medium-high heat. Cover grill; cook 10 to 12 minutes, turning after 5 minutes, until juice of chicken is clear when center of thickest part is cut (170°F).

4) Meanwhile, in small bowl, mix dressing, blue cheese and sour cream. Place grilled chicken on platter; serve with celery and dressing mixture.

HIGH ALTITUDE (3500-6500 FT.): Grill chicken over medium-low heat 13 to 15 minutes.

Nutrition Information Per Serving:	
Calories: 310	From Fat: 180
Total Fat	20g
Saturated Fat	3.5g
Trans Fat	0g
Cholesterol	80mg
Sodium	600mg
Total Carbohydrate	4g
Dietary Fiber	0g
Sugars	3g
Protein	29g

Country Rhubarb Crostata

PREP TIME: 20 MINUTES (READY IN 4 HOURS 20 MINUTES)
SERVINGS: 8

e EASY

CRUST

1 Pillsbury® refrigerated pie crust
  (from 15-oz box), softened as
  directed on box

FILLING

1 cup sugar

3 tablespoons all-purpose flour

$1/2$ teaspoon grated orange peel

3 eggs, slightly beaten

$1/2$ cup sour cream

$3^1/2$ cups sliced fresh or frozen rhubarb

TOPPING

$1/4$ cup sugar

$1/4$ cup all-purpose flour

2 tablespoons butter or margarine,
  softened

1) Heat oven to 375°F. Place pie crust in
   9-inch glass pie plate as directed on box
   for One-Crust Filled Pie (do not trim or
   flute crust).

2) In medium bowl, mix 1 cup sugar,
   3 tablespoons flour and the orange peel.
   Stir in eggs and sour cream. Add the
   rhubarb; toss gently. Spoon into the
   crust-lined pie plate. Fold edges of crust
   over filling, ruffling decoratively.

3) In small bowl, mix topping ingredients
   until crumbly. Sprinkle over filling.

4) Bake 50 to 60 minutes or until crust is
   light golden brown. Cool 3 hours before
   serving. Cover and refrigerate any
   remaining tart.

   HIGH ALTITUDE (3500-6500 FT.): Bake 55 to
   65 minutes.

Nutrition Information Per Serving:

Calories:	350	From Fat:	130
Total Fat		15g	
Saturated Fat		7g	
Trans Fat		0g	
Cholesterol		100mg	
Sodium		160mg	
Total Carbohydrate		51g	
Dietary Fiber		0g	
Sugars		32g	
Protein		4g	

Lemon Mini Tarts

PREP TIME: 15 MINUTES (READY IN 25 MINUTES)
SERVINGS: 16 TARTS

 EASY

1 cup milk

1 box (4-serving size) lemon instant pudding and pie filling mix

1 teaspoon grated lemon peel

1 crust from 1 box (15 oz) Pillsbury® refrigerated pie crusts

Strawberry halves, lemon slices or other fresh fruit

Fresh mint leaves

Powdered sugar, if desired

1) In medium bowl, beat milk and pudding mix 2 minutes with electric mixer at medium speed or 2 to 3 minutes with wire whisk until well blended. Stir in lemon peel. Refrigerate.

2) Allow 1 pie crust pouch to stand at room temperature 15 to 20 minutes. (Refrigerate the remaining pie crust for another use.)

3) Heat oven to 450°F. Remove pie crust from pouch. Using rolling pin, roll crust to 15-inch diameter. With lightly floured 3-inch round cutter, cut 16 rounds from crust; discard scraps. Fit rounds into 16 (2¾-inch) ungreased muffin cups, pressing in gently. Generously prick crusts with fork. Bake 5 to 7 minutes or until very light golden brown. Remove from pan; cool completely.

4) Spoon lemon filling into tart shells. Garnish with sliced fruit and mint leaves. If desired, sprinkle with powdered sugar.

HIGH ALTITUDE (3500-6500 FT.): No change.

Nutrition Information Per Serving:		
Calories: 90	From Fat:	30
Total Fat		3.5g
Saturated Fat		1.5g
Trans Fat		0g
Cholesterol		0mg
Sodium		140mg
Total Carbohydrate		14g
Dietary Fiber		0g
Sugars		7g
Protein		0g

Raspberry-Almond Puff Bites

PREP TIME: 1 HOUR (READY IN 1 HOUR 30 MINUTES)
SERVINGS: 36

1 sheet frozen puff pastry (from 17.3-oz box), thawed as directed on box

1 container (6 oz) fresh raspberries

1/3 cup powdered sugar

3/4 cup whipping cream

1/2 teaspoon almond extract

Nutrition Information Per Serving:

Calories:	60	From Fat:	40
Total Fat			4g
Saturated Fat			2g
Trans Fat			0g
Cholesterol			15mg
Sodium			20mg
Total Carbohydrate			5g
Dietary Fiber			0g
Sugars			1g
Protein			0g

1) Heat oven to 400°F. On lightly floured surface, roll the puff pastry with rolling pin into 12-inch square. Cut square into 6 rows by 6 rows to make 36 squares. On ungreased cookie sheet, place squares 1/2 inch apart.

2) Bake 10 to 12 minutes or until puffed and golden brown. Remove from cookie sheet to cooling rack. Cool completely, about 15 minutes.

3) Reserve 36 of the smallest raspberries. In small bowl, mash remaining raspberries (about 1/2 cup) with fork. Reserve 2 teaspoons of the powdered sugar. In medium bowl, beat whipping cream, remaining powdered sugar and the almond extract with electric mixer on high speed until stiff peaks form. Fold mashed raspberries into whipped cream.

4) Split each puff pastry square into 2 layers. Spread about 1/2 tablespoon of the whipped cream mixture on the bottom layers; replace tops. Top each square with tiny dollop (about 1/4 teaspoon) whipped cream mixture; add reserved raspberry. (If desired, squares can be refrigerated up to 2 hours at this point.) Just before serving, place reserved powdered sugar in small fine-mesh strainer and sift over tops of squares.

HIGH ALTITUDE (3500-6500 FT.): Bake 8 to 10 minutes.

Fall & Winter Favorites

Celebrate the season and festive occasions with these Halloween treats, Christmastime goodies and more.

BLACK CATS
PG. 228

PORK CHOPS AND APPLES
WITH STUFFING
PG. 238

CHEESY CHILI CASSEROLE
PG. 233

HOWLING WINGS
PG. 234

Creamy Candy Corn Puddings

PREP TIME: 30 MINUTES (READY IN 1 HOUR)
SERVINGS: 6

1 box (4-serving size) butterscotch instant pudding and pie filling mix

4 cups milk

20 drops red food color

45 drops yellow food color

1 box (4-serving size) banana cream instant pudding and pie mix

1 cup whipping cream, whipped

12 pieces candy corn

1) Make butterscotch pudding as directed on box, using 2 cups of the milk. Stir in 20 drops red food color and 25 drops yellow food color. Refrigerate 30 minutes. Make banana cream pudding as directed on box, using remaining 2 cups milk. Stir in remaining 20 drops yellow food color. Refrigerate until ready to use.

2) To assemble, place about ¼ cup banana cream pudding in bottom of each of 6 (8-oz) martini glasses. (Cover and refrigerate remaining banana cream pudding for another use.) Top each with about ⅓ cup butterscotch pudding and about ⅓ cup whipped cream. Garnish with candy corn.

HIGH ALTITUDE (3500-6500 FT.): No change.

Nutrition Information Per Serving:

Calories:	310	From Fat:	140
Total Fat			15g
Saturated Fat			10g
Trans Fat			0.5g
Cholesterol			55mg
Sodium			490mg
Total Carbohydrate			37g
Dietary Fiber			0g
Sugars			33g
Protein			6g

Save time by using purchased frozen whipped topping instead of making your own.

Halloween Madness Chili Bake

PREP TIME: 20 MINUTES (READY IN 40 MINUTES)
SERVINGS: 6

 EASY

1¼ lb lean (at least 90%) ground turkey

1 can (16 oz) spicy chili beans in sauce, undrained

1½ cups shredded Cheddar cheese (6 oz)

1 can (8 oz) Pillsbury® refrigerated reduced-fat crescent dinner rolls

1 tablespoon cornmeal

Nutrition Information Per Serving:	
Calories: 470	From Fat: 210
Total Fat	23g
Saturated Fat	11g
Trans Fat	1g
Cholesterol	95mg
Sodium	1100mg
Total Carbohydrate	30g
Dietary Fiber	3g
Sugars	5g
Protein	34g

1) Heat oven to 375°F. In 10-inch skillet, cook turkey over medium-high heat 7 to 9 minutes, stirring frequently, until no longer pink; drain if necessary. Stir in beans; heat until hot. Pour hot mixture into ungreased 11x7-inch or 8x8-inch (2-quart) glass baking dish. Sprinkle with cheese.

2) Unroll dough onto flat surface; firmly press perforations to seal. Using small Halloween-shaped cutter, cut shape out of center of dough. Place dough sheet evenly over top (for 8x8-inch dish, fold under the short sides to fit). Sprinkle cornmeal all over dough, except on cutout area.

3) Bake 18 to 20 minutes or until golden brown.

HIGH ALTITUDE (3500-6500 FT.): No change.

Fresh Pear Crostata

PREP TIME: 25 MINUTES (READY IN 1 HOUR)
SERVINGS: 8

 EASY

½ cup sugar

3 tablespoons all-purpose flour

4 cups chopped peeled ripe pears (8 to 9 medium)

1 Pillsbury® refrigerated pie crust (from 15-oz box), softened as directed on box

1 teaspoon sugar

2 tablespoons sliced almonds

1) Heat oven to 450°F. In medium bowl, mix ½ cup sugar and the flour. Gently stir in pears to coat. Unroll pie crust into ungreased 15x10x1-inch pan.

2) Spoon the pear mixture onto the center of crust to within 2 inches of edge. Carefully fold 2-inch edge of crust up over the pear mixture, pleating crust slightly as necessary. Sprinkle 1 teaspoon sugar over crust edge.

Nutrition Information Per Serving:	
Calories: 240	From Fat: 70
Total Fat	8g
Saturated Fat	2.5g
Trans Fat	0g
Cholesterol	0mg
Sodium	110mg
Total Carbohydrate	41g
Dietary Fiber	3g
Sugars	21g
Protein	0g

3) Bake 14 to 20 minutes, sprinkling almonds over pear mixture during last 5 minutes of bake time, until pears are tender and crust is golden brown. Cool 15 minutes. Cut into wedges; serve warm. Cover and refrigerate any remaining tart.

HIGH ALTITUDE (3500-6500 FT.): Bake 20 to 26 minutes.

Black Cats

PREP TIME: 20 MINUTES (READY IN 20 MINUTES)
SERVINGS: 4

 EASY

3 strands pull-apart black licorice twists

1 can (6.4 oz) black decorating icing

4 individually wrapped chocolate-covered créme-filled cake rolls (from 10-oz box)

4 pieces black gumdrops, cut in half crosswise

12 miniature candy-coated chocolate baking bits

1) Cut the licorice strands into 24 (½-inch) pieces for whiskers and 4 (4-inch) pieces for tails.

2) Using icing to secure the candies, make face on top of each cake roll. Use black gumdrops for ears, baking bits for eyes and nose, and licorice for whiskers. Poke licorice in back end of each for tail.

3) Let stand 5 minutes to set.

HIGH ALTITUDE (3500-6500 FT.): No change.

Nutrition Information Per Serving:

Calories:	300	From Fat:	110
Total Fat			12g
Saturated Fat			5g
Trans Fat			1g
Cholesterol			10mg
Sodium			140mg
Total Carbohydrate			47g
Dietary Fiber			0g
Sugars			37g
Protein			2g

Feel free to let your imagination run wild and customize your cats using your choice of candy decorations...or create your own creature entirely.

Scarecrow Tostadas

PREP TIME: 45 MINUTES (READY IN 45 MINUTES)
SERVINGS: 6

- 1 lb lean (at least 80%) ground beef
- 1 can (16 oz) Old El Paso® vegetarian refried beans
- 2 teaspoons ground cumin
- ½ teaspoon garlic salt
- 6 Old El Paso® tostada shells (from 4.5-oz box)
- 6 ready-to-eat baby-cut carrots
- 6 red bell pepper slices
- 12 cherry tomatoes
- About 3 teaspoons sour cream
- 12 ripe olive slices
- 1½ cups finely shredded Mexican or taco-seasoned cheese blend (6 oz)
- 1½ cups chopped leaf lettuce
- 6 triangle-shaped tortilla chips (about 3 inch)

1) In 10-inch skillet, cook beef over medium-high heat 5 to 7 minutes, stirring frequently, until thoroughly cooked; drain. Add beans, cumin and garlic salt. Reduce heat to low; cook 3 to 4 minutes, stirring occasionally, until hot.

2) Meanwhile, heat tostada shells as directed on box.

3) To assemble tostadas, spread ½ cup beef mixture onto each tostada shell. Place carrots in center of each for nose, pepper slice for mouth and 2 tomatoes for eyes. Spoon ¼ teaspoon sour cream on each tomato eye; top with the ripe olive slices. Sprinkle ¼ cup cheese and ¼ cup lettuce around top edge of each tostada. Place tortilla chip on top of each tostada for hat. Serve immediately.

HIGH ALTITUDE (3500-6500 FT.): No change.

Nutrition Information Per Serving:

Calories:	440	From Fat:	230
Total Fat		25g	
Saturated Fat		11g	
Trans Fat		2g	
Cholesterol		85mg	
Sodium		1140mg	
Total Carbohydrate		26g	
Dietary Fiber		6g	
Sugars		3g	
Protein		26g	

Confetti Popcorn Bars

PREP TIME: 15 MINUTES (READY IN 15 MINUTES)
SERVINGS: 16 BARS

 EASY

1 bag (3.5 oz) Pop•Secret® microwave popcorn, popped

½ cup small gumdrops

⅓ cup unsalted peanuts

2 cups miniature marshmallows

3 tablespoons butter or margarine

Nutrition Information Per Serving:		
Calories: 120	From Fat:	50
Total Fat		6g
Saturated Fat		2g
Trans Fat		0.5g
Cholesterol		5mg
Sodium		25mg
Total Carbohydrate		14g
Dietary Fiber		0g
Sugars		7g
Protein		2g

1) Grease 8- or 9-inch square pan. Remove any unpopped kernels from the popcorn. In large greased bowl, mix the popcorn, gumdrops and peanuts.

2) In 4-cup microwavable measuring cup, microwave marshmallows and butter uncovered on High 1½ to 2 minutes or until melted and smooth, stirring once halfway through microwave time. Pour marshmallow mixture over popcorn mixture; toss until evenly coated.

3) With buttered hands, press mixture in pan. Refrigerate until firm. For bars, cut into 4 rows by 4 rows.

HIGH ALTITUDE (3500-6500 FT.): No change.

Spooky Berry Shakes

PREP TIME: 15 MINUTES (READY IN 15 MINUTES)
SERVINGS: 4 SHAKES

 EASY

1 tablespoon white vanilla baking chips

¼ teaspoon vegetable oil

2 drops green food color

4 clear plastic cups (8- to 9-oz size)

2 cups vanilla ice cream (about 4 scoops)

1 cup frozen blueberries

1 cup frozen raspberries

2 cups milk

Nutrition Information Per Serving:		
Calories: 330	From Fat:	110
Total Fat		12g
Saturated Fat		7g
Trans Fat		0g
Cholesterol		40mg
Sodium		115mg
Total Carbohydrate		48g
Dietary Fiber		5g
Sugars		39g
Protein		7g

1) In small microwavable bowl, microwave vanilla chips and oil uncovered on High about 1 minute or until chips can be stirred smooth. Stir in green food color. With tip of knife, spread on inside of each cup to look like eyes and mouth.

2) In blender, place remaining ingredients. Cover; blend until smooth. Pour into cups. Serve immediately.

HIGH ALTITUDE (3500-6500 FT.): No change.

Chicken Enchilada Mummies

PREP TIME: 30 MINUTES (READY IN 1 HOUR 20 MINUTES)
SERVINGS: 12 ENCHILADAS

2 teaspoons vegetable oil

6 boneless, skinless chicken breasts (about 2½ lb), cut into 1-inch pieces

1 medium onion, chopped (½ cup)

1 teaspoon ground cumin

1 teaspoon garlic salt

½ teaspoon dried oregano leaves

1½ cups sour cream

¾ cup chopped roasted red bell peppers (from a jar)

1 can (4.5 oz) Old El Paso® chopped green chiles

3 cups finely shredded Mexican cheese blend (12 oz)

12 Old El Paso® flour tortillas (8 inch)

2 cans (10 oz each) Old El Paso® enchilada sauce

1) Heat oven to 350°F. Spray 13x9-inch (3-quart) and 8x8-inch (2-quart) baking dishes with cooking spray.

2) In 12-inch skillet, heat the oil over medium-high heat. Add chicken and onion; cook and stir 4 to 5 minutes or until chicken is no longer pink in center. Stir in cumin, garlic salt and oregano. Cook 1 minute longer; drain if necessary. Pour chicken mixture into large bowl.

3) Reserve 2 tablespoons sour cream in small bowl; refrigerate. Into bowl of chicken mixture, stir remaining sour cream, roasted peppers, chiles and 1½ cups of the cheese blend.

4) Spread heaping ¾ cup chicken mixture in the center of each tortilla. Roll up tortillas; arrange 8 seam-side down in 13x9-inch baking dish and 4 seam-side down in 8x8-inch baking dish.

5) Top each baking dish evenly with enchilada sauce. Sprinkle with remaining 1½ cups cheese. Spray 2 sheets of foil with cooking spray; cover each baking dish with foil, sprayed side down.

6) Bake about 50 minutes or until enchiladas are hot. Place the reserved 2 tablespoons sour cream in small resealable food-storage plastic bag. Seal bag; cut off 1 corner of bag. Squeeze bag to pipe eyes and mouth on each mummy.

HIGH ALTITUDE (3500-6500 FT.): Heat oven to 375°F.

Nutrition Information Per Serving:	
Calories: 390	From Fat: 190
Total Fat	21g
Saturated Fat	10g
Trans Fat	1g
Cholesterol	105mg
Sodium	880mg
Total Carbohydrate	19g
Dietary Fiber	1g
Sugars	4g
Protein	30g

Cheesy Crescent Ghosts

PREP TIME: 20 MINUTES (READY IN 30 MINUTES)
SERVINGS: 16 APPETIZERS

 EASY   LOW FAT

1 can (8 oz) Pillsbury® refrigerated crescent dinner rolls

1 cup shredded mozzarella cheese or Colby-Monterey Jack cheese blend (4 oz)

Assorted sliced olives, as desired

1) Heat oven to 375°F. Spray large cookie sheet with cooking spray, or cover with cooking parchment paper.

2) On cutting board, unroll dough; separate into 8 triangles. From center of longest side to opposite point, cut each triangle in half, making 16 triangles. Shape each as needed to look like ghost shape. Arrange the triangles on cookie sheet, folding the narrow point under about ½ inch to form head of ghost.

3) Bake about 7 minutes or until slightly puffed and just beginning to brown. Sprinkle each ghost with 1 tablespoon cheese; top with sliced olives to form mouth and eyes. Bake 2 to 3 minutes longer or until cheese is melted.

HIGH ALTITUDE (3500-6500 FT.): No change.

Nutrition Information Per Serving:

Calories:	45	From Fat:	25
Total Fat			2.5g
Saturated Fat			1g
Trans Fat			0g
Cholesterol			0mg
Sodium			90mg
Total Carbohydrate			4g
Dietary Fiber			0g
Sugars			0g
Protein			2g

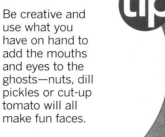

tip

Be creative and use what you have on hand to add the mouths and eyes to the ghosts—nuts, dill pickles or cut-up tomato will all make fun faces.

Cheesy Chili Casserole

PREP TIME: 45 MINUTES (READY IN 45 MINUTES)
SERVINGS: 8 (ABOUT 1-1/4 CUPS EACH)

1½ cups uncooked regular long-grain white rice

2½ cups water

1 lb lean (at least 80%) ground beef

½ cup chopped onion

1 small green bell pepper, seeded and diced

2 garlic cloves, finely chopped

½ cup water

1 can (28 oz) diced tomatoes

1 can (15 oz) Progresso® dark red kidney beans, drained, rinsed

1 cup (4 oz) cubed Mexican prepared cheese product with jalapeño peppers (from a loaf)

1 tablespoon chili powder

1 teaspoon ground cumin

½ teaspoon salt

3 tablespoons chopped fresh cilantro

Tortilla chips, as desired

1) Cook rice as directed on package, using 2½ cups water.

2) In 12-inch skillet, cook the beef over medium-high heat 5 to 7 minutes, stirring frequently, until thoroughly cooked; drain. Stir in onion, bell pepper, garlic, ½ cup water, the tomatoes and beans; cook about 6 minutes, stirring occasionally, until onion and bell pepper are tender. Stir in cheese product until melted. Stir in chili powder, cumin and salt. Cook 3 minutes longer.

3) Just before serving, gently stir in cooked rice and cilantro. Garnish with additional chopped cilantro, if desired. Serve warm with tortilla chips.

HIGH ALTITUDE (3500-6500 FT.): Increase second cook time to 8 minutes on medium. After adding spices, continue cooking on medium 3 minutes longer.

Nutrition Information Per Serving:	
Calories: 590	From Fat: 150
Total Fat	17g
Saturated Fat	7g
Trans Fat	1g
Cholesterol	75mg
Sodium	1490mg
Total Carbohydrate	77g
Dietary Fiber	8g
Sugars	8g
Protein	32g

Howling Wings

PREP TIME: 1 HOUR (READY IN 5 HOURS)
SERVINGS: 30 DRUMMETTES

 EASY   LOW FAT

30 chicken wing drummettes (about 3 lb)

1 can (7 oz) chipotle chiles in adobo sauce, chopped

1 cup zesty Italian dressing

1 jar (12 to 17 oz) caramel topping (³⁄₄ to 1 cup)

Nutrition Information Per Serving:

Calories:	80	From Fat:	20
Total Fat			2g
Saturated Fat			0g
Trans Fat			0g
Cholesterol			20mg
Sodium			160mg
Total Carbohydrate			8g
Dietary Fiber			0g
Sugars			6g
Protein			6g

1) Cut off excess skin from each drummette; discard. Place drummettes in large resealable food-storage plastic bag. Add chopped chipotle chiles with adobo sauce and Italian dressing; seal bag. Turn bag to mix the ingredients and coat the drummettes. Refrigerate at least 4 hours but no longer than 24 hours, turning bag occasionally.

2) Heat oven to 425°F. Place sheet of foil in bottom of broiler pan. Arrange drummettes on foil. Bake 15 minutes; drain if necessary. Meanwhile, to make sauce, transfer the marinade from bag to 2-quart saucepan; stir in caramel topping. Heat to boiling over medium-high heat; reduce heat to medium-low and simmer.

3) Reduce oven temperature to 375°F; brush the drummettes with sauce and bake about 30 minutes longer, brushing every 15 minutes with sauce, until browned and juice is clear when thickest part is cut to bone (180°F). Serve drummettes with sauce.

HIGH ALTITUDE (3500-6500 FT.): No change.

Monster Munch

PREP TIME: 20 MINUTES (READY IN 35 MINUTES)
SERVINGS: 9 (1 CUP EACH)

 EASY

4 cups Chex® cereal

4 cups popped Pop•Secret® microwave popcorn

1 cup honey-roasted cashews

1 cup roasted salted pumpkin seeds

¼ cup butter or margarine

6 tablespoons packed brown sugar

2 tablespoons light corn syrup

¼ teaspoon vanilla

¼ teaspoon pumpkin pie spice

1 cup candy corn

1) In 4-quart microwavable bowl, mix cereal, popcorn, cashews and pumpkin seeds; set aside.

2) In medium microwavable bowl, microwave butter, brown sugar, corn syrup and vanilla uncovered on High about 2 minutes or until mixture is boiling, stirring after 1 minute; stir in pumpkin pie spice. Pour over the cereal mixture, stirring until evenly coated.

3) Microwave 5 to 6 minutes, stirring and scraping bowl after every minute. Spread on waxed paper to cool, about 15 minutes, stirring occasionally to break up.

4) Stir in candy corn. Store in airtight container.

HIGH ALTITUDE (3500-6500 FT.): No change.

Nutrition Information Per Serving:

Calories:	510	From Fat:	230
Total Fat			26g
Saturated Fat			7g
Trans Fat			0.5g
Cholesterol			15mg
Sodium			430mg
Total Carbohydrate			57g
Dietary Fiber			2g
Sugars			34g
Protein			12g

Wormy Apple Bars

PREP TIME: 10 MINUTES (READY IN 1 HOUR)
SERVINGS: 12 BARS

EASY

1¼ cups all-purpose flour

⅓ cup packed brown sugar

½ cup butter or margarine, softened

1 can (21 oz) apple pie filling

⅓ cup granulated sugar

1 teaspoon ground cinnamon

1 box (15 oz) Pillsbury® refrigerated pie crusts

1) Heat oven to 425°F (400°F for dark or nonstick pan). In large bowl, beat the flour, brown sugar and butter with electric mixer on medium speed until well blended. Press mixture in bottom of ungreased 13x9-inch pan.

2) Spoon and spread filling over crust. Bake 10 minutes.

3) Meanwhile, in large bowl, mix granulated sugar and cinnamon. Cut 1 cold rolled crust lengthwise in half (keep the remaining crust refrigerated). Cut into ¼-inch slices. Repeat with remaining crust. Separate pieces and toss with sugar mixture. Sprinkle cut-up crust mixture evenly over filling.

4) Bake 18 to 22 minutes or until crust is golden brown. Cool completely, about 30 minutes. For bars, cut into 4 rows by 3 rows. Cover and refrigerate any remaining bars.

HIGH ALTITUDE (3500-6500 FT.): Bake 22 to 26 minutes.

Nutrition Information Per Serving:

Calories:	370	From Fat:	150
Total Fat			17g
Saturated Fat			8g
Trans Fat			0g
Cholesterol			25mg
Sodium			200mg
Total Carbohydrate			52g
Dietary Fiber			1g
Sugars			23g
Protein			2g

"Devilicious" Eggs

PREP TIME:	30 MINUTES (READY IN 30 MINUTES)
SERVINGS:	12

 EASY

6 eggs

Assorted cut-up herbs, olives, baby-cut carrots, bell pepper, green onion and other vegetables of choice, as desired

¼ cup mayonnaise or salad dressing

2 teaspoons Dijon mustard

Paprika, as desired

1) In 3-quart saucepan, place eggs in single layer; add enough cold water to cover eggs by 1 inch. Cover; heat to boiling. Remove from heat; let stand covered 15 minutes. While eggs stand, cut assorted herbs and vegetables for decorating. Drain eggs; immediately place in cold water with ice cubes, or run cold water over eggs until completely cooled. To remove shell, crackle it by tapping gently all over; roll between hands to loosen. Peel, starting at large end.

2) Cut each egg lengthwise in half. Slip out yolks into small bowl; mash with fork.

3) Stir mayonnaise and mustard into yolks. Fill the whites with egg yolk mixture, heaping it lightly.

4) Sprinkle with paprika and garnish with desired herbs and vegetables to make faces. Cover loosely and refrigerate up to 24 hours.

HIGH ALTITUDE (3500-6500 FT.): Place eggs in saucepan. Add enough water to cover eggs by 1 inch. Add a pinch of salt. After heating salt water to boiling, boil 5 minutes. Remove from heat, cover and let stand 15 minutes. Drain; rinse with cold water.

Nutrition Information Per Serving:

Calories:	70	From Fat:	60
Total Fat			6g
Saturated Fat			1.5g
Trans Fat			0g
Cholesterol			110mg
Sodium			80mg
Total Carbohydrate			0g
Dietary Fiber			0g
Sugars			0g
Protein			3g

Cheese-Filled Jack-o'-Lantern

PREP TIME: 40 MINUTES (READY IN 1 HOUR 35 MINUTES)
SERVINGS: 28 SLICES (1/2 INCH EACH)

1 block 8 oz Colby cheese

6 tablespoons butter or margarine, melted

1/2 teaspoon garlic powder

3 cans (12 oz each) Pillsbury® Golden Layers® refrigerated flaky original biscuits

7 slices (1/2 oz each) American cheese

1 red or orange bell pepper

1 green bell pepper, cut into strips

1) Heat oven to 350°F. Heavily grease 12-cup fluted tube cake pan with shortening.

2) Cut Colby cheese into 30 one-inch cubes. Mix melted butter and garlic powder in small bowl.

3) Using 1 can at a time, wrap 1 biscuit around 1 cube of Colby cheese, forming ball shape, pinching tightly to seal. Dip entire ball into garlic butter. Place in pan; continue with remaining biscuits.

4) Bake 35 to 40 minutes or until top is golden brown. Immediately turn pan upside down onto heatproof serving plate. Top with American cheese slices; cover with pan. Let stand 10 to 15 minutes or until cheese is melted.

5) Cut eyes, nose and mouth from red bell pepper; place on cheese to make jack-o'-lantern face. Place small glass in center opening of jack-o'-lantern; fill glass with bell pepper strips. Slice to serve, or pull apart.

HIGH ALTITUDE (3500-6500 FT.): Bake 40 to 45 minutes.

Nutrition Information Per Serving:	
Calories: 180	From Fat: 100
Total Fat	11g
Saturated Fat	5g
Trans Fat	2g
Cholesterol	20mg
Sodium	500mg
Total Carbohydrate	15g
Dietary Fiber	0g
Sugars	2g
Protein	5g

R.I.P. Banana PB&J Sandwiches

PREP TIME: 30 MINUTES (READY IN 30 MINUTES)
SERVINGS: 8

 EASY

16 slices bread

9 tablespoons creamy peanut butter

9 teaspoons grape jelly

1 small banana, cut into 24 slices

1) Place 1 piece of bread on top of another. Cut 4-inch by 2½-inch casket shape from the longest part of the bread slices. Cut ½ inch off both corners of the top of bread slice. Repeat with the remaining bread slices for 8 caskets.

2) Separate bread slices. Spread 1 tablespoon peanut butter on bottom slice of each. Top with 1 teaspoon jelly, 3 banana slices and top slice of bread.

3) Place remaining tablespoon peanut butter and teaspoon jelly in small resealable food-storage plastic bag. Seal bag; gently knead to mix peanut butter and jelly. Cut ⅛ inch off 1 corner of bag. Pipe RIP (rest in peace) on each casket sandwich. Cover and refrigerate until ready to serve.

HIGH ALTITUDE (3500-6500 FT.): No change.

Nutrition Information Per Serving:		
Calories: 280	From Fat: 100	
Total Fat		11g
Saturated Fat		2g
Trans Fat		0g
Cholesterol		0mg
Sodium		430mg
Total Carbohydrate		37g
Dietary Fiber		2g
Sugars		9g
Protein		9g

Pork Chops and Apples with Stuffing

PREP TIME: 15 MINUTES (READY IN 1 HOUR 10 MINUTES)
SERVINGS: 4

 EASY

3 cups herb-seasoned stuffing cubes

1 jar (12 oz) pork gravy

1 medium onion, cut into ⅛-inch slices

4 bone-in pork loin chops, ½ inch thick (about 1½ lb)

1 medium red apple, sliced

Nutrition Information Per Serving:		
Calories: 430	From Fat: 120	
Total Fat		13g
Saturated Fat		4.5g
Trans Fat		0g
Cholesterol		80mg
Sodium		1120mg
Total Carbohydrate		45g
Dietary Fiber		4g
Sugars		7g
Protein		35g

1) Heat oven to 375°F. Spray 12x8- or 13x9-inch (3-quart) glass baking dish with cooking spray. Place stuffing cubes in dish; stir in gravy.

2) Top with onion, pork chops and apple. Cover with foil.

3) Bake 40 minutes. Uncover; bake 10 to 15 minutes longer or until pork is no longer pink in center.

HIGH ALTITUDE (3500-6500 FT.): No change.

Brownie Pumpkin Cheesecake

PREP TIME:	15 MINUTES (READY IN 4 HOURS 10 MINUTES)
SERVINGS:	12

 EASY

BROWNIE BASE

- 1 box (1 lb 3.9 oz) dark chocolate fudge brownie mix

  Water, vegetable oil and eggs called for on brownie mix box

FILLING

- 2 packages (8 oz each) cream cheese, softened
- ½ cup sugar
- ½ cup canned pumpkin (not pumpkin pie mix)
- 2 eggs
- ½ teaspoon vanilla
- ½ teaspoon pumpkin pie spice
- ½ cup semisweet chocolate chips, melted

1) Heat oven to 350°F. Spray 10-inch springform pan with cooking spray. Make brownie batter as directed on box for basic recipe; spread in pan. Bake 28 to 30 minutes or until toothpick inserted 2 inches from side of pan comes out almost clean.

2) Meanwhile, in large bowl, beat cream cheese and sugar with electric mixer on medium speed until smooth and creamy. Beat in pumpkin until well blended. On low speed, beat in eggs 1 at a time, just until combined. Stir in vanilla and pumpkin pie spice. Reserve ½ cup filling in small bowl. Pour remaining filling over baked brownie base.

3) Stir the melted chocolate chips into reserved filling; place chocolate in large resealable food-storage plastic bag. Seal the bag; cut off 1 corner of bag. Squeeze bag to pipe jack-o'-lantern face on cheesecake.

4) Bake 40 to 45 minutes or until center is almost set. Cool 30 minutes. Run knife around edge of pan to loosen cheesecake. Cool 30 minutes longer. Refrigerate at least 2 hours before serving. Cover and refrigerate any remaining cheesecake.

HIGH ALTITUDE (3500-6500 FT.): Follow High Altitude brownie mix directions for batter. In Step 1, bake brownie about 35 minutes.

Nutrition Information Per Serving:

Calories:	510	From Fat:	260
Total Fat			29g
Saturated Fat			11g
Trans Fat			0g
Cholesterol			110mg
Sodium			290mg
Total Carbohydrate			55g
Dietary Fiber			2g
Sugars			40g
Protein			7g

Pumpkin Cheese Tart

PREP TIME: 40 MINUTES (READY IN 1 HOUR 20 MINUTES)
SERVINGS: 10

CRUST

1/3 cup quick-cooking oats, ground, if desired

1 cup gingersnap cookie crumbs (about 20 cookies)

3 tablespoons butter or margarine, melted

1/4 teaspoon ground cinnamon

CREAM CHEESE FILLING

2 containers (8 oz each) reduced-fat cream cheese

1/3 cup granulated sugar

2 tablespoons fat-free (skim) milk

1 tablespoon all-purpose flour

1/2 teaspoon vanilla

1 egg

PUMPKIN FILLING

1 cup canned pumpkin (not pumpkin pie mix)

1/3 cup packed brown sugar

1/2 teaspoon pumpkin pie spice

CARAMEL SAUCE

1/2 cup packed brown sugar

1/4 cup fat-free (skim) milk

1/4 cup corn syrup

2 tablespoons water

1 tablespoon butter or margarine

1/4 teaspoon vanilla

1) Heat oven to 375°F. Spray 10-inch tart pan with removable bottom with cooking spray. In small bowl, mix the crust ingredients. Press in bottom and up side of pan. Bake 6 to 8 minutes or until set; set aside.

2) In large bowl, beat the cream cheese filling ingredients with electric mixer on medium speed until smooth and creamy. Reserve 2/3 cup cream cheese filling; set aside.

3) In small bowl, mix pumpkin filling ingredients. Add to remaining cream cheese filling; mix well. Spoon into crust. Spoon dollops of reserved cream cheese filling randomly over pumpkin filling. Swirl with knife to marble mixtures. Bake 25 to 30 minutes or until set. Cool 10 minutes. Remove side of pan. Serve warm, or cool 1 hour and refrigerate until serving time.

4) Just before serving, in 1-quart saucepan, heat caramel sauce ingredients to boiling over medium heat, stirring constantly. Boil 1 minute. Remove from heat. Serve warm over tart. Cover and refrigerate any remaining tart.

HIGH ALTITUDE (3500-6500 FT.): No change.

Nutrition Information Per Serving:		
Calories: 370	From Fat:	160
Total Fat		17g
Saturated Fat		10g
Trans Fat		1g
Cholesterol		70mg
Sodium		310mg
Total Carbohydrate		47g
Dietary Fiber		1g
Sugars		35g
Protein		7g

Halloween Marsh-Monsters

PREP TIME:	25 MINUTES (READY IN 25 MINUTES)
SERVINGS:	8 SNACKS

 EASY   LOW FAT

8 thick pretzel rods

8 large marshmallows

Candy corn, miniature candy-coated chocolate baking bits, string licorice, Bugles® corn snacks, gummy peach rings, fruit snacks, candy sprinkles, as desired

1 container (1 lb) vanilla creamy ready-to-spread frosting

Assorted food colors

For best results, work with one color at a time so the frosting does not set. If you like, use chocolate frosting for the cats.

1) Gently push 1 pretzel into 1 flat side of each marshmallow; set aside. Plan and assemble the decorations for each marshmallow.

2) In 1-cup microwavable measuring cup, microwave ½ cup frosting uncovered on High 10 to 20 seconds or until smooth and melted when stirred. Add 1 to 2 drops food color as desired—green for witches or Frankenstein, red for devils and yellow for pumpkins or cats.

3) Dip and decorate 1 marshmallow at a time. Hold the pretzel and dip the marshmallow into frosting to coat all sides. Immediately add decorations to create features—candy corn for noses, baking bits for eyes and licorice for whiskers. To make witch's hat, push corn snack through center of peach ring. For devil's or witch's cape, use fruit snack cut in half crosswise at an angle; attach at base of marshmallow while frosting is soft. Set pretzels in drinking glass to dry before storing. Store in airtight container.

HIGH ALTITUDE (3500-6500 FT.): No change.

Nutrition Information Per Serving:

Calories:	80	From Fat:	0
Total Fat			0g
Saturated Fat			0g
Trans Fat			0g
Cholesterol			0mg
Sodium			200mg
Total Carbohydrate			17g
Dietary Fiber			0g
Sugars			4g
Protein			2g

Peanutty Halloween Cookie Pizza

PREP TIME: 15 MINUTES (READY IN 1 HOUR 5 MINUTES)
SERVINGS: 16

e EASY

1 roll (16.5 oz) Pillsbury® Create 'n Bake® refrigerated chocolate chip cookies

½ cup creamy peanut butter

1 cup Halloween-colored candy-coated chocolate candies

½ cup dry-roasted peanuts

¼ cup vanilla creamy ready-to-spread frosting (from 1-lb container)

1) Heat oven to 350°F. Line 12-inch pizza pan with foil; grease foil with shortening. Break cookie dough into 2-inch pieces; arrange evenly in pan. With floured fingers, press to form crust.

2) Bake 16 to 18 minutes or until deep golden brown. Cool completely, about 30 minutes.

3) Use foil to lift crust from pan. Carefully remove foil from crust; place crust on serving platter or tray. Spread peanut butter over crust. Sprinkle with chocolate candies and peanuts.

4) In small microwavable bowl, microwave the frosting uncovered on High 10 to 15 seconds or until thin enough to drizzle. Transfer to small resealable food-storage plastic bag. Cut small hole in 1 corner of bag; drizzle over cookie pizza. Cut into wedges or squares.

HIGH ALTITUDE (3500-6500 FT.): No change.

Nutrition Information Per Serving:

Calories:	280	From Fat:	130
Total Fat			15g
Saturated Fat			4.5g
Trans Fat			1.5g
Cholesterol			5mg
Sodium			180mg
Total Carbohydrate			32g
Dietary Fiber			1g
Sugars			22g
Protein			5g

Game Day Chili

PREP TIME: 2 HOURS 10 MINUTES (READY IN 2 HOURS 10 MINUTES)
SERVINGS: 10 (1-1/4 CUPS EACH)

1 tablespoon vegetable oil

2 lb beef stew meat, cut into ¾-inch cubes

4 medium garlic cloves, finely chopped

1 package (1⅜ oz) Old El Paso® chili seasoning mix

1 can (28 oz) Progresso® crushed tomatoes, undrained

1 can (14 oz) beef broth

1 can or bottle (12 oz) beer or beef broth

1 can (6 oz) tomato paste

2 cans (15 oz each) spicy chili beans in sauce, undrained

1 cup sour cream

1 cup shredded Cheddar cheese (4 oz)

1) In 5-quart Dutch oven or saucepan, heat oil over medium-high heat until hot. Add the beef stew meat and garlic; cook, stirring occasionally, until beef is browned. Stir in the chili seasoning mix. Stir in the tomatoes, beef broth, beer and tomato paste. Heat to boiling. Reduce heat to low; cover and simmer 2 hours, stirring once halfway through cooking.

2) About 15 minutes before serving, stir in the beans. Cook 10 to 15 minutes longer or until beans are hot. Top individual servings with sour cream and cheese.

HIGH ALTITUDE (3500-6500 FT.): No change.

Nutrition Information Per Serving:		
Calories: 400	From Fat: 190	
Total Fat		22g
Saturated Fat		10g
Trans Fat		0.5g
Cholesterol		80mg
Sodium		1270mg
Total Carbohydrate		24g
Dietary Fiber		6g
Sugars		8g
Protein		27g

Golden Cornbread

PREP TIME: 10 MINUTES (READY IN 35 MINUTES)
SERVINGS: 6 TO 8

 EASY

2 eggs, slightly beaten

1 cup milk

¼ cup vegetable oil or melted shortening

1½ cups yellow cornmeal

1 cup all-purpose flour

¼ cup sugar

2¼ teaspoons baking powder

¾ teaspoon salt

Nutrition Information Per Serving:		
Calories: 360	From Fat: 110	
Total Fat		12g
Saturated Fat		2.5g
Trans Fat		0g
Cholesterol		75mg
Sodium		520mg
Total Carbohydrate		54g
Dietary Fiber		2g
Sugars		11g
Protein		9g

1) Heat oven to 450°F. Grease or spray 8- or 9-inch square pan.

2) In large bowl, mix all ingredients. Pour into pan.

3) Bake 20 to 25 minutes or until toothpick inserted in center comes out clean. Serve warm if desired.

HIGH ALTITUDE (3500-6500 FT.): Decrease baking powder to 1-3/4 teaspoons.

Witches' Brew Punch

PREP TIME: 10 MINUTES (READY IN 4 HOURS 10 MINUTES)
SERVINGS: 12 (1 CUP EACH)

 EASY   LOW FAT

ICE RING

6 packages (.09 oz each) chewy fruit flavored snacks

2 plastic gloves

Cold water

PUNCH

1 cup boiling water

1 box (4-serving size) orange-flavored gelatin

1 can (46 oz) pineapple juice, chilled

1 quart (4 cups) apple cider, chilled

¼ cup lemon juice

1 bottle (33.8 oz) ginger ale, chilled

1) Place 3 packages of fruit snacks in each plastic glove. Pour cold water over fruit snacks, filling to within 1 inch of top; tie end of each glove. Freeze until solid, 4 to 5 hours.

2) In 3-quart pitcher or bowl, pour boiling water on the gelatin; stir until gelatin is dissolved. Stir in the pineapple juice, apple cider and lemon juice. Cover and refrigerate.

3) Just before serving, peel off the gloves; place hands in punch bowl, fruit snack side up.

4) Pour punch into punch bowl over hands. Gently stir in ginger ale.

HIGH ALTITUDE (3500-6500 FT.): No change.

Nutrition Information Per Serving:

Calories:	190	From Fat:	0
Total Fat		0g	
Saturated Fat		0g	
Trans Fat		0g	
Cholesterol		0mg	
Sodium		60mg	
Total Carbohydrate		47g	
Dietary Fiber		0g	
Sugars		38g	
Protein		1g	

Banana Split Bark

PREP TIME: 40 MINUTES (READY IN 1 HOUR 10 MINUTES)
SERVINGS: ABOUT 40 (1-1/2X1-1/2-INCH) PIECES

 EASY

16 oz chocolate-flavored candy coating, chopped

 2 dried pineapple rings, coarsely chopped ($\frac{1}{2}$ cup)

$\frac{3}{4}$ cup dried sweetened banana chips, broken into large pieces

$\frac{1}{2}$ cup chopped pecans, toasted

$\frac{1}{3}$ cup dried cherries

$\frac{1}{2}$ cup white vanilla baking chips

To toast pecans, sprinkle them in an ungreased heavy skillet. Cook them over medium heat 5 to 7 minutes, stirring frequently until the nuts begin to brown, then stirring constantly until they are light brown.

1) Line large cookie sheet with waxed paper. In 2-quart saucepan, melt candy coating over low heat, stirring constantly.

2) In medium bowl, mix pineapple, banana chips, pecans and cherries; reserve $\frac{1}{2}$ cup. Add remaining fruit mixture to melted candy coating; toss to coat. Cool 5 minutes at room temperature. Gently fold in baking chips. Spread mixture evenly into 12x9-inch rectangle on waxed paper-lined cookie sheet; sprinkle with reserved fruit mixture. Cool until set, about 30 minutes.

3) Break into 1$\frac{1}{2}$x1$\frac{1}{2}$-inch pieces. Store in airtight container.

HIGH ALTITUDE (3500-6500 FT.): No change.

Nutrition Information Per Serving:

Calories:	100	From Fat:	50
Total Fat			6g
Saturated Fat			3.5g
Trans Fat			0g
Cholesterol			0mg
Sodium			15mg
Total Carbohydrate			11g
Dietary Fiber			0g
Sugars			11g
Protein			1g

Chocolate Cat Cookies

PREP TIME: 15 MINUTES (READY IN 30 MINUTES)
SERVINGS: 12 COOKIES

 EASY

1 package (18 oz) Pillsbury® Ready To Bake® Big Deluxe Classics® triple chocolate cookies

Assorted candy sprinkles, as desired

Candy-coated chocolate candies, candy corn, string licorice

1) Heat oven to 350°F. Onto ungreased cookie sheet, place cookies 2 inches apart; flatten cookies slightly to make smooth tops.

2) Use fingers to press dough inward at top of each cookie, forming V shape; press resulting tips into points for cat ears.

3) Sprinkle cookies with candy sprinkles. Bake as directed on package. While cookies are baking, plan and assemble decorations. Immediately decorate the hot cookies with candy-coated chocolate candies for eyes, candy corn for noses and string licorice for whiskers. Remove cookies to cooling rack. Cool completely. Store in airtight container.

HIGH ALTITUDE (3500-6500 FT.): No change.

Nutrition Information Per Serving:		
Calories: 200	From Fat:	90
Total Fat		10g
Saturated Fat		3g
Trans Fat		1.5g
Cholesterol		10mg
Sodium		115mg
Total Carbohydrate		25g
Dietary Fiber		1g
Sugars		16g
Protein		2g

tip

It is hard to tell when these cookies are done. Take them out at the time given on the package, even if they look soft. They will firm up when cooled.

Meringue Candy Canes

PREP TIME: 20 MINUTES (READY IN 1 HOUR 20 MINUTES)
SERVINGS: ABOUT 3-1/2 DOZEN COOKIES

⊖ EASY   🌡 LOW FAT

3 egg whites

½ teaspoon cream of tartar

¾ cup sugar

¼ teaspoon peppermint extract

Red or pink food color

Nutrition Information Per Serving:

Calories:	15	From Fat:	0
Total Fat			0g
Saturated Fat			0g
Trans Fat			0g
Cholesterol			0mg
Sodium			0mg
Total Carbohydrate			4g
Dietary Fiber			0g
Sugars			4g
Protein			0g

1) Heat oven to 200°F. Line 2 cookie sheets with cooking parchment paper or foil. In large bowl, beat egg whites and cream of tartar with electric mixer on high speed until foamy. Gradually add sugar, 1 tablespoon at a time, beating until meringue is stiff and glossy. Beat in peppermint extract.

2) Fit large decorating bag with ¼-inch star tip. With small brush, paint 3 to 4 evenly spaced stripes of food color on inside of decorating bag, from tip to upper edge. Carefully spoon meringue into bag. Pipe 2½-inch candy canes onto paper-lined cookie sheets.

3) Bake about 1 hour or until dry but not brown.

HIGH ALTITUDE (3500-6500 FT.): No change.

Happy Reindeer

PREP TIME: 15 MINUTES (READY IN 15 MINUTES)
SERVINGS: 12 COOKIES

⊖ EASY

2 tablespoons chocolate creamy ready-to-spread frosting (from 1-lb container)

24 miniature candy-coated semisweet chocolate baking bits

1 package (12 oz) chocolate-covered marshmallow pinwheel cookies (12 cookies)

12 small gumdrops

24 pretzel twists

Nutrition Information Per Serving:

Calories:	210	From Fat:	50
Total Fat			6g
Saturated Fat			1.5g
Trans Fat			1g
Cholesterol			0mg
Sodium			190mg
Total Carbohydrate			36g
Dietary Fiber			1g
Sugars			12g
Protein			4g

1) Spread frosting on 1 side of each baking bit; attach 2 to top of each cookie for eyes.

2) Spread frosting on the wide end of each gumdrop; attach at hole of each cookie for nose.

3) Break pretzels to look like antlers (see photo). Insert 2 pretzel pieces in top of each cookie for antlers.

HIGH ALTITUDE (3500-6500 FT.): No change.

Cranberry-Chocolate Tart

PREP TIME: 50 MINUTES (READY IN 2 HOURS 25 MINUTES)
SERVINGS: 10

PASTRY

  1/3 cup shortening

1 1/4 cups all-purpose or unbleached flour

  1 teaspoon vinegar

  2 to 4 tablespoons cold water

  1/2 cup semisweet chocolate chips

  1/4 cup half-and-half

TOPPING

  2 cups fresh or frozen cranberries

  1 cup sugar

  1/2 cup water

FILLING

  3/4 cup milk

  1 box (4-serving size) vanilla instant pudding and pie filling mix

  1 cup sour cream

  1 tablespoon grated orange peel or 2 tablespoons orange-flavored liqueur

1) Heat oven to 450°F. In medium bowl, using pastry blender, cut shortening into flour until mixture looks like coarse crumbs. Sprinkle flour mixture with vinegar; add cold water, 1 tablespoon at a time, while tossing and mixing lightly with fork. Add cold water until dough is just moist enough to hold together.

2) Shape dough into ball. With floured fingers, press dough evenly over bottom and up side of 10-inch tart pan with removable bottom or 9-inch glass pie plate. Flute edge, if desired. Prick bottom and sides of pastry generously with fork. Bake 8 to 12 minutes or until lightly browned. In 1-quart saucepan, melt chocolate chips and half-and-half, stirring until smooth. Spread in shell. Cool slightly; refrigerate until chocolate is firm, about 15 minutes.

3) Meanwhile, in 1-quart saucepan, heat the topping ingredients to boiling, stirring until sugar is dissolved. Boil gently 3 to 4 minutes or until most of cranberries pop. Cool at least 30 minutes.

4) In small bowl, beat milk and vanilla pudding with electric mixer on low speed about 1 minute or until blended; stir in the sour cream and orange peel. Let stand 5 minutes. Pour over the chocolate layer in shell, spreading to cover evenly. Spoon the cooled cranberries over the filling, covering completely. Refrigerate tart at least 1 hour until serving time. Let stand at room temperature 10 minutes before serving. Cover and refrigerate any remaining tart.

HIGH ALTITUDE (3500-6500 FT.): Increase cold water in pastry to 4 to 6 tablespoons. Bake 12 to 16 minutes.

Nutrition Information Per Serving:		
Calories: 350	From Fat:	140
Total Fat		15g
Saturated Fat		7g
Trans Fat		1.5g
Cholesterol		20mg
Sodium		160mg
Total Carbohydrate		51g
Dietary Fiber		2g
Sugars		35g
Protein		3g

White Chocolate Gingerbread Bears

PREP TIME: 1 HOUR 45 MINUTES (READY IN 2 HOURS 45 MINUTES)
SERVINGS: ABOUT 8 DOZEN COOKIES

 LOW FAT

1½ cups sugar

1 cup butter or margarine, softened

⅓ cup molasses

1 egg

2 cups all-purpose or unbleached flour

1 cup whole wheat flour

2 teaspoons baking soda

2 teaspoons ground ginger

2 teaspoons ground cinnamon

½ teaspoon salt

3 oz (½ cup) white vanilla baking chips or vanilla-flavored candy coating, melted

Decorating icing, if desired

Nutrition Information Per Serving:		
Calories: 50	From Fat:	20
Total Fat		2.5g
Saturated Fat		1.5g
Trans Fat		0g
Cholesterol		5mg
Sodium		55mg
Total Carbohydrate		8g
Dietary Fiber		0g
Sugars		4g
Protein		0g

1) In large bowl, beat sugar and butter until light and fluffy. Add molasses and egg; blend well. Stir in all-purpose flour, whole wheat flour, baking soda, ginger, cinnamon and salt; mix well. Cover the dough with plastic wrap; refrigerate 1 hour for easier handling.

2) Heat oven to 350°F. On lightly floured surface, roll out dough, ¼ at a time, to ⅛-inch thickness. Refrigerate remaining dough until ready to roll. Cut dough with floured 4½-inch bear-shaped cookie cutter. Place 1 inch apart on ungreased cookie sheets. Using small heart-shaped canapé cutter, cut design from center of each bear.

3) Bake heart shapes on separate cookie sheet 5 to 7 minutes or until set. Bake bears 6 to 9 minutes or until set. Cool 1 minute; remove from cookie sheets. Cool completely. Line large cookie sheet with sides with waxed paper. Spread backs of cooled cookies with melted chocolate; place on cookie sheet. Refrigerate to set. Dip gingerbread hearts into chocolate and press onto bear's paw. Add facial features with decorating icing. Allow the frosting to set. Store between sheets of waxed paper in loosely covered container.

HIGH ALTITUDE (3500-6500 FT.): No change.

Chocolate Chip-Almond-Cherry Cups

PREP TIME: 45 MINUTES (READY IN 1 HOUR 45 MINUTES)
SERVINGS: 48 COOKIES

(f) LOW FAT

1 roll (16.5 oz) Pillsbury® Create 'n Bake® refrigerated chocolate chip cookies

½ cup almond paste, crumbled

½ cup dried cherries

½ cup cherry preserves

ICING

1 cup powdered sugar

¼ teaspoon almond extract

4 to 5 teaspoons milk

Powdered sugar, if desired

1) Heat oven to 350°F. Grease 48 miniature muffin cups with shortening; lightly flour. In large bowl, break up cookie dough. With hands, knead in almond paste and dried cherries.

2) Divide dough into 48 pieces. Shape each piece into ball; place in muffin cup. With thumb, make indentation in the center of each ball.

3) Bake 6 to 8 minutes or until edges are golden brown. Cool in pan on cooling rack 5 minutes. Run knife around edge of cookie to loosen; cool 1 to 2 minutes longer. Remove from muffin cups; place on cooling rack to cool.

4) Spoon ½ teaspoon preserves into each cooled cup. In small bowl, mix powdered sugar, almond extract and enough milk for desired drizzling consistency; blend until smooth. Drizzle over cookies; let stand until set, about 30 minutes. Sprinkle with powdered sugar.

HIGH ALTITUDE (3500-6500 FT.): Bake 10 to 12 minutes.

Nutrition Information Per Serving:		
Calories: 80	From Fat:	20
Total Fat		2.5g
Saturated Fat		0.5g
Trans Fat		0g
Cholesterol		0mg
Sodium		30mg
Total Carbohydrate		13g
Dietary Fiber		0g
Sugars		10g
Protein		0g

Star Santa Cookies

PREP TIME: 1 HOUR 20 MINUTES (READY IN 1 HOUR 50 MINUTES)
SERVINGS: 17 COOKIES

1 roll (16.5 oz) Pillsbury® Create 'n Bake® refrigerated sugar cookies

¼ cup all-purpose flour

1 cup vanilla creamy ready-to-spread frosting (from 1-lb container)

Red food color (liquid or paste)

2⅓ cups miniature marshmallows, halved

34 miniature chocolate chips

17 red miniature candy-coated chocolate baking bits

1) Heat oven to 350°F. In large bowl, break up cookie dough. Stir or knead in flour until well blended. With rolling pin, roll out dough to ¼-inch thickness.

2) Cut dough into 17 stars, using 3-inch star-shaped cookie cutter. On ungreased cookie sheets, place stars 2 inches apart.

3) Bake 6 to 8 minutes or until light golden brown. Immediately remove from cookie sheets to cooling racks. Cool completely, about 15 minutes.

4) In small bowl, mix ⅓ cup of the frosting and the red food color until well blended and desired red color. Frost 1 point of each star for Santa's hat. Place 1 marshmallow half on tip of hat. Avoiding area under hat for the face, spread vanilla frosting on remaining cookie for the beard. Top with marshmallow halves. Place dots of frosting on 2 chocolate chips; place on face for eyes. Place dot of frosting on baking bit and position for nose.

HIGH ALTITUDE (3500-6500 FT.): No change.

Nutrition Information Per Serving:		
Calories: 230	From Fat:	80
Total Fat		9g
Saturated Fat		2.5g
Trans Fat		2.5g
Cholesterol		10mg
Sodium		120mg
Total Carbohydrate		35g
Dietary Fiber		0g
Sugars		23g
Protein		1g

Cranberry Mousse Mini-Tarts

PREP TIME: 45 MINUTES (READY IN 2 HOURS 5 MINUTES)
SERVINGS: 24 MINI TARTS

1 envelope unflavored gelatin

2/3 cup water

1/2 cup sugar

1 cup whole cranberries, chopped

1/2 teaspoon grated orange peel

1 box (15 oz) Pillsbury® refrigerated pie crusts, softened as directed on box

1/4 cup whipping cream

2 teaspoons powdered sugar

1 teaspoon powdered sugar

1) Sprinkle gelatin on water to soften, set aside about 15 minutes. In 1½-quart saucepan, heat ½ cup sugar and the cranberries just to boiling over medium heat, stirring occasionally. Remove from heat; stir in gelatin mixture and orange peel. Refrigerate 30 to 40 minutes or until mixture just starts to thicken.

2) Heat oven to 425°F. Spray 24 miniature muffin cups with cooking spray. Unroll crusts on work surface. With 2½-inch scalloped round cutter, cut 15 rounds from 1 crust and 9 from the other. From the remaining crust, cut 24 1-inch star shapes. Fit rounds into muffin cups, pressing in gently. Generously prick crusts with fork. Bake crusts 6 to 9 minutes or until light golden brown. Cool completely, about 15 minutes; remove from muffin cups. Bake star shapes 3 to 4 minutes or until light golden brown.

3) In small bowl, beat whipping cream until soft peaks form. Add 2 teaspoons powdered sugar; beat until stiff peaks form. Fold in the cranberry mixture; refrigerate about 10 minutes or until thickened. Spoon about 1 tablespoon into each crust; top each with 1 star. Store in refrigerator. Just before serving, sprinkle with 1 teaspoon powdered sugar.

HIGH ALTITUDE (3500-6500 FT.): No change.

Nutrition Information Per Serving:		
Calories: 80	From Fat:	35
Total Fat		3.5g
Saturated Fat		1.5g
Trans Fat		0g
Cholesterol		0mg
Sodium		45mg
Total Carbohydrate		10g
Dietary Fiber		0g
Sugars		5g
Protein		0g

Chocolate-Covered Cheesecake Trees

PREP TIME: 1 HOUR 10 MINUTES (READY IN 5 HOURS 15 MINUTES)
SERVINGS: 28 TREES

1 cup chocolate wafer crumbs

¼ cup butter or margarine, melted

2 packages (8 oz each) cream cheese, softened

½ cup sugar

¼ cup sour cream

1 teaspoon vanilla

2 eggs

28 paper lollipop sticks or flat wooden sticks with round ends

3½ cups semisweet chocolate chips (from 24-oz bag)

3 tablespoons shortening

2 oz vanilla-flavored candy coating (almond bark), chopped

½ teaspoon vegetable oil

1 to 2 drops green paste food color, if desired

1) Heat oven to 300°F. Line 8-inch pan with heavy-duty foil so foil extends over sides of pan. In small bowl, mix wafer crumbs and butter. Press in bottom of foil-lined pan.

2) In large bowl, beat cream cheese and sugar with electric mixer on medium speed until smooth. Beat in sour cream, vanilla and eggs. Pour over crust.

3) Bake 30 to 40 minutes or until edges are set (center will be soft but will set when cool). Cool in pan on cooling rack 30 minutes. Cover; freeze 2 hours. Meanwhile, cover 1 large cookie sheet with waxed paper.

4) Remove cheesecake from pan by lifting foil. Cut lengthwise into four long pieces. Cut each piece into 7 triangles, working with 1 long piece at a time (keep corner pieces for snacking). Insert sticks into bottoms of triangles. Place on waxed paper-lined cookie sheet. Freeze 30 minutes. If making ahead, cover and freeze until ready to coat with chocolate.

5) Meanwhile, in 2-quart saucepan, melt chocolate chips and shortening over medium-low heat, stirring frequently, until smooth. Place in medium bowl.

6) Working in 2 batches of 14 (keep remaining in freezer until ready to coat), dip each tree quickly into melted chocolate to coat, letting excess drip off. Use knife or spatula to spread chocolate around stick entrance. Place crust side down on waxed paper.

7) In small microwavable bowl, microwave candy coating and oil uncovered on High 1 minute, stirring every 15 seconds, until melted. Stir in food color. Spoon into 1-quart resealable food-storage plastic bag. Seal bag; cut tiny hole in corner of bag. Pipe melted coating over trees to look like garland. Store covered in freezer.

HIGH ALTITUDE (3500-6500 FT.): Heat oven to 325°F.

Nutrition Information Per Serving:		
Calories: 250	From Fat:	150
Total Fat		17g
Saturated Fat		10g
Trans Fat		0.5g
Cholesterol		40mg
Sodium		90mg
Total Carbohydrate		21g
Dietary Fiber		1g
Sugars		18g
Protein		3g

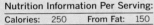

Little Drummer Boy Drums

PREP TIME: 50 MINUTES (READY IN 1 HOUR 15 MINUTES)
SERVINGS: 18 DRUMS

 EASY

1 roll (16.5 oz) Pillsbury® Create 'n Bake® refrigerated sugar cookies

1/4 cup all-purpose flour

1/2 cup vanilla creamy ready-to-spread frosting (from 1-lb container)

1/2 cup red, blue, yellow, pink or green sugar

18 pretzel sticks, broken in half

36 miniature marshmallows

1) Heat oven to 350°F. In large bowl, break up the cookie dough. Stir or knead in the flour until well blended. Shape rounded teaspoonfuls of the cookie dough into 36 balls; place 1 inch apart on ungreased cookie sheets.

2) Bake 8 to 10 minutes or until set and the edges are light golden brown. Cool 1 minute; remove from cookie sheets to cooling racks. Cool completely, about 15 minutes.

3) For each drum, spread about 1 rounded teaspoon frosting between 2 cookies. With additional frosting, spread outsides, but not top of stack, with frosting. Roll outsides in sugar.

4) Poke 1 end of each pretzel stick into marshmallow. Spread a little frosting on the side of each marshmallow. Place 2 marshmallows, frosting side down, on top of each drum, crisscrossing pretzels to look like drumsticks. Let stand until frosting is set, about 1 hour. Store in tightly covered container.

HIGH ALTITUDE (3500-6500 FT.): No change.

Nutrition Information Per Serving:

Calories:	180	From Fat:	60
Total Fat			7g
Saturated Fat			2g
Trans Fat			2g
Cholesterol			10mg
Sodium			95mg
Total Carbohydrate			29g
Dietary Fiber			0g
Sugars			19g
Protein			1g

Marzipan Snow People

PREP TIME: 45 MINUTES (READY IN 45 MINUTES)
SERVINGS: 8 SNOW PEOPLE

 EASY

1 package (7 or 8 oz) marzipan or almond paste

56 slivered almonds (about 2 tablespoons)

8 round chocolate-covered peppermint candies (1½ inches each), unwrapped

Multi-colored oblong candy sprinkles

2 packages (0.75 oz each) fruit snack in three-foot rolls (any flavor)

8 small gumdrops

Nutrition Information Per Serving:		
Calories: 220	From Fat:	80
Total Fat		9g
Saturated Fat		1.5g
Trans Fat		0g
Cholesterol		0mg
Sodium		15mg
Total Carbohydrate		33g
Dietary Fiber		2g
Sugars		27g
Protein		3g

1) Roll marzipan into log shape; divide into 8 portions. Divide each portion into large (1¼-inch) ball, medium (1-inch) ball and small (¾-inch) ball.

2) For each person, poke 1 slivered almond into center of chocolate-covered peppermint candy. Place large ball over almond, gently pushing downward to attach. Gently push 2 almonds in center of large ball; attach medium ball, gently pushing down. Gently push 1 almond in center of medium ball; place small ball over almond, gently pushing down to attach.

3) Using toothpick, make holes in face of snowman for eyes and nose. Place 2 brown oblong sprinkles into holes to look like eyes. Place 1 oblong sprinkle in hole to look like nose. If desired, make holes for buttons and add colored oblong sprinkles. Place 2 slivered almonds in center of middle ball to look like arms.

4) Unroll fruit snacks. For scarf; cut eight 5x½-inch strips. Fold each strip in half horizontally, leaving 1 inch on each end unfolded; make small cuts at ends for fringe. Wrap around neck, slightly overlapping at shoulder. To make base of hats, cut eight ¾-inch-diameter circles of fruit snack. Place fruit snack round on snowman's head. Insert slivered almond halfway down into center. Cut off and discard ⅛ inch off the bottom of gumdrop; flatten bottom slightly. Attach onto slivered almond to finish hat.

HIGH ALTITUDE (3500-6500 FT.): No change.

Porcelain Cookies

PREP TIME: 1 HOUR 30 MINUTES (READY IN 3 HOURS 30 MINUTES)
SERVINGS: ABOUT 32 COOKIES

COOKIES

- ¾ cup butter, softened
- ¾ cup granulated sugar
- 1 egg
- 1 tablespoon finely grated lemon peel
- 2 tablespoons lemon juice
- 2½ cups all-purpose flour
- 1 teaspoon baking soda
- ¼ teaspoon salt

ROYAL ICING

- 3 cups powdered sugar
- 2 tablespoons meringue powder
- 5 teaspoons lemon juice
- 4 to 5 tablespoons water

DECORATIONS

- Colored sugars
- Colored candy sprinkles

Nutrition Information Per Serving:

Calories:	150	From Fat:	40
Total Fat			4.5g
Saturated Fat			3g
Trans Fat			0g
Cholesterol			20mg
Sodium			100mg
Total Carbohydrate			25g
Dietary Fiber			0g
Sugars			16g
Protein			2g

1) In large bowl, beat butter and granulated sugar with electric mixer on medium speed until creamy. On low speed, beat in egg, lemon peel and 2 tablespoons juice. Stir in flour, baking soda and salt until well blended.

2) Divide dough into 4 parts; flatten each part into ½-inch-thick round. Wrap each in waxed paper or plastic wrap; refrigerate 30 minutes.

3) Heat oven to 350°F. Remove 1 round of dough at a time from refrigerator. Between sheets of floured waxed paper or plastic wrap, roll dough until ¼ to ⅜ inch thick. Cut with 3-inch cookie cutters in various shapes. On ungreased cookie sheets, place cutouts 1 inch apart.

4) Bake 10 to 12 minutes or just until the edges are golden. Cool on cookie sheets about 1 minute before removing to cooling rack. To make cookies for hanging, using a toothpick or end of plastic straw, carefully poke a hole in the top of each cookie while cookies are still hot. Cool 10 to 15 minutes before frosting.

5) In medium bowl, stir together powdered sugar and meringue powder. Stir in 5 teaspoons lemon juice and enough of the 4 to 5 tablespoons water to make a thin icing. Transfer ½ cup of the icing into small bowl; set aside. Using a flexible pastry brush, paint cookies to the edges with icing. Place on cooling rack to dry completely, about 30 minutes.

6) Beat reserved icing with electric mixer on high speed 5 to 7 minutes or until peaks form. Place in small resealable food-storage plastic bag; cut a very small hole in the bottom of the bag with the plain white icing. Squeeze icing onto the glazed cookies. Before icing dries, sprinkle with decorations, and tap off excess. Dry thoroughly on cooling rack. Thread cookies with narrow ribbon for hanging.

HIGH ALTITUDE (3500-6500 FT.): No change.

Linzer Sandwich Cookies

PREP TIME: 1 HOUR (READY IN 4 HOURS)
SERVINGS: ABOUT 26 SANDWICH COOKIES

¾ cup hazelnuts (filberts)

½ cup packed light brown sugar

2½ cups all-purpose flour

2 teaspoons cream of tartar

1 teaspoon baking soda

½ teaspoon salt

¼ teaspoon ground cinnamon

1 cup butter, softened

1 egg

1 teaspoon vanilla

Powdered sugar, powdered sugar icing, colored sugars or decors, if desired

½ cup seedless raspberry jam

Nutrition Information Per Serving:

Calories: 170	From Fat: 80
Total Fat	9g
Saturated Fat	4.5g
Trans Fat	0g
Cholesterol	25mg
Sodium	150mg
Total Carbohydrate	18g
Dietary Fiber	0g
Sugars	7g
Protein	2g

1) Heat oven to 350°F. Spread hazelnuts in ungreased shallow baking pan. Bake uncovered about 6 minutes, stirring occasionally. Rub the nuts in a kitchen towel to remove loose skins (some skins may not come off); cool 5 to 10 minutes. Turn off oven.

2) In food processor bowl with metal blade, place nuts and ¼ cup of brown sugar. Cover; process with about 10 on-and-off pulses, 2 to 3 seconds each, until nuts are finely ground but not oily.

3) In small bowl, mix flour, cream of tartar, baking soda, salt and cinnamon; set aside.

4) In large bowl, beat butter and remaining ¼ cup brown sugar with electric mixer on medium speed about 3 minutes or until smooth. Add the nut mixture; beat about 1 minute or until mixed. Beat in egg and vanilla. With spoon, stir in flour mixture about 1 minute or just until blended. Shape dough into 2 balls; flatten each ball into a disk. Wrap separately in plastic wrap; refrigerate at least 2 hours until firm.

5) Heat oven to 425°F. Remove 1 dough disk from refrigerator. On well-floured surface, roll dough with floured rolling pin until about 1/8 inch thick. Cut with 2½-inch cookie cutter in desired shape. On ungreased cookie sheets, place cutouts about 1 inch apart.

6) Roll and cut other half of dough. Using a 1-inch square or round cutter, cut out the center of half of the cookies. Reroll the dough centers and cut out more cookies.

7) Bake 4 to 5 minutes or until edges are light golden brown. Remove from cookie sheets to cooling rack. Cool about 10 minutes.

8) Lightly sprinkle powdered sugar over cookies with center cutouts. Or drizzle with powdered sugar icing, and sprinkle with colored sugars or decors. Spread about 1 teaspoon raspberry jam over bottom side of each whole cookie. Top with a cutout cookie. Cool completely, about 1 hour.

HIGH ALTITUDE (3500-6500 FT.): No change.

Sweet Penguins

PREP TIME:	40 MINUTES (READY IN 40 MINUTES)
SERVINGS:	12 PENGUINS

 EASY

36 pecan halves

6 oz chocolate-flavored candy coating, coarsely chopped

12 large marshmallows

12 miniature chocolate-covered peanut butter cup candies, unwrapped

12 pieces candy corn

Nutrition Information Per Serving:

Calories:	170	From Fat:	80
Total Fat			9g
Saturated Fat			3.5g
Trans Fat			0g
Cholesterol			0mg
Sodium			35mg
Total Carbohydrate			19g
Dietary Fiber			0g
Sugars			17g
Protein			2g

1) Line 2 cookie sheets with waxed paper. On 1 cookie sheet, arrange pecan halves in 12 clusters of 3 to form base of each penguin—2 face forward for feet and 1 perpendicular across back.

2) In 1-cup microwavable measuring cup or narrow glass, microwave candy coating uncovered on High 45 seconds; stir. Continue heating and stirring every 10 seconds, just until smooth.

3) Insert wooden or metal skewer into one flat side of marshmallow; dip first 1 side, then turn and dip other side into melted chocolate, to look like wings, leaving center of marshmallow white for breast of penguin. Place dipped marshmallow (for body) on top of 1 peanut butter cup candy (for head), using open tips of kitchen scissors or knife to push marshmallow off skewer. Place on other cookie sheet (penguin will be upside down). Repeat with remaining marshmallows and candies. Let stand until chocolate is set, about 5 minutes.

4) Using remaining melted chocolate, spoon a small amount onto each cluster of pecans to hold them together; allow chocolate to set, about 5 minutes.

5) To finish each penguin, turn penguin body and head right side up (candy on top). Attach to pecan cluster using a small amount of melted candy coating. After about 5 minutes or when set, make small opening in the marshmallow with tip of knife at top of breast, and firmly press 1 piece of candy corn in for beak.

HIGH ALTITUDE (3500-6500 FT.): No change.

Peppermint Pretzel Canes

PREP TIME: 15 MINUTES (READY IN 45 MINUTES)
SERVINGS: 12 PRETZELS

 EASY

- 6 oz vanilla-flavored candy coating (almond bark), cut into pieces
- 2 tablespoons shortening
- 2/3 cup finely crushed peppermint candies (24 candies)
- 12 (8 1/2-inch) pretzel rods (from 11-oz package)

1) Line cookie sheet with waxed paper. In 2-quart saucepan, melt the almond bark pieces and shortening over low heat, stirring occasionally. Pour into 11x7-inch (2-quart) glass baking dish or other shallow dish; carefully set baking dish in hot water to keep almond bark soft. (Do not get any water into almond bark.)

2) Sprinkle crushed candy over separate sheet of waxed paper. Dip pretzels into melted almond bark; allow excess to drip off. Roll in crushed candy. Place on cookie sheet. Let stand until set, about 30 minutes.

HIGH ALTITUDE (3500-6500 FT.): No change.

Nutrition Information Per Serving:

Calories:	190	From Fat:	60
Total Fat		7g	
Saturated Fat		3.5g	
Trans Fat		0g	
Cholesterol		0mg	
Sodium		210mg	
Total Carbohydrate		30g	
Dietary Fiber		0g	
Sugars		19g	
Protein		2g	

tip To easily crush the candies, place them inside a double thickness of heavy-duty resealable plastic bags and seal. Place them on a cutting board and hit them with a hammer to crush.

Crescent Angel Wings

| PREP TIME: | 25 MINUTES (READY IN 1 HOUR 5 MINUTES) |
| SERVINGS: | 16 COOKIES |

 EASY

3 tablespoons gold decorator sugar crystals

1 can (8 oz) Pillsbury® refrigerated crescent dinner rolls

1 teaspoon grated lemon peel

2 tablespoons butter or margarine, melted

Nutrition Information Per Serving:

Calories:	80	From Fat:	40
Total Fat			4.5g
Saturated Fat			2g
Trans Fat			1g
Cholesterol			0mg
Sodium			120mg
Total Carbohydrate			8g
Dietary Fiber			0g
Sugars			3g
Protein			1g

1) Line cookie sheets with cooking parchment paper. Sprinkle cutting board with half of sugar crystals. Unroll dough and separate into 4 rectangles; place on sugar-sprinkled board, firmly pressing perforations to seal. Lightly press dough into sugar. In small bowl, mix the remaining half of sugar and the lemon peel. Brush rectangles with 1 tablespoon of the melted butter; sprinkle with sugar mixture.

2) Place 1 rectangle on top of another. Starting with both of the shortest sides, roll up each side jelly-roll fashion until rolls meet in center. Repeat with remaining 2 rectangles. Cover; refrigerate dough rolls about 30 minutes or until dough is firm.

3) Heat oven to 375°F. With serrated knife, cut each roll into 8 slices, making 16 slices total. Place slices, cut side down, 2 inches apart on cookie sheets. Brush with remaining tablespoon melted butter.

4) Bake 9 to 13 minutes or until golden brown. If necessary, gently reroll the cookies. Immediately remove from cookie sheets to cooling rack. Cool completely. Store in airtight container.

HIGH ALTITUDE (3500-6500 FT.): Bake 7 to 11 minutes.

Cranberry-Cheesecake Tart

JAMES SLOBODEN | PUYALLUP, WASHINGTON

BAKE-OFF® CONTEST 34, 1990 | PRIZE WINNER

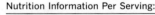

PREP TIME: 30 MINUTES (READY IN 5 HOURS 30 MINUTES)
SERVINGS: 10

CRUST

1 Pillsbury® refrigerated pie crust (from 15-oz box), softened as directed on box

FILLING

1 can (16 oz) whole berry cranberry sauce

¼ cup chopped pecans

6 tablespoons sugar

1 tablespoon cornstarch

1 package (8 oz) cream cheese, softened

⅓ cup sugar

1 egg

TOPPING

1 cup sour cream

2 tablespoons sugar

½ teaspoon vanilla

1) Heat oven to 450°F. Bake pie crust as directed on box for One-Crust Baked Shell, using 10-inch tart pan with removable bottom or 9-inch glass pie plate. Cool 5 minutes. Reduce oven temperature to 375°F.

2) In medium bowl, mix cranberry sauce, pecans, 6 tablespoons sugar and the cornstarch. Spread in crust.

3) In medium bowl, beat cream cheese, ⅓ cup sugar and egg with electric mixer on medium speed until smooth. Spoon evenly over cranberry mixture. Bake at 375°F 25 to 30 minutes or until set.

4) In small bowl, mix sour cream, 2 tablespoons sugar and the vanilla. Spoon evenly over filling. Bake at 375°F 5 minutes longer. Cool slightly. Refrigerate 3 to 4 hours or until set. Cover and refrigerate any remaining pie.

HIGH ALTITUDE (3500-6500 FT.): No change.

Nutrition Information Per Serving:		
Calories: 390	From Fat: 180	
Total Fat		20g
Saturated Fat		10g
Trans Fat		0g
Cholesterol		65mg
Sodium		180mg
Total Carbohydrate		47g
Dietary Fiber		0g
Sugars		35g
Protein		3g

Marshmallow Santas

PREP TIME: 1 HOUR 10 MINUTES (READY IN 1 HOUR 10 MINUTES)
SERVINGS: 10 SANTAS

10 small pretzel twists

5 oz vanilla-flavored candy coating (almond bark) from 16- or 20-oz package, chopped (slightly less than 1 cup)

20 large marshmallows

¼ cup red sugar

40 miniature chocolate chips

½ cup shredded coconut

¼ teaspoon pink sugar

10 red cinnamon candies

10 red or green foil-wrapped milk chocolate candy bells

10 miniature marshmallows

5 large green gumdrops, cut in half

20 candy-coated chocolate candies

Nutrition Information Per Serving:		
Calories: 230	From Fat:	70
Total Fat		8g
Saturated Fat		5g
Trans Fat		0g
Cholesterol		0mg
Sodium		60mg
Total Carbohydrate		39g
Dietary Fiber		0g
Sugars		31g
Protein		2g

1) Place cooking parchment paper or waxed paper on cookie sheet; place pretzels on paper for feet of Santas.

2) In 1-cup microwavable measuring cup, microwave candy coating uncovered on High 35 seconds; stir. Continue heating 10 seconds at a time until coating is smooth after stirring.

3) Using wooden skewer inserted into 1 flat end of marshmallow, dip marshmallow into melted coating. Allow excess to drip off; sprinkle with red sugar and place on pretzel. Place 2 chocolate chips on front for buttons (where feet extend). Insert another marshmallow on skewer; dip and allow excess to drip off. Sprinkle with coconut; sprinkle with bit of pink sugar for face; add eyes (chocolate chips) and nose (cinnamon candy). Place on top of other marshmallow. Set aside to cool, or refrigerate. Repeat with remaining marshmallows.

4) When the coating is firm, attach the hats (wrapped candy bells), tassels (miniature marshmallows) and bags (gumdrops) with small amount of melted coating. Use toothpick to make small opening for arms (candy-coated chocolate candies); insert arms into marshmallows with small amount of melted coating.

HIGH ALTITUDE (3500-6500 FT.): No change.

Peppermint Mousse Cups

PREP TIME: 35 MINUTES (READY IN 35 MINUTES)
SERVINGS: 24 MOUSSE CUPS

 EASY

1½ cups semisweet chocolate chips

½ cup white vanilla baking chips

1 cup whipping cream

½ teaspoon peppermint extract

2 drops red food color

2 tablespoons crushed candy canes
(about 6 miniature candy canes)

You can purchase the chocolate shells instead of making them; look for the shells at your supermarket.

1) Line 24 mini muffin cups with petit four paper cups. In 1-quart saucepan, melt semisweet chips over low heat, stirring frequently. Spoon about 2 teaspoons of the chocolate into each paper cup. With back of small measuring spoon, spread chocolate up sides to within ⅛ inch of top. Chocolate should be warm enough to spread. Refrigerate about 20 minutes or until completely set.

2) Meanwhile, in small microwavable bowl, microwave vanilla baking chips uncovered on High 1 minute. Stir in 3 tablespoons of the whipping cream; microwave about 30 seconds longer or until chips are melted. Stir in peppermint extract and food color. Cool slightly, about 5 minutes. Carefully remove paper cups from chocolate cups.

3) In medium bowl, beat remaining whipping cream with electric mixer on high speed until stiff peaks form. Fold melted vanilla chip mixture into whipped cream. Spoon or pipe whipped cream mixture into chocolate cups. Refrigerate until serving. Just before serving, sprinkle with candy.

HIGH ALTITUDE (3500-6500 FT.): No change.

Nutrition Information Per Serving:		
Calories: 110	From Fat:	70
Total Fat		8g
Saturated Fat		5g
Trans Fat		0g
Cholesterol		10mg
Sodium		15mg
Total Carbohydrate		11g
Dietary Fiber		0g
Sugars		10g
Protein		0g

FAMILY-SIZE
CHICKEN POT PIE
PG. 283

Cooking For Kids

You'll see smiles (and clean plates!) when you treat children to these fun-filled and wholesome foods.

TACO MONSTER MOUTHS
PG. 267

BEEF AND BEAN TACO CASSEROLE
PG. 278

CANDY-TOPPED CREAMY
PEANUT BUTTER BARS
PG. 271

Mini Chicken Pot Pies

PREP TIME: 15 MINUTES (READY IN 30 MINUTES)
SERVINGS: 4 POT PIES

 EASY

1½ cups frozen peas and carrots

1 cup cubed (½ inch) cooked chicken

1 cup refrigerated diced cooked potatoes with onions (from 20-oz bag)

¼ cup milk

½ teaspoon dried thyme leaves

1 can (10¾ oz) condensed cream of chicken soup

1 can (4 oz) Pillsbury® refrigerated crescent dinner rolls

1 egg

1 tablespoon water

⅛ teaspoon dried thyme leaves

1) Heat oven to 400°F. In 2-quart saucepan, mix peas and carrots, chicken, potatoes, milk, ½ teaspoon thyme and the cream of chicken soup. Heat to boiling over medium-high heat, stirring occasionally. Divide the mixture evenly among 4 ungreased 10-oz custard cups.

2) Unroll crescent dough. Place 1 crescent over each custard cup.

3) In small bowl, mix the egg and water. Brush mixture over crescent dough. Sprinkle ⅛ teaspoon thyme over dough. Bake 11 to 13 minutes or until crusts are golden brown.

HIGH ALTITUDE (3500-6500 FT.): No change.

Nutrition Information Per Serving:		
Calories: 330	From Fat:	140
Total Fat		15g
Saturated Fat		5g
Trans Fat		1.5g
Cholesterol		90mg
Sodium		920mg
Total Carbohydrate		31g
Dietary Fiber		2g
Sugars		5g
Protein		18g

Taco Monster Mouths

PREP TIME: 20 MINUTES (READY IN 30 MINUTES)
SERVINGS: 6 (1 TACO EACH)

 EASY

2 plum (Roma) tomatoes

12 large pimiento-stuffed green olives

3 slices (1/2 oz each) American cheese

6 Old El Paso® Stand 'N Stuff® taco shells (from 4.7 oz box)

1/2 lb lean (at least 80%) ground beef

2 tablespoons Old El Paso® 40% less sodium taco seasoning mix

1/3 cup water

Shredded lettuce, if desired

1) Cut each tomato lengthwise into 3 pieces. Remaining inside of tomato may be chopped for additional taco filling, if desired.

2) Cut slit into 1 side of each olive to make a flat side. Cut each of the slices of cheese in half vertically in a zigzag line to look like teeth.

3) Heat oven to 350°F. Arrange the taco shells on ungreased cookie sheet. Bake 5 to 7 minutes or until hot. Meanwhile, in 10-inch skillet, cook the ground beef over medium-high heat 5 to 7 minutes, stirring frequently, until thoroughly cooked; drain. Stir in the taco seasoning mix and water. Reduce heat to medium; cook about 5 minutes, stirring frequently until the water has evaporated.

4) To assemble, fill tacos with desired fillings so that the beef is on the top. Placing each taco on its side on serving plate, insert 1 tomato slice into meat filling to look like tongue. Place 1 cheese slice with zigzag edge toward meat along top side of taco between the shell and the filling. Place 2 olives, flat sides down, to look like eyes on top of shell.

HIGH ALTITUDE (3500-6500 FT.): No change.

Nutrition Information Per Serving:		
Calories: 180	From Fat:	100
Total Fat		11g
Saturated Fat		3.5g
Trans Fat		1.5g
Cholesterol		30mg
Sodium		490mg
Total Carbohydrate		12g
Dietary Fiber		1g
Sugars		0g
Protein		9g

Meatball Creepy Crawlers

PREP TIME: 35 MINUTES (READY IN 50 MINUTES)
SERVINGS: 10 (2 APPETIZERS EACH)

e EASY

MEATBALLS

1 can (12 oz) Pillsbury® Golden Layers® refrigerated flaky original biscuits

20 frozen cooked beef meatballs, thawed (from 16-oz bag)

1/4 cup shoestring potatoes (from 1 3/4-oz can) or chow mein noodles

Sliced olives, pickles and carrots, as desired

DIPS, IF DESIRED

1/4 cup ketchup

1/4 cup mustard

1/2 cup cheese dip

1) Heat oven to 375°F. Spray large cookie sheet with cooking spray, or cover with cooking parchment paper.

2) Separate dough into 10 biscuits. Separate each biscuit into 2 layers. Wrap 1 biscuit piece around each meatball; seal. To make 1 creepy crawler, line up 10 wrapped meatballs on cookie sheet, making sure each is touching, to make a curved line. Poke shoestring potatoes in both sides of each ball for legs, at the head for antennae and tongue, and at the end for tail. Repeat with the remaining 10 wrapped meatballs to make second crawler.

3) Bake 13 to 16 minutes or until golden brown. Garnish with olives for eyes and mouth. Top every other section with layer of pickle, carrot and olive. In small bowl, mix ketchup and mustard for dip. Serve crawlers with dips.

HIGH ALTITUDE (3500-6500 FT.): No change.

Nutrition Information Per Serving:

Calories:	180	From Fat:	80
Total Fat			9g
Saturated Fat			2.5g
Trans Fat			1.5g
Cholesterol			30mg
Sodium			570mg
Total Carbohydrate			18g
Dietary Fiber			0g
Sugars			3g
Protein			8g

Pizza Dipping Sticks

PREP TIME: 10 MINUTES (READY IN 25 MINUTES)
SERVINGS: 4 (4 STRIPS EACH)

e EASY

1 can (13.8 oz) Pillsbury® refrigerated classic pizza crust

30 slices pepperoni (from 3.5-oz package)

1 1/2 cups shredded mozzarella cheese (6 oz)

1 to 1 1/2 cups pizza sauce, warmed

Nutrition Information Per Serving:

Calories:	580	From Fat:	250
Total Fat			28g
Saturated Fat			13g
Trans Fat			0g
Cholesterol			70mg
Sodium			1940mg
Total Carbohydrate			55g
Dietary Fiber			1g
Sugars			10g
Protein			28g

1) Heat oven to 400°F. Grease or spray cookie sheet. Unroll dough; place on cookie sheet. Starting at center, press out dough into 13x9-inch rectangle.

2) Bake 7 minutes. Top with pepperoni and cheese.

3) Bake 8 to 10 minutes longer or until cheese is melted. Cool 2 minutes. Cut pizza in half lengthwise, then cut into a total of 16 (1 1/2-inch) strips. Serve with pizza sauce for dipping.

HIGH ALTITUDE (3500-6500 FT.): Heat oven to 425°F.

Sloppy Joe Biscuit Rounds

PREP TIME: 30 MINUTES (READY IN 50 MINUTES)
SERVINGS: 8

¾ lb lean (at least 80%) ground beef

¼ cup chopped onion

¼ cup chopped green bell pepper

⅓ cup ketchup

1 tablespoon yellow mustard

1 teaspoon Worcestershire sauce

¼ teaspoon salt

⅛ teaspoon pepper

1 can (16.3 oz) Pillsbury® Grands!® homestyle refrigerated buttermilk biscuits

1 egg yolk

¼ teaspoon water

½ cup shredded Monterey Jack or Cheddar cheese (2 oz)

1) Heat oven to 375°F. Spray large cookie sheet with cooking spray. In 10-inch skillet, cook ground beef, onion and bell pepper over medium-high heat until beef is thoroughly cooked; drain. Stir in the ketchup, mustard, Worcestershire sauce, salt and pepper.

2) Separate dough into 8 biscuits. Place 2½ inches apart on cookie sheet. With bottom of flat 2-inch diameter glass or fingers, press out each biscuit to 3½-inch round with ¼-inch rim around outside edge. In small bowl, beat egg yolk and water with fork. Brush over tops and sides of biscuits.

3) Spoon about ⅓ cup beef mixture into indentation in each biscuit. Sprinkle each biscuit with 1 tablespoon cheese.

4) Bake 12 to 17 minutes or until biscuits are golden brown and cheese is melted.

HIGH ALTITUDE (3500-6500 FT.): No change.

Nutrition Information Per Serving:

Calories:	310	From Fat:	140
Total Fat			16g
Saturated Fat			6g
Trans Fat			3.5g
Cholesterol			60mg
Sodium			870mg
Total Carbohydrate			28g
Dietary Fiber			0g
Sugars			7g
Protein			14g

For a complete meal, serve these hearty biscuit rounds with a green salad and glasses of milk.

4-Square Family Pizza

PREP TIME: 20 MINUTES (READY IN 35 MINUTES)
SERVINGS: 16 SERVINGS

Cornmeal, if desired

1 can (13.8 oz) Pillsbury® refrigerated classic pizza crust

2 teaspoons olive oil

½ cup shredded Cheddar cheese (2 oz)

1½ cups shredded mozzarella cheese (6 oz)

HAWAIIAN PIZZA SQUARE

2 tablespoons pizza sauce

2 slices Canadian bacon, quartered

¼ cup pineapple tidbits, well drained (from 8-oz can)

BBQ CHICKEN PIZZA SQUARE

1 tablespoon chopped red onion

½ cup refrigerated honey hickory barbecue sauce with shredded chicken, large pieces cut up

MARGHERITA PIZZA SQUARE

1 tablespoon shredded fresh Parmesan cheese

3 to 4 plum (Roma) tomatoes, sliced

1 tablespoon thin fresh basil strips

PEPPERONI PIZZA SQUARE

2 tablespoons pizza sauce

8 to 10 slices pepperoni (from 3-oz package)

Using this recipe as a general guideline, you can create any combination of pizza squares you like for your family pizza night or a party.

1) Heat oven to 425°F. Spray cookie sheet with cooking spray; sprinkle with cornmeal. Unroll dough; place on cookie sheet. Starting at center, press out dough into 14x12-inch rectangle. Brush dough with olive oil.

2) Bake 6 to 8 minutes. Sprinkle Cheddar cheese in the shape of a "plus sign" on crust, dividing the crust into four squares. Top each square with 1 of the 4 variations listed above to make 4 different squares. Top entire pizza with mozzarella cheese.

3) Bake 10 to 13 minutes longer or until crust is deep golden brown and cheese is melted and bubbly. Cut pizza into 4 squares; cut each square into 4 squares to make a total of 16 squares.

HIGH ALTITUDE (3500-6500 FT.): No change.

Nutrition Information Per Serving:		
Calories: 150	From Fat:	60
Total Fat		6g
Saturated Fat		3g
Trans Fat		0g
Cholesterol		15mg
Sodium		420mg
Total Carbohydrate		15g
Dietary Fiber		0g
Sugars		4g
Protein		8g

Candy-Topped Creamy Peanut Butter Bars

PREP TIME: 30 MINUTES (READY IN 2 HOURS 20 MINUTES)
SERVINGS: 36 BARS

1 roll (16.5 oz) Pillsbury® Create 'n Bake™ refrigerated chocolate chip cookies

³/₄ cup butter or margarine, softened

½ cup peanut butter

2 cups powdered sugar

2 tablespoons milk

1 cup salted peanuts

1 cup semisweet chocolate chips

¼ cup whipping cream

½ cup miniature candy-coated chocolate baking bits

2 teaspoons colored sprinkles

1) Heat oven to 350°F. In ungreased 13x9-inch pan, break up cookie dough. With floured fingers, press dough evenly in bottom of pan to form crust. Bake 12 to 16 minutes or until light golden brown. Cool completely, about 30 minutes.

2) In medium bowl, beat ½ cup of the butter, the peanut butter, powdered sugar and milk until smooth. Stir in the peanuts. Spread mixture over the cooled crust.

3) In 1-quart saucepan, cook chocolate chips and remaining ¼ cup butter over low heat, stirring frequently, until melted and smooth. Remove from heat. Cool 10 minutes.

4) Stir whipping cream into chocolate mixture until well blended. Spread over peanut butter mixture. Immediately sprinkle baking bits and colored sprinkles over chocolate. Refrigerate until chocolate is set, about 1 hour. For bars, cut into 6 rows by 6 rows. Store bars in refrigerator.

HIGH ALTITUDE (3500-6500 FT.): Bake crust 16 to 19 minutes.

Nutrition Information Per Serving:

Calories:	210	From Fat:	110
Total Fat			13g
Saturated Fat			5g
Trans Fat			0.5g
Cholesterol			15mg
Sodium			100mg
Total Carbohydrate			21g
Dietary Fiber			0g
Sugars			16g
Protein			3g

tip

To make this yummy treat speedier and cross an ingredient off of your shopping list, omit the peanuts and replace the regular peanut butter with the crunchy variety.

Southwest Sloppy Joe Pizza

CHRIS BATTON | NORTH IRWIN, PENNSYLVANIA

BAKE-OFF® CONTEST 43, 2008

PREP TIME: 20 MINUTES (READY IN 45 MINUTES)
SERVINGS: 8

ⓔ EASY

1 can (13.8 oz) Pillsbury® refrigerated classic pizza crust

1 lb lean (at least 80%) ground beef

1 medium onion, chopped (¹⁄₂ cup)

¹⁄₄ cup diced jalapeño chiles

¹⁄₄ teaspoon ground mustard

¹⁄₄ teaspoon garlic powder

1¹⁄₂ teaspoons Worcestershire sauce

1 cup Old El Paso® Thick 'n Chunky salsa

¹⁄₂ cup Smucker's® Concord Grape jelly

2 cups shredded mild Cheddar cheese (8 oz)

1) Heat oven to 400°F. Spray large cookie sheet with Crisco® Original No-Stick cooking spray. Unroll the pizza crust dough on cookie sheet; press dough into 15x10-inch rectangle. Bake 8 to 10 minutes or until light golden brown.

2) In 10-inch skillet, cook beef, onion and chiles over medium heat 8 to 10 minutes, stirring occasionally, until the beef is thoroughly cooked; drain well.

3) Stir the mustard, garlic powder, Worcestershire sauce, salsa and jelly into the beef mixture. Cook over medium heat 5 to 6 minutes, stirring occasionally, until slightly thickened.

4) Spread beef mixture over partially baked crust. Sprinkle with cheese.

5) Bake 8 to 16 minutes longer or until cheese is melted and crust is golden brown. Let pizza stand 5 minutes before cutting.

HIGH ALTITUDE (3500-6500 FT.): No change.

Nutrition Information Per Serving:	
Calories: 400	From Fat: 160
Total Fat	17g
Saturated Fat	9g
Trans Fat	0.5g
Cholesterol	65mg
Sodium	800mg
Total Carbohydrate	41g
Dietary Fiber	0g
Sugars	14g
Protein	21g

If less heat is desired, remove the ribs and seeds from the chiles before dicing them.

Easy Crescent Taco Bake

PREP TIME: 25 MINUTES (READY IN 50 MINUTES)
SERVINGS: 6

1 can (8 oz) Pillsbury® refrigerated crescent dinner rolls

1 lb lean (at least 80%) ground beef

¾ cup Old El Paso® thick 'n chunky salsa

2 tablespoons Old El Paso® taco seasoning mix (from 1.25-oz package)

1 cup shredded Cheddar cheese (4 oz)

Shredded lettuce, as desired

Diced tomato, as desired

Nutrition Information Per Serving:

Calories:	370	From Fat:	200
Total Fat			23g
Saturated Fat			10g
Trans Fat			2.5g
Cholesterol			65mg
Sodium			960mg
Total Carbohydrate			20g
Dietary Fiber			0g
Sugars			4g
Protein			21g

1) Heat oven to 375°F. Unroll dough; separate into 8 triangles. Place in ungreased 9-inch square pan or 10-inch pie plate; press over bottom and up sides to form crust.

2) In 10-inch skillet, cook the beef over medium heat 8 to 10 minutes, stirring occasionally, until thoroughly cooked; drain. Stir in salsa and taco seasoning mix; simmer 5 minutes. Spoon meat mixture in crust-lined pan; sprinkle with cheese.

3) Bake 20 to 25 minutes or until crust is deep golden brown and cheese is melted. Serve topped with lettuce and tomato.

HIGH ALTITUDE (3500-6500 FT.): No change.

No-Bake Cereal Bars

PREP TIME: 25 MINUTES (READY IN 55 MINUTES)
SERVINGS: 36 BARS

 EASY

1 cup light corn syrup

1 cup sugar

1¼ cups peanut butter

6 cups Cheerios® cereal

1 bag (12 oz) semisweet chocolate chips (2 cups)

Nutrition Information Per Serving:

Calories:	180	From Fat:	70
Total Fat			8g
Saturated Fat			2.5g
Trans Fat			0g
Cholesterol			0mg
Sodium			85mg
Total Carbohydrate			24g
Dietary Fiber			1g
Sugars			15g
Protein			3g

1) Lightly butter 13x9-inch pan. In 4- to 5-quart Dutch oven, heat the corn syrup and sugar to boiling over medium-high heat, stirring constantly. Cook until the sugar is dissolved; remove from heat. Add 1 cup of the peanut butter; stir until smooth. Add cereal; mix well. Immediately press in buttered pan.

2) In 2-quart saucepan over low heat, melt chocolate chips with remaining ¼ cup peanut butter, stirring constantly. Spread evenly over the bars. Refrigerate about 30 minutes or cool completely at room temperature until chocolate is set. For bars, cut into 9 rows by 4 rows.

HIGH ALTITUDE (3500-6500 FT.): No change.

Peanuttiest Peanut Butter Brownie Bars

SHEILAH FIOLA | KENT, WASHINGTON

Pillsbury Bake-Off®   BAKE-OFF® CONTEST 43, 2008

PREP TIME: 30 MINUTES (READY IN 3 HOURS 55 MINUTES)
SERVINGS: 24 BARS

1 box (13.3 oz) Pillsbury® Peanut Butter Swirl Jif® brownie mix

2 cups crushed chocolate or regular graham crackers (28 squares)

½ cup plus 3 tablespoons Land O Lakes® butter

1 can (14 oz) sweetened condensed milk (not evaporated)

⅓ cup Jif® creamy peanut butter

1¼ cups peanut butter chips

¾ cup milk chocolate chips

1 cup Fisher® Spanish peanuts, finely chopped

Nutrition Information Per Serving:

Calories:	350	From Fat:	180
Total Fat			20g
Saturated Fat			9g
Trans Fat			0.5g
Cholesterol			20mg
Sodium			190mg
Total Carbohydrate			35g
Dietary Fiber			1g
Sugars			27g
Protein			7g

1) Heat oven to 350°F (325°F for dark or nonstick pan). Lightly spray 13x9-inch pan with Crisco® Original No-Stick cooking spray.

2) In large bowl, stir dry brownie mix and graham cracker crumbs until well mixed; set aside.

3) Into medium microwavable bowl, squeeze peanut butter from peanut butter packet (from brownie mix). Add butter. Microwave uncovered on High 1 minute to 1 minute 30 seconds, stirring once, until butter is melted. Stir until smooth.

4) Pour peanut butter mixture over brownie mixture; stir until well mixed. Press evenly in pan.

5) In same medium microwavable bowl, mix milk, ⅓ cup peanut butter and ½ cup of the peanut butter chips. Microwave uncovered on High 1 minute, stirring once, until mixture is melted. Stir until smooth.

6) Gently pour milk mixture evenly over brownie layer in pan; spread evenly. Sprinkle remaining ¾ cup peanut butter chips, the chocolate chips and peanuts over milk mixture; press in lightly.

7) Bake 18 to 22 minutes or until edges are golden brown and center is just set when lightly touched (do not overbake). Cool completely in pan on cooling rack, about 3 hours. For bars, cut into 6 rows by 4 rows.

HIGH ALTITUDE (3500-6500 FT.): Bake 25 to 30 minutes.

Frozen Banana-Split Dessert

PREP TIME: 25 MINUTES (READY IN 4 HOURS 5 MINUTES)
SERVINGS: 9

^{2}/$_3$ cup crushed chocolate graham
    crackers (8 squares)

2 tablespoons sugar

2 tablespoons butter or margarine,
    melted

1 box (4-serving size) vanilla pudding
    and pie filling mix (not instant)

^{1}/$_2$ cup sugar

2 cups milk

2 ripe bananas, mashed

1^3/$_4$ cups frozen whipped topping,
    thawed

^{1}/$_3$ cup hot fudge topping

1^1/$_4$ cups fresh whole strawberries, cut
    into ^{1}/$_2$-inch pieces

1^1/$_4$ cups ^{1}/$_2$-inch pieces fresh pineapple

1) Spray 8-inch square pan with cooking
   spray. In small bowl, mix crushed
   crackers and 2 tablespoons sugar. Stir in
   melted butter until crumbly and well
   blended. Press mixture in bottom of pan.
   Freeze about 10 minutes or until set.

2) Meanwhile, in 2-quart saucepan, mix
   pudding mix, ^{1}/$_2$ cup sugar and the milk
   with wire whisk. Cook over medium heat,
   stirring constantly, until mixture comes to
   a full boil. Cool 10 minutes at room
   temperature. Refrigerate 30 minutes.

3) Stir bananas into pudding. Fold in 1 cup
   of the whipped topping. Spread over
   crust. Freeze at least 3 hours or overnight.

4) Cut into serving pieces; place on dessert
   plates. Top each piece with 2 teaspoons
   fudge topping, generous tablespoonful
   of the remaining whipped topping,
   2 tablespoons berries and 2 tablespoons
   pineapple. Serve immediately.

HIGH ALTITUDE (3500-6500 FT.): No change.

Nutrition Information Per Serving:

Calories:	290	From Fat:	70
Total Fat			8g
Saturated Fat			6g
Trans Fat			0g
Cholesterol			10mg
Sodium			130mg
Total Carbohydrate			51g
Dietary Fiber			2g
Sugars			40g
Protein			3g

tip

Having a party?
Serve each piece
of dessert without
toppings, then let
guests add their
own hot fudge,
strawberries,
pineapple and
whipped topping.

Flaky Pizza Snacks

PREP TIME: 25 MINUTES (READY IN 35 MINUTES)
SERVINGS: 16 SNACKS

 EASY

1 can (8 oz) Pillsbury® refrigerated crescent dinner rolls

1/3 cup pizza sauce

1/4 cup grated Parmesan cheese

1 cup finely chopped tomato

1/3 cup shredded mozzarella cheese

Chopped fresh basil leaves, if desired

Nutrition Information Per Serving:	
Calories: 70	From Fat: 35
Total Fat	4g
Saturated Fat	1.5g
Trans Fat	1g
Cholesterol	0mg
Sodium	170mg
Total Carbohydrate	7g
Dietary Fiber	0g
Sugars	2g
Protein	2g

1) Heat oven to 375°F. Spray cookie sheet with cooking spray. Unroll dough into 1 large rectangle; press perforations to seal.

2) Spread the pizza sauce evenly over rectangle to within 1 inch of the edges. Sprinkle with Parmesan cheese. Starting at short side, roll up rectangle, jelly-roll fashion. With sharp knife, cut into 16 slices. Place slices cut side down on cookie sheet. Top each slice with 1 tablespoon tomato and about 1 teaspoon mozzarella cheese.

3) Bake 9 to 11 minutes or until the edges are golden brown and the cheese is melted. (Bottoms will be very deep golden brown.) Top with basil.

HIGH ALTITUDE (3500-6500 FT.): Bake 10 to 12 minutes.

Weeknight Stroganoff

PREP TIME: 20 MINUTES (READY IN 20 MINUTES)
SERVINGS: 4 (1-1/2 CUPS EACH)

 EASY

1 medium onion, sliced (1/2 cup)

1 cup water

1 can (14 oz) beef broth

4 1/2 cups uncooked wide egg noodles (8 oz)

1 cup Green Giant® frozen sweet peas

1 teaspoon paprika

1/2 lb cooked roast beef, cut into thin bite-size strips

1 container (8 oz) sour cream

2 medium green onions, sliced (2 tablespoons), if desired

1) Spray 12-inch skillet or 5-quart Dutch oven with cooking spray; heat over medium-high heat. Add the onion; cook and stir 2 to 3 minutes or until crisp-tender.

2) Stir in water, beef broth, uncooked noodles, frozen peas and paprika. Heat to boiling. Reduce heat to medium-low; cover and simmer 6 to 8 minutes, stirring occasionally, until the noodles are desired doneness and the liquid is almost absorbed.

3) Stir in beef and sour cream. Cook 1 to 2 minutes longer, stirring constantly, just until hot. Sprinkle with green onions.

HIGH ALTITUDE (3500-6500 FT.): No change.

Nutrition Information Per Serving:	
Calories: 500	From Fat: 210
Total Fat	23g
Saturated Fat	11g
Trans Fat	1g
Cholesterol	125mg
Sodium	520mg
Total Carbohydrate	47g
Dietary Fiber	3g
Sugars	5g
Protein	25g

California Cheeseburger Pie

PREP TIME: 25 MINUTES (READY IN 1 HOUR 15 MINUTES)
SERVINGS: 8

1 box (15 oz) Pillsbury® refrigerated pie crusts, softened as directed on box

1½ lb lean (at least 80%) ground beef

2 large onions, chopped (1 cup)

12 oz prepared cheese product (from 16-oz loaf), cubed (about 2 cups)

½ cup Thousand Island dressing

2 teaspoons yellow mustard

16 round dill pickle chips or 8 oblong dill pickle slices

¼ teaspoon sesame seed

Lettuce leaves

2 plum (Roma) tomatoes, sliced

1) Heat oven to 375°F. Make pie crusts as directed on box for Two-Crust Pie using 9-inch glass pie plate.

2) In 12-inch skillet, cook ground beef and onions over medium-high heat, stirring frequently, until the beef is thoroughly cooked; drain.

3) Stir in the cheese, dressing and mustard. Reduce heat to low; cook 2 to 3 minutes, stirring occasionally, until the cheese is melted. Spoon beef mixture into crust-lined pie plate. Arrange pickle chips over beef mixture.

4) Top with second crust; seal edge and flute. Sprinkle with sesame seed. Cut slits in several places in top crust. Cover crust edge with 2- to 3-inch-wide strips of foil to prevent excessive browning; remove foil during the last 15 minutes of baking.

5) Bake 30 to 40 minutes or until crust is golden brown. Let stand 10 minutes before serving. Top pie with lettuce and tomatoes. Serve with ketchup and mustard if desired.

HIGH ALTITUDE (3500-6500 FT.): No change.

Nutrition Information Per Serving:		
Calories: 600	From Fat:	370
Total Fat		41g
Saturated Fat		16g
Trans Fat		1g
Cholesterol		100mg
Sodium		1330mg
Total Carbohydrate		35g
Dietary Fiber		0g
Sugars		7g
Protein		23g

Beef and Bean Taco Casserole

PREP TIME: 20 MINUTES (READY IN 50 MINUTES)
SERVINGS: 5 (1-1/2 CUPS EACH)

e EASY

1 lb lean (at least 80%) ground beef

1 can (16 oz) Old El Paso® refried beans

1 jar (16 oz) Old El Paso® Thick 'n Chunky salsa

1 package (1.25 oz) Old El Paso® 40% less-sodium taco seasoning mix

2½ cups coarsely broken tortilla chips

½ medium green bell pepper, chopped (¾ cup)

4 medium green onions, sliced (¼ cup)

2 medium tomatoes, chopped (1½ cups)

1 cup shredded Cheddar or Monterey Jack cheese (4 oz)

¼ cup sliced ripe olives

1 cup shredded lettuce

1) Heat oven to 350°F. In 12-inch skillet, cook beef over medium-high heat 5 to 7 minutes, stirring occasionally, until thoroughly cooked; drain. Stir in refried beans, salsa and taco seasoning mix. Reduce heat to medium. Heat to boiling, stirring occasionally.

2) In ungreased 2-quart casserole, place 2 cups of the broken tortilla chips. Top evenly with beef mixture. Sprinkle with bell pepper, onions, 1 cup of the tomato, the cheese and olives.

3) Bake uncovered 20 to 30 minutes or until hot and bubbly and cheese is melted. Top baked casserole with lettuce, remaining ½ cup tomato and remaining ½ cup tortilla chips.

HIGH ALTITUDE (3500-6500 FT.): Bake uncovered 25 to 35 minutes.

Nutrition Information Per Serving:

Calories:	510	From Fat:	220
Total Fat			24g
Saturated Fat			10g
Trans Fat			1g
Cholesterol			85mg
Sodium			1720mg
Total Carbohydrate			44g
Dietary Fiber			7g
Sugars			6g
Protein			29g

Rocky Road Crescent Bars

LORRAINE AUSTIN | ANAHEIM, CALIFORNIA

BAKE-OFF® CONTEST 28, 1978

PREP TIME: 20 MINUTES (READY IN 1 HOUR 50 MINUTES)
SERVINGS: 36 BARS

⊜ EASY

1 can (8 oz) Pillsbury® refrigerated crescent dinner rolls

1 package (8 oz) cream cheese, softened

1/2 cup sugar

3/4 cup peanut butter

1/2 cup corn syrup

1 teaspoon vanilla

1 egg

1 1/2 cups miniature marshmallows

3/4 cup salted peanuts, chopped

1 bag (6 oz) semisweet chocolate chips (1 cup)

1) Heat oven to 375°F. Unroll dough and separate into 2 long rectangles. Place in ungreased 15x10x1-inch pan or 13x9-inch pan; press over bottom of pan to form crust. Press the edges and perforations to seal.

2) In medium bowl, mix cream cheese, sugar and peanut butter until smooth. Add corn syrup, vanilla and egg; blend well. Pour peanut butter mixture over crust. Sprinkle with marshmallows, peanuts and chocolate chips.

3) Bake 15x10x1-inch pan 18 to 22 minutes, 13x9-inch pan 25 to 30 minutes or until filling is puffed and edges are deep golden brown. Cool completely, about 1 hour. For bars, cut into 9 rows by 4 rows.

HIGH ALTITUDE (3500-6500 FT.): After pouring peanut butter mixture over crust, bake 15x10x1-inch pan 22 to 25 minutes, 13x9-inch pan 28 to 30 minutes. Sprinkle with marshmallows, peanuts and chocolate chips. Bake 10 minutes longer.

Nutrition Information Per Serving:		
Calories: 160	From Fat:	80
Total Fat		9g
Saturated Fat		3.5g
Trans Fat		0g
Cholesterol		15mg
Sodium		110mg
Total Carbohydrate		15g
Dietary Fiber		0g
Sugars		9g
Protein		4g

tip Corn syrup is available in a light and dark variety. Light corn syrup, which has a milder, sweet flavor, has been clarified to remove color and cloudiness.

Cheesy Chicken and Bean Quesadillas

PREP TIME: 40 MINUTES (READY IN 1 HOUR)
SERVINGS: 8 QUESADILLAS

2 cups shredded or finely chopped deli rotisserie chicken (from 2- to 2½-lb chicken)

½ cup chopped red bell pepper

4 medium green onions, thinly sliced (¼ cup)

1 can (15 oz) Progresso® black beans, drained, rinsed

½ cup cooked white rice

1 package (11.5 oz) Old El Paso® flour tortillas for burritos (8 tortillas)

3 cups shredded Monterey Jack cheese (12 oz)

Cooking spray

1 teaspoon olive oil

1 cup Old El Paso® Thick 'n Chunky salsa

½ cup sour cream

1) In medium bowl, mix the chicken, bell pepper, green onions, beans and rice. Top half of each tortilla with ½ cup chicken mixture and ½ cup of the cheese. Fold other half of each tortilla over filling, press down slightly. Spray top halves of tortillas with cooking spray.

2) Heat 12-inch skillet over medium-low heat. Place 2 filled tortillas at a time, sprayed sides down, in skillet. Cook 4 to 5 minutes, turning once, until golden brown and hot. Cut into wedges. Serve with salsa and sour cream.

HIGH ALTITUDE (3500-6500 FT.): No change.

Nutrition Information Per Serving:

Calories: 480	From Fat: 210
Total Fat	24g
Saturated Fat	12g
Trans Fat	1.5g
Cholesterol	75mg
Sodium	970mg
Total Carbohydrate	39g
Dietary Fiber	5g
Sugars	3g
Protein	28g

Cookie-Peanut-Ice Cream Pizza

PREP TIME: 15 MINUTES (READY IN 1 HOUR 30 MINUTES)
SERVINGS: 10

 EASY

1 roll (16.5 oz) Pillsbury® Create 'n Bake™ refrigerated chocolate chip cookies

1 jar (16 oz) hot fudge topping

½ gallon (8 cups) vanilla ice cream

1 cup salted Spanish peanuts

Nutrition Information Per Serving:

Calories: 680	From Fat: 290
Total Fat	32g
Saturated Fat	13g
Trans Fat	2g
Cholesterol	60mg
Sodium	440mg
Total Carbohydrate	87g
Dietary Fiber	3g
Sugars	60g
Protein	12g

1) Heat oven to 350°F. Spray 12-inch pizza pan with cooking spray. Break up cookie dough onto pan. Press dough in bottom and up side of pan to form crust. Bake 10 to 14 minutes or until light golden brown. Cool completely, about 30 minutes.

2) Stir hot fudge topping to soften. Spoon and spread about half of topping over cookie crust. Cover with scoops of ice cream, leaving ½ inch around the edge.

3) Drizzle remaining topping over ice cream, heating topping if necessary. Sprinkle with peanuts. Freeze 30 minutes. Cut into wedges to serve.

HIGH ALTITUDE (3500-6500 FT.): Heat oven to 375°F. Bake 12 to 14 minutes.

Chili-Cheese Dog Pizza

ROBIN HYDE | DELAND, FLORIDA

Pillsbury Bake-Off®

BAKE-OFF® CONTEST 43, 2008

PREP TIME: 20 MINUTES (READY IN 45 MINUTES)
SERVINGS: 6

ℯ EASY

1 can (13.8 oz) Pillsbury® refrigerated classic pizza crust

5 all-beef hot dogs

1 tablespoon Crisco® 100% extra virgin or pure olive oil

1 garlic clove, finely chopped

1 cup chili with beans (from 15-oz can)

1 medium onion, chopped (1/2 cup)

1/2 cup chopped dill pickles

1 cup shredded mild Cheddar cheese (4 oz)

1 to 2 tablespoons ketchup

1 to 2 tablespoons yellow mustard

1) Heat oven to 400°F. Spray large cookie sheet with Crisco® Original No-Stick cooking spray. Unroll pizza crust dough on cookie sheet; press dough into 13x9-inch rectangle. Pinch edges of dough to form rim.

2) Generously prick hot dogs with fork to prevent curling; cut diagonally into 1/4-inch slices (about 9 to 10 slices per hot dog). Place slices on dough; press down gently. Mix oil and garlic; drizzle over dough and hot dogs.

3) Bake 15 to 18 minutes or until crust is golden brown. Meanwhile, in 1-quart saucepan, heat the chili over medium-low heat 4 to 5 minutes, stirring occasionally, until hot.

4) Spoon chili randomly over hot dog slices; spread evenly to cover. Sprinkle with onion, pickles and cheese.

5) Bake 2 to 3 minutes longer or until cheese is melted. Drizzle ketchup and mustard in diagonal pattern over pizza.

HIGH ALTITUDE (3500-6500 FT.): No change.

Nutrition Information Per Serving:	
Calories: 430	From Fat: 200
Total Fat	22g
Saturated Fat	9g
Trans Fat	0.5g
Cholesterol	40mg
Sodium	1360mg
Total Carbohydrate	42g
Dietary Fiber	2g
Sugars	8g
Protein	16g

Double-Delight Peanut Butter Cookies

CAROLYN GURTZ | GAITHERSBURG, MARYLAND

PREP TIME: 45 MINUTES (READY IN 45 MINUTES)
SERVINGS: 24 COOKIES

¼ cup Fisher® dry-roasted peanuts, finely chopped

¼ cup Domino® or C&H® granulated sugar

½ teaspoon ground cinnamon

½ cup Jif® creamy peanut butter

½ cup Domino® or C&H® confectioners' powdered sugar

1 roll (16.5 oz) Pillsbury® Create 'n Bake® refrigerated peanut butter cookies, well chilled

1) Heat oven to 375°F. In small bowl, mix chopped peanuts, granulated sugar and cinnamon; set aside.

2) In another small bowl, stir the creamy peanut butter and powdered sugar until completely blended. Shape mixture into 24 (1-inch) balls.

3) Cut roll of cookie dough into 12 slices. Cut each slice in half crosswise to make 24 pieces; flatten slightly. Shape 1 cookie dough piece around 1 peanut butter ball, covering completely. Repeat with remaining dough and balls.

4) Roll each covered ball in peanut mixture; gently pat mixture completely onto balls. On ungreased large cookie sheets, place balls 2 inches apart. Spray bottom of drinking glass with Crisco® Original No-Stick cooking spray; press into remaining peanut mixture. Flatten each ball to ¼-inch thickness with bottom of glass. Sprinkle any remaining peanut mixture evenly on tops of cookies; gently press into dough.

5) Bake 7 to 12 minutes or until edges are golden brown. Cool 1 minute; remove from cookie sheets to cooling rack. Store tightly covered.

HIGH ALTITUDE (3500-6500 FT.): No change.

Nutrition Information Per Serving:

Calories:	150	From Fat: 70
Total Fat		7g
Saturated Fat		1.5g
Trans Fat		0.5g
Cholesterol		0mg
Sodium		125mg
Total Carbohydrate		17g
Dietary Fiber		0g
Sugars		11g
Protein		3g

Family-Size Chicken Pot Pie

PREP TIME: 1 HOUR (READY IN 1 HOUR 40 MINUTES)
SERVINGS: 12

1½ lb boneless skinless chicken breasts or thighs

12 oz baby red potatoes, quartered (about 2 cups)

½ lb ready-to-eat baby-cut carrots (about 2 cups)

2 cans (14 oz each) chicken broth

1 lb fresh asparagus spears, trimmed, cut into 2-inch pieces

5 tablespoons butter or margarine

1 box (10.6 oz) Pillsbury® refrigerated Italian garlic with herb breadsticks

1 cup chopped onions (1 large)

6 tablespoons all-purpose flour

½ teaspoon seasoned salt

1½ cups whipping cream

1 tablespoon finely chopped fresh rosemary leaves

1 package (8 oz) sliced fresh mushrooms (3 cups)

Nutrition Information Per Serving:

Calories:	340	From Fat:	170
Total Fat		19g	
Saturated Fat		10g	
Trans Fat		1g	
Cholesterol		80mg	
Sodium		680mg	
Total Carbohydrate		23g	
Dietary Fiber		2g	
Sugars		4g	
Protein		18g	

1) Heat oven to 350°F. Spray bottom only of 13x9-inch (3-quart) glass baking dish with cooking spray.

2) In 5- to 6-quart Dutch oven, heat chicken, potatoes, carrots and broth to boiling over medium-high heat. Cover and simmer 18 minutes. Add asparagus; cook 2 minutes longer. Using slotted spoon, remove potatoes, carrots and asparagus to colander to drain. Check doneness of chicken; if juice of chicken is clear when center of thickest part is cut, remove to cutting board. Measure out and reserve 2 cups broth for sauce; discard any remaining broth. Return vegetables to Dutch oven; cover. When chicken is cool enough to handle, tear into large shreds. Place chicken in Dutch oven.

3) In 3-quart saucepan, melt butter and half the garlic butter from breadsticks box over medium heat. Cook onions in butter 2 minutes. Using wire whisk, stir in flour and seasoned salt. Cook, stirring constantly, about 1 minute or until flour bubbles. Do not let flour turn brown.

4) Gradually stir in 2 cups reserved chicken broth; heat to boiling. Boil and stir 1 minute. Reduce heat to low. Stir in the whipping cream; cook 4 to 5 minutes, stirring constantly, until thickened. Stir in rosemary. Pour the sauce over the vegetables and chicken. Spread in baking dish; sprinkle with the mushrooms.

5) Separate breadstick dough into 10 strips. Pinch 2 strips together, forming 1 long strip; repeat, making 2 additional strips, and use these longer strips for the 13-inch length of baking dish. Create lattice pattern over mixture by twisting and gently stretching each strip of dough over mixture, tucking ends of strips under. With cover removed from remaining garlic butter; microwave on High 5 seconds to soften. Lightly brush butter over strips.

6) Bake 30 to 40 minutes or until bubbly around edges. If necessary, loosely cover with foil after 20 minutes to prevent excessive browning.

HIGH ALTITUDE (3500-6500 FT.): Bake 35 to 40 minutes.

Cookies, Bars & Candies

Sweet tooths will be thrilled when you surprise them with these irresistible homemade goodies.

GINGER MACAROONS
PG. 305

WAKE-UP ESPRESSO CEREAL BARS
PG. 305

CHOCOLATE TRUFFLE
MERINGUES
PG. 294

FUDGY CHOCOLATE-PEANUT BUTTER
THUMBPRINTS
PG. 306

Coconut-Hazelnut Dream Bars

PREP TIME: 30 MINUTES (READY IN 2 HOURS 20 MINUTES)
SERVINGS: 36 BARS

CRUST

¾ cup all-purpose or unbleached flour

⅓ cup granulated sugar

¼ cup unsweetened baking cocoa

5 tablespoons cold butter or margarine

2 teaspoons ice water

FILLING

⅓ cup ginger or orange marmalade

⅓ cup packed brown sugar

¼ teaspoon vanilla

1 egg

¾ cup coarsely chopped toasted hazelnuts (filberts)

½ cup coconut

¼ teaspoon baking powder

⅛ teaspoon salt

TOPPING

2 tablespoons dark chocolate chips

¼ teaspoon vegetable oil

1) Heat oven to 350°F. Line 8-inch square pan with foil. In medium bowl, mix flour, sugar and cocoa. Using pastry blender or fork, cut in butter until mixture looks like coarse crumbs. Stir in ice water to form crumbly mixture. Press the mixture in foil-lined pan. Bake 12 to 15 minutes or until set. Cool 10 minutes on cooling rack.

2) Spread marmalade over crust. In small bowl, beat brown sugar, vanilla and egg with electric mixer on medium speed until well blended and light in color. Stir in remaining filling ingredients; mix well. Carefully spoon mixture over marmalade. Bake 23 to 28 minutes or until golden brown. Cool 1 hour.

3) In small microwavable bowl, microwave chocolate chips and oil uncovered on High 20 seconds. Stir; microwave in additional 20-second increments until mixture can be stirred smooth. Drizzle over bars. Cut into 6 rows by 6 rows.

HIGH ALTITUDE (3500-6500 FT.): No change.

Nutrition Information Per Serving:		
Calories: 80	From Fat:	35
Total Fat		4g
Saturated Fat		1.5g
Trans Fat		0g
Cholesterol		10mg
Sodium		30mg
Total Carbohydrate		9g
Dietary Fiber		0g
Sugars		6g
Protein		1g

 tip

To toast hazelnuts, heat oven to 350°F. Spread hazelnuts in an ungreased shallow pan. Bake uncovered 6 to 7 minutes, stirring occasionally, until light brown.

Cranberry-Orange Biscotti

PREP TIME: 1 HOUR 5 MINUTES (READY IN 1 HOUR 45 MINUTES)
SERVINGS: ABOUT 4 DOZEN COOKIES

½ cup sugar

½ cup firmly packed brown sugar

¼ cup butter or margarine, softened

2 teaspoons grated orange peel

3 eggs

3 cups all-purpose flour

3 teaspoons baking powder

¾ cup sweetened dried cranberries, chopped

¼ cup chopped almonds

GLAZE

8 oz white chocolate baking bar, chopped

1 cup dark chocolate chips

1 teaspoon grated orange peel

Nutrition Information Per Serving:

Calories:	110	From Fat:	40
Total Fat			4.5g
Saturated Fat			2.5g
Trans Fat			0g
Cholesterol			15mg
Sodium			45mg
Total Carbohydrate			17g
Dietary Fiber			0g
Sugars			11g
Protein			2g

1) Heat oven to 350°F. Spray 1 large or 2 small cookie sheets with cooking spray.

2) In 4-quart bowl, beat sugar, brown sugar and butter with electric mixer on medium speed until well blended. Add 2 teaspoons orange peel and the eggs; beat well. Stir in the flour and baking powder; mix well. Stir in the cranberries and almonds.

3) Shape the dough into 3 rolls, each about 7 inches long. Place the rolls at least 3 inches apart on cookie sheet; flatten each to form ¾-inch-thick rectangle, about 3 inches wide and 7 inches long.

4) Bake 20 to 25 minutes or until rectangles are light golden brown and centers are firm to the touch. Place rectangles on cooling racks; cool 5 minutes.

5) Wipe cookie sheet clean. With serrated knife, cut each rectangle into ½-inch slices; place, cut side up, on cookie sheet.

6) Bake 6 to 8 minutes or until top surface is slightly dry. Turn cookies over; bake 6 to 8 minutes longer or until top surface is slightly dry. Remove cookies from cookie sheets; cool completely on cooling racks.

7) Melt white chocolate in 2-quart heavy saucepan over low heat, stirring until smooth. Remove from heat; dip 1 long side of each of 24 cookies into chocolate. Place on waxed paper until chocolate is set. In another 2-quart heavy saucepan, melt dark chocolate over low heat, stirring until smooth. Remove from heat; dip 1 long side of remaining 24 cookies into chocolate. Place on waxed paper until chocolate is set. Store tightly covered.

HIGH ALTITUDE (3500-6500 FT.): No change.

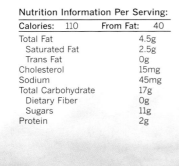

Dark Chocolate Brownies with Chunky Peanut Butter Filling

PREP TIME: 35 MINUTES (READY IN 2 HOURS 50 MINUTES)
SERVINGS: 36 BROWNIES

BROWNIES

- 1/2 cup dark corn syrup
- 1/2 cup butter
- 6 oz bittersweet baking chocolate, coarsely chopped
- 3 eggs
- 1 cup all-purpose flour
- 3/4 cup granulated sugar
- 1 teaspoon vanilla

FILLING

- 2 cups chunky peanut butter
- 1/2 cup butter, softened
- 2 cups powdered sugar
- 1 tablespoon vanilla

FROSTING

- 1/2 cup whipping cream
- 6 oz bittersweet baking chocolate, coarsely chopped
- 1 teaspoon vanilla
- Chopped roasted peanuts, if desired

1) Heat oven to 325°F. Grease bottom and sides of 13x9-inch pan with shortening and lightly flour, or spray with baking spray with flour.

2) In 2-quart saucepan, heat the corn syrup, 1/2 cup butter and 6 oz chocolate over low heat, stirring frequently, until chocolate is melted. Remove from heat. Beat in eggs, one at a time, using wire whisk. Add flour, granulated sugar and 1 teaspoon vanilla; beat with wire whisk until batter is smooth and shiny. Spread in pan.

3) Bake 23 to 25 minutes or just until toothpick inserted in center comes out clean (do not overbake). Cool completely, about 45 minutes.

4) Meanwhile, in large bowl, beat the peanut butter and 1/2 cup butter with electric mixer on medium speed until blended. Add powdered sugar and 1 tablespoon vanilla; beat until smooth and fluffy. Spread over brownies.

5) In 1-quart saucepan, heat whipping cream and 6 oz chocolate over low heat, stirring frequently, until chocolate is melted and mixture is smooth. Stir in 1 teaspoon vanilla. Cool 5 minutes. Spread frosting over peanut butter filling. Sprinkle with peanuts. Refrigerate until firm, about 1 hour. For brownies, cut into 6 rows by 6 rows.

HIGH ALTITUDE (3500-6500 FT.): Heat oven to 350°F. Bake 27 to 29 minutes.

Nutrition Information Per Serving:		
Calories: 290	From Fat:	170
Total Fat		19g
Saturated Fat		9g
Trans Fat		0g
Cholesterol		35mg
Sodium		115mg
Total Carbohydrate		23g
Dietary Fiber		2g
Sugars		14g
Protein		6g

Lemon Butter Flutes

PREP TIME: 1 HOUR 15 MINUTES (READY IN 1 HOUR 15 MINUTES)
SERVINGS: ABOUT 4 DOZEN COOKIES

COOKIES

1¼ cups powdered sugar

1 cup butter or margarine, softened

1 tablespoon grated lemon peel

1 tablespoon lemon juice

1 egg

2½ cups all-purpose or unbleached flour

¼ teaspoon salt

GLAZE

1 cup powdered sugar

4 to 5 teaspoons lemon juice

2 teaspoons powdered sugar

1) Heat oven to 400°F. In large bowl, beat 1¼ cups powdered sugar and the butter with electric mixer on medium speed until light and fluffy. Add lemon peel, lemon juice and egg; blend well. Stir in flour and salt until well mixed. Fill cookie press with dough. Using the cookie press and bar plate, press a long ribbon of dough onto ungreased cookie sheet. Score the cookie dough at 2¼-inch intervals.

2) Bake 5 to 8 minutes or until set but not brown. Cut cookies at score lines with sharp knife. Immediately remove from cookie sheets. Cool completely.

3) In small bowl, mix 1 cup powdered sugar and enough lemon juice for desired drizzling consistency. Drizzle over cookies; let stand until set. Sprinkle with 2 teaspoons powdered sugar.

HIGH ALTITUDE (3500-6500 FT.): No change.

Nutrition Information Per Serving:

Calories:	80	From Fat:	35
Total Fat			4g
Saturated Fat			2.5g
Trans Fat			0g
Cholesterol			15mg
Sodium			40mg
Total Carbohydrate			11g
Dietary Fiber			0g
Sugars			6g
Protein			0g

Scandinavian Almond Bars

PREP TIME: 10 MINUTES (READY IN 1 HOUR 5 MINUTES)
SERVINGS: 48 BARS

 EASY   LOW FAT

1 roll (16.5 oz) Pillsbury® Create 'n Bake® refrigerated sugar cookies

½ teaspoon ground cinnamon

1 teaspoon almond extract

1 egg white

1 tablespoon water

1 cup sliced almonds

¼ cup sugar

Nutrition Information Per Serving:

Calories:	60	From Fat:	25
Total Fat			3g
Saturated Fat			0.5g
Trans Fat			0.5g
Cholesterol			0mg
Sodium			30mg
Total Carbohydrate			7g
Dietary Fiber			0g
Sugars			4g
Protein			0g

1) Heat oven to 350°F. Grease 15x10x1-inch pan with shortening. In large bowl, break up cookie dough. Stir in cinnamon and almond extract until well blended. With floured fingers, press dough mixture evenly in bottom of pan to form crust.

2) In small bowl, beat egg white and water until frothy. Brush over dough. Sprinkle evenly with almonds and sugar.

3) Bake 17 to 22 minutes or until the edges are light golden brown. Cool completely, about 30 minutes. For triangle shapes, cut bars into 4 rows by 6 rows to make 24 squares; cut each square in half diagonally.

HIGH ALTITUDE (3500-6500 FT.): No change.

Brazilian Jubilee Cookies

PREP TIME: 1 HOUR 15 MINUTES (READY IN 1 HOUR 15 MINUTES)
SERVINGS: ABOUT 3 DOZEN COOKIES

¾ cup granulated sugar

¼ cup packed brown sugar

½ cup shortening

2 teaspoons vanilla

1 egg

1½ cups all-purpose flour

1 to 2 tablespoons instant coffee granules or crystals

1 teaspoon baking powder

½ teaspoon salt

½ teaspoon ground cinnamon

1 cup chopped Brazil nuts

36 milk chocolate stars (from 14-oz bag)

Additional chopped Brazil nuts, if desired

1) Heat oven to 350°F. Grease cookie sheets with shortening or cooking spray. In large bowl, beat the sugars and shortening with electric mixer on medium speed, scraping the bowl occasionally, until well blended. Beat in vanilla and egg. On low speed, beat in flour, instant coffee, baking powder, salt, cinnamon and 1 cup chopped nuts until dough forms.

2) Shape dough by tablespoonfuls into balls. Place 2 inches apart on cookie sheets.

3) Bake 12 to 15 minutes or until golden brown. Immediately top each cookie with 1 chocolate star. Remove from the cookie sheets to cooling rack; cool 5 minutes (chocolate will soften). Spread chocolate over cookies to frost. Sprinkle with additional chopped nuts.

HIGH ALTITUDE (3500-6500 FT.): No change.

Nutrition Information Per Serving:

Calories:	120	From Fat:	60
Total Fat			7g
Saturated Fat			2g
Trans Fat			0g
Cholesterol			5mg
Sodium			50mg
Total Carbohydrate			13g
Dietary Fiber			0g
Sugars			8g
Protein			2g

Apricot-Caramel-Coconut Bars

LINDA HICKAM | HEALDSBURG, CALIFORNIA

Bake-Off® CONTEST 43, 2008

PREP TIME:	10 MINUTES (READY IN 3 HOURS)
SERVINGS:	36 BARS

 EASY

1 cup Fisher® Chef's Naturals® slivered blanched almonds

2 cups Pillsbury BEST® all-purpose unbleached flour

1/2 cup Domino® or C&H® granulated sugar

1 cup Land O Lakes® butter, cut up

1 cup Smucker's® apricot preserves

1/3 cup Smucker's® caramel ice cream topping

3/4 cup unsweetened or sweetened shredded coconut

1) Heat oven to 350°F.

2) In food processor bowl with metal blade, place the almonds. Cover; process with on-and-off pulses until finely chopped. Add flour, sugar and butter to almonds. Cover; process with on-and-off pulses until mixture looks like coarse crumbs. (Or, finely chop almonds. In large bowl, mix chopped almonds, flour and sugar; cut in butter with pastry blender until mixture looks like coarse crumbs.)

3) In bottom of ungreased 13x9-inch pan, evenly press half of crumb mixture (about 2½ cups).

4) In medium bowl, mix preserves, caramel topping and coconut. Spread over crumb mixture to within ½ inch of the edges. Sprinkle remaining crumb mixture evenly over apricot mixture to edges of pan.

5) Bake 40 to 50 minutes or until edges are golden brown. Cool completely, about 2 hours. For bars, cut into 6 rows by 6 rows.

HIGH ALTITUDE (3500-6500 FT.): No change.

Nutrition Information Per Serving:

Calories:	140	From Fat:	70
Total Fat			8g
Saturated Fat			4.5g
Trans Fat			0g
Cholesterol			15mg
Sodium			50mg
Total Carbohydrate			16g
Dietary Fiber			0g
Sugars			8g
Protein			2g

Mocha-Walnut Bars with Dark Chocolate Ganache

ELIZABETH BENNETT | MILL CREEK, WASHINGTON

BAKE-OFF® CONTEST 43, 2008

PREP TIME: 30 MINUTES (READY IN 3 HOURS 10 MINUTES)
SERVINGS: 24 BARS

2½ cups very finely chopped Fisher®
    Chef's Naturals® walnuts

6 tablespoons Domino® or C&H®
    granulated sugar

6 tablespoons Land O Lakes® butter,
    melted

1 roll (16.5 oz) Pillsbury® Create 'n
    Bake® refrigerated sugar cookies

1 tablespoon instant espresso coffee
    granules

1½ cups dark chocolate chips

¼ cup plus 2 tablespoons whipping
    cream

Nutrition Information Per Serving:

Calories:	190	From Fat:	80
Total Fat			9g
Saturated Fat			1.5g
Trans Fat			1.5g
Cholesterol			10mg
Sodium			140mg
Total Carbohydrate			27g
Dietary Fiber			0g
Sugars			17g
Protein			2g

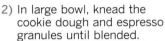

1) Heat oven to 350°F. In medium bowl, stir walnuts, sugar and butter until moistened. Press mixture evenly on bottom of ungreased 13x9-inch pan or 12x8-inch (2-quart) glass baking dish. Bake 8 to 15 minutes or until edges are just golden brown. Cool 30 minutes.

2) In large bowl, knead the cookie dough and espresso granules until blended. Drop small spoonfuls of dough evenly over walnut crust. Gently press dough together evenly over crust. (If dough is sticky, use floured fingers.)

3) Bake 20 to 25 minutes or until golden brown. Cool 30 minutes.

4) In medium microwavable bowl, microwave chocolate chips and whipping cream uncovered on High 1 minute, stirring after 30 seconds; stir until chips are melted and mixture is smooth. Spread chocolate mixture over bars. Refrigerate 1 hour. For bars, cut into 6 rows by 4 rows. Cover and refrigerate any remaining bars.

HIGH ALTITUDE (3500-6500 FT.): No change.

Rocky Road Pretzels

PREP TIME: 20 MINUTES (READY IN 20 MINUTES)
SERVINGS: 24

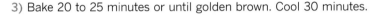 EASY

6 oz milk chocolate, chopped

2 oz bittersweet baking chocolate or mildly sweet dark chocolate, chopped

⅓ cup coarsely chopped cashews

⅓ cup miniature marshmallows

24 lattice pretzels or small pretzel twists

Nutrition Information Per Serving:

Calories:	70	From Fat:	40
Total Fat			4g
Saturated Fat			2g
Trans Fat			0g
Cholesterol			0mg
Sodium			25mg
Total Carbohydrate			7g
Dietary Fiber			0g
Sugars			4g
Protein			

1) Line large cookie sheet with waxed paper or cooking parchment paper. In medium microwavable bowl, microwave chocolates uncovered on High about 1 minute or until chocolates can be stirred smooth. Fold in cashews and marshmallows.

2) Arrange pretzels on cookie sheet 2 inches apart. Spoon heaping teaspoon chocolate onto each pretzel. Let stand in cool place until set, about 15 minutes (do not refrigerate).

HIGH ALTITUDE (3500-6500 FT.): No change.

Chocolate Swirl Almond Toffee

PREP TIME: 30 MINUTES (READY IN 1 HOUR)
SERVINGS: ABOUT 42 PIECES

TOFFEE

- 1 cup butter or margarine
- 2 tablespoons light corn syrup
- 2 tablespoons water
- 1 cup sugar
- 1 cup chopped almonds

TOPPING

- $\frac{1}{2}$ cup semisweet chocolate chips
- $\frac{1}{2}$ cup white vanilla baking chips

1) Line 15x10x1-inch pan with foil. Butter the foil.

2) In 2-quart saucepan, mix butter, corn syrup, water and sugar. Cook over medium heat until sugar dissolves and mixture boils, stirring constantly. Cook until candy thermometer reaches soft-crack stage (290°F). Remove the saucepan from heat. Quickly stir in almonds. Pour the mixture into buttered foil-lined pan. Let stand 2 to 3 minutes to harden.

3) Sprinkle chips over hot toffee; let stand 1 to 1½ minutes to soften. With knife, swirl the softened chips over toffee. Refrigerate about 30 minutes or until chocolate is set. Break toffee into serving-sized pieces.

HIGH ALTITUDE (3500-6500 FT.): Cook until candy thermometer reaches high altitude soft-crack stage (260°F to 286°F).

Nutrition Information Per Serving:

Calories:	110	From Fat:	70
Total Fat			7g
Saturated Fat			4g
Trans Fat			0g
Cholesterol			10mg
Sodium			40mg
Total Carbohydrate			9g
Dietary Fiber			0g
Sugars			8g
Protein			0g

Chocolate Truffle Meringues

PREP TIME: 25 MINUTES (READY IN 2 HOURS 10 MINUTES)
SERVINGS: 24 COOKIES

MERINGUES

2 egg whites

⅓ cup granulated sugar

½ cup powdered sugar

2 tablespoons unsweetened baking cocoa

FILLING

¼ cup whipping cream

3 oz bittersweet baking chocolate, chopped, or ½ cup dark chocolate chips

2 tablespoons butter or margarine, cut into small pieces

Nutrition Information Per Serving:

Calories:	60	From Fat:	35
Total Fat			3.5g
Saturated Fat			2.5g
Trans Fat			0g
Cholesterol			5mg
Sodium			15mg
Total Carbohydrate			7g
Dietary Fiber			0g
Sugars			5g
Protein			0g

1) Heat oven to 200°F. Line cookie sheet with cooking parchment paper. In medium bowl, beat egg whites with electric mixer on medium speed until soft peaks form. Gradually add granulated sugar, beating at high speed just until stiff peaks form.

2) In small bowl, mix powdered sugar and cocoa. Fold cocoa mixture, ⅓ at a time, into beaten egg whites. Spoon the mixture into decorating bag fitted with star tip. Draw 1½-inch-diameter circle on white paper; place under the parchment paper as a guide for piping the rounds. Pipe the mixture into twenty-four 1½-inch rounds on parchment-lined cookie sheet. With back of teaspoon, make an indentation in each to hold filling. (Or, mixture can be spooned into dollops on parchment paper.)

3) Bake 1 to 1¼ hours or until crisp. Cool completely, about 10 minutes.

4) Meanwhile, in 1-quart heavy saucepan, heat the whipping cream just to simmering over medium-low heat. Remove from heat; stir in chocolate with wire whisk until melted. Stir in butter pieces, a few at a time, until melted. Refrigerate until thickened, about 30 minutes.

5) Just before serving, spoon or pipe about 1 teaspoon filling into indentation of each meringue.

HIGH ALTITUDE (3500-6500 FT.): Heat oven to 225°F. Bake 1-1/4 to 1-1/2 hours.

 Parchment paper is a grease- and moisture-resistant paper that prevents baked goods from sticking to pans. It also keeps the pans clean. Look for it near the foil at the grocery store.

Rich Espresso Bars with Buttercream Frosting

PREP TIME: 25 MINUTES (READY IN 3 HOURS 50 MINUTES)
SERVINGS: 32 BARS

BARS

- ½ cup butter
- 1 cup packed light brown sugar
- 1 teaspoon vanilla
- 2 eggs
- ¾ cup all-purpose flour
- 2 tablespoons plus 2 teaspoons instant espresso coffee powder
- ¼ teaspoon baking powder
- ¼ teaspoon salt
- ¾ cup finely chopped pecans or walnuts, if desired

ESPRESSO BUTTERCREAM FROSTING

- ⅓ cup whipping cream
- ¼ cup butter
- 1 cup white vanilla baking chips
- 1 tablespoon instant espresso coffee powder
- ½ teaspoon vanilla
- ½ cup powdered sugar

GARNISH

- 32 chocolate-covered espresso coffee beans

1) Heat oven to 350°F. Lightly grease bottom and sides of 13x9-inch pan with shortening or cooking spray.

2) In 2-quart saucepan, heat ½ cup butter and the brown sugar over medium heat, stirring frequently, until butter is melted and sugar is moistened. Remove from heat. Add 1 teaspoon vanilla and the eggs; beat with spoon until smooth.

3) In small bowl, stir together flour, 2 tablespoons plus 2 teaspoons espresso powder, the baking powder and salt. Add to egg mixture. Beat with spoon until well blended. Stir in pecans. Spread evenly in pan.

4) Bake 15 to 20 minutes or until toothpick inserted in center comes out clean. Cool in pan on cooling rack about 30 minutes.

5) In 2-quart saucepan, heat whipping cream, ¼ cup butter and the vanilla baking chips over medium heat, stirring frequently, until chips and butter are melted. Remove from heat. Stir in 1 tablespoon espresso powder, ½ teaspoon vanilla and the powdered sugar; beat well with spoon (mixture will be lumpy). Refrigerate until chilled, about 30 minutes.

6) Beat chilled mixture with electric mixer on high speed 2 to 3 minutes or until light and fluffy. Spread evenly over bars. Refrigerate at least 2 hours. For bars, cut into 8 rows by 4 rows. Top each bar with 1 coffee bean. Cover and refrigerate any remaining bars.

HIGH ALTITUDE (3500-6500 FT.): No change.

Nutrition Information Per Serving:	
Calories: 140	From Fat: 70
Total Fat	8g
Saturated Fat	5g
Trans Fat	0g
Cholesterol	30mg
Sodium	75mg
Total Carbohydrate	17g
Dietary Fiber	0g
Sugars	14g
Protein	1g

tip

If you like, you can use instant coffee granules and put the granules through a fine sieve. The flavor will not be as pronounced as with espresso powder.

Cappuccino Fudge Brownies

PREP TIME: 40 MINUTES (READY IN 2 HOURS 30 MINUTES)
SERVINGS: 36 BROWNIES

BROWNIES

5 oz unsweetened baking chocolate, cut into pieces

¾ cup butter or margarine

2 tablespoons instant coffee granules or crystals

1 tablespoon vanilla

2¼ cups sugar

1 teaspoon ground cinnamon

4 eggs

1⅓ cups all-purpose flour

1½ cups coarsely chopped pecans

FROSTING

½ cup butter or margarine, softened

2 cups powdered sugar

½ teaspoon vanilla

2 tablespoons brewed coffee

GLAZE

1 oz semisweet baking chocolate, chopped

1 teaspoon shortening

1) Heat oven to 375°F. Grease 13x9-inch pan. In 1-quart saucepan, melt the unsweetened chocolate and ¾ cup butter over low heat, stirring occasionally. Remove from heat. Stir in coffee granules and 1 tablespoon vanilla; set aside.

2) In large bowl, beat sugar, cinnamon and eggs about 7 minutes or until sugar is dissolved. Fold chocolate mixture, flour and pecans into egg mixture just until blended. Pour batter into pan. Bake 25 to 35 minutes. Do not overbake. Cool completely, about 1 hour.

3) In small bowl, beat ½ cup butter until light and fluffy. Add powdered sugar, ½ teaspoon vanilla and brewed coffee. Beat until smooth. Spread over cooled brownies.

4) In 1-quart saucepan, melt semisweet chocolate with shortening over low heat, stirring occasionally. Drizzle glaze in horizontal parallel lines about 1 inch apart over top of brownies. Immediately draw knife through the glaze in straight vertical lines to form pattern. Refrigerate until firm, about 15 minutes. For brownies, cut into 9 rows by 4 rows. Cover and refrigerate any remaining brownies.

HIGH ALTITUDE (3500-6500 FT.): No change.

Nutrition Information Per Serving:	
Calories: 230	From Fat: 110
Total Fat	13g
Saturated Fat	6g
Trans Fat	0g
Cholesterol	40mg
Sodium	55mg
Total Carbohydrate	25g
Dietary Fiber	1g
Sugars	20g
Protein	2g

tip

For super-quick cleanup after making this recipe, line the 13x9-inch baking pan with foil before pouring the brownie batter into the pan.

Lemon-Ginger Shortbread

PREP TIME: 30 MINUTES (READY IN 1 HOUR 20 MINUTES)
SERVINGS: 32 COOKIES

COOKIES

1 cup butter, softened

1/3 cup sugar

2 cups all-purpose flour

1/3 cup finely chopped crystallized ginger

1 tablespoon grated lemon peel

GLAZE

4 oz white chocolate baking bar, chopped

1) Heat oven to 325°F. In large bowl, beat butter and sugar with electric mixer on medium speed until light and fluffy.

2) Add flour, ginger and lemon peel; mix well. Shape dough into ball; divide into 4 pieces. On ungreased cookie sheets, flatten each piece to 6-inch round; press edges to smooth.

3) Bake 15 to 25 minutes or until edges are light golden brown. Cool 5 minutes. Cut each round into 8 wedges; pierce surface with fork if desired. Cool completely on cookie sheet, about 15 minutes.

4) In small microwavable bowl, microwave white chocolate uncovered on High 30 seconds. Stir; continue microwaving, stirring every 10 seconds until melted and stirred smooth. Place in small resealable food-storage plastic bag; seal bag. Cut off small corner of bag. Squeeze chocolate decoratively onto cooled cookies.

HIGH ALTITUDE (3500-6500 FT.): Increase flour to 2-1/3 cups.

Nutrition Information Per Serving:	
Calories: 110	From Fat: 60
Total Fat	7g
Saturated Fat	4.5g
Trans Fat	0g
Cholesterol	15mg
Sodium	45mg
Total Carbohydrate	11g
Dietary Fiber	0g
Sugars	4g
Protein	1g

Pecan-Rum Bars

PREP TIME: 40 MINUTES (READY IN 2 HOURS 15 MINUTES)
SERVINGS: 32 BARS

CRUST

1 cup butter, softened

1 cup packed brown sugar

2 cups all-purpose flour

FILLING

2 eggs

1/2 cup packed brown sugar

1/2 cup dark corn syrup

1 tablespoon rum or 1 teaspoon rum extract

2 cups pecan halves

ICING

1/2 cup powdered sugar

1 tablespoon butter, softened

2 teaspoons rum or 1/2 teaspoon rum extract plus 2 teaspoons water

1) Heat oven to 375°F. Grease the bottom and sides of 13x9-inch pan with shortening or cooking spray (do not use dark pan).

2) In medium bowl, beat 1 cup butter and 1 cup brown sugar with electric mixer on low speed until creamy. Stir in flour. Press evenly in pan.

3) Bake 12 to 14 minutes or until edges are golden brown and center springs back when touched lightly.

4) Meanwhile, in medium bowl, mix all filling ingredients except pecans. Stir in pecans. Pour over crust, spreading pecans evenly.

5) Bake 12 to 15 minutes or until filling is set. Cool completely, about 1 hour.

6) In small bowl, mix the icing ingredients (add additional rum or water, 1/2 teaspoon at a time, if icing is too thick to drizzle). Drizzle icing over bars. For bars, cut into 8 rows by 4 rows.

HIGH ALTITUDE (3500-6500 FT.): No change.

Nutrition Information Per Serving:	
Calories: 200	From Fat: 100
Total Fat	11g
Saturated Fat	4.5g
Trans Fat	0g
Cholesterol	30mg
Sodium	55mg
Total Carbohydrate	23g
Dietary Fiber	0g
Sugars	14g
Protein	2g

Chai-Spiced Cookies

PREP TIME: 1 HOUR 30 MINUTES (READY IN 1 HOUR 30 MINUTES)
SERVINGS: ABOUT 4 DOZEN COOKIES

COOKIES

1	cup butter, softened
1/2	cup powdered sugar
2	cups all-purpose flour
1 1/2	teaspoons ground cardamom
1 1/2	teaspoons ground allspice
1	teaspoon ground cinnamon
1	teaspoon ground nutmeg
1/2	teaspoon ground ginger
1/2	teaspoon ground cloves
1/2	teaspoon salt
4	teaspoons vanilla
2	egg yolks

COATING

1 1/2	cups powdered sugar
1/2	teaspoon ground cardamom
1/2	teaspoon ground cinnamon

1) Heat oven to 350°F. In large bowl, beat the butter and 1/2 cup powdered sugar with electric mixer on low speed until blended. Stir in the remaining cookie ingredients.

2) Shape dough by tablespoonfuls into balls. On ungreased cookie sheets, place balls 1 1/2 inches apart.

3) Bake 12 to 15 minutes or until very lightly browned. Remove from cookie sheets to cooling rack; cool 5 minutes.

4) In medium bowl, mix coating ingredients. Working in batches, gently roll warm cookies in coating mixture. Cool on cooling rack 5 minutes. Roll in mixture again.

HIGH ALTITUDE (3500-6500 FT.): No change.

Nutrition Information Per Serving:		
Calories: 80	From Fat:	35
Total Fat		4g
Saturated Fat		2.5g
Trans Fat		0g
Cholesterol		20mg
Sodium		50mg
Total Carbohydrate		9g
Dietary Fiber		0g
Sugars		5g
Protein		0g

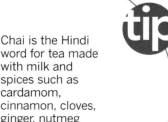

Chai is the Hindi word for tea made with milk and spices such as cardamom, cinnamon, cloves, ginger, nutmeg and pepper.

Dulce de Leche Cookies

PREP TIME: 1 HOUR 15 MINUTES (READY IN 1 HOUR 45 MINUTES)
SERVINGS: ABOUT 40 SANDWICH COOKIES

GARNISH
1 cup flaked coconut

COOKIES
1 cup butter, softened

^{2}/$_3$ cup sugar

2 egg yolks

3 tablespoons dark rum or ^{1}/$_2$ teaspoon rum extract plus 2^1/$_2$ tablespoons water

1 teaspoon vanilla

2^1/$_2$ cups all-purpose flour

1 teaspoon baking powder

^{1}/$_4$ teaspoon salt

^{1}/$_4$ cup sugar

FILLING
1 cup caramel apple dip (from 16-oz container)

Nutrition Information Per Serving:	
Calories: 120	From Fat: 50
Total Fat	6g
Saturated Fat	3.5g
Trans Fat	0g
Cholesterol	25mg
Sodium	95mg
Total Carbohydrate	17g
Dietary Fiber	0g
Sugars	9g
Protein	1g

1) Heat oven to 350°F. Spread the coconut in ungreased shallow pan. Bake uncovered 5 to 7 minutes, stirring occasionally, until golden brown. Turn off oven. In food processor bowl with metal blade, place the cooled coconut. Cover; process until ground. Set aside.

2) Meanwhile, in large bowl, beat butter and ^{2}/$_3$ cup sugar with electric mixer on medium speed about 1 minute or until smooth. Add egg yolks, rum and vanilla. On high speed, beat about 1 minute or until blended.

3) In medium bowl, stir together the flour, baking powder and salt. Stir the flour mixture into the butter mixture until well blended. Cover; refrigerate 30 minutes.

4) Heat oven to 350°F. Shape dough into ^{3}/$_4$-inch balls. On ungreased nonstick (not insulated) cookie sheets, place balls about 2 inches apart. Dip bottom of small glass into ^{1}/$_4$ cup sugar; press on cookies to make about 1^1/$_2$ inches in diameter.

5) Bake 10 to 11 minutes or just until edges begin to brown. Remove from cookie sheets to cooling rack. Cool completely, about 15 minutes.

6) For each sandwich cookie, spread about 1 teaspoon of the caramel apple dip on bottom of 1 cookie, spreading to edge of cookie. Top with second cookie. Gently squeeze until filling oozes out a little around the side. Roll edges of cookies in ground coconut.

HIGH ALTITUDE (3500-6500 FT.): No change.

Fudgy Peanut Butter Sandwich Cookies

BEVERLEY ROSSELL | MORGANTOWN, INDIANA

BAKE-OFF® CONTEST 43, 2008

PREP TIME: 1 HOUR 10 MINUTES (READY IN 1 HOUR 55 MINUTES)
SERVINGS: 18 SANDWICH COOKIES

COOKIES

- 1 roll (16.5 oz) Pillsbury® Create 'n Bake® refrigerated peanut butter cookies
- 1 cup plus 2 tablespoons Fisher® honey-roasted peanuts, coarsely ground

PEANUT BUTTER FUDGE FILLING

- $\frac{1}{2}$ cup Land O Lakes® unsalted or salted butter
- $\frac{1}{2}$ cup Jif® creamy peanut butter
- 2 teaspoons vanilla
- $2\frac{1}{3}$ cups Domino® or C&H® confectioners' powdered sugar

GANACHE

- 1 cup semisweet chocolate chips
- 2 tablespoons whipping cream

1) In large bowl, break up cookie dough. Mix in 1 cup of the peanuts. Cover; refrigerate about 30 minutes or until well chilled.

2) Heat oven to 375°F. Spray cookie sheets with Crisco® Original No-Stick cooking Spray, or line with cooking parchment paper. Shape the chilled dough into 36 (1¼-inch) balls. Place balls 2 inches apart on the cookie sheets. Flatten to ½-inch thickness with lightly floured metal spatula or drinking glass. Bake 9 to 11 minutes or until edges are golden brown. Cool 5 minutes; remove from cookie sheets to cooling rack. Cool completely, about 30 minutes.

3) Meanwhile, in 2-quart saucepan, melt the butter and peanut butter over medium heat, stirring occasionally. Remove from heat; stir in vanilla. Cool 1 minute. Stir in powdered sugar. When cool enough to handle, knead filling several times until sugar is thoroughly blended. Shape into log, about 9 inches long and 2 inches in diameter. Cut into 18 (½-inch) slices, reshaping slices into round shape if necessary. Cover with plastic wrap; set aside.

4) When ready to assemble cookies, place 1 filling slice on bottom of 1 cookie; top with another cookie, bottom side down, and press together slightly. Repeat with remaining cookies.

5) In medium microwavable bowl, microwave chocolate chips and whipping cream uncovered on High about 1 minute, stirring twice, until melted. Spoon heaping 1 teaspoonful on top of each cookie. Sprinkle with the remaining ground peanuts. Let stand 10 minutes or until ganache is set. Store tightly covered in single layer at room temperature.

HIGH ALTITUDE (3500-6500 FT.): No change.

Nutrition Information Per Serving:	
Calories: 380	From Fat: 200
Total Fat	22g
Saturated Fat	8g
Trans Fat	1g
Cholesterol	20mg
Sodium	190mg
Total Carbohydrate	40g
Dietary Fiber	2g
Sugars	30g
Protein	7g

Chocolate Peppermint Chews

PREP TIME: 45 MINUTES (READY IN 2 HOURS 15 MINUTES)
SERVINGS: 36 CHEWS

 EASY   LOW FAT

1 bag (12 oz) semisweet chocolate chips (2 cups)

1/3 cup corn syrup

1/2 teaspoon peppermint or almond extract

1/2 teaspoon vanilla

36 (6 x 6-inch) pieces clear plastic wrap or waxed paper

1) Line 9x5-inch loaf pan with plastic wrap.

2) In 2-quart saucepan, melt the chocolate over low heat, stirring constantly. Remove from heat. Add the corn syrup, extract and vanilla; mix well. Quickly pour into pan; spread evenly.

3) Refrigerate uncovered 30 minutes or until firm. Cut chews into 9 rows by 4 rows for 36 square pieces.

4) Place 1 chew in center of 1 end of individual plastic wrap square; roll up, folding up and twisting ends. Repeat to use up chews.

HIGH ALTITUDE (3500-6500 FT.): No change.

Nutrition Information Per Serving:

Calories: 60	From Fat: 25
Total Fat	3g
Saturated Fat	1.5g
Trans Fat	0g
Cholesterol	0mg
Sodium	0mg
Total Carbohydrate	8g
Dietary Fiber	0g
Sugars	6g
Protein	0g

Caramel Chai Bars

KERSTIN SINKEVICIUS | SOMERVILLE, MASSACHUSETTS   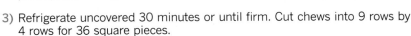 BAKE-OFF® CONTEST 43, 2008

PREP TIME: 20 MINUTES (READY IN 2 HOURS 40 MINUTES)
SERVINGS: 16 BARS

 EASY

1 roll (16.5 oz) Pillsbury® Create 'n Bake® refrigerated sugar cookies

1 package (1.1 oz) chai tea latte mix (from 8.8-oz box)

1/2 cup Smucker's® caramel sundae syrup™

2 tablespoons Pillsbury BEST® all-purpose flour

1/2 cup Fisher® Chef's Naturals® fine ground walnuts

1) Heat oven to 350°F. In large bowl, knead the cookie dough and dry chai mix until well blended.

2) Break up 3/4 of the chai dough in ungreased 8-inch square pan. Press dough evenly in bottom of pan. (If dough is sticky, use floured fingers.) Bake 12 to 17 minutes or until light golden brown.

3) Meanwhile, in small bowl, mix caramel syrup and flour. In another small bowl, knead remaining 1/4 of chai dough and the walnuts.

4) Gently drizzle caramel mixture evenly over partially baked crust. Crumble walnut chai dough evenly over caramel.

5) Bake 22 to 29 minutes longer or until top is golden brown and firm to the touch and caramel is bubbly. Cool completely, about 1 hour 30 minutes. For bars, cut into 4 rows by 4 rows.

HIGH ALTITUDE (3500-6500 FT.): In Step 2, bake 15 to 20 minutes. In Step 5, bake 29 to 32 minutes.

Nutrition Information Per Serving:

Calories: 190	From Fat: 80
Total Fat	9g
Saturated Fat	1.5g
Trans Fat	1.5g
Cholesterol	10mg
Sodium	140mg
Total Carbohydrate	27g
Dietary Fiber	0g
Sugars	17g
Protein	2g

Quick Crescent Baklava

ANNETTE ERBECK (MRS. GAIL) | MASON, OHIO | Pillsbury Bake-Off® | BAKE-OFF® CONTEST 29, 1980

PREP TIME: 25 MINUTES (READY IN 2 HOURS 25 MINUTES)
SERVINGS: 36 BARS

2 cans (8 oz each) Pillsbury®
  refrigerated crescent dinner rolls

3 to 4 cups walnuts, finely chopped

¾ cup sugar

1 teaspoon ground cinnamon

½ cup honey

2 tablespoons butter or margarine

2 teaspoons lemon juice

Nutrition Information Per Serving:

Calories:	150	From Fat:	90
Total Fat			10g
Saturated Fat			2g
Trans Fat			0.5g
Cholesterol			0mg
Sodium			105mg
Total Carbohydrate			14g
Dietary Fiber			0g
Sugars			9g
Protein			2g

1) Heat oven to 350°F. Unroll 1 can of dough and separate into 2 long rectangles. Place in ungreased 13x9-inch pan; press in the bottom and ½ inch up the sides to form crust, firmly pressing the perforations to seal. Bake 5 minutes. Meanwhile, in large bowl, mix walnuts, ½ cup of the sugar and the cinnamon.

2) Spoon walnut mixture evenly over crust. Separate remaining can of dough into 2 long rectangles. Place over walnut mixture; press out to edges of pan. With tip of sharp knife, score dough with 6 lengthwise and 6 diagonal markings to form 36 diamond-shaped pieces, using dough edges and perforations as a guide.

3) In 1-quart saucepan, mix remaining ¼ cup sugar, the honey, butter and lemon juice. Heat to boiling. Remove from heat; spoon half of sugar mixture evenly over dough.

4) Bake 25 to 30 minutes longer or until golden brown. Spoon remaining sugar mixture evenly over hot baklava. Cool completely, about 1 hour. Refrigerate until thoroughly chilled, about 30 minutes. For diamond shapes, cut 6 straight parallel lines down length of pan; cut 6 diagonal lines across straight lines.

HIGH ALTITUDE (3500-6500 FT.): No change.

Triple-Layered Brownies

PREP TIME: 35 MINUTES (READY IN 2 HOURS 35 MINUTES)
SERVINGS: 48 BROWNIES

BROWNIES

½ cup butter

2 oz unsweetened baking chocolate

2 eggs

1 cup packed light brown sugar

½ cup all-purpose flour

1 teaspoon vanilla

FILLING

½ cup whipping cream

1 bag (12 oz) white vanilla baking chips (2 cups)

1 cup dried cherries, chopped

GLAZE

½ cup semisweet chocolate chips

2 tablespoons butter

Nutrition Information Per Serving:	
Calories: 120	From Fat: 60
Total Fat	6g
Saturated Fat	4g
Trans Fat	0g
Cholesterol	20mg
Sodium	40mg
Total Carbohydrate	13g
Dietary Fiber	0g
Sugars	11g
Protein	1g

1) Heat oven to 350°F. Grease bottom and sides of 9-inch square pan with shortening and lightly flour, or spray with baking spray with flour.

2) In 2-quart saucepan, melt ½ cup butter and the unsweetened chocolate over medium heat, stirring constantly. Remove from heat; cool 5 minutes. Stir in the eggs, brown sugar, flour and vanilla until smooth. Spread evenly in the pan.

3) Bake 25 to 30 minutes or until toothpick inserted in center comes out clean. Cool in pan on cooling rack about 30 minutes.

4) Meanwhile, in 1-quart saucepan, heat whipping cream and white baking chips just to boiling over medium heat, stirring frequently. Remove from heat. Stir in the cherries. Spread filling over brownies. Refrigerate about 30 minutes or until set.

5) In small microwavable bowl, place chocolate chips and 2 tablespoons butter. Microwave uncovered on High 30 seconds; stir. Microwave 15 seconds longer; stir until melted and smooth. Spread glaze evenly over filling. Refrigerate at least 30 minutes. For brownies, cut into 8 rows by 6 rows. Cover and refrigerate any remaining brownies.

HIGH ALTITUDE (3500-6500 FT.): No change.

tip

If you like, you can replace the cherries in these rich treats with chopped cherry-flavored, dried sweetened cranberries.

Chocolate Buttersweets

VANCE FLETCHER | INDIANAPOLIS, INDIANA

BAKE-OFF® CONTEST 16, 1964

PREP TIME: 1 HOUR 35 MINUTES (READY IN 2 HOURS 15 MINUTES)
SERVINGS: ABOUT 3 DOZEN COOKIES

COOKIES
- ½ cup butter or margarine, softened
- ½ cup powdered sugar
- ¼ teaspoon salt
- 1 teaspoon vanilla
- 1 to 1½ cups all-purpose flour

FILLING
- 1 package (3 oz) cream cheese, softened
- 1 cup powdered sugar
- 2 tablespoons all-purpose flour
- 1 teaspoon vanilla
- ½ cup chopped walnuts
- ½ cup flaked coconut

FROSTING
- ½ cup semisweet chocolate chips
- 2 tablespoons butter or margarine
- 2 tablespoons water
- ½ cup powdered sugar

1) Heat oven to 350°F. In large bowl, beat ½ cup butter, ½ cup powdered sugar, the salt and 1 teaspoon vanilla with electric mixer on medium speed, scraping bowl occasionally, until blended. Gradually beat in 1 to 1¼ cups flour until soft dough forms.

2) Shape teaspoonfuls of dough into balls. On ungreased cookie sheets, place balls 2 inches apart. With thumb or handle of wooden spoon, make indentation in center of each.

3) Bake 12 to 15 minutes or until edges are lightly browned. Meanwhile, in small bowl, beat cream cheese, 1 cup powdered sugar, 2 tablespoons flour and 1 teaspoon vanilla on medium speed until well blended. Stir in walnuts and coconut.

4) Immediately remove the cookies from the cookie sheets to cooling racks. Spoon about ½ teaspoon filling into each cookie. Cool completely, about 30 minutes.

5) In 1-quart saucepan, heat chocolate chips, 2 tablespoons butter and the water over low heat, stirring occasionally, until chips are melted. Remove from heat. With spoon, beat in ½ cup powdered sugar until smooth. Frost cooled cookies. Store covered in refrigerator.

HIGH ALTITUDE (3500-6500 FT.): Bake 9 to 12 minutes.

Nutrition Information Per Serving:		
Calories: 110	From Fat:	60
Total Fat		6g
Saturated Fat		3.5g
Trans Fat		0g
Cholesterol		10mg
Sodium		50mg
Total Carbohydrate		12g
Dietary Fiber		0g
Sugars		8g
Protein		0g

Ginger Macaroons

PREP TIME: 1 HOUR (READY IN 1 HOUR 25 MINUTES)
SERVINGS: ABOUT 2-1/2 DOZEN COOKIES

 LOW FAT

3 egg whites

²/₃ cup sugar

3 tablespoons all-purpose flour

1 teaspoon pumpkin pie spice

¹/₈ to ¹/₄ teaspoon ground ginger

¹/₄ teaspoon salt

¹/₄ cup finely chopped candied ginger

2 cups flaked coconut

¹/₃ cup semisweet chocolate chips

1 teaspoon shortening

Nutrition Information Per Serving:

Calories:	50	From Fat:	15
Total Fat			2g
Saturated Fat			1.5g
Trans Fat			0g
Cholesterol			0mg
Sodium			40mg
Total Carbohydrate			8g
Dietary Fiber			0g
Sugars			6g
Protein			0g

1) Heat oven to 325°F. Spray cookie sheets with baking spray with flour.

2) In large bowl, beat egg whites with electric mixer on high speed until frothy. Gradually beat in sugar until stiff. In small bowl, stir together flour, pumpkin pie spice, ground ginger and salt; fold into beaten egg whites. Fold in candied ginger and coconut.

3) Drop by tablespoonfuls 2 inches apart onto cookie sheets.

4) Bake 15 to 20 minutes or until macaroons feel firm and are very lightly browned. Cool 10 minutes; remove from cookie sheets to cooling rack. Cool completely, about 15 minutes.

5) In small microwavable bowl, place chocolate chips and shortening. Microwave uncovered on High 30 seconds; stir until melted and smooth. Drizzle over cookies.

HIGH ALTITUDE (3500-6500 FT.): No change.

Wake-Up Espresso Cereal Bars

PREP TIME: 20 MINUTES (READY IN 2 HOURS 20 MINUTES)
SERVINGS: 12 BARS

 EASY

1) Butter bottom and sides of 8-inch square pan.

2) In 3-quart saucepan, heat corn syrup and brown sugar to boiling over medium-high heat, stirring constantly. Remove from heat. In small bowl, stir coffee granules into boiling water until dissolved; stir into corn syrup mixture along with peanut butter until smooth. Add cereal and pretzels, stirring until evenly coated.

3) Press evenly in pan. Let stand about 2 hours or until set. For bars, cut into 4 rows by 3 rows. Store covered.

HIGH ALTITUDE (3500-6500 FT.): No change.

¹/₂ cup corn syrup

¹/₃ cup packed brown sugar

2 teaspoons instant espresso coffee granules or instant coffee granules

2 teaspoons boiling water

¹/₂ cup creamy peanut butter

2 cups Basic 4® cereal

1 cup broken pretzel sticks

Nutrition Information Per Serving:

Calories:	190	From Fat:	50
Total Fat			6g
Saturated Fat			1g
Trans Fat			0g
Cholesterol			0mg
Sodium			160mg
Total Carbohydrate			29g
Dietary Fiber			1g
Sugars			15g
Protein			4g

Fudgy Chocolate-Peanut Butter Thumbprints

STEPHANIE HOLLOWELL | DALLAS, TEXAS

BAKE-OFF® CONTEST 43, 2008

PREP TIME:	1 HOUR (READY IN 1 HOUR)
SERVINGS:	ABOUT 2 DOZEN COOKIES

COOKIES

1 box (20 oz) Pillsbury® chocolate frosted brownie mix

¹/₂ cup Jif® extra crunchy peanut butter

2 Eggland's Best eggs

1 teaspoon vanilla

²/₃ cup milk chocolate chips

TOPPING

Frosting packet from brownie mix

¹/₃ cup Jif® extra crunchy peanut butter

¹/₄ cup Land O Lakes® unsalted or salted butter, softened

2 tablespoons Fisher® dry-roasted peanuts, finely chopped

1) Heat oven to 350°F. Lightly spray large cookie sheets with Crisco® Original No-Stick Cooking Spray, or line with cooking parchment paper.

2) Reserve frosting packet from brownie mix. In large bowl, beat brownie mix, ¹/₂ cup peanut butter, the eggs and vanilla with electric mixer on low speed 20 seconds. Beat on high speed 30 to 40 seconds or until completely mixed. Stir in chocolate chips.

3) Drop 24 heaping tablespoons of dough 2 inches apart onto cookie sheets. Press thumb into center of each cookie to make indentation, but do not press all the way to the cookie sheet (if dough sticks to thumb, spray thumb with cooking spray). Bake 9 to 11 minutes or until almost no indentation remains when touched. Cool 1 minute; remove from cookie sheets to cooling rack. Cool completely, about 20 minutes.

4) In small bowl, beat contents of reserved frosting packet, ¹/₃ cup peanut butter and the butter with electric mixer on medium speed until smooth. Fill each thumbprint indentation with 2 teaspoons frosting mixture, spreading slightly; sprinkle with peanuts. Let stand until the frosting mixture is set. Store loosely covered in single layer.

HIGH ALTITUDE (3500-6500 FT.): No change.

Nutrition Information Per Serving:		
Calories: 120	From Fat: 80	
Total Fat		9g
Saturated Fat		3g
Trans Fat		0g
Cholesterol		20mg
Sodium		60mg
Total Carbohydrate		6g
Dietary Fiber		0g
Sugars		4g
Protein		3g

Mexican Chocolate Crunch Brownies

VALERIE SCHUCHT | GLASTONBURY, CONNECTICUT

BAKE-OFF® CONTEST 43, 2008

PREP TIME: 20 MINUTES (READY IN 3 HOURS)
SERVINGS: 24 BROWNIES

EASY

1 box (12.8 oz) Cinnamon Toast Crunch® cereal (about 8 cups)

½ cup Land O Lakes® butter, melted

1 tablespoon corn syrup

1 box (19.5 oz) Pillsbury® traditional fudge brownie mix

½ cup Crisco® pure vegetable oil

¼ cup water

2 Eggland's Best eggs

½ teaspoon ground cinnamon

1⅓ cups semisweet chocolate chips

3 tablespoons cinnamon-sugar (from 3.62-oz jar)

1) Heat oven to 350°F. Spray 13x9-inch pan with Crisco® Original No-Stick cooking spray. Place the cereal in food processor bowl with metal blade (crush cereal in 2 batches if necessary). Cover; process until finely crushed (about 4 cups). Or place the cereal in large resealable food-storage plastic bag; crush with rolling pin.

2) In large bowl, stir butter and corn syrup until well blended. Add crushed cereal; mix thoroughly. Press evenly in pan.

3) In large bowl, make brownie mix as directed on box, using oil, water and eggs and adding cinnamon. Stir in ⅔ cup of the chocolate chips. Pour brownie batter over cereal mixture. Sprinkle remaining ⅔ cup chocolate chips evenly over batter.

4) Bake 20 minutes. Sprinkle cinnamon-sugar evenly over brownies. Bake 14 to 18 minutes longer or until brownies are set when lightly touched in center. Cool 10 minutes; loosen edges but do not cut. Cool completely, about 2 hours. For brownies, cut into 6 rows by 4 rows.

HIGH ALTITUDE (3500-6500 FT.): In Step 2, bake crust 5 to 8 minutes. Make brownie mix following High Altitude directions on box.

Nutrition Information Per Serving:	
Calories: 280	From Fat: 130
Total Fat	15g
Saturated Fat	5g
Trans Fat	0g
Cholesterol	25mg
Sodium	190mg
Total Carbohydrate	35g
Dietary Fiber	1g
Sugars	22g
Protein	2g

tip

If you're out of cinnamon-sugar, just substitute 3 tablespoons sugar mixed with 1/2 teaspoon ground cinnamon.

Toffee-Banana Brownies

GWEN BEAUCHAMP | LANCASTER, TEXAS   BAKE-OFF® CONTEST 43, 2008

PREP TIME: 20 MINUTES (READY IN 3 HOURS 10 MINUTES)
SERVINGS: 24 BROWNIES

🅴 EASY

1 box (19.5 oz) Pillsbury® traditional fudge brownie mix

½ cup Crisco® pure vegetable oil

¼ cup water

3 Eggland's Best eggs

1½ cups toffee bits

1 cup Fisher® macadamia nuts, chopped

2 firm ripe medium bananas, cut into ¼-inch pieces (2 cups)

⅓ cup Smucker's® caramel ice cream topping

1) Heat oven to 350°F. Generously spray 13x9-inch pan with Crisco® Original No-Stick cooking spray.

2) In medium bowl, stir brownie mix, oil, water and eggs 50 strokes with spoon. Add 1 cup of the toffee bits, the nuts and bananas; stir just until well blended. Pour into pan. Sprinkle remaining ½ cup toffee bits over top.

3) Bake 38 to 48 minutes or until center is set when lightly touched, top is slightly dry and edges just start to pull away from sides of pan. Cool completely, about 2 hours. For brownies, cut into 6 rows by 4 rows. To serve, drizzle each brownie with caramel topping. Cover and refrigerate any remaining brownies.

HIGH ALTITUDE (3500-6500 FT.): Increase water to 1/3 cup. Add 1/2 cup all-purpose flour to dry brownie mix.

Nutrition Information Per Serving:

Calories: 260	From Fat: 130
Total Fat	15g
Saturated Fat	3g
Trans Fat	0g
Cholesterol	105mg
Sodium	75mg
Total Carbohydrate	30g
Dietary Fiber	0g
Sugars	23g
Protein	2g

Jumbo Honey-Roasted Peanut Butter Cookies

KARRY EDWARDS | SANDY, UTAH

BAKE-OFF® CONTEST 43, 2008

PREP TIME: 25 MINUTES (READY IN 1 HOUR 10 MINUTES)
SERVINGS: 8 SANDWICH COOKIES

 EASY

2 packages (8 oz each) cream cheese, softened

½ cup Jif® creamy peanut butter

2 tablespoons honey

1 cup Domino® or C&H® confectioners' powdered sugar

1 roll (16.5 oz) Pillsbury® Create 'n Bake® refrigerated peanut butter cookies

¾ to 1 cup Fisher® honey-roasted dry roasted peanuts, coarsely chopped

1) In large bowl, beat cream cheese, peanut butter and honey with electric mixer on medium speed until smooth. Add powdered sugar; beat just until smooth. Cover; refrigerate at least 1 hour while baking and cooling cookies.

2) Heat oven to 350°F. Make cookies as directed on package. Cool completely.

3) Spread ⅓ cup cream cheese mixture on bottom of 1 cookie; top with another cookie, bottom side down. Press the cookies together slightly so the cream cheese mixture just extends past the edges of cookies. Roll edge of cream cheese mixture in chopped peanuts to generously coat. Repeat with remaining cookies.

4) Serve immediately, or store in single layer tightly covered in refrigerator up to 4 hours (cookies stored longer become very soft).

HIGH ALTITUDE (3500-6500 FT.): No change.

Nutrition Information Per Serving:

Calories: 730	From Fat: 420
Total Fat	47g
Saturated Fat	18g
Trans Fat	2.5g
Cholesterol	70mg
Sodium	560mg
Total Carbohydrate	60g
Dietary Fiber	2g
Sugars	41g
Protein	16g

White Chocolate-Cherry Blondies

PREP TIME: 30 MINUTES (READY IN 4 HOURS 55 MINUTES)
SERVINGS: 36 BLONDIES

2 cups packed brown sugar

½ cup butter or margarine, softened

2 teaspoons vanilla

½ teaspoon almond extract

2 eggs

2 cups all-purpose flour

1 teaspoon baking powder

¼ teaspoon salt

2 packages (6 oz each) white chocolate baking bars, cut into chunks

½ cup slivered almonds

½ cup chopped dried cherries or cranberries

½ teaspoon vegetable oil

1) Heat oven to 350°F. Grease or spray 13x9-inch pan. In large bowl, beat brown sugar, butter, vanilla, almond extract and eggs with electric mixer on medium speed until light and fluffy.

2) On low speed, beat in flour, baking powder and salt until well blended. Set aside ¼ cup of white chocolate bar chunks. Stir in remaining chunks, almonds and cherries. Spread batter evenly in pan.

3) Bake 20 to 25 minutes or until the top is golden brown and set. Cool completely, about 1 hour.

4) In small microwavable bowl, microwave the reserved white chocolate bar chunks and oil uncovered on High 30 to 60 seconds, stirring every 15 seconds, until melted; stir well. Drizzle glaze over bars. Or if desired, place glaze in small food-storage plastic bag and cut off small tip from one corner of bag; drizzle glaze in diagonal lines over bars. Let stand until glaze is set, about 3 hours. For bars, cut into 6 rows by 6 rows.

HIGH ALTITUDE (3500-6500 FT.): Spread batter in pan to within 1/2 inch from edges (batter will spread during baking). Bake 30 to 35 minutes.

Nutrition Information Per Serving:		
Calories: 170	From Fat:	60
Total Fat		7g
Saturated Fat		3.5g
Trans Fat		0g
Cholesterol		20mg
Sodium		65mg
Total Carbohydrate		25g
Dietary Fiber		0g
Sugars		19g
Protein		2g

tip

To make cutting the bars easier, line the pan with foil, and then grease the foil. Bake the bars in the foil-lined pan. When the bars are cool, use the foil to lift them from the pan and onto a flat surface for cutting.

Raspberry-Filled Brownie Delights

TERESA RALSTON | NEW ALBANY, OHIO

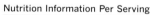

BAKE-OFF® CONTEST 43, 2008

PREP TIME: 35 MINUTES (READY IN 1 HOUR 20 MINUTES)
SERVINGS: 12 SANDWICH COOKIES

1 box (15.5 oz) Pillsbury® chocolate chunk brownie mix

1/4 cup Pillsbury BEST® all-purpose flour

1/2 cup Land O Lakes® unsalted or salted butter, melted

1 Eggland's Best egg

1 teaspoon vanilla

1/4 cup plus 2 tablespoons Smucker's® red raspberry preserves

2 to 4 teaspoons Domino® or C&H® confectioners' powdered sugar

12 fresh raspberries (about 1/2 cup)

1) Heat oven to 375°F. In large bowl, stir together brownie mix and flour. Add butter, egg and vanilla; stir until blended. Let dough stand 15 minutes for easier handling.

2) Shape dough into 24 (about 1½-inch) balls (dough will be soft). Place 2 inches apart on ungreased large cookie sheet.

3) Bake 10 to 13 minutes or until set and tops appear dry. Cool on cookie sheet 1 minute; remove from cookie sheet to cooling rack. Cool completely, about 30 minutes.

4) Spread 1½ teaspoons preserves on bottom of 1 cookie; top with another cookie, bottom side down. Repeat with the remaining cookies. Sprinkle powdered sugar through fine-mesh strainer or sieve over cookies. Place on serving platter; garnish as desired with raspberries.

HIGH ALTITUDE (3500-6500 FT.): Heat oven to 350°F. Decrease butter to 1/3 cup.

Nutrition Information Per Serving:	
Calories: 280	From Fat: 110
Total Fat	13g
Saturated Fat	7g
Trans Fat	1g
Cholesterol	35mg
Sodium	105mg
Total Carbohydrate	39g
Dietary Fiber	0g
Sugars	25g
Protein	2g

Choco-Caramel Nut Puddles

PREP TIME: 30 MINUTES (READY IN 50 MINUTES)
SERVINGS: 24 CANDIES

7 oz milk chocolate chips

7 oz chocolate-flavored candy coating, cut into pieces

12 dried papaya or pineapple pieces or apricots

12 pecan halves

10 caramels, unwrapped

2 teaspoons milk

1) Using pencil, draw twenty-four 1½-inch circles on waxed paper-lined cookie sheets, 2 inches apart. In medium microwavable bowl, mix chocolate chips and candy coating. Microwave uncovered on Medium 3 to 4 minutes, stirring once halfway through. Stir until smooth. Spoon and spread 1 tablespoon chocolate mixture onto each circle. Refrigerate about 10 minutes or until chocolate is set. Place 12-inch piece of waxed paper on work surface. Dip fruit pieces and pecan halves into chocolate; place on waxed paper.

2) In small microwavable bowl, microwave caramels and milk uncovered on Medium 2½ to 3 minutes, stirring once every minute, until melted. Stir until smooth. Spoon about ½ teaspoon caramel mixture onto each chocolate circle, leaving ½ inch chocolate showing around edge. Decorate each with dried fruit or nut; press down lightly. Refrigerate just until set.

3) Gently remove candies from waxed paper. Store in single layer in airtight container.

HIGH ALTITUDE (3500-6500 FT.): No change.

Nutrition Information Per Serving:	
Calories: 80	From Fat: 35
Total Fat	4g
Saturated Fat	1.5g
Trans Fat	0g
Cholesterol	0mg
Sodium	20mg
Total Carbohydrate	10g
Dietary Fiber	0g
Sugars	8g
Protein	0g

Ooey-Gooey Turtle Bars

GRETCHEN WANEK | OSHKOSH, WISCONSIN

BAKE-OFF® CONTEST 43, 2008

PREP TIME: 20 MINUTES (READY IN 4 HOURS 25 MINUTES)
SERVINGS: 24 BARS

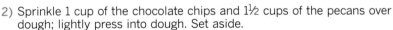 EASY

1 roll (16.5 oz) Pillsbury® Create 'n Bake® refrigerated sugar cookies

1 bag (12 oz) semisweet chocolate chips (2 cups)

3 cups Fisher® Chef's Naturals® chopped pecans

½ cup Land O Lakes® butter

½ cup packed Domino® or C&H® light brown sugar

1 jar (12.25 oz) Smucker's® caramel ice cream topping

1 cup graham cracker crumbs (16 squares)

1) Heat oven to 350°F (325°F for dark or nonstick pan). Press cookie dough evenly in bottom of ungreased 13x9-inch pan.

2) Sprinkle 1 cup of the chocolate chips and 1½ cups of the pecans over dough; lightly press into dough. Set aside.

3) In 2-quart saucepan, melt butter over medium-high heat. Stir in brown sugar, caramel topping and graham cracker crumbs. Heat to boiling, stirring constantly. Pour over crust in pan; spread evenly. Sprinkle with remaining 1 cup chocolate chips and 1½ cups pecans.

4) Bake 25 to 32 minutes or until the edges are deep golden brown and pecans are lightly toasted. Cool on cooling rack 30 minutes; loosen sides from pan, but do not cut. Cool completely, about 3 hours longer. (For firmer bars, let stand an additional 2 hours.) For bars, cut into 6 rows by 4 rows.

HIGH ALTITUDE (3500-6500 FT.): Bake 27 to 34 minutes.

Nutrition Information Per Serving:	
Calories: 370	From Fat: 200
Total Fat	22g
Saturated Fat	7g
Trans Fat	1.5g
Cholesterol	15mg
Sodium	160mg
Total Carbohydrate	40g
Dietary Fiber	2g
Sugars	28g
Protein	3g

BUSTER SUNDAE PIE
PG. 335

All-American Pies & Treats

Home sweet home is just a taste away when you whip up these memorable, family-favorite desserts.

NUTTY CARAMEL COOKIE TART
PG. 341

CHOCOLATE SURPRISE PECAN PIE
PG. 327

COFFEE ICE CREAM PIE
PG. 319

Black-Bottom Banana Cream Pie

PREP TIME: 30 MINUTES (READY IN 4 HOURS 30 MINUTES)
SERVINGS: 8

1 box (4-serving size) vanilla pudding and pie filling mix (not instant)

2 cups milk

1 Pillsbury® refrigerated pie crust (from 15-oz box), softened as directed on box

2/3 cup hot fudge topping

2 cups sliced ripe bananas (about 2 large bananas)

1 cup whipping cream, whipped

Chocolate curls, if desired

1) Make pudding mix with milk as directed on box for pie. Cool 30 minutes, stirring 2 or 3 times.

2) Meanwhile, heat oven to 450°F. Bake pie crust as directed on box for One-Crust Baked Shell, using 9-inch glass pie plate. Cool on cooling rack 10 minutes.

3) Spread fudge topping in bottom of shell. Top with bananas, pudding and whipped cream. Refrigerate at least 4 hours until serving time. Garnish with chocolate curls. Cover and refrigerate any remaining pie.

HIGH ALTITUDE (3500-6500 FT.): No change.

Nutrition Information Per Serving:		
Calories: 400	From Fat:	180
Total Fat		20g
Saturated Fat		10g
Trans Fat		0g
Cholesterol		40mg
Sodium		300mg
Total Carbohydrate		51g
Dietary Fiber		1g
Sugars		29g
Protein		4g

Cherry-Blueberry Pie

PREP TIME: 30 MINUTES (READY IN 3 HOURS 25 MINUTES)
SERVINGS: 8

CRUST

1 box (15 oz) Pillsbury® refrigerated pie crusts, softened as directed on box

FILLING

1/2 cup sugar

2 tablespoons cornstarch

1/4 teaspoon ground cinnamon

1 can (21 oz) cherry pie filling

1 1/2 cups fresh blueberries or raspberries

CRUST GLAZE

1 egg white

1 teaspoon water

2 teaspoons sugar

1) Heat oven to 425°F. Make pie crusts as directed on box for Two-Crust Pie, using 9-inch glass pie plate.

2) In large bowl, mix 1/2 cup sugar, the cornstarch and cinnamon. Stir in pie filling and blueberries; spoon into the crust-lined pie plate. Top with second crust; seal edge and flute. Cut slits or shapes in several places in top crust.

3) In small bowl, beat egg white and water with fork until blended; brush over top of pie (discard any remaining egg white mixture). Sprinkle with 2 teaspoons sugar. Cover edge with 2- to 3-inch-wide strips of foil to prevent excessive browning; remove foil during the last 15 minutes of bake time.

4) Bake 45 to 55 minutes or until crust is golden brown. Cool on cooling rack at least 2 hours before serving.

HIGH ALTITUDE (3500-6500 FT.): No change.

Nutrition Information Per Serving:		
Calories: 340	From Fat: 130	
Total Fat		14g
Saturated Fat		5g
Trans Fat		0g
Cholesterol		5mg
Sodium		230mg
Total Carbohydrate		53g
Dietary Fiber		1g
Sugars		22g
Protein		1g

Creamy Mojito Pie

AYOFEMI WRIGHT | ATLANTA, GEORGIA

 Pillsbury Bake-Off®   BAKE-OFF® CONTEST 43, 2008

PREP TIME: 15 MINUTES (READY IN 1 HOUR 45 MINUTES)
SERVINGS: 8

🄴 EASY

CRUST

1 Pillsbury® refrigerated pie crust (from 15-oz box), softened as directed on box

FILLING

1 package (8 oz) cream cheese, softened

1 cup whole or 2% milk

1 box (4-serving size) vanilla instant pudding and pie filling mix

1/2 cup frozen (thawed) limeade concentrate

1 1/2 teaspoons rum extract

TOPPING

1 1/2 cups whipping cream

1/4 cup Domino® or C&H® confectioners' powdered sugar

3/4 to 1 1/2 teaspoons mint extract

GARNISHES, IF DESIRED

Fresh mint sprigs

Lime slices

1) Heat oven to 450°F. Make pie crust as directed on box for One-Crust Baked Shell using 9-inch glass pie plate. Bake 10 to 12 minutes or until light golden brown. Cool completely on cooling rack, about 15 minutes.

2) In large bowl, beat the cream cheese with electric mixer on low speed until creamy. Add remaining filling ingredients; beat on low speed about 30 seconds or until blended. Beat on medium speed 2 minutes, scraping bowl occasionally, until thickened and creamy. Spoon filling evenly into pie crust; refrigerate while making topping.

3) In same bowl, beat the topping ingredients on medium speed until stiff peaks form. Spread topping evenly over filling. Refrigerate about 1 hour or until set.

4) Garnish pie with mint sprigs and lime slices. Cover and refrigerate any remaining pie.

HIGH ALTITUDE (3500-6500 FT.): No change.

Nutrition Information Per Serving:	
Calories: 480 From Fat: 290	
Total Fat	32g
Saturated Fat	18g
Trans Fat	1g
Cholesterol	90mg
Sodium	400mg
Total Carbohydrate	43g
Dietary Fiber	0g
Sugars	24g
Protein	4g

Pistachio Mousse Brownie Torte

JANE ESTRIN | GAINESVILLE, FLORIDA

BAKE-OFF® CONTEST 43, 2008

PREP TIME: 1 HOUR (READY IN 2 HOURS 45 MINUTES)
SERVINGS: 16

CAKE

- 1 box (19.5 oz) Pillsbury® traditional fudge brownie mix
- ½ cup Crisco® pure canola oil
- ¼ cup water
- 3 Eggland's Best eggs

MOUSSE

- 1 box (4-serving size) pistachio instant pudding and pie filling mix
- ¾ cup cold whole milk
- 1 cup cold whipping cream
- ½ cup pistachio nuts, coarsely chopped

GLAZE

- ½ cup whipping cream
- 4 oz semisweet baking chocolate, finely chopped
- 1 teaspoon vanilla
- 1 teaspoon light corn syrup

GARNISH

- ½ cup whipping cream
- 2 tablespoons Domino® or C&H® confectioners' powdered sugar
- Reserved 1 tablespoon pistachio instant pudding and pie filling mix

1) Heat oven to 350°F. Lightly spray bottom of 2 (8-inch) round cake pans with Crisco® Original No-Stick cooking spray. Line bottoms of pans with cooking parchment paper; lightly spray paper with cooking spray. In large bowl, stir brownie mix, oil, water and eggs 50 strokes with spoon. Spread half of batter (1½ cups) evenly in each pan.

2) Bake 27 to 30 minutes or until toothpick inserted 2 inches from edge of pan comes out clean. Cool in pans on cooling racks 10 minutes. Run knife around edge of pans to loosen. Place cooling rack upside down on 1 pan; turn rack and pan over. Remove pan and parchment paper. Repeat with second brownie layer. Place racks with brownie layers in refrigerator to cool completely, about 20 minutes.

3) Meanwhile, measure 1 tablespoon of the pudding mix; reserve for garnish. In large bowl, beat remaining pudding mix, the milk and 1 cup cream with electric mixer on high speed about 2 minutes or until mixture is thick and creamy. Stir in nuts. Cover; refrigerate.

4) Carefully cut each brownie layer horizontally in half, using long serrated knife, to make 4 layers. On serving plate, place 1 brownie layer, cut side down. Spread ⅓ of pistachio mousse (¾ cup) evenly to edge of brownie. Repeat layering twice, using 2 brownie layers (place cut sides down) and remaining mousse. Top with remaining brownie layer, cut side down. Refrigerate torte while making glaze.

5) In 1-quart saucepan, heat ½ cup cream over medium heat, stirring occasionally, just until bubbles start to form at edge of pan. Remove from heat. Add chocolate; stir constantly until smooth. Stir in vanilla and corn syrup; let stand 10 minutes. Stir glaze; spoon over top of torte, allowing some to run down side. Return torte to refrigerator while making garnish.

6) In medium bowl, beat ½ cup cream, the powdered sugar and reserved 1 tablespoon pudding mix on high speed until stiff peaks form. Spoon mixture into decorating bag fitted with star tip and pipe rosettes on top of torte, or spoon dollops of mixture on torte. Refrigerate at least 30 minutes before serving. Cover and refrigerate any remaining torte.

HIGH ALTITUDE (3500-6500 FT.): For cake, increase water to 1/3 cup and add 1/2 cup all-purpose flour.

Nutrition Information Per Serving:		
Calories: 380	From Fat: 220	
Total Fat		25g
Saturated Fat		9g
Trans Fat		0g
Cholesterol		70mg
Sodium		200mg
Total Carbohydrate		34g
Dietary Fiber		1g
Sugars		23g
Protein		5g

Apple-Blueberry Pie with Strawberry Sauce

PREP TIME: 30 MINUTES (READY IN 3 HOURS 30 MINUTES)
SERVINGS: 8

PIE

5 cups peeled, cored and thinly sliced apples

2 cups fresh or frozen (thawed) blueberries

1 cup sugar

½ teaspoon ground cinnamon

3 tablespoons quick-cooking tapioca

1 box (15 oz) Pillsbury® refrigerated pie crusts, softened as directed on box

2 tablespoons butter or margarine

1 egg

1 teaspoon water

STRAWBERRY SAUCE

2 cups fresh strawberries

½ cup sugar

1 tablespoon sweet Marsala wine or water

1 tablespoon cornstarch

2 tablespoons water

½ cup whipping cream

1) Heat oven to 400°F. In large bowl, stir together apples, blueberries, 1 cup sugar, the cinnamon and tapioca; let stand 15 minutes. Make pie crusts as directed on box for Two-Crust Pie, using 9-inch glass pie plate.

2) Spoon apple mixture into crust-lined pie plate. Dot with butter. Top with second crust; seal edge and flute. Cut slits in several places in top crust. Stir together egg and 1 teaspoon water; brush on top of crust.

3) Bake 15 minutes. Cover the edge of crust with strips of foil; reduce oven temperature to 350°F. Bake 40 to 45 minutes longer or until apples are tender. Cool on cooling rack at least 2 hours.

4) Meanwhile, to make Strawberry Sauce, in 1-quart saucepan, crush enough strawberries to make ⅓ cup. Stir in ½ cup sugar and the wine. Heat to boiling over medium heat. Dissolve cornstarch in 2 tablespoons water; stir into strawberry mixture. Boil and stir 2 minutes. Remove from heat; cool to room temperature. Stir in whipping cream. Slice remaining berries; stir into sauce. Refrigerate until serving time. Top individual servings with sauce.

HIGH ALTITUDE (3500-6500 FT.): In Step 3, increase first bake time to 20 minutes.

Nutrition Information Per Serving:		
Calories: 550	From Fat: 200	
Total Fat		22g
Saturated Fat		10g
Trans Fat		0g
Cholesterol		60mg
Sodium		250mg
Total Carbohydrate		85g
Dietary Fiber		2g
Sugars		50g
Protein		2g

Coffee Ice Cream Pie

PREP TIME: 20 MINUTES (READY IN 2 HOURS 35 MINUTES)
SERVINGS: 8

 EASY

CRUST

30 chocolate wafers, crushed (about 1½ cups)

½ cup butter or margarine, softened

¼ cup coconut

3 tablespoons finely chopped cashews or macadamia nuts

FILLING

1 quart (4 cups) coffee ice cream, slightly softened

TOPPING

1 cup hot fudge topping, warmed

Whole cashews or macadamia nuts, if desired

1) In medium bowl, mix crushed chocolate wafers, butter, coconut and chopped cashews. Press mixture in bottom and side of 9-inch glass pie plate; refrigerate 15 minutes. Carefully spoon softened ice cream into chilled crust. Cover and freeze about 2 hours or until firm.

2) Top individual servings with fudge topping; garnish with whole cashews. Cover and freeze any remaining pie.

HIGH ALTITUDE (3500-6500 FT.): No change.

Nutrition Information Per Serving:

Calories:	520	From Fat:	250
Total Fat			28g
Saturated Fat			16g
Trans Fat			1.5g
Cholesterol			55mg
Sodium			400mg
Total Carbohydrate			61g
Dietary Fiber			3g
Sugars			41g
Protein			7g

Chocolate-Hazelnut Pizza

PREP TIME: 15 MINUTES (READY IN 40 MINUTES)
SERVINGS: 12

 EASY

1 can (13.8 oz) Pillsbury® refrigerated classic pizza crust

½ cup hazelnut spread with cocoa

¼ cup dark chocolate chips

2 tablespoons semisweet chocolate chips

2 tablespoons white vanilla baking chips

1 teaspoon vegetable oil

¼ cup hazelnuts (filberts), toasted, skins removed, chopped

1) Heat oven to 400°F. Grease or spray 12-inch pizza pan. Unroll dough in pan. Starting at center, press out dough with hands, forming ½-inch rim.

2) Bake 12 to 15 minutes or until golden brown. Immediately spread with hazelnut spread; sprinkle with dark chocolate and semisweet chocolate chips. Bake 1 to 2 minutes, just until chocolate begins to melt.

3) In small microwavable bowl, microwave the white vanilla baking chips and vegetable oil uncovered on High 30 to 60 seconds, stirring every 15 seconds, until melted. Sprinkle hazelnuts on pizza. Drizzle with melted white chips. Cool 5 minutes. Cut into wedges. Serve warm.

HIGH ALTITUDE (3500-6500 FT.): No change.

Nutrition Information Per Serving:

Calories:	210	From Fat:	80
Total Fat			9g
Saturated Fat			2.5g
Trans Fat			0g
Cholesterol			0mg
Sodium			250mg
Total Carbohydrate			28g
Dietary Fiber			1g
Sugars			13g
Protein			4g

Chai Cream Pie

PREP TIME: 25 MINUTES (READY IN 2 HOURS 50 MINUTES)
SERVINGS: 8

CRUST

1 Pillsbury® refrigerated pie crust (from 15-oz box), softened as directed on box

FILLING

1 cup water

1 package (1.1 oz) chai tea latte mix

1 bag (10 1/2 oz) miniature marshmallows (6 cups)

1 tablespoon butter or margarine

2 tablespoons caramel-flavored sundae syrup

1 1/2 cups whipping cream

1/4 cup chopped pecans

Shaved chocolate

1) Heat oven to 450°F. Bake pie crust as directed on box for One-Crust Baked Shell, using 9-inch glass pie plate. Cool on cooling rack 15 minutes or until completely cool.

2) In 3-quart saucepan, heat water to boiling over high heat. Stir in chai mix; reduce heat to low. Using wire whisk, stir in marshmallows and butter. Continue stirring just until the marshmallows are melted. Stir in the caramel syrup. Refrigerate about 30 minutes or until cool and thickened.

3) In chilled medium bowl, beat whipping cream with electric mixer on high speed until stiff peaks form. Set aside 1 cup whipped cream. Fold remaining whipped cream into cooled filling. Pour into cooled pie crust. Sprinkle with pecans. Cover; refrigerate 2 hours or until filling is set. Garnish with reserved whipped cream and shaved chocolate. Cover and refrigerate any remaining pie.

HIGH ALTITUDE (3500-6500 FT.): Bake crust 10 to 12 minutes.

Nutrition Information Per Serving:

Calories:	440	From Fat:	230
Total Fat			25g
Saturated Fat			12g
Trans Fat			0.5g
Cholesterol			60mg
Sodium			210mg
Total Carbohydrate			51g
Dietary Fiber			0g
Sugars			27g
Protein			2g

Southern Peach–Almond Pie with Berry Sauce

PREP TIME: 30 MINUTES (READY IN 3 HOURS)
SERVINGS: 8

CRUST

- 1 box (15 oz) Pillsbury® refrigerated pie crusts, softened as directed on box
- 1 tablespoon sliced almonds, if desired

FILLING

- 5½ to 6 cups sliced peeled peaches (8 to 9 medium)
- 1 tablespoon lemon juice
- 1 cup sugar
- ¼ cup cornstarch
- ¼ teaspoon ground nutmeg
- ¼ teaspoon salt

SAUCE

- ¼ cup sugar
- 1 tablespoon cornstarch
- 1 bag (12 oz) frozen whole raspberries or blackberries, thawed, drained and liquid reserved
- ½ teaspoon almond extract

1) Heat oven to 400°F. Make pie crusts as directed on box for Two-Crust Pie, using 9-inch glass pie plate. Sprinkle sliced almonds over second crust; roll in with rolling pin.

2) In large bowl, gently mix peaches and lemon juice to coat. Gently stir in the remaining filling ingredients. Spoon into crust-lined pan. Carefully place second crust, almond side up, over filling; seal edge and flute. Cut slits in several places in top crust.

3) Bake 35 to 45 minutes or until golden brown. Cover edge of crust with strips of foil after 15 to 20 minutes of bake time to prevent excessive browning. Cool at least 1 hour before serving.

4) Meanwhile, in 2-quart saucepan, mix ¼ cup sugar and 1 tablespoon cornstarch. If necessary, add water to reserved raspberry liquid to measure ½ cup. Gradually stir liquid into sugar mixture, cooking and stirring over medium heat until thickened. Gently fold in raspberries; stir in almond extract. Cool completely, about 1 hour.

5) Top individual servings with sauce.

HIGH ALTITUDE (3500-6500 FT.): Bake 45 to 55 minutes.

Nutrition Information Per Serving:	
Calories: 440	From Fat: 230
Total Fat	25g
Saturated Fat	11g
Trans Fat	2g
Cholesterol	85mg
Sodium	1140mg
Total Carbohydrate	26g
Dietary Fiber	6g
Sugars	3g
Protein	26g

Lemon Cream Cheese-Blueberry Pie

PREP TIME: 20 MINUTES (READY IN 1 HOUR 35 MINUTES)
SERVINGS: 8

CRUST

1 Pillsbury® refrigerated pie crust (from 15-oz box), softened as directed on box

FILLING

1 package (8 oz) cream cheese, softened

1½ cups milk

1 box (4-serving size) lemon instant pudding and pie filling mix

TOPPING

1 can (21 oz) blueberry pie filling with more fruit

1 cup frozen (thawed) whipped topping

Lemon wedges, if desired

1) Heat oven to 450°F. Bake pie crust as directed on box for One-Crust Baked Shell, using 9-inch glass pie plate. Cool on cooling rack 15 minutes.

2) Meanwhile, in small bowl, beat cream cheese with electric mixer on medium speed until fluffy. In medium bowl, beat milk and pudding mix with electric mixer on medium speed until well blended. Add cream cheese; beat until smooth.

3) Spread cream cheese-pudding mixture in shell. Refrigerate 1 hour.

4) Top individual servings with blueberry pie filling; garnish with whipped topping and lemon peel. Cover and refrigerate any remaining pie.

HIGH ALTITUDE (3500-6500 FT.): No change.

Nutrition Information Per Serving:	
Calories: 390	From Fat: 180
Total Fat	20g
Saturated Fat	11g
Trans Fat	0g
Cholesterol	40mg
Sodium	390mg
Total Carbohydrate	50g
Dietary Fiber	0g
Sugars	31g
Protein	4g

tip

To make this yummy pie a day ahead, prepare the recipe through Step 3. Cover and refrigerate the pie overnight, then top it as directed.

Heavenly Caramel Pie

RUTH-ANNE O'GORMAN | KODIAK, ALASKA

BAKE-OFF® CONTEST 43, 2008

 EASY

PREP TIME: 15 MINUTES (READY IN 2 HOURS 45 MINUTES)
SERVINGS: 10

1 Pillsbury® refrigerated pie crust (from 15-oz box), softened as directed on box

1½ cups Smucker's® caramel ice cream topping (from two 12.25-oz jars)

¼ cup Fisher® Chef's Naturals® chopped pecans

2 packages (8 oz each) cream cheese, softened

1 container (8 oz) frozen whipped topping, thawed (3 cups)

½ cup Fisher® Chef's Naturals® pecan halves

1) Heat oven to 450°F. Make pie crust as directed on box for One-Crust Baked Shell using 9-inch glass pie plate. Bake 10 to 12 minutes or until light golden brown. Cool completely on cooling rack, about 15 minutes.

2) In small bowl, mix ¼ cup of the caramel topping and the chopped pecans. Spread mixture over bottom of cooled pie crust.

3) In large bowl, beat cream cheese and 1 cup of the caramel topping with electric mixer on medium speed until well blended. Fold in the whipped topping just until blended (do not overmix). Spoon cream cheese mixture into pie crust. Refrigerate at least 2 hours until set.

4) Arrange pecan halves on top of pie; drizzle the remaining ¼ cup caramel topping over pie. Cover and refrigerate any remaining pie.

HIGH ALTITUDE (3500-6500 FT.): No change.

Nutrition Information Per Serving:

Calories: 500	From Fat: 280
Total Fat	31g
Saturated Fat	16g
Trans Fat	0g
Cholesterol	55mg
Sodium	400mg
Total Carbohydrate	51g
Dietary Fiber	1g
Sugars	29g
Protein	5g

Easy Apple Pie Foldover

PREP TIME: 25 MINUTES (READY IN 1 HOUR 15 MINUTES)
SERVINGS: 4

FILLING

1½ cups thinly sliced, peeled apples (1½ medium)

¼ cup packed brown sugar

1 tablespoon water

1 teaspoon lemon juice

1 tablespoon all-purpose flour

1 tablespoon granulated sugar

¼ teaspoon salt

1 tablespoon butter or margarine

½ teaspoon vanilla

CRUST

1 Pillsbury® refrigerated pie crust (from 15-oz box), softened as directed on box

1 egg

1 tablespoon water

1 teaspoon granulated sugar

⅛ teaspoon ground cinnamon

Nutrition Information Per Serving:	
Calories: 380	From Fat: 160
Total Fat	18g
Saturated Fat	7g
Trans Fat	0g
Cholesterol	70mg
Sodium	410mg
Total Carbohydrate	51g
Dietary Fiber	0g
Sugars	22g
Protein	2g

Tart apples such as Granny Smith and Haralson make flavorful pies. Braeburn and Gala apples provide a good texture and slightly sweeter flavor.

1) In 2-quart saucepan, mix apples, brown sugar, 1 tablespoon water and the lemon juice. Cook over medium heat, stirring occasionally, until bubbly. Reduce heat to low; cover and cook 6 to 8 minutes, stirring occasionally, until apples are tender.

2) In small bowl, mix flour, 1 tablespoon granulated sugar and the salt. Gradually stir into apple mixture, cooking and stirring until mixture thickens. Remove from heat; stir in butter and vanilla. Cool 15 minutes.

3) Meanwhile, heat oven to 375°F. Unroll pie crust on ungreased cookie sheet. Spoon cooled fruit mixture evenly onto half of crust to within ½ inch of the edge.

4) In small bowl, beat egg and 1 tablespoon water; brush over edge of crust. Fold untopped half of crust over apple mixture; firmly press edge to seal. Flute edge; cut small slits in several places in top crust. Brush top with remaining egg mixture. In another small bowl, mix 1 teaspoon granulated sugar and the cinnamon; sprinkle over crust.

5) Bake 25 to 35 minutes or until crust is golden brown. Cool on cooling rack at least 10 minutes before serving.

HIGH ALTITUDE (3500-6500 FT.): Bake 23 to 28 minutes.

Chocolate-Strawberry Pie

PREP TIME: 30 MINUTES (READY IN 2 HOURS 30 MINUTES)
SERVINGS: 8

CRUST

1 Pillsbury® refrigerated pie crust (from 15-oz box), softened as directed on box

FILLING

1 cup semisweet chocolate chips (6 oz)

2 tablespoons butter or margarine

¼ cup powdered sugar

3 tablespoons kirsch or water

1 package (8 oz) cream cheese, softened

1½ to 2 pints (3 to 4 cups) whole strawberries

GLAZE

3 tablespoons red currant jelly

2 teaspoons kirsch or water

1) Heat oven to 450°F. Bake pie crust as directed on box for One-Crust Baked Shell, using 9-inch glass pie plate or 10-inch tart pan with removable bottom. Cool on cooling rack 15 minutes.

2) In 2-quart saucepan, melt chocolate chips and butter over low heat, stirring constantly. Stir in the powdered sugar, 3 tablespoons kirsch and the cream cheese until well blended. Pour into pie shell. Arrange strawberries over the chocolate mixture.

3) In 1-quart saucepan, heat jelly with 2 teaspoons kirsch until warm; spoon or brush over strawberries. Refrigerate at least 2 hours until serving time. Cover and refrigerate any remaining pie.

HIGH ALTITUDE (3500-6500 FT.): No change.

Nutrition Information Per Serving:

Calories:	420	From Fat:	240
Total Fat			26g
Saturated Fat			14g
Trans Fat			0g
Cholesterol			45mg
Sodium			220mg
Total Carbohydrate			41g
Dietary Fiber			2g
Sugars			22g
Protein			3g

Orange Mousse Pie

PREP TIME: 30 MINUTES (READY IN 2 HOURS 45 MINUTES)
SERVINGS: 8

CRUST

1 Pillsbury® refrigerated pie crust (from 15-oz box), softened as directed on box

FILLING

1 envelope unflavored gelatin

¾ cup orange juice

1 package (8 oz) cream cheese, softened

1 cup powdered sugar

1 teaspoon grated orange peel

2 cups whipping cream

2 large oranges, chopped, drained (2 cups)

TOPPING

1 container (6 oz) Yoplait® Original 99% Fat-Free French vanilla yogurt

1) Heat oven to 450°F. Bake pie crust as directed on box for One-Crust Baked Shell, using 9-inch glass pie plate. Cool on cooling rack 15 minutes.

2) Meanwhile, in 1-quart saucepan, mix the gelatin and orange juice; let stand 1 minute. Cook and stir over medium heat until dissolved. In small bowl, beat cream cheese, powdered sugar and orange peel with electric mixer on medium speed until smooth and fluffy. Gradually add softened gelatin; blend well. Refrigerate until slightly thickened, about 15 minutes.

3) In large bowl, beat whipping cream with electric mixer on high speed until stiff peaks form. Fold whipped cream into orange mixture; gently fold in chopped oranges. Spoon into crust. Refrigerate until firm, about 2 hours. Garnish with orange peel. Top each serving with dollop of yogurt. Cover and refrigerate any remaining pie.

HIGH ALTITUDE (3500-6500 FT.): No change.

Nutrition Information Per Serving:		
Calories: 520	From Fat: 320	
Total Fat		36g
Saturated Fat		20g
Trans Fat		1g
Cholesterol		100mg
Sodium		230mg
Total Carbohydrate		45g
Dietary Fiber		1g
Sugars		28g
Protein		6g

Chocolate Surprise Pecan Pie

PREP TIME: 25 MINUTES (READY IN 3 HOURS 45 MINUTES)
SERVINGS: 10

CRUST

1 Pillsbury® refrigerated pie crust (from 15-oz box), softened as directed on box

FILLING

1 package (8 oz) cream cheese, softened

⅓ cup sugar

Dash salt

1 teaspoon vanilla

1 egg

1 cup chopped pecans

½ cup semisweet chocolate chips

TOPPING

3 eggs

¼ cup sugar

1 cup light corn syrup

1 teaspoon vanilla

1 oz unsweetened baking chocolate, melted, cooled

GARNISH

½ cup whipping cream

1 tablespoon chocolate-flavor syrup

Nutrition Information Per Serving:

Calories:	540	From Fat:	280
Total Fat			31g
Saturated Fat			13g
Trans Fat			0g
Cholesterol			125mg
Sodium			220mg
Total Carbohydrate			58g
Dietary Fiber			2g
Sugars			31g
Protein			6g

tip

To quickly soften the cream cheese, simply place it in a microwavable bowl and microwave it uncovered on Low 1 to 2 minutes or until softened, checking it every 30 seconds.

1) Heat oven to 375°F. Place pie crust in 9-inch glass pie plate as directed on box for One-Crust Filled Pie. In small bowl, beat cream cheese, ⅓ cup sugar, the salt, 1 teaspoon vanilla and 1 egg with electric mixer on low speed until well blended. Spread cream cheese mixture into bottom of crust-lined pie plate. Sprinkle with pecans and chocolate chips.

2) In small bowl, beat the topping ingredients on medium speed just until blended. Carefully pour topping over pecans and chocolate chips. Cover the crust edge with 2- to 3-inch-wide strips of foil to prevent excessive browning; remove foil during last 15 minutes of bake time.

3) Bake 40 to 45 minutes or until center is set. Cool on cooling rack at least 2 hours before serving.

4) In chilled small bowl, beat whipping cream on high speed until stiff peaks form. Drizzle each pie wedge with chocolate syrup. Spoon dollop of whipped cream on each wedge. Cover and refrigerate any remaining pie.

HIGH ALTITUDE (3500-6500 FT.): Bake 60 to 65 minutes.

Coffee Crunch Chocolate Tart

VESTA FRIZZEL | INDEPENDENCE, MISSOURI

Bake-Off — Pillsbury | BAKE-OFF® CONTEST 32, 1986

PREP TIME: 25 MINUTES (READY IN 3 HOURS 15 MINUTES)
SERVINGS: 12

CRUST

1 Pillsbury® refrigerated pie crust (from 15-oz box), softened as directed on box

CRUMB LAYER

1/2 cup crisp coconut cookie crumbs (3 to 4 cookies)

2 tablespoons all-purpose flour

2 tablespoons packed brown sugar

1 to 2 teaspoons instant coffee granules or crystals

1 tablespoon butter or margarine

FILLING

1 cup powdered sugar

1 package (3 oz) cream cheese, softened

1 1/2 teaspoons vanilla

2 oz unsweetened baking chocolate, melted

2 cups whipping cream

GARNISH, IF DESIRED

6 to 8 dark roasted or chocolate-coated coffee beans or crushed coconut cookies

Unsweetened baking cocoa

1) Heat oven to 450°F. Place pie crust in 10-inch tart pan with removable bottom or 9-inch glass pie plate; press in bottom and up side of pan. Trim edges if necessary. Generously prick crust with fork. In small bowl, mix cookie crumbs, flour, brown sugar and instant coffee. Using fork or pastry blender, cut in butter until mixture is crumbly. Sprinkle over bottom of pie crust-lined pan. Bake 12 to 16 minutes or until light golden brown. Cool completely, about 30 minutes.

2) In large bowl, beat powdered sugar, cream cheese and vanilla until well blended. Add chocolate; beat until smooth. Gradually add whipping cream, beating until firm peaks form. Spread the filling into crust. Refrigerate 2 to 3 hours. Remove side of pan; garnish as desired. Cover and refrigerate any remaining tart.

HIGH ALTITUDE (3500-6500 FT.): No change.

Nutrition Information Per Serving:

Calories:	330	From Fat:	210
Total Fat			23g
Saturated Fat			14g
Trans Fat			0.5g
Cholesterol			55mg
Sodium			125mg
Total Carbohydrate			26g
Dietary Fiber			0g
Sugars			14g
Protein			2g

Stuffed-Crust Strawberry Cream Pie

PREP TIME: 25 MINUTES (READY IN 2 HOURS 35 MINUTES)
SERVINGS: 8

CRUST

- 1 box (15 oz) Pillsbury® refrigerated pie crusts, softened as directed on box
- 1 package (7 oz) almond paste
- 1 teaspoon cornstarch
- 1 egg white

FILLING

- ½ cup granulated sugar
- 3 tablespoons cornstarch
- 3 cups sliced fresh strawberries

TOPPING

- 1 cup whipping cream
- 2 tablespoons powdered sugar
- ¼ teaspoon vanilla
- 8 fresh whole strawberries, if desired

1) Heat oven to 400°F. Unroll 1 crust on work surface. Into medium bowl or food processor, crumble almond paste. Add 1 teaspoon cornstarch and the egg white. Mix or cover and process until smooth. Spread on crust to within 1¼ inches of edge. Unroll second crust; place on top and pat together gently. Place stuffed crust in ungreased 9-inch glass pie plate. Seal edges; flute. Cover edge with foil; fit second pie plate inside first pie plate on top of crust.

2) Bake 10 minutes. Remove top pie plate; gently prick the crust surface over filling about 15 times with fork. Bake uncovered about 15 minutes longer or until crust is light golden brown. Cool completely, about 1 hour.

3) Meanwhile, in 2-quart saucepan, mix granulated sugar and 3 tablespoons cornstarch. Stir in strawberries. Heat to boiling over medium heat, stirring constantly. Cook and stir 3 to 5 minutes or until filling thickens. Refrigerate about 30 minutes, stirring once, until cool.

4) Just before serving, spread the strawberry filling in crust. In medium bowl, beat the whipping cream, powdered sugar and vanilla with electric mixer on high speed until soft peaks form. Spread on top of pie. Garnish with whole strawberries.

HIGH ALTITUDE (3500-6500 FT.): No change.

Nutrition Information Per Serving:		
Calories: 540	From Fat: 270	
Total Fat		30g
Saturated Fat		11g
Trans Fat		0g
Cholesterol		40mg
Sodium		240mg
Total Carbohydrate		63g
Dietary Fiber		3g
Sugars		30g
Protein		4g

Crunchy Crust Blueberry Swirl Pie

MRS. RICHARD FURRY | LA MESA, CALIFORNIA

BAKE-OFF® CONTEST 23, 1972

PREP TIME: 30 MINUTES (READY IN 3 HOURS 30 MINUTES)
SERVINGS: 8

e EASY

CRUST
- ½ cup butter or margarine
- ¾ cup all-purpose or self-rising flour
- ½ cup quick-cooking oats
- ½ cup chopped nuts
- 2 tablespoons sugar

FILLING
- 1 box (4-serving size) lemon-flavored gelatin
- ½ cup boiling water
- 1 can (21 oz) blueberry pie filling
- ½ cup sour cream

TOPPING, IF DESIRED
Whipped cream

1) Heat oven to 400°F. Butter 9-inch glass pie plate.

2) In 2½-quart microwavable bowl, microwave ½ cup butter uncovered on High 30 seconds, adding 10 seconds as needed until butter melts. Stir in flour, oats, nuts and sugar. Press in bottom and side of the buttered pie plate. Bake 11 to 13 minutes or until the edges are golden brown.

3) Meanwhile, in 1½-quart bowl, dissolve gelatin in boiling water. Stir in pie filling. Refrigerate until thickened, about 1 hour.

4) Pour the filling mixture into crust. Spoon sour cream by tablespoonfuls on top. Cut through sour cream and lightly fold filling over it, making swirls. Refrigerate 2 hours or until cold. Top individual servings with whipped cream. Cover and refrigerate any remaining pie.

HIGH ALTITUDE (3500-6500 FT.): Bake 13 to 15 minutes.

Nutrition Information Per Serving:	
Calories: 380	From Fat: 180
Total Fat	20g
Saturated Fat	10g
Trans Fat	0.5g
Cholesterol	40mg
Sodium	140mg
Total Carbohydrate	47g
Dietary Fiber	2g
Sugars	31g
Protein	5g

Raspberry Mousse Pie

PREP TIME: 25 MINUTES (READY IN 3 HOURS 20 MINUTES)
SERVINGS: 8

1 Pillsbury® refrigerated pie crust (from 15-oz box), softened as directed on box

½ cup almond paste (from 8-oz tube)

2 cups whipping cream

1 envelope unflavored gelatin

2 tablespoons cold water

1 tablespoon lemon juice

4 cups fresh or frozen raspberries (from two 12-oz bags)

¾ cup sugar

3 tablespoons sugar

3 tablespoons frozen cranberry raspberry juice concentrate, thawed

Mint sprigs, if desired

Nutrition Information Per Serving:

Calories:	510	From Fat:	270
Total Fat			29g
Saturated Fat			14g
Trans Fat			0.5g
Cholesterol			70mg
Sodium			135mg
Total Carbohydrate			57g
Dietary Fiber			5g
Sugars			38g
Protein			4g

1) Heat oven to 450°F. Bake pie crust as directed on box for One-Crust Baked Shell, using 9-inch glass pie plate.

2) Meanwhile, in small microwavable bowl, place the almond paste and 2 tablespoons of the whipping cream. Microwave uncovered on High 30 seconds or until almond paste is softened; stir until smooth. Spread almond paste mixture over bottom of warm pie crust. Cool 45 minutes.

3) In small bowl, mix gelatin with cold water and lemon juice; stir with fork to soften. In 2-quart saucepan, mix 3 cups of raspberries and ¾ cup sugar; add the softened gelatin. Cook over medium heat 6 to 8 minutes, stirring constantly, until gelatin is dissolved and mixture is warm. Refrigerate until cool, about 30 minutes.

4) In large bowl, beat remaining whipping cream with electric mixer on high speed until soft peaks form. Gently fold raspberry mixture into whipped cream mixture. Spoon mixture over almond paste mixture. Refrigerate at least 2 hours until chilled.

5) In medium bowl, place remaining 1 cup raspberries, 3 tablespoons sugar and the juice concentrate. Crush raspberries with fork and stir well to dissolve sugar. Drizzle crushed raspberry mixture over individual servings of pie. Garnish with fresh mint. Cover and refrigerate any remaining pie.

HIGH ALTITUDE (3500-6500 FT.): No change.

Lemon Truffle Pie

PATRICIA KIEWIET | LAGRANGE, ILLINOIS   BAKE-OFF® CONTEST 35, 1992

PREP TIME: 1 HOUR 10 MINUTES (READY IN 3 HOURS 10 MINUTES)
SERVINGS: 10

CRUST

1 Pillsbury® refrigerated pie crust (from 15-oz box), softened as directed on box

LEMON LAYER

1 cup sugar

2 tablespoons cornstarch

2 tablespoons all-purpose flour

1 cup water

2 egg yolks, beaten

1 tablespoon butter or margarine

½ teaspoon grated lemon peel

¼ cup lemon juice

CREAM CHEESE LAYER

1 cup white vanilla baking chips or chopped white chocolate baking bar (6 oz)

1 package (8 oz) ⅓-less-fat cream cheese (Neufchâtel), softened

TOPPING

½ cup whipping cream

1 tablespoon sliced almonds, toasted

1) Heat oven to 450°F. Bake pie crust as directed on box for One-Crust Baked Shell, using 9-inch glass pie plate. Cool on cooling rack 15 minutes.

2) Meanwhile, in 2-quart saucepan, mix sugar, cornstarch and flour. Gradually stir in the water until smooth. Heat to boiling over medium heat, stirring constantly. Reduce heat to low; cook 2 minutes, stirring constantly. Remove from heat. Stir about ¼ cup hot mixture into egg yolks until well blended. Stir egg yolk mixture into mixture in saucepan. Heat to boiling over low heat, stirring constantly. Cook 2 minutes, stirring constantly. Remove from heat. Stir in butter, lemon peel and lemon juice.

3) Place ⅓ cup hot lemon mixture in 1-quart saucepan; cool the remaining lemon mixture 15 minutes. Into hot mixture in saucepan, stir vanilla baking chips. Cook and stir over low heat just until chips are melted.

4) In small bowl, beat cream cheese with electric mixer on medium speed until fluffy. Beat in melted vanilla chip mixture until well blended. Spread in bottom of crust. Spoon lemon mixture evenly over cream cheese layer. Refrigerate until set, 2 to 3 hours.

5) Just before serving, in small bowl, beat whipping cream with electric mixer on high speed until stiff peaks form. Pipe or spoon whipped cream over pie. Garnish with toasted almonds. Cover and refrigerate any remaining pie.

HIGH ALTITUDE (3500-6500 FT.): No change.

Nutrition Information Per Serving:		
Calories: 500	From Fat: 190	
Total Fat		22g
Saturated Fat		7g
Trans Fat		0g
Cholesterol		40mg
Sodium		310mg
Total Carbohydrate		75g
Dietary Fiber		2g
Sugars		40g
Protein		2g

Cookies 'n Cream Mini Cheesecakes

PREP TIME: 25 MINUTES (READY IN 2 HOURS 10 MINUTES)
SERVINGS: 24

16 creme-filled chocolate sandwich cookies, crushed (about 1 1/2 cups)

2 tablespoons butter or margarine, melted

1 package (8 oz) cream cheese, softened

1/4 cup milk

2 tablespoons sugar

1 teaspoon vanilla

1 egg

4 creme-filled chocolate sandwich cookies, cut into 1/4-inch pieces (about 1/2 cup)

3 tablespoons semisweet chocolate chips

1 teaspoon shortening

1) Heat oven to 325°F. Line 24 miniature muffin cups with paper baking cups. In small bowl, mix the crushed cookies and melted butter. Press 1 teaspoon cookie mixture firmly in the bottom of each muffin cup.

2) In large bowl, beat cream cheese, milk and sugar with electric mixer on medium speed until light and fluffy. Add vanilla and egg; beat well. Fold in cut-up cookies. Spoon 1 heaping tablespoon cream cheese mixture into each crust-lined muffin cup.

3) Bake 12 to 14 minutes or until edges are set and centers are still soft. Cool in pan on cooling rack 30 minutes. Refrigerate at least 1 hour or up to 48 hours before serving.

4) Just before serving, in 1-cup microwave-safe measuring cup, combine the chocolate chips and shortening. Microwave on High for 30 to 45 seconds or until melted, stirring once. Drizzle chocolate over tops of cheesecakes. Store in refrigerator.

HIGH ALTITUDE (3500-6500 FT.): No change.

Nutrition Information Per Serving:

Calories:	100	From Fat:	60
Total Fat			6g
Saturated Fat			3.5g
Trans Fat			0.5g
Cholesterol			20mg
Sodium			95mg
Total Carbohydrate			8g
Dietary Fiber			0g
Sugars			5g
Protein			2g

Sweet Potato Pie with Macadamia Praline

PREP TIME: 25 MINUTES (READY IN 2 HOURS 25 MINUTES)
SERVINGS: 8

CRUST

1 Pillsbury® refrigerated pie crust (from 15-oz box), softened as directed on box

FILLING

¾ cup granulated sugar

1 teaspoon ground cinnamon

½ teaspoon ground ginger

½ teaspoon ground nutmeg

¼ teaspoon salt

1 teaspoon vanilla

1 can (23 oz) sweet potatoes in syrup, drained and mashed (about 2 cups)

1 can (12 oz) evaporated milk

2 eggs, beaten

TOPPING

3 tablespoons packed brown sugar

3 tablespoons corn syrup

1 tablespoon butter or margarine

½ teaspoon vanilla

1 jar (3½ oz) macadamia nuts, coarsely chopped, or ¾ cup coarsely chopped pecans

1 cup crème fraîche or whipped cream

1) Heat oven to 425°F. Place pie crust in 9-inch glass pie plate as directed on box for One-Crust Filled Pie.

2) In large bowl, mix filling ingredients. Pour into crust-lined pie plate. Bake 15 minutes. Reduce oven temperature to 350°F. Bake 25 minutes longer. Meanwhile (during the last 5 minutes of bake time), in 1-quart saucepan, mix brown sugar, corn syrup and butter. Heat to boiling over low heat. Reduce heat; simmer 2 minutes. Remove from heat; stir in vanilla. Sprinkle nuts evenly over pie; drizzle with topping mixture.

3) Bake 20 to 30 minutes longer or until knife inserted in center comes out clean. (Place foil or cookie sheet on lowest oven rack during baking to guard against spillage.) Cover the crust edge with strips of foil during last 10 minutes of baking to prevent excessive browning. Cool 1 hour. Garnish with crème fraîche. Cover and refrigerate any remaining pie.

HIGH ALTITUDE (3500-6500 FT.): No change.

Nutrition Information Per Serving:	
Calories: 580	From Fat: 290
Total Fat	32g
Saturated Fat	13g
Trans Fat	0.5g
Cholesterol	105mg
Sodium	300mg
Total Carbohydrate	67g
Dietary Fiber	3g
Sugars	45g
Protein	7g

tip

Crème fraîche is a thick, extremely rich, slightly tangy cream. Look for it in your store's dairy department. Or, make your own by combining 1 cup whipping cream and 3 tablespoons buttermilk. Cover and let it stand at room temperature up to 24 hours or until very thick.

Turtle Cheesecake Tartlets

PREP TIME: 35 MINUTES (READY IN 2 HOURS 35 MINUTES)
SERVINGS: 24 TARTLETS

- 1 box (15 oz) Pillsbury® refrigerated pie crusts, softened as directed on box
- ½ cup milk chocolate chips
- 4 oz cream cheese (from 8-oz package), softened
- ¼ cup packed brown sugar
- 2 tablespoons caramel topping
- 1 egg
- ½ teaspoon vegetable oil
- 2 tablespoons finely chopped pecans

Nutrition Information Per Serving:

Calories:	110	From Fat:	60
Total Fat			7g
Saturated Fat			3g
Trans Fat			0g
Cholesterol			15mg
Sodium			80mg
Total Carbohydrate			12g
Dietary Fiber			0g
Sugars			5g
Protein			0g

1) Heat oven to 450°F. Remove 1 pie crust from pouch; unroll on work surface. Roll lightly with rolling pin. Cut 12 rounds from crust with 2½- to 2¾-inch cookie cutter. Press the rounds in the bottom and up the sides of 12 mini muffin cups, with edges extending above cups about ⅛ inch. Repeat with remaining pie crust. Place about 5 of the chocolate chips in each crust.

2) Bake 6 minutes. Leave crusts in pan. Reduce oven temperature to 375°F.

3) Meanwhile, in medium bowl, beat the cream cheese, brown sugar, caramel topping and egg with electric mixer on medium speed until creamy. Spoon evenly over chocolate chips, about 1½ teaspoons for each tartlet.

4) Bake at 375°F 10 to 12 minutes or until cheesecake is set. Cool in pan on cooling rack 10 minutes; remove from pan.

5) In small custard cup or other small microwavable bowl, place remaining chocolate chips and the oil. Microwave uncovered on High 30 seconds; stir. Microwave about 30 seconds longer or until melted; stir. Drizzle over each cheesecake; immediately sprinkle with pecans. Refrigerate at least 2 hours before serving. Cover and refrigerate any remaining tartlets.

HIGH ALTITUDE (3500-6500 FT.): Bake 12 to 14 minutes.

Buster Sundae Pie

PREP TIME: 25 MINUTES (READY IN 4 HOURS 40 MINUTES)
SERVINGS: 8

⊜ EASY

CRUST

- 1 Pillsbury® refrigerated pie crust (from 15-oz box), softened as directed on box

FILLING

- 4 cups (1 quart) vanilla ice cream, slightly softened
- ½ cup caramel topping
- ½ cup fudge topping
- ¾ cup Spanish peanuts (4 oz)

  Additional peanuts, if desired

1) Heat oven to 450°F. Bake pie crust as directed on box for One-Crust Baked Shell, using 9-inch glass pie plate. Cool on cooling rack 15 minutes.

2) Layer 2 cups of the ice cream in crust. Drizzle with ¼ cup of the caramel topping and ¼ cup of the fudge topping. Sprinkle with peanuts. Layer remaining 2 cups ice cream over peanuts. Freeze 4 hours or overnight.

3) Drizzle individual servings with remaining caramel topping and fudge topping. Sprinkle with peanuts. Cover and freeze any remaining pie.

HIGH ALTITUDE (3500-6500 FT.): No change.

Nutrition Information Per Serving:

Calories:	700	From Fat:	340
Total Fat			38g
Saturated Fat			16g
Trans Fat			0.5g
Cholesterol			70mg
Sodium			470mg
Total Carbohydrate			77g
Dietary Fiber			3g
Sugars			44g
Protein			11g

Candy Bar Pie

TRACEY CHRENKO | OWOSSO, MICHIGAN

Pillsbury **Bake-Off**

BAKE-OFF® CONTEST 35, 1992

PREP TIME: 20 MINUTES (READY IN 3 HOURS 40 MINUTES)
SERVINGS: 10

⊖ EASY

CRUST

1 Pillsbury® refrigerated pie crust (from 15-oz box), softened as directed on box

FILLING

5 bars (2.07 oz each) chocolate-covered peanut, caramel and nougat candy

4 packages (3 oz each) cream cheese, softened

½ cup sugar

2 eggs

⅓ cup sour cream

⅓ cup creamy peanut butter

TOPPING

3 tablespoons whipping cream

⅔ cup milk chocolate chips

1) Heat oven to 450°F. Place pie crust in 9-inch glass pie plate as directed on the box for One-Crust Filled Pie. Bake 5 to 7 minutes or until very light golden brown; cool. Reduce oven temperature to 325°F.

2) Cut candy bars in half lengthwise; cut into ¼-inch pieces. Place candy bar pieces over bottom of partially baked crust. In small bowl, beat the cream cheese and sugar with electric mixer on medium speed until smooth. Beat in 1 egg at a time until well blended. Add the sour cream and peanut butter, beating until mixture is smooth. Pour over candy bar pieces. Bake at 325°F 30 to 40 minutes or until center is set. Cool completely.

3) In 1-quart saucepan, heat whipping cream until very warm. Remove from heat; stir in chocolate chips until melted and smooth. Spread over top of pie. Refrigerate 2 to 3 hours before serving. Cover and refrigerate any remaining pie.

HIGH ALTITUDE (3500-6500 FT.): In Step 1, bake 6 to 8 minutes. In Step 2, bake 35 to 45 minutes.

Nutrition Information Per Serving:

Calories: 560	From Fat: 330
Total Fat	36g
Saturated Fat	18g
Trans Fat	0g
Cholesterol	95mg
Sodium	320mg
Total Carbohydrate	48g
Dietary Fiber	1g
Sugars	34g
Protein	9g

Plum Peachy Pie

PREP TIME: 25 MINUTES (READY IN 2 HOURS 45 MINUTES)
SERVINGS: 8

1 box (15 oz) Pillsbury® refrigerated pie crusts, softened as directed on box

1 tablespoon peach-flavored gelatin (from a box)

¼ cup cornstarch

1 cup sugar

4 cups sliced peeled fresh peaches or frozen (thawed) sliced peaches

2 medium red plums, peeled, pitted and thinly sliced

1 tablespoon butter or margarine

½ teaspoon sugar

1) Heat oven to 400°F. Make pie crusts as directed on box for Two-Crust Pie, using 9-inch glass pie plate.

2) In large bowl, mix gelatin, cornstarch and 1 cup sugar; stir in peaches. Spoon into crust-lined pie plate. Top with plum slices. Dot with butter. Top with second crust; seal edge and flute. Cut slits in several places in top crust.

3) Brush small amount of water over top crust; sprinkle lightly with ½ teaspoon sugar. Cover edge of crust with strips of foil to prevent excessive browning.

4) Bake 10 minutes. Reduce oven to 350°F; bake 35 to 40 minutes longer or until crust is golden brown and peaches are tender. Cool pie on cooling rack 1 hour 30 minutes before serving.

HIGH ALTITUDE (3500-6500 FT.): In Step 4, increase second bake time to 40 to 45 minutes.

Nutrition Information Per Serving:

Calories:	410	From Fat:	140
Total Fat			16g
Saturated Fat			6g
Trans Fat			0g
Cholesterol			10mg
Sodium			240mg
Total Carbohydrate			66g
Dietary Fiber			1g
Sugars			35g
Protein			1g

Grands!® Little Pies

S. LEA MEAD | SAN MATEO, CALIFORNIA   BAKE-OFF® CONTEST 40, 2002 | PRIZE WINNER

PREP TIME: 20 MINUTES (READY IN 55 MINUTES)
SERVINGS: 16   EASY

¾ cup all-purpose flour

½ cup packed brown sugar

1 teaspoon ground cinnamon

½ cup butter or margarine

½ cup chopped nuts, if desired

1 can (16.3 oz) Pillsbury® Grands!® Flaky Layers refrigerated original or buttermilk biscuits

1 can (21 oz) apple, blueberry or cherry pie filling

1 to 1½ cups whipping cream

Cinnamon-sugar

1) Heat oven to 350°F. In medium bowl, mix flour, brown sugar and cinnamon. With pastry blender or fork, cut in butter until the mixture looks like coarse crumbs. Stir in nuts.

2) Separate dough into 8 biscuits. Split each biscuit in half to make 16 rounds. With floured fingers, flatten each to form 4-inch round. Press each biscuit round in ungreased 2¾x1¼-inch muffin cup. Spoon 2 tablespoons pie filling into each biscuit-lined cup. Sprinkle each with about 2 tablespoons flour mixture. (Cups will be full.)

3) Bake 15 to 22 minutes or until golden brown. Cool 5 minutes. Remove from the muffin cups to cooling rack. Cool 10 minutes.

4) In small bowl, beat the whipping cream with electric mixer on high speed until stiff peaks form. Top each serving with the whipped cream; sprinkle with the cinnamon-sugar. Cover and refrigerate any remaining pies.

HIGH ALTITUDE (3500-6500 FT.): Bake 17 to 22 minutes.

Nutrition Information Per Serving:

Calories:	280	From Fat:	130
Total Fat			15g
Saturated Fat			8g
Trans Fat			2g
Cholesterol			30mg
Sodium			320mg
Total Carbohydrate			34g
Dietary Fiber			0g
Sugars			18g
Protein			3g

tip

Depending on the juiciness of the fruit, this pie has the potential to bubble over, which is why the recipe suggests using a cookie sheet beneath it in the oven.

Orchard Medley Pie

PREP TIME: 20 MINUTES (READY IN 3 HOURS 20 MINUTES)
SERVINGS: 8

EASY

FILLING

1 1/2 cups diced peeled apples

3/4 cup fresh red raspberries

3/4 cup fresh blackberries

3/4 cup fresh blueberries

3/4 cup chopped rhubarb

3/4 cup sugar

3 tablespoons quick-cooking tapioca

1 tablespoon lemon juice

CRUST

1 box (15 oz) Pillsbury® refrigerated pie crusts, softened as directed on box

1 1/2 tablespoons butter or margarine

1) Place cookie sheet or foil on lowest oven rack to guard against spillage. Heat oven to 400°F. In large bowl, stir together filling ingredients. Let stand 15 minutes, stirring occasionally.

2) Make pie crusts as directed on box for Two-Crust Pie, using 9-inch glass pie plate. Spoon filling into crust-lined pie plate; dot with butter. Top with second crust; seal edge and flute. Cut slits in several places in top crust. Cover crust edge with 2- to 3-inch-wide strips of foil to prevent excessive browning; remove foil during last 15 minutes of bake time.

3) Bake 15 minutes; reduce the oven temperature to 350°F. Bake 30 to 35 minutes longer or until the filling bubbles in the slits. Cool pie 2 hours before serving.

HIGH ALTITUDE (3500-6500 FT.): No change.

Nutrition Information Per Serving:	
Calories: 370	From Fat: 150
Total Fat	16g
Saturated Fat	6g
Trans Fat	0g
Cholesterol	15mg
Sodium	240mg
Total Carbohydrate	56g
Dietary Fiber	2g
Sugars	23g
Protein	0g

Orange Cream Dessert Squares

BONNY BOYD | DUBUQUE, IOWA

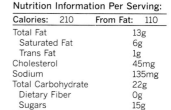

BAKE-OFF® CONTEST 43, 2008

PREP TIME: 25 MINUTES (READY IN 3 HOURS 35 MINUTES)
SERVINGS: 24

1 roll (16.5 oz) Pillsbury® Create 'n Bake® refrigerated sugar cookies

2 tablespoons grated orange peel (from 2 large oranges)

2 packages (8 oz each) cream cheese, softened

¼ cup Domino® or C&H® granulated sugar

½ cup Smucker's® sweet orange marmalade

1 teaspoon orange-flavored liqueur or ¼ teaspoon orange extract

2 Eggland's Best eggs

3 tablespoons whipping cream

2 drops orange food color (or 2 drops yellow and 1 drop red food color)

1½ teaspoons Land O Lakes® butter

½ cup white vanilla baking chips

1) Heat oven to 350°F. Press cookie dough evenly on bottom and 1 inch up sides of ungreased 13x9-inch (3-quart) glass baking dish. (If dough is sticky, use floured fingers.) Sprinkle evenly with orange peel.

2) In medium bowl, beat cream cheese, sugar, marmalade and liqueur with electric mixer on medium-high speed about 1 minute or until well blended. Add eggs; beat about 2 minutes or until well blended and mixture is creamy. Spread evenly in crust.

3) Bake 29 to 36 minutes or until crust is golden brown and center is set. Cool 1 hour.

4) In small microwavable bowl, microwave whipping cream and food color uncovered on High about 30 seconds or just until boiling. Add butter and baking chips; stir until chips are melted. Spread mixture evenly over bars. Refrigerate about 1½ hours or until chilled and firm.

5) To serve, cut into 6 rows by 4 rows, using thin, sharp knife and wiping blade occasionally. Cover and refrigerate any remaining dessert squares.

HIGH ALTITUDE (3500-6500 FT.): No change.

Nutrition Information Per Serving:	
Calories: 210	From Fat: 110
Total Fat	13g
Saturated Fat	6g
Trans Fat	1g
Cholesterol	45mg
Sodium	135mg
Total Carbohydrate	22g
Dietary Fiber	0g
Sugars	15g
Protein	3g

Nutty Caramel Cookie Tart

SHANNON KOHN | SIMPSONVILLE, SOUTH CAROLINA

Bake-Off® BAKE-OFF® CONTEST 43, 2008

PREP TIME: 20 MINUTES (READY IN 2 HOURS 5 MINUTES)
SERVINGS: 16

💬 EASY

1 roll (16.5 oz) Pillsbury® Create 'n Bake® refrigerated sugar cookies

⅓ cup Fisher® dry-roasted peanuts

⅓ cup Smucker's® caramel ice cream topping

¼ cup Jif® creamy peanut butter

½ teaspoon ground cinnamon

½ cup peanut butter chips

¼ cup white vanilla baking chips

1) Heat oven to 350°F. Press cookie dough evenly in bottom of ungreased 9-inch springform pan. (If dough is sticky, use floured fingers.) Bake 17 to 22 minutes or until light golden brown.

2) Meanwhile, place peanuts in resealable food-storage plastic bag; seal bag. Crush peanuts with rolling pin or meat mallet; set aside.

3) In medium microwavable bowl, microwave caramel topping, peanut butter and cinnamon uncovered on High 30 to 60 seconds or until hot and bubbly; stir well. Drizzle mixture evenly over partially baked crust. Sprinkle with peanut butter chips, vanilla baking chips and crushed peanuts.

4) Bake 12 to 18 minutes longer or until the edges are golden brown. Cool completely, about 1 hour 30 minutes.

5) Run sharp knife carefully around the edge of the tart to loosen; remove the side of the pan. To serve, cut the tart into wedges. Store tightly covered at room temperature.

HIGH ALTITUDE (3500-6500 FT.): No change.

Nutrition Information Per Serving:

Calories:	240	From Fat:	110
Total Fat			12g
Saturated Fat			3g
Trans Fat			1.5g
Cholesterol			10mg
Sodium			180mg
Total Carbohydrate			29g
Dietary Fiber			0g
Sugars			19g
Protein			4g

Spiced Creamy Caramel-Peanut Torte

JENNIFER HOWETH | NEWCASTLE, OKLAHOMA

 BAKE-OFF® CONTEST 43, 2008

PREP TIME: 20 MINUTES (READY IN 1 HOUR 55 MINUTES)
SERVINGS: 16

E EASY

1 roll (16.5 oz) Pillsbury® Create 'n Bake® refrigerated chocolate chip cookies

2 packages (8 oz each) cream cheese, softened

1 jar (12.25 oz) Smucker's® caramel ice cream topping

½ cup Jif® creamy peanut butter

⅓ cup Domino® or C&H® confectioners' powdered sugar

1 teaspoon vanilla

¼ teaspoon ground cinnamon

⅛ teaspoon freshly grated nutmeg or regular ground nutmeg

1 container (8 oz) frozen whipped topping, thawed

1¼ cups Fisher® honey-roasted peanuts

1) Heat oven to 350°F. Spray 10- or 9-inch springform pan with Crisco® Original No-Stick cooking spray. Press cookie dough on bottom and ¼ inch up side of pan. Bake 16 to 23 minutes or until golden brown. Cool completely, about 45 minutes.

2) Meanwhile, in large bowl, beat cream cheese, ⅔ cup of the caramel topping, the peanut butter and powdered sugar with electric mixer on medium speed until smooth. Beat in vanilla, cinnamon and nutmeg. Fold in whipped topping until well mixed. Fold in 1 cup of the peanuts. Cover; refrigerate until crust is completely cooled.

3) Spoon cream cheese mixture over cookie crust. Freeze at least 30 minutes until set.

4) Just before serving, top cheesecake with remaining ¼ cup peanuts and drizzle with remaining ⅓ cup caramel topping. For easier cutting, wipe knife after each cut. Cover and refrigerate any remaining cheesecake.

HIGH ALTITUDE (3500-6500 FT.): No change.

Nutrition Information Per Serving:

Calories:	460	From Fat:	250
Total Fat			28g
Saturated Fat			12g
Trans Fat			1.5g
Cholesterol			35mg
Sodium			330mg
Total Carbohydrate			43g
Dietary Fiber			2g
Sugars			29g
Protein			9g

Warm and Fudgy Raspberry Pudding Cake

KAREN BOWLDEN | BOISE, IDAHO

BAKE-OFF® CONTEST 43, 2008

Bake-Off

PREP TIME: 20 MINUTES (READY IN 1 HOUR 40 MINUTES)
SERVINGS: 12

e EASY

1 box (19.5 oz) Pillsbury® classic milk chocolate brownie mix

½ cup Crisco® pure canola oil

¼ cup water

4 Eggland's Best eggs

1 package (8 oz) cream cheese, softened

1 cup Smucker's® seedless red raspberry jam

¼ cup sour cream

1 teaspoon vanilla

1 jar (11.75 oz) Smucker's® hot fudge ice cream topping

½ cup fresh red raspberries

Fresh mint sprigs

1 quart vanilla ice cream, if desired

1) Heat oven to 350°F. Spray 13x9-inch (3-quart) glass baking dish with Crisco® Original No-Stick cooking spray.

2) In large bowl, stir brownie mix, oil, water and 2 of the eggs 50 strokes with spoon. Pour into baking dish.

3) In medium bowl, beat cream cheese and jam with electric mixer on medium speed until well mixed. Beat in remaining 2 eggs, the sour cream and vanilla until well mixed (mixture will be runny). Pour over brownie batter. Swirl mixtures slightly with a spoon or tip of knife for marbled design.

4) Bake 35 to 50 minutes or until the edges are golden brown and the center is puffed and set when lightly touched.

5) Warm jar of fudge topping as directed on label. Pour evenly over cake, spreading to cover if necessary. Cool 30 to 45 minutes before serving. Garnish with raspberries and mint sprigs. Serve with ice cream.

HIGH ALTITUDE (3500-6500 FT.): Make brownies following High Altitude package directions. Bake 40 to 50 minutes.

Nutrition Information Per Serving:		
Calories: 540	From Fat:	210
Total Fat		24g
Saturated Fat		7g
Trans Fat		0g
Cholesterol		85mg
Sodium		300mg
Total Carbohydrate		74g
Dietary Fiber		1g
Sugars		54g
Protein		7g

Alphabetical Index

General Recipe Index

This handy index lists every recipe by food category, major ingredient and/or cooking method, so you can easily locate recipes to suit your needs.